THE FUTURE OF URBAN FORM

THE FUTURE OF URBAN FORM

THE IMPACT OF NEW TECHNOLOGY

**EDITED BY JOHN BROTCHIE,
PETER NEWTON, PETER HALL &
PETER NIJKAMP**

CROOM HELM
London & Sydney

NICHOLS PUBLISHING COMPANY
New York

© 1985 John Brotchie, Peter Newton, Peter Hall and Peter Nijkamp
Croom Helm Ltd, Provident House, Burrell Row,
Beckenham, Kent BR3 1AT
Croom Helm Australia Pty Ltd, First Floor, 139 King Street,
Sydney, NSW 2001, Australia

British Library Cataloguing in Publication Data

The Future of urban form.
    1. City planning – Technological innovations
    I. Brotchie, John
    307',14   HT391
    ISBN 0-7099-3255-3

First published in the United States of America 1985 by
Nichols Publishing Company, Post Office Box 96
New York, NY 10024

Library of Congress Cataloing in Publication Data
Main entry under title:

The Future of urban form.

    Papers from a workshop held in Waterloo, Canada,
July 1983, which was organized by the Working Commission
72 of the International Council for Building Research,
Studies, and Documentation.
    1. Cities and towns – Effect of technological
innovations on –Congresses. I. Brotchie, J.F.
II. International Council for Building Research, Studies,
and Documentation. Working Commission 72.
HT119.F88   1985   307.7'6   84-29448
ISBN 0-89397-213-4

Printed and bound in Great Britain
by Billing & Sons Limited, Worcester.

CONTENTS

FIGURES

Tables

ACKNOWLEDGEMENTS

The editors are most grateful to Professor Bruce Hutchinson, University of Waterloo, for hosting and participating in the workshop from which this book has emerged; to Dr Guyla Sebestyen, Secretary General, International Council for Building Research Studies and Documentation, for inviting the study; to Australia's Commonwealth Scientific and Industrial Research Organization and The Canadian Mortgage and Housing Corporation for financial support; to Rhyll Pahud for typing the manuscript; and to the contributors for their enthusiastic participation in discussion and manuscript preparation.

PREFACE

This book of exploratory essays is produced as an outcome of a workshop held in Waterloo, Canada, in July 1983 as part of an international study on technological change and urban form convened by the International Council for Building Research Studies and Documentation (CIB) as Working Commission 72 (CIBW72).

The meeting and associated background studies were concerned with those technological, economic and social changes occurring nationally and internationally which impact on cities and the communities which comprise them. These technological changes included automation in the secondary sector, the combination of the microprocessor and telecommunications in the tertiary and quaternary sectors, the effects of energy price rises and threats of shortage, and substitution effects in the energy and vehicle technology areas. Social and economic consequences included unemployment, increasing income differentials, changes in employment patterns, urban activities and lifestyles, and their interactions. Of foremost concern, however, was the manner in which socio-technical changes had a capability for altering the direction of urban development via changing space needs and locational requirements of industry and transport (supply induced) as well as of individuals and families (demand induced).

Almost without exception the chapters in this volume are future-oriented (with due recognition to the contribution that the past and present make to shaping the future) and are concerned with exploring, often speculatively, the transition of technologically advanced Western societies to an information-based post-industrial state and the impact that such a transition is likely to have on national settlement systems.

As such, the study has important implications for industry and community including building, transport, communications and other service sectors; all industries making investment, location and planning decisions, and all those concerned with the future of our cities and the communities they accommodate and support.

The Plan of the Book

Chapter 1 takes an overview. It notes that the microelectronic-information technology revolution is producing changes in our patterns of living and working at least as profound as did the industrial revolution but within a shorter timeframe. The industrial revolution extended human musculature. The information revolution is extending the mind and nervous system. It is knowledge-based rather than energy-based, and knowledge is a cumulative resource, contributing to the increasing rate of change. Increasing diversity of opportunities and increasing informality of organisation of activities in space and time are among further consequences expected to occur. A model of urban change is outlined which recognises the interplay of supply (technology and profit-based) and demand (human needs-based) factors; the locational consequences of technological change are represented as two-dimensional trajectories in an activity and interaction space.

Part One provides an international and regional perspective. In Chapter 2, resulting changes in industrial and living patterns are viewed at the world and European levels. The new information based industries are reported to be bypassing the industrial cities in favour of high-amenity areas in the sunbelt and pre-industrial towns, raising the issue of whether these 'rustbowl' cities are restorable or disposable (along with the future of their inhabitants). Chapter 3 views the North American industrial scene. It classifies industry as 'routine' and 'non-routine'. Routine industries are seen to be seeking locations with low-factor costs and to be subject to automation, deskilling and job loss. Non-routine activities are considered to be seeking locations with high amenity and, in the case of 'high tech', further requirements include access to high-quality communications, international transport and knowledge centres. Other features are the growth of the quaternary and quinary sectors, and the number of new small firms setting up. It notes a reversal of the rule 'people follow jobs', substituting 'jobs follow people' in post-industrial society.

Part Two views future impacts on industry, providing a contrast between the UK and USA. For Britain (Chapter 4), the prospect of cities without manufacturing industry is raised, and a transition from supply-determined development to consumer-led development patterns is perceived. For the US (Chapter 5), the factors influencing the future of manufacturing are discussed; and a scenario of continued increase in capital substitution, automation and growth in high-technology industries is examined, with continued dispersal of industry and workforce. A less likely, politically imposed, 'low tech', labour-intensive alternative is also considered. Chapter 6 gives an overview which focuses on the quaternary sector (and on California in particular), which is enmeshed in the information-technology development wave.

Part Three examines the role of innovation in development. Chapter 7 explores the dynamics of the process of industrial and urban change including long-wave or cyclic effects. The place of innovation in this process and its implications for the urban system are considered and modelled. Chapter 8 views spatial patterns of biotechnology industries, which are at the front of the wave of the next technological revolution, and the different locational behaviours exhibited in their development and production stages.

Part Four treats communication and transport and their interactions. Chapter 9 evaluates the role of information technology (particularly telecommunications) in the urban system, including the changes in activity patterns that this is generating and the needs that it is meeting. The importance of trust as a factor in the development and operation of urban systems and the (initially inhibiting) role of information technology in this regard are discussed. Chapter 10 reviews the impacts of previous transport improvements on urban development and looks at transport innovations currently in the development pipeline (largely information-related), speculating upon their impacts on the urban system and its future form. Chapter 11 examines transport-communication interactions and the implications for growth in each. Chapter 12 discusses the impacts of energy price changes, scarcity concerns and associated transport and energy technologies on the urban system, arguing for better integration of work and residential activities through planning and policy initiatives.

Part Five considers information systems and their impacts. Chapter 13 discusses trends in both 'high tech' and 'low tech' ('high touch') service industries. Chapter 14 considers 'teleshopping' systems and their impacts on shopping-centre development. Chapter 15 proposes the concept of key factors in the urban system for use in urban planning, and information systems based on these factors to provide an early warning system for monitoring and analysing urban impacts of technological change. Chapter 16 discusses the reaction developing in many urban communities to perceived threats from high-technology and information systems, with the consequence that personal information for use in planning may not be collected in future.

Part Six discusses institutional influences: first from the viewpoint of the state as a facilitator of technological change and the role of planning authorities as regulators (Chapter 17); and secondly, the role of the state as a safety net (Chapter 18). The increasing roles of the informal sector and self-help networks and the responsibilities of industry itself in periods of societal transition are also noted.

Part Seven focuses on approaches to modelling urban systems under selected change processes. Chapter 19 considers metropolitan implications of technological change using a transport-land use interaction model, with rearrangement of activities being projected under various scenarios. Chapter 20 studies energy impacts and policies for a metropolitan region and a non-metropolitan region using transport-land use interaction models. Chapter 21 discusses the resulting dynamics of urban change and new techniques for its modelling. Chapter 22 takes an overview of the urban change process and its relationship to the process of modelling that change, indicating the need to seek for a 'deep structure' of urban systems.

Part Eight considers the future urban system — firstly, to the extent that it is determined by decisions already made, and therefore predictable, and secondly, to the extent that it may be influenced by decisions yet to be made, and is therefore choosable. In Chapter 23, a study of current and emerging socio-technical trends and impacts, and their interactions, is reported. In Chapter 24 the criteria for a desirable urban system are discussed in the context of a better spatial balance between work and residence, with implementation via the co-ordination of various public sector investment decisions and planning controls.

Part Nine takes an overview of the future urban system and its implications for planning. Chapter 25 examines the various forces which operate to increase concentration of activities, and those working to increase their dispersal, and the various urban forms resulting. Dispersal at the national and regional levels and decentralisation at the metropolitan level are expected due to the influence of the information revolution; but redistribution of activity and concentration around urban sub-centres within the metropolis are also projected. Chapter 26 looks at planning strategies for the future and the reasons for both optimism and pessimism in this regard. The pessimism comes from projection of present trends in the short term. Cautious optimism relates to the potential for human intervention as a response to these projections, in selection of and working towards a more desirable future in the longer term.

1. INTRODUCTION

J. Brotchie, P. Newton, P. Hall and P. Nijkamp

This book is about a revolution and its likely consequences. The information revolution is, as yet, in its very early stages. But the indications are that it will cause changes in patterns of living and working at least as fundamental and comprehensive as those induced by the industrial revolution of the eighteenth and nineteenth centuries. However, this time the rate of change is certain to be greater. Two examples reflecting the leading edge of this change are indicative:

> Mr. Toshio Iguchi lives on the outskirts of Tokyo. His small factory nearby produces moulded plastics. On arriving there in the morning, he switches on the machine which heats the plastic and starts up the three robots which he recently acquired to replace his previous staff of four. He then goes to golf. Every four hours, his wife refills the machine with plastic and removes the finished products. After dinner at night, he returns to switch off the machines, and set up for the following morning.[1]

> In the foothills of the Sierras in California, Meryl Jackson checks the weather report before deciding whether to spend the day on the ski slopes or developing software on her home computer. Once or twice a week she travels to Silicon Valley for a project meeting but most of her communications with her firm are electronic.[2]

In 1984, these modes of living and working are still exceptional, but they foreshadow the changing patterns of human activity possible in post-industrial society.

In fact advanced Western industrial societies are experiencing a series of technological revolutions which are in the process of profoundly changing societal structure and economy. All major societal transitions until now (such as the neolithic revolution where hunting and gathering gave way to sedentary farming, and the industrial revolution where manufacturing displaced agriculture as the dominant source of work) have been linked primarily to technological change, whereby new materials, products, production processes and organisational processes have been substituted for old. The basket of technologies which characterise any particular society (whether agrarian, industrial or post-industrial) has always served essentially the same function: providing production, transport, communication and living arrangements. The spatial patterns which have characterised these various societal epochs are however vastly different. In preindustrial society, production was predominantly agricultural and occurred outside the cities. The industrial revolution reversed this pattern with manufacturing production emerging as the major activity and occurring in inner city areas. In the post-industrial era, this pattern is again reversing with production moving largely to the metropolitan periphery and beyond (see Chapters 3, 4, 6 and 25).

Ever since the invention of the plough and wheel, technological change has facilitated the reorganisation of human activities and their interactions. The industrial revolution, with its concentration on the hardware and mechanics of production and of transport, increased the formality of such organisation. It resulted in the industrial city. The smokestack became a symbol of production, and the subsequent development of the urban railway became a means of escape to cleaner, suburban air. These technological changes resulted in industrial concentration and made commuting both desirable and feasible. Subsequent land-use zoning made it virtually compulsory. Distributed electric power allowed some deconcentration and environmental improvement. The motor car added further flexibility to activity-interaction patterns. By the middle of the twentieth century advanced Western industrial societies began changing yet again under the impact of a further technological revolution, the 'electronic technology revolution' (Stonier 1979). A further stage of this revolution is the computer-based 'information revolution' which is the subject of this book. These technological advances underlie what has come to be termed the post-industrial economy (Bell 1980; Jones 1982), where industry and agriculture remain important sectors of production, but have sharply diminished labour requirements compared to the service and knowledge — or information-based industries. Further freedom of location of activities and interactions is occurring as a result.

Industrial society represents an extreme in several ways, from which the information society is retreating. In the US and Britain, the smokestack cities are declining as newer industries bypass them in favour of higher amenity environments, in the sunbelt, mountain or coastal areas, in newer cities and in non-metropolitan towns, that is in those places that escaped the force of the industrial revolution (see Chapters 2 and 3). The same pattern is beginning to appear in other Western European countries. The process of reducing formality and increasing personalised ('do it yourself') activity has been a feature of this century. The partial displacement of public transport (with its paid labour force) by private transport, of telephone operators by direct dialling, of servants by kitchen appliances, of the theatre by radio, TV and video, of formal working hours by flexi-time and part-time employment, of the guest house by the weekend cottage, of the coffee house by the home percolator, of large main-frame computers by personal computers, of inhouse production by subcontracting, of the conventional office by home work stations, of shopping by teleshopping and of commuting by telecommuting, are all components of this shift. Paradoxically, the rejection by some of high technology (Chapter 16), due perhaps to lifestyle preference or inability to effectively compete in the contemporary workplace, in favour of (pre-industrial) low-technology activities such as crafts, is also a move in this direction of informality and diversity.

Many of the growth activities, of the high-technology and low-technology variety, are environmentally benign. Thus both facilitate a partial return to a cottage industry pattern. The difference between the two, however, lies in the interconnectivities that are involved. Low technology involves little interaction. High technology involves considerable interaction on electronic networks and to a lesser extent on other transport-communication modes. Another difference is the faster rates of change of high technology.

In fact a feature of the chronology of technological change over the ages has been its generally accelerating pace: from the development of stone age tools to the age of metals took tens of thousands of years, further progress to the age of steam took thousands of years, to oil and electricity just a century, and to electronics merely decades (in relation to specific technologies, such as information processing, similar trends are evident; see Grosch 1973). The present rate of change is such that another major technological revolution, biotechnology, has already begun (Chapter 8).

Technologies

Post-industrial society is predicated upon the emergence of several new technologies. The technologies spawned by the industrial revolution contrast markedly with those from the electronic revolution in that the former produced devices which extended human musculature whereas the latter deal with devices which extend the human nervous system:

> Radio and telephone were an extension of the ear, film was initially
> an extension of sight, then coupled to sound, television an extension
> of sight and sound, and finally the computer an extension of the
> brain. It has always been the function of technology to extend human
> capabilities. To extend human neurological capabilities is qualita-
> tively different from extending the human musculature. This new
> technology was bound to create profound changes in society.
> (Stonier 1979:1)

Information technology represents an outgrowth of developments in
electronics and microelectronics, the technologies of which are central
to both communications and computing. Information storage has been
facilitated by recent developments in large-capacity memories, information processing capacity has increased markedly with linkages to
computers, and information dissemination is enhanced by linkage to
telecommunications networks; the ability of these technologies to
operate in combination adds substantially to their impacts (see Chapters
9 and 25). Examples of areas where information technology has
exerted, or is likely to initiate, major economic and social changes are
numerous; they include, at one extreme, the increasing global integration of national and regional economies and, at the other, progress
towards the electronic or 'paperless' office. A further feature of
information technology is its ability to separate flows of information
from the movement and processing of goods and materials, or from
traffic flows, that they define. This facilitates the centralisation of this
information and its manipulation by systems methods, so as to maximise the effectiveness of production, distribution and travel to meet a
diverse range of user needs.

In addition, new energy-based technology has developed in response
to the finiteness of oil resources and associated cost increases; this
includes transport-system changes (Chapter 10) such as smaller, more
efficient cars, electric vehicles, new or improved public transport
systems such as new mass-transit metro systems, and small-vehicle
systems such as personal rapid transit. Also relevant are alternative
energy production systems, particularly solar[3] (see also Chapter 5).
These energy-based technology changes (and net increases in energy
cost), although initially more visible and with greater initial income
effects, are likely to have smaller long-term influence and less fundamental impact than information technology (and its decreasing cost).
The use of electronic information systems for traffic management,
including road-pricing systems, represents an effective combination of
the two (see Chapters 10 and 11).

There is a dark side to technology however. The change process and especially the speed of this change is leaving widespread societal disruption in its wake. Deskilling and job loss in the more routine secondary and tertiary activities are affecting large numbers of people of all ages but particularly the young (see Chapters 3 and 4) and especially in the older industrial areas. The aspirations and opportunities of these groups to meet even basic human needs are threatened (except where underwritten by the State — Chapter 18), providing little hope of meeting higher social and psychological needs. Disenchantment with the capacity of new technology to meet these needs is also well established along with a suspicion of its more detrimental physical (e.g. atomic energy) and informational (privacy) effects (see Chapter 16).

Even for those with jobs, the information revolution is initiating major organisational changes within firms and government organisations, affecting tasks, relationships, and organisational status for many. Relative changes in influence and income will result both at the level of individuals and institutions. As spatial and informational constraints are overcome, relative shifts of competitive advantage will occur, such as from the unskilled and semi-skilled groups to knowledge workers, from material and energy based industries, to information based industries, from regions of low amenity (rust bowls, frost belt) to those of high amenity, and even from sovereign states to multi-national organisations. Thus some groups will lose substantially and even devastatingly while others gain.

Challenges for planning will grow (as noted by Gertler in Chapter 17 and Hall in Chapter 26) as these rates of technological, economic and social change increase and as the formality of the industrial era both spatially and temporally gives way to the relative informality of post-industrial society. Problems of directing and accommodating change are not restricted to metropolitan planning authorities, although they constitute a principal focus in this book (see Chapters 15 and 22). It is also apparent that the viability of private organisations will depend, in part, upon the appropriateness of their built form and locational decisions in an era of rapid technological change.

Urban Form and Activity Patterns

Urban form is treated here as the pattern of residential and non-residential urban activities and their interactions as expressed by the built environment which accommodates them.

In post-industrial society, non-residential urban activities might usefully be classed as routine or non-routine (see Chapter 3). Information technology has the capacity for initiating significant change in each of these areas of activity. One major impact is on information industries where many routine white-collar tasks may be handled automatically in the electronic office, thus eliminating middle-management and basic processing jobs. Another major impact is in the processing of goods and services where routine blue-collar tasks may be handled by automation; and even variations to these tasks may be controlled by a microprocessor quickly adjusting tool settings and so on to facilitate 'flexible manufacturing' or 'production on demand'. This allows a fundamental change in the production process from 'economies of scale' to 'economies of scope', increasing diversity of goods and services to better match individual needs. It also facilitates continuous (24-hour) production, but reduces or deskills blue collar jobs (Chapters 3 and 5). A further major area of impact is in the movement of goods and people, where traffic and freight flows can be optimally controlled or advised (on routes, speeds or destinations) to minimise congestion, energy cost or travel time (Chapters 10 and 11). Routine industries (both manufacturing and clerical) are likely to seek locations with low-factor costs and also to exhibit increasing automation, deskilling and job loss. Some industries, and the urban areas they support, will suffer obsolescence and decline.

Non-routine industries are seeking locations with higher amenities such as the sunbelt, the coastal areas and the non-industrial towns and in the case of research and development, access to universities and research institutions, transport, including an international airport, and high-quality communications. A net result of the information revolution has been to make non-routine activities more 'footloose'. Their benign nature allows decreasing emphasis on zonal separation and commuting, and, in some cases, a return to a cottage-industry pattern as noted earlier. Thus non-routine tasks, including research and development and other specialised industry support services, such as software production, can be performed from remote work stations which may be in the home. Increasing employment, reducing formality, increasing specialisation and increasing diversity are features in this case (see Toffler 1981, and Table 1.1 for a profile of settlement-sensitive characteristics of industrial and post-industrial societies).

High-technology industries appear to be concentrating in a limited number of locations within each country which possess the locational attributes outlined above. Apparently, these jobs follow people (reversing the rule for industrial location of 'people follow jobs'), or locations attractive to skilled employees are selected (see Chapters 3, 5 and 25).

Table 1.1 Settlement-sensitive Characteristics of Industrial and Post-industrial Societies.

Industrial society	Information society
Routine employment dominant	Non-routine employment dominant
Polluting	Clean
Energy based, constrained resource	Information based, cumulative resource
Formality	Informality
Special zones	Mixed zones
Rigid schedules	Flexible schedules
Specialist operator	Do-it-yourself
Public transport	Private transport
Telegraph	Telephone
Regular hours	Flexi time
Bank teller	Flexi teller
Theatre	TV, video
Office	Home work situation
Main frame computer	Personal computer
'Economies of scale'	'Economies of scope'
Uniformity	Diversity
Industrial cities	Post-industrial urban systems

At the national and regional levels, activities are dispersing, facilitated by information technology. The virtual city (alternatively labelled the global village and the non place urban realm) is made feasible by information technology (see Chapter 25). Electronic technology links cities, multinational firms, dispersed components of an industry, or other complex activities. When urban centres are economically disadvantaged by congestion, information technology facilitates dispersal to the fringe, to rural areas, or even offshore. Thus information technology, by reducing spatial constraints, can have a polarising effect on activities with different locational needs, such as routine and non-routine industries and the people they employ.

At the metropolitan level, particular subgroups of the population and certain classes of jobs have generally been moving outwards to the periphery of development and beyond, assisted by transport and communications technology. But some major urban centres are also growing in terms of new commercial space and, in some cases, new residential space. The forces encouraging this intrametropolitan concentration include at one end of the spectrum financial entrapment of low-skilled unemployed, at the other, preference for inner-city living for lifestyle and journey-to-work reasons on the part of some higher income groups, and, regarding industrial use, the space-saving features of new technologies (see Chapters 13 and 23).

Different activities are responding variously to information technology change. Banking activities involving high levels of trust (such as loan negotiations) continue to require face-to-face transactions and are staying in the centre of the city (Chapter 6), while back office functions such as credit card operations (requiring levels of trust that can be mechanised) are moving to more decentralised and dispersed locations. Insurance companies operating largely on documents are moving to the suburbs. High-technology industries are demonstrably footloose (Chapters 3 and 6), and associated software production tends to disperse more widely into surrounding (high-amenity) regions. The net result is a dispersal of activities involving the processing of information, some to residential areas in the suburbs and beyond, whereas other face-to-face transactions involving trust remain in the central city along with their service support. Meanwhile, information technology has allowed more routine production of goods or services to move to areas of low-factor costs, such as rural areas or offshore. Thus the impacts of technological change are variable, affecting different urban areas in different ways, depending upon their particular labour force-amenity mix.

The Process of Change

The motivational forces for technological change are twofold: on the supply side, sustaining economic growth and profit-for-private-sector industry; on the demand side, meeting human needs and aspirations. Supply-induced change and innovation have been an integral part of all economic systems. Technological change and economic growth are linked through the capacity of new technology to lower costs, to improve products and to increase output and profitability (Chapter 7). Demand-induced change is linked to the appetite among the population for an increasing array of 'needs'. Maslow (1970) has suggested a hierarchy of five human needs commencing at the lowest level with physiological needs and proceeding to safety (security), belonging (social), esteem (ego), and self-actualisation (self-fulfillment). He suggests the motivation for change is the sequential satisfaction of these unmet needs (Chapter 13).

Human progress then is a stepwise or branching path into the future as one need is met and another substituted, and as new innovations are developed and other opportunities close. (Maslow considered that for the average US citizen in the 1950s the lower-level human needs were largely met, but the upper-level needs only partially met.)

The industries developed to meet these needs might be identified as food, shelter, transport, recreation, communication and knowledge or, more conventionally, as primary, secondary, tertiary, quaternary and quinary (see Jones 1982). The lower-level needs (and their industries) are mainly land- and energy-based and were largely met as a consequence of the agricultural and industrial revolutions. The upper-level needs are largely information- or knowledge-based and come within the scope of the information revolution. Land and energy are finite resources, or a continuing resource in the case of solar energy, but information and *knowledge* are cumulative resources and this contributes to the increasing rate of change.

In the information society, Batty (Chapter 4) and others (Naisbitt 1982; Hawkins 1983) perceive a fundamental shift occurring from supply-induced changes to demand-induced changes, as the means for expression and realisation of these needs are developed, and as locational choices are freed from technological constraints.

Thus a possible model of the change process is indicated in Figure 1.1. On the supply side, resources are shifting from materials and energy to knowledge. Technological breakthroughs require research and development and then production, and locational decisions are required at each stage. Technological change leads to changes in the resource inputs used in production. This is resulting in less input of materials, energy and labour and greater input of knowledge. Consequences include reduction in demand for materials and energy, and job loss in production. Job loss thereby accrues to cities unevenly as location decisions also change. On the demand side, emerging higher order human needs and aspirations are seen to play an increasing role in this process, and will, in turn, involve locational decisions associated with residential development and infrastructural provision.

In this process the state undertakes two principal functions: as an associate of capital it establishes the appropriate conditions or environment for private enterprise to operate profitably; and via public expenditure programmes it seeks to address the human needs generated by technological and structural change, drawing upon increased societal capacity linked to economic growth. Thus the state provides a safety net for the mismatches between supply and demand for labour (and infrastructure) that changing technology is inducing (see Chapter 18). It is complemented by an informal sector comprised partly of those displaced (particularly when an economic downswing accompanies structural change) and by self-help networks which are establishing at the grass roots level (see Chapter 18 and Naisbitt 1982).

Figure 1.1   A Structural Model of Technological and Urban
             Change
             (Highlighting the shift from energy to knowledge
             base, lower to higher order human needs and
             from supply-induced change to demand-induced
             change in urban development)

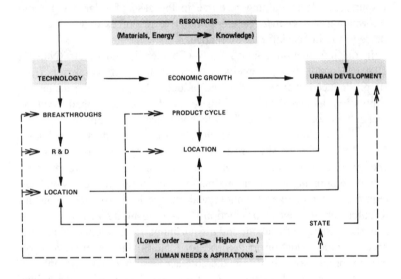

The state is an organisation with the requisite level of power and resources to institute fundamental and widespread change in the lives of individuals, groups, regions and entire nations (see Chapter 16).[4] Some major multinational companies have similar powers. The manner in which both utilise land, capital, human resources and technology to achieve their respective corporate objectives will affect future patterns of urban and regional development. State (or federal) governments and city administrations are further involved in a role of competing with each other to provide infrastructure and venture capital packages capable of attracting private development (especially the footloose high-technology industry) to a particular locality (see Figure 1.2). The manner in which information technology is harnessed in this process is examined in the succeeding chapters. However, to the extent that there

Figure 1.2 State and Capital Inputs to Local Development

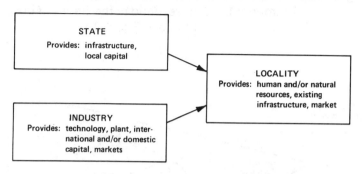

is a shift from supply-induced change to demand-induced change, the influence of large private companies and the state may be decreasing.

Modifying the impacts of change at the urban system level is a further set of factors. The net urban change depends on the cost-effectiveness of an innovation, the number of opportunities so offered, their diversity, and the information available on them. In the case of information technology, processing capabilities are almost doubling annually while unit costs are decreasing at a similar rate, facilitating rapid market penetration. This technology enables a diverse range of new and existing goods and services to be produced at low cost, along with dissemination of information on them. These changes are affecting the organisational arrangements for working and living and hence the spaces and locations required for these activities and the interactions between them. One further factor affecting the spatial impact of the change process is the adaptability of the community, of its administration, and of the private and public sectors which comprise the industrial and employment base of the urban system, to accept or respond to the changes occurring around it.

A Model of Urban Form and Change

The urban system may be expressed in terms of residential and non-residential activities, and of the interactions, such as transport and communications, which occur between them. At the metropolitan level the spatial arrangement or form of the system may be expressed in terms of two key parameters: the spatial dispersal of non-residential activities; and the spatial dispersal or extent of their interactions. The dispersal of

Figure 1.3 Trajectory of Metropolitan Development
(Numbers 1 to 5 correspond to the stages of urban
development identified in Figure 2.1)

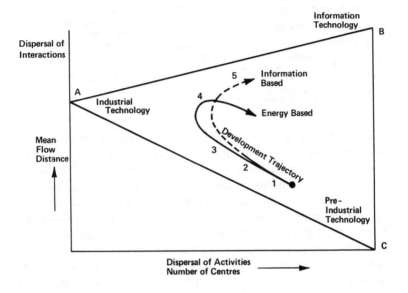

non-residential activities may be measured by their mean distance from
the urban centre or by the number of (dispersed) centres within the
metropolitan area, and the dispersal of interactions by the mean flow
distance.

These two parameters may be expressed as the two axes of a graph
(Figure 1.3) representing an activity-versus-interaction space. The
triangle ABC defines the feasible limits of this space. The point A
represents a single-centred city, the line BC represents the other
extreme of complete dispersal of non-residential activities, or cottage
industries. The line AB represents the extreme of zero flow cost where
interactions are (randomly distributed and) independent of distance; the
line AC represents the other extreme of infinite flow cost or interactions
with the closest activity only. A particular city may be presented as a
point in this space.

The spatial impacts of technological change may be expressed as a movement of this point in the two-dimensional space. Increasing energy costs would result in shorter trips and hence a movement downwards in Figure 1.3. Reducing communications costs on the other hand would result in a movement upwards. Increasing concentration of industry is represented by a movement to the left. Increasing decentralisation is indicated by a movement to the right.

Urban technology may also be expressed in terms of these parameters: the point C in Figure 1.3 represents pre-industrial or low urban technology, such as pedestrian or horsedrawn travel, and low density construction. The point A represents the extreme of concentrated industrial technology, supported by public and private radial mass transport systems, and high rise buildings with elevator systems. The point B represents an urban system based on information technology in which dispersed activities interact electronically — that is, the fully interconnected, wired city.

Thus in terms of the changes considered above, point C represents pre-industrial or the alternative society, independence, 'low tech' (or 'high touch' — Naisbitt 1982), self-help and the informal sector; point A represents industrial society and its organisational structures, dependence, hierarchies, concentration, limited choice, representative democracy and institutional help; and point B represents the information society, interdependence, networks, diversity and participatory democracy.

A possible trajectory of the urban system over time within this parameter space is indicated in Figure 1.3. The early stages of metropolitan development are indicated by a movement inwards, or concentration. The later industrial and post-industrial development is accompanied by a movement outwards (see Chapter 2). Information-based industries may be expected to move towards the point B, particularly where the interactions are primarily electronic. But this movement may be slowed by the need for some of these industries to retain 'high touch', face-to-face interaction for transactions needing trust. Material- and energy-based industries, too, may be expected to take a lower trajectory, particularly when the interactions are largely energy-based, and especially when the movement of heavy materials is involved. Thus the changes that are occurring in society and its urban systems as a consequence of the information revolution are by no means similar or unidirectional. On the contrary, they are diverse, profound and multifaceted. The task of this book is to try to explore them in more detail.

Notes

1. From Hamish McDonald (1983), 'Robots in Japan', *Airways Inflight*, Qantas, Sydney, July-August.
2. From Richard Meier, see Chapter 6.
3. Here, Ryan (1980) identifies the following energy transitions: from animate energy in pre-industrial (agrarian) society to fossil fuels in industrial society and the coming transition to solar-based energy systems in post-industrial society. The combination of microelectronics and energy technology in thin film photovoltaics is producing a reducing cost trend which is rapidly increasing the viability of this process. The above trends, together with lighter materials and miniaturisation, are reducing, for post-industrial society, the limitations previously imposed by energy.
4. The state apparatus, according to Green (1983), is vulnerable to control by key groups who tend to use the machinery of government in their own favour, often at the expense of those in need: 'many [government] programmes . . . assisted the professionals who ran them but did little for the intended beneficiaries'. Likewise, the introduction into a region of new technology is controlled, at global level by large corporations (Baranson 1978), at metropolitan level by economically and politically powerful groups (see, e.g., Jones's (1982:214) account of the transformation of Los Angeles into a car-based city; also Winner's (1980:123) account of bridge-building in New York).

References

Baranson, J. (1978) *Technology and the Multinationals. Corporate Strategies in a Changing World Economy,* D.C. Heath & Co., Lexington, Massachusetts

Bell, D. (1980) 'The Social Framework of the Information Society' in M.L. Dertouzos and J. Moses (eds) *The Computer Age: a Twenty-Year View,* The MIT Press, Cambridge, Massachusetts

Green, D.G. (1983) 'The Attack on the Welfare State', *Australian Journal of Social Issues, 18*(3), 157-70

Grosch, H.R.J. (1973) 'The Information Explosion', in W.A. Hahn and K.F. Gordon (eds) *Assessing the Future and Policy Making,* Gordon and Breach, New York

Hawkins, P. (1983) *The Next Economy,* Holt, Rinehart and Winston, New York

Jones, B. (1982) *Sleepers, Wake! Technology and the Future of Work,* Oxford University Press, Melbourne

Maslow, A.H. (1970) *Motivation and Personality,* Harper and Row, London

Naisbitt, J. (1982) *Megatrends,* Warner, New York

Ryan, C.J. (1980) 'The Choices in the Next Energy and Social Revolution', *Technological Forecasting and Social Change, 16,* 191-208

Stonier, T. (1979) 'The Third Industrial Revolution: Microprocessors and Robots', paper prepared for The International Metal Workers Federation Central Committee Meeting, Vienna, 19 October

Toffler, A. (1981) *The Third Wave,* Bantam Books, New York

Winner, L. (1980) 'Do Artifacts Have Politics?' *Daedalus, 109*(1), 121-36

PART ONE

INTERNATIONAL AND REGIONAL PERSPECTIVES

2. THE WORLD AND EUROPE
P. Hall

In this chapter four tasks are attempted in increasing order of difficulty, or as some might say impossibility. First, for the recent past — defined as the period 1950-80 — the chapter tries to identify the main features of urban-regional change, setting Europe within a broad international context. It then asks how far these trends can be attributed to technological developments that were occurring within the same period, relating these to parallel changes in economy, society, lifestyles and values. Thirdly it asks how far any of these factors might be expected to change in the immediate future — defined as the period 1980-2010. Finally it considers the impact of such changes, again, on the pattern of urban-regional change.

The Recent Past: Main Trends

Recent American work (Berry 1976; Vining and Kontuly 1977; Vining and Strauss 1977) suggests that in the US at least four major trends are simultaneously occurring. First, for several decades urban regions have been decentralising: people and jobs are diminishing in central cities, continuing to increase in suburbs. Secondly, and more recently, the decentralisation process has gone a stage further: city regions (SMSAs) have tended to grow more slowly than before, while non-metropolitan growth has accelerated. While some of this non-metropolitan growth represents continued outward wave-like movement to counties just outside SMSA borders (which may thus be included at the next Census redefinition), about one-half is taking place in more distant locations, away from major cities. Thirdly, returns to urban scale appear negative: larger SMSAs are tending to stagnate and even to decline, while smaller SMSAs show the fastest rates of growth. Fourthly, within larger polycentric urban regions (the so-called Standard Consolidated Statistical Areas, SCSAs), growth is notably moving away from the larger central SMSAs (New York, Detroit, San Francisco, Los Angeles) to smaller peripheral SMSAs (Long Branch-Ashbury Park, Ann Arbor, San Jose, Oxnard-Simi Valley-Ventura).

These trends are quite powerfully modified by regional effects: growth is passing from older-settled and older-industrialised regions (the North East and East North Central regions) to the sunbelt (especially the West South Central, Mountain and Pacific regions). The combined result is, for instance, that larger SMSAs forming the centre of SCSAs in the older regions are tending to decline, while smaller SMSAs in the sunbelt show most vigorous growth; but all tend to show outward decentralisation from core to ring.

It appears that the trends are predictably very similar for population and for employment, an exception appearing only where population decentralises before employment, thus producing longer commuting distances. Some evidence, for instance from the New York region, suggests that this may be a transitional phase: eventually, after a time lag of perhaps one or two decades, the very scale of population out-movement generates new suburban employment, not only in residentiary services, but in basic industries too. Associated with this, there has been a notable tendency in older regions and cities for contraction of employment in manufacturing and goods-handling services (transportation, freight movement, distribution); the parallel growth of so-called quaternary industry, mainly in offices, has typically failed to compensate. By contrast, in newer cities and regions, both manufacturing and service industries have continued to generate new jobs.

In Western Europe the evidence is not so clear-cut (Hall and Hay 1980; Hall 1980). There, at any rate down to 1975, different parts of the continent appear to have reached different stages of evolution. Great Britain and Ireland ('Atlantic Europe' in Table 2.1) behaved most like the US. Here there was a clear tendency, even in the 1950s but very markedly after 1960, for core-to-ring decentralisation, either relative (ring growing faster than core) or absolute (core declining, ring growing). The largest SMSAs had reached the point of decentralisation during loss from the whole metropolitan areas; here population was decentralising outwards to neighbouring metropolitan areas. But the growth of the latter was much stronger in prosperous, less traditionally industrialised regions (like the south-east of Great Britain) than in the older industrial regions like the north-east or north–west. Northern Europe (Scandinavia), Western Europe (Benelux, France) and Central Europe (Federal Republic of Germany, Switzerland, Austria) appeared to be transitional: they began to decentralise, but later than Britain. Southern Europe was actually centralising down to 1970, and this process even affected relatively large cities which were growing. But here, too, there was some counter-movement after 1970. It will be noticed that as the eye goes down Table 2.1, the movement across from centralisation to decentralisation seems to be progressively more tardy.

The evidence for Japan, assembled by Glickman (1978), gives

Table 2.1 Europe: Pattern of Population Shift, 1950-75

	% of all metro areas exhibiting type of shift					
	LC	AC	RC	RD	AD	LD
Atlantic Europe						
1950-60	7.0	5.6	39.2	27.3	10.5	10.5
1960-70	2.8	1.4	21.7	40.6	25.2	8.4
1960-70*	2.9	0.7	21.7	41.3	24.6	8.8
1970-75*	2.2	0.7	23.2	39.1	18.1	16.7
Northern Europe						
1950-60	6.8	34.1	43.2	13.6	2.3	0.0
1960-70	6.8	9.1	63.6	13.6	6.8	0.0
1970-75	4.6	0.0	6.8	36.4	43.2	9.1
Western Europe						
1950-60	4.2	39.2	34.2	18.3	3.3	0.8
1960-70	2.5	17.5	49.2	20.8	8.3	1.7
1960-70*	2.5	17.7	49.6	20.2	8.4	1.7
1970-75*	9.2	7.6	33.6	21.9	25.2	2.5
Southern Europe						
1950-60	23.1	26.9	42.3	7.7	0.0	0.0
1960-70	18.4	24.6	40.8	14.6	1.5	0.0
1960-70*	17.6	25.6	40.8	15.2	0.8	0.0
1970-75*	11.2	7.2	20.8	32.0	20.8	8.0
Central Europe						
1950-60	25.4	12.8	43.1	15.7	1.0	2.0
1960-70	1.0	2.0	24.5	49.0	22.6	1.0
1960-70*	3.9	7.7	23.1	53.9	11.5	0.0
1970-75*	0.0	3.9	23.1	15.4	42.3	15.4

Key: LC Centralisation during decline in population
     AC Absolute centralisation
     RC Relative centralisation
     RD Relative decentralisation
     AD Absolute decentralisation
     LD Decentralisation during decline in population
     * Based on restricted sample of metropolitan areas. Refer also to Figure
     2.1.
Source: Hall and Hay (1980)

similar results. During the 1950s and 1960s, there was a quite uniform growth of the urban system, with few observable negative returns to scale in the largest metropolitan areas; and there was no notable tendency towards decentralisation. Only after 1970 did these effects become very pronounced.

This strongly suggests that urban areas tend to pass through some kind of continuum over time. The key elements in this process appear to be the degree of primacy (the relation between the growth of the largest city, or cities, and the rest), the relationship between cores and rings within metropolitan areas, and the relationship between metropolitan and non-metropolitan growth. In the earlier stages of economic development, corresponding to less-developed countries today, there is growing metropolitanisation, growing primacy and growing centralisation. At a later stage, corresponding to the stage of rapid industrialisation, though metropolitan growth continues, the primacy rate begins to drop (because of the development of lower-order cities) and decentralisation sets in, led always by the leading metropolitan area. During the period 1950-80, while Great Britain had already arrived at a late stage of this process, much of Europe was still passing through earlier phases. In particular, it should be realised that in this period some 7 million people in the European Economic Community left the land and migrated to the cities for work in factories or offices. Many of them flooded into the major cities, where a disproportionate part of the available job opportunities in secondary and tertiary activities was to be found.

Employment data are much more difficult to assemble on a uniform, comparable basis than are residential population data. The evidence suggests that the outward movement of population precedes that of employment, generally by a decade or more. Some parts of Europe (for instance Central Europe) had reached a stage of general population deconcentration by the 1970s but their central city employment levels were at worst stable. The evidence for Great Britain, which is particularly interesting since clearly it has led the deconcentration process in Europe, indicates that after the mid-1960s there was a sharp contraction of employment in manufacturing and in associated goods-handling tertiary activities (transportation, warehousing, port activities), particularly in inner urban areas.

The reasons are complex and still to some extent open to debate (Keeble 1976; Fothergill and Gudgin 1982; Massey and Meegan 1982). It is generally accepted that, at least until the early 1980s, this contraction was abnormally evident in inner-city areas and thus may have resulted from sheer lack of space in which to restructure production at a time when, under competitive pressure, British industry was being forced to change traditional production processes. It is generally accepted also that the same pressures drove many traditional inner-city firms to the wall, causing their total closure. Further, there is widespread agreement that actual physical movement of plants was not very important, as Dennis (1978) has shown for London. What is still debatable is the extent to which the decline is attributable to changes in corporate ownership and control which, some observers argue, massively contributed to the process through closure of inner-city plants and transfer of production to newer greenfield or urban-periphery sites. Whatever the balance between these different factors, the dominant underlying one was the forced restructuring of production, through substitution of capital for labour and the development of more efficient flow techniques of production, requiring greater space per worker and newer, generally single-storey, plants. Similarly, in the docks, containerisation massively accelerated the movement from congested inner dock basins to sites nearer the estuary mouths.

Other types of employment have shown a greater affinity for city-centre locations — in particular, the fast-growing group of producer service industries that includes educational services, the media, finance, insurance and real estate, advertising and many other office-based activities. However, the location of these industries appears to depend to a considerable extent on the urban hierarchy in each country. This hierarchy shows notable differences within Europe from one nation-state to another, depending on accidents of history. Thus France and the Federal Republic of Germany — two nations very similar in their levels of economic development — have totally contrasting urban patterns, the first heavily primate, the second strongly dispersed among a number of strong regional capitals. Britain and Belgium both have so-called rank-size distributions characteristic of mature industrial countries, though in Britain the presence of a ring of about 20 small metropolitan areas around London could be said to give rise to a modified primate effect. Germany, the Netherlands, Switzerland, Spain and Italy all exhibit what might be called shared primacy, with a number of equally important middle-sized urban areas dominating the picture. This distinction is vital in understanding the growth of producer service employment. In Britain for instance there is clear evidence that the major provincial cities are weakening as office centres (Daniels 1977) and that producer services are weakly developed in provincial regions (Northern Ireland Economic Council 1982), while in Germany the reverse appears to be true (Burtenshaw *et al.* 1981). The result is that whereas in Germany an outward shift of manufacturing can be countered by increases in city-centre producer service employment, in British provincial cities this fails to happen.

A further noticeable trend is that more routine producer-service employment shifts locally, within higher-order metropolitan areas, from centre to periphery in search of rent and salary savings. Such a trend has been noticeable for instance within the New York region, taking office development outward to commuter cities such as Stamford and New

Haven. In the case of London it first (in the 1950s) resulted in development at Croydon 20 kilometres south of central London, and then in a ring of medium-sized cities in the 50-65 kilometres ring, such as Southend-on-Sea and Reading. These cities now form the centres of some of the fastest-growing metropolitan areas in Britain, and some of them have tended to exhibit rapid employment growth in their central cities.

In some countries these shifts are reinforced by regional contrasts. Europe contains a number of well-defined major industrial regions, based in the nineteenth century on coalfields and associated port cities (South Wales, North West England, North East England, Central Scotland, Wallonia, Lorraine, the Ruhrgebiet, Silesia). Most of these areas have exhibited major employment losses during the 1960s and 1970s because of the structural contraction of their basic industries. In them, most urban areas — both big and small — have tended to stagnate or even to decline in population and employment. In Great Britain, for instance, both the London and Manchester metropolitan areas declined, reflecting the general tendency to contraction of bigger urban areas; but while in London this decline was compensated by increases in the smaller metropolitan areas all around, in Manchester no such compensating increase occurred (Spence *et al.* 1982).

We can sum up the available evidence on trends in a series of propositions. First, the form of the urban hierarchy in Europe markedly depends on inertia — some of it reflecting fairly ancient history. Secondly, shifts in that hierarchy seem to reflect the stage of industrialisation/urbanisation that has been reached, with Great Britain in the van and Southern (and Eastern) Europe in the rear. The most advanced countries share the American tendencies: stagnation and decline of larger metropolitan areas, gains in smaller areas and even (in Great Britain during the 1970s) in non-metropolitan areas such as Cornwall and Mid-Wales, outward movement from city to suburb. The less advanced countries still tend to exhibit rapid growth of larger urban areas and even of their central cities, reflecting the concentration there of development impulses in earlier stages of development; this process may be enhanced in periods of rapid economic growth of the world economy, such as the 1950s and 1960s. All this suggests that nations pass through some kind of continuum from urbanisation to de-urbanisation over time; the earlier phases are characterised by increasing urbanisation, increasing primacy, and ring-to-core centralisation, the later phases by the reverse processes (Figure 2.1). Finally, regional shifts may emphasise or distort these patterns. The most advanced

Figure 2.1 Schematic Model of Urban Development
(For key, refer to Table 2.1)

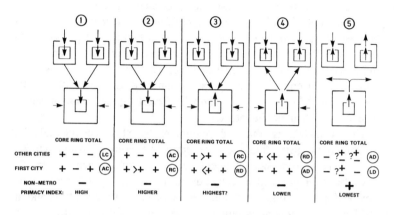

countries (Great Britain, the US) show a decline of older-industrialised regions (the 'rustbowl' effect) and a growth of new high-technology industry in smaller cities in formerly agricultural regions (Silicon Valley, the Research Triangle of North Carolina, the M4 Corridor in Britain).

The Recent Past: The Impact of Technological Change

Undoubtedly, technological change has had some influence on these shifts. First, as already seen above, capital substitution in manufacturing and in goods-handling tertiaries has played a major role in the contraction of those industries in congested inner-city locations and in older-industrialised regions. Secondly, with subtle exceptions and qualifications, all European countries have experienced rapid technological development, during the period 1950-80, in transportation and communications technology. All European nations have built motorway and associated high-speed, free-access highway systems, giving most of them national networks that link up all large and medium-sized cities. Germany and Italy had such systems in place even by 1950, but have extended them; Great Britain, Belgium, the Netherlands, France, Spain, Switzerland and Austria have constructed them. Similarly, nearly all European countries have modernised their inter-city rail systems, creating high-speed links (Britain's 125s, the TEEs on the mainland of Europe) between the major business cities. Some European cities have invested massively in new or improved rapid transit systems. Airports have been reconstructed and inter-city air services, both internally and internationally, have been greatly developed — though, because of regulation, invariably at a much higher cost per kilometre than in the US. Telecommunications have been massively extended and improved, with universal direct-dial services to all parts of the world at a much lower cost than the operator-connected services of the 1950s. Europe has taken a lead in some aspects of new communications technology, such as Videotext.

The spatial effects of these developments have been considerable, but an important distinction must be drawn between inter-regional and intra-urban impacts. At inter-regional scale, within each country the effect has been to shrink effective distance through big reductions in the time and cost of communication. Motorways, high-speed trains and air services have brought provincial cities effectively closer to national capitals; highway and train times have typically been cut by about half in 30 years. Though this cannot be established with precision, it appears that the main effect has been to reduce the role of provincial cities to subsidiary centres, controlled from national capitals. Work by Goddard and Morris (1975) in Britain, for instance, has clearly established that workers in decentralised offices have fewer contacts than those remaining in London. This effect however will depend on the precise form of the national urban hierarchy already discussed; it is strong in Britain, weak or non-existent in Germany.

At intra-urban level, the effects are more varied and complex. Some nations and some cities have tended to invest heavily in urban motorways, some less so or hardly at all; the contrast between London and Paris is striking. Similarly, some nations and cities have invested more heavily than others in rail rapid transit: most major German cities now have modern rail systems, while some major cities (Birmingham, Manchester) have invested almost nothing. Only a little systematic work has been undertaken on the impacts of such investments. Whereas American work (the BART impact study) suggests that they have been negligible, isolated German studies indicate a contrary result. In Britain, studies of the Glasgow and Newcastle upon Tyne systems indicate that they have concentrated shopping patterns, the major regional centre gaining, the smaller centres losing. Certainly the major German cities, which have combined new rail systems with extensive pedestrianisation and general environmental upgrading, appear to be more prosperous than some of their British equivalents. But to link cause and effect is extremely difficult.

Similarly, those cities that have failed to build urban highway systems may have raised transportation costs for industry and may thus have indirectly encouraged industrial contraction. Though numerous studies have shown that transportation costs are not in general a very large part of total production costs, nevertheless the extra time involved in distributing goods over congested urban streets may prove to have been a telling factor. In small European countries, it may make a critical difference in the ability to make a return delivery trip within one day. A detailed survey of industrialists in a congested part of south London, for instance, showed that traffic difficulties were regarded as significant (Department of the Environment 1977). In London, expert judgement is that completion of the 187 kilometre London beltway, the M25, in the mid-1980s, will exert a further strong outward pull for factories, warehouses and offices (Lichfield and Partners 1981). The two similar Paris beltways, the A86 and A87, which connect suburban nodes and new towns, may well play a similar role.

What is supremely difficult is to filter out these effects as against those resulting from general social and economic changes. Thus the M25 may well attract London industry to sites 20 or more kilometres from the centre — but so may availability of the right kinds of skilled labour, a good physical and social environment, good access to airport facilities and presence of the right kinds of specialised services. The problem is that social preferences and locational needs are all working in the same direction — outwards.

There has been much comment in the urban literature on an apparent contrary phenomenon: gentrification. First recognised and named in London in the early 1960s (Glass *et al.* 1964:xviii), it has continued to spread there and to invade many smaller British cities. Similar phenomena are noticeable in Dutch and German cities. The trend is undoubtedly widespread; the paradox is that, since the incomers live at more generous space standards than those they displace, its invariable result is to increase the outflow of people from the city. It may help generate labour-intensive service activities of a residentiary or semi-residentiary character, such as boutiques, wine bars and restaurants, but the total effect on employment is a matter for speculation.

The Future: Likely Technologies

Forecasting is an inherently risky and usually unprofitable business, especially where, as here, it involves the interrelationship of technological, economic, social and even national-cultural trends. The only possible comfort is that some of the main lines of technological advance seem to be well set. All observers agree that the next two decades shall see a vast expansion of information-processing technology, which may have an effect on tertiary industry — especially on producer services — at least as great as the impact of earlier technological advances on manufacturing industry. What seems certain also is that these systems will first be developed and used in the three major advanced industrial areas of the world: the US, Japan and Western Europe. The pattern of diffusion of the new technologies, in its early years, already demonstrates this. It is inherently difficult to say whether any one of these areas will take a dominating lead; more likely since all have areas of strength and all are able to import new technology almost instantaneously, the diffusion will be fairly uniform.

Equally clear is the likely development of biotechnology, based on the techniques of fermentation and recombinant DNA. Nearly all observers are agreed that this technology is still in its developmental stage and that it is unlikely to produce major industrial applications, with consequent effects on employment, for some years — perhaps until the turn of the century (see Chapter 8). There are possibilities of interesting synergistic relationships between developments in biotechnology and information technology, especially in the field of artificial intelligence.

Thus, though the broad shape of the new technology is fairly clear, its eventual outcomes are not. From past experience (Jewkes *et al.* 1969), an important proposition can be derived: the precise application of new technologies is not usually appreciated at first. The steam engine, and over a hundred years later the internal combustion engine, were both initially viewed as stationary sources of power; their application to locomotion came only belatedly. Similarly, the radio and later the computer were not originally viewed as sources of mass entertainment. So we do not know exactly what the industrial implications of the new technologies may be, even in the relatively short term.

The Future: Impacts on Settlement

The really difficult problem, given this uncertainty, is to predict the effects of the new technologies, through their economic impacts on both production and consumption, on future patterns of living and working. Here, another insight of Jewkes and his colleagues is relevant: major bursts of technological advance have invariably been followed by upheavals in the system of production. Steam power rapidly led to the displacement of the domestic system of production by the factory system; the development of the automobile was accompanied by assembly-line production, first on Ford's magneto line at Highland Park in 1913 (Nevins 1954). Some observers have suggested that the characteristic feature of the post-Second World War period has been the growth of unpaid domestic production to replace paid services; thus television and video-recorders have replaced cinemas and music halls, the car has replaced buses and trams and trains. The home computer could represent a dramatic extension of this principle, whereby a very large part of all activity transfers into the home (Gershuny 1978; Gershuny and Miles 1983). Interestingly, such activity is not included in estimates of GDP with the result that, as it increases in importance, the real GDP is under-estimated.

Such developments, in Gershuny's view, depend on provision of appropriate infrastructure as well as on specialist servicing facilities; thus cars demanded surfaced highways as well as filling stations and repair shops. Interestingly, though the infrastructure needed for the revolution in information technology is either in place or is in course of being provided (telephone lines, fibre optic cables, satellites, two-way cable transmission), it is not yet freely available to users; the analogy is with the automobile around 1910. However within the next few years, as the infrastructure does become widely accessible, it is quite feasible to visualise substantial areas of production transferring from central-ised, specialised buildings back into the home; routine typing and record-keeping are obvious candidates. Employers would effect major savings in rents and presumably also in salaries, since commuting costs would be eliminated; employees would effect major economies in their own time-budgets and thereby gain flexibility in reconciling work and domestic responsibilities (cf. Carlstein *et al.* 1978). The optimal location for such activities will depend to some degree on telecom-munications' charging policies; in both the US and Great Britain, deregulation of telecommunications monopolies is already leading to a two-level system of charging whereby larger urban centres, with their more dense traffic, enjoy lower rates than smaller, remoter places.

Such shifts are likely to eliminate a proportion of present-day personal travel — especially regular peak-hour commuting — and of mail traffic. There may however be compensating increases in other forms of travel. A paradox in the history of communications is that major technological improvements have invariably been followed by an increase in travel rather than the reverse; witness the impact of the telephone which, by greatly facilitating fairly routine contacts, led to vastly increased demand for follow-up face-to-face contact. If information technology led to a great increase in the exchange of written material, this might well generate a demand for face-to-face meetings to discuss it. And other technological advances, such as video-conferencing, do not necessarily allow for the serendipity effect of random face-to-face encounters. Advances in information exchange are likely therefore to be followed, as in the recent past, by an explosion in the demand for conferences, conventions, seminars, workshops and other forms of direct encounter. Paradoxically, the most highly favoured locations for such encounters are likely to be either the centres of major national or regional cities, with well-developed restaurant and entertainment facilities, or environmentally favoured university or resort towns. The least favoured sites will be the old, decaying industrial cities.

The curious prospect in Europe, therefore, is one of a partial return to the spatial patterns of the agrarian Middle Ages. With the uniformly available high-technology infrastructure, a high degree of residential dispersal will be possible. Many people will be free to express a preference for isolated farms, villages or small towns (Hall 1977). Negative externalities of crowding in the larger metropolitan areas may mean that, for those workers free to choose, preferred locations will tend to be the older, more rural settlements in regions unaffected by the first industrial revolution. The exceptions will be a few larger cities with good environmental qualities and highly developed social infrastructure, including the national capital cities, which also in most cases will be old-established places. These trends are already observable in the European country most advanced along this road, Great Britain; here, the migration patterns of the 1970s are almost the obverse of those of 100 years ago.

Such trends do not mean the complete disappearance of the traditional urban hierarchy. Even with a wide variety of goods and services available via an electronic supply system, there will continue to be a need for physical concentration in central places. Electronic mail order will not prove a substitute for window shopping, any more than in the Edwardian 'Raj the Army and Navy Catalogue was a substitute for home leave and the trip to Harrods. Electronic medical diagnosis is unlikely to obviate the need for visits to hospital laboratories, let alone the intensive care unit. Electronic education will not remove the need for face-to-face seminars and tutorials, as Britain's Open University has found. This paper was typed at home directly on to a computer and could — had the networking technology been sufficiently diffused — have been circulated directly worldwide to fellow-conferees by telephone. But that would not, and will not, remove the age-old need to meet and to communicate face-to-face in conferences and workshops.

References

Berry, B.J.L. (1976) 'The Counter-Urbanization Process: Urban America Since 1970' in Berry, B.J.L. (ed.) *Urbanization and Counter-Urbanization*, Sage Urban Affairs Annual Reviews No. 11, Sage, Beverly Hills

Burtenshaw, D.J., Bateman, M. and Ashworth, G.J. (1981) *The City in West Europe*, John Wiley, New York

Carlstein, T., Parkes, D. and Thrift, N. (1978) *Human Activity and Time Geography: Timing Space and Spacing Time*, (vol. 2), Edward Arnold, London

Daniels, P.W. (1977) 'Office Location in the British Conurbations: Trends and Strategies', *Urban Studies, 14*, 261-74

Dennis, R. (1978) 'The Decline of Manufacturing Employment in Inner London: 1966-74', *Urban Studies, 15*, 63-73

Department of the Environment (1977) *Inner London: Policies for Dispersal and Balance*, HMSO, London

Fothergill, S. and Gudgin, G. (1982) *Unequal Growth: Urban and Regional Employment Change in the UK*, Heinemann Educational Books, London

Gershuny, J. (1978) *After Industrial Society?: The Emerging Self-Service Economy*, Macmillan, London

Gershuny, J. and Miles, I. (1983) *The New Service Economy: The Transformation of Employment in Industrial Societies*, Frances Pinter, London

Glass, R. *et al.* (1964) *London: Aspects of Change*, Centre for Urban Studies Report No. 3, Macgibbon and Kee, London

Glickman, N.J. (1978) *The Growth and Management of the Japanese Urban System*, Academic Systems, New York

Goddard, J.B. and Morris, D. (1975) *The Communications Factor in Office Decentralization*, Pergamon Press, Oxford

Hall, P. (1977) *Europe 2000*, Duckworth, London

Hall, P. (1980) 'New Trends in European Urbanization', *The Annals of the American Academy of Political and Social Science, 451*, 45-51

Hall, P. and Hay, D. (1980) *Growth Centres in the European Urban System*, Heinemann Educational Books, London

Jewkes, J., Sawyers, D. and Stillerman, R. (1969) *The Sources of Invention* (2nd ed.), W.A. Norton, New York

Keeble, D. (1976) *Industrial Location and Planning in the United Kingdom*, Methuen, London

Lichfield, N. and Partners, Goldstein Leigh Associates (1981) *M25 London Orbital: Property Market Effects*, Nathaniel Lichfield Associates, London

Massey, D. and Meegan, R. (1982) *The Anatomy of Job Loss*, Methuen, London

Nevins, A. (1954) *Ford: The Man, the Times, the Company*, Charles Scribners Sons, New York

Northern Ireland Economic Council (1982) *Private Services in Economic Development*, Paper No. 30, Northern Ireland Economic Council, Belfast

Spence, N., Gillespie, A., Goddard, J., Kennett, S., Pinch, S. and Williams A. (1982) *British Cities: An Analysis of Urban Change*, Urban and Regional Planning Series (vol. 26), Pergamon, Oxford

Vining, D.R. and Kontuly, T. (1977) 'Increasing Returns to City Size in the Face of an Impending Decline in the Size of large Cities: Which is the Bogus Fact?' *Environment and Planning A, 9,* 59-62

Vining, D.R. and Strauss, A. (1977) 'A Demonstration that the Current Deconcentration of Population in the United States is a Clean Break with the Past' *Environment and Planning A, 9,* 751-58

3. NORTH AMERICA
E. Malecki

This chapter addresses some recent trends and mechanisms relating to technological change in the urban and regional systems of Canada and the US, thus complementing Chapters 2 and 5 in this collection. It concludes by discussing the effects of technological change and its challenges for planning.

Urban and Regional Trends in North America

Any discussion of urban and regional dynamics in North America must recognise the evolution of the well-ordered system of regional and subregional centres that exists in both countries (Borchert 1972, 1978; Pred 1977; Simmons 1976). The major cities in each country dominate their surrounding market areas, and decisions and economic activities are channelled through these centres before filtering down to places below them in the hierarchy. City size is no longer the best indicator of the status of a city, because many large North American cities have lost population as their manufacturing bases have deteriorated (for example, St Louis, Pittsburgh and Cleveland). The rise of the service sector as the major source of employment and the economic base of many younger cities has altered the traditional foundation of urban growth (Hirschhorn 1979). In so doing, the advantages of cities and of regions have begun to be compared against standards relating to education and research, cultural and environmental amenities, and accessibility in the wider national and international system (Ullman 1958; Freidmann and Wolff 1982).

A useful shorthand description of North American urban-regional growth during the 1950-80 period is *decentralised concentrated dispersion* (Richardson 1973:135). All three components of this term have played major roles in the shifts identified in the location of economic activity in North America. *Dispersion* is a fair description of the spread of population and employment out of the manufacturing belt in both the US and Canada. The impetus behind this dispersion is a complex set of social and economic forces, including technological changes such as the improvement of highway and communication networks, the rapid expansion of air travel for inter-urban transportation, and the development of air conditioning which made habitable on a wide scale parts of the southern US. Social and political forces would include the growth of income maintenance programmes, especially for retirees, which has increased mobility to move to more hospitable or desirable locations (Beyers 1979). Finally, rapid changes in technologies have permitted manufacturing to take place in isolated rural and foreign locations that could not even be considered until the past 20 years or so (Bluestone and Harrison 1982:115-18). Transportation and communication technologies have obviously served to reduce or almost eliminate the barrier that distance once presented. But perhaps more influential have been changes in production technology that have helped to standardise the manufacture of large-volume products by an increasingly less-skilled (and lower-wage) workforce, which most often can be found in developing countries and in backward areas of many countries. The size of Canada and the US allows these low-cost sites to be found within national borders, unlike in Europe where some countries function as the periphery in contrast to core regions found in other countries. As Levy suggests in Chapter 5, the international migration of industry away from even the least-developed regions of North America is likely to be more significant in the future. Population dispersion based on non-wage income (e.g. retirees) and its pull for market-oriented employment is unlikely to slow down as the population continues to age. The dispersion of manufacturing oriented toward low wages has perhaps seen its peak; automation is likely to replace labour intensity of production and alter at least that part of the pressure toward dispersion of economic activity.

The *decentralisation* of economic activity refers to the marked suburbanisation of manufacturing, distribution and office functions within metropolitan regions over the past few decades. The sprawl found in all North American urban areas, but particularly those whose growth has been most rapid since 1950, is a product of the highway-based transportation system and its impacts on the distribution of housing, shopping and employment opportunities. Canadian and American cities are different in the extent to which these changes have affected urban form (Goldberg and Mercer 1980). Specifically, Canadian cities have remained much more centralised, in part because of different housing policies and greater support for intra-urban transport than is found in the US. In the US the decentralisation of urban areas has had the effect of increasing the racial and economic disparity between cities and their suburbs (Muller 1981; Sternlieb and Hughes 1977).

The *concentration* of regional growth in North America has taken place at the same time as the dispersion away from the traditional north-eastern core. As economic opportunities have spread into other regions, notably the 'sunbelt' of the south and west, there is a distinct dichotomy or polarisation in the type of growth that has occurred. Both Hall and Levy (in Chapters 2 and 5) point to the selectivity of recent growth, wherein some cities prosper as centres of corporate and financial power, innovation and regional prominence, while others struggle to maintain their dominance over a surrounding hinterland. A vivid example is provided by the recent growth of Houston and the decline of New Orleans on the southern coast of the US. Growth in the sunbelt has been most pronounced and most varied in a relatively small number of urban regions. Rural areas and small towns are sharing the overall growth of the region, but it is of a perceptibly different kind and described here as the dispersion of production from the north-east. Sunbelt cities, on the other hand, are becoming integrated into the higher-order communication and control networks that are increasingly represented by the service and information activities (the tertiary and quaternary sectors).

The service sector and its growth have received relatively little attention from urban and regional researchers, especially in light of their dominance as a source of employment. The work that has been done in a North American context points to the hierarchical pattern evident in the distribution of service employment, a pattern that is less evident for manufacturing (Stanback *et al.* 1981). In addition, especially when the non-routine, quaternary services are included, the service sector can be seen to have an urban location pattern, in stark contrast to the increasingly rural pattern found in manufacturing. This *dualism* or spatial division of labour is among the most important trends emerging from recent technological changes in the location of production and corporate control (Stanback and Noyelle 1982). Consequently, the distribution of job opportunities and rewards varies greatly among regions and cities. Low-skill production jobs have replaced agriculture in many peripheral regions, but the widest variety of opportunities is available primarily only in and near a few major cities.

As technological changes take place, new sectors, activities and 'growth industries' exhibit a marked bias in their location in an urban-regional system. This is because these new activities are different from the manufacturing and service sectors commonly dichotomised in urban and regional models (Hirschhorn 1979). These activities may be divided into two types: quaternary sector activities related to information and control; and research and development (R & D) directed toward new products and services. Both types are properly considered as quaternary activities (see Chapter 4), although R & D is frequently classified with the manufacturing sectors that it serves. Locationally, at the level of decision-making and administration within firms, only certain types of locations provide the necessary infrastructure, including frequent, well-connected air service and high-level communication linkages, as well as residential amenities for administrative and professional employees. The infrastructure factors may be interpreted as technological, but their geographical distribution is far from uniform or ubiquitous, and cumulative advantages in certain regions seem to persist for a rather long time.

A persistent feature of urban systems noted earlier is the presence of some degree of hierarchical structure, especially for control and innovation, which tends to focus on large urban regions first and peripheral regions only later (Pred 1977). In addition to obvious market-related reasons, this is due to the level of business support services, the density of information present in large cities, and the cumulative know-how and prior innovations there. Lasuen (1973) made this point a decade ago in the context of developing countries; it is becoming equally true for advanced economies (Freidmann and Wolff 1982). This is not to say that some information-related innovations (especially consumer products) are not widely available, but the fullest bundles of technologies and information tend to consistently gravitate toward the large urban regions favoured by large companies for administrative activities (Borchert 1978; Pred 1977; Stanback and Noyelle 1982). The hierarchical structure is not fixed across firms or inflexible over space, however, as Pred (1976) has shown, because each firm has its own individual control network. It is the overlap of many such corporate networks that generates the spatial regularities increasingly found in empirical studies.

The second type of economic activity that stems directly from technological change is R & D, and R & D is not markedly different from administration and control in its locational factors. In addition to infrastructure and residential and recreational attractiveness common to quaternary sector location, university and government research facilities are attractions for R & D location. Furthermore, *for R & D activities, more than for perhaps any other economic activity, jobs seem to follow people rather than the reverse.* Scientific and technical workers appear to exert a large influence in corporate location, which is not true for unskilled workers performing routine tasks. Still, the locational preferences of R & D workers may change or be changed in ways that are not well understood. The spatial result reinforces regional specialisation, since few places or regions other than large agglomerations and attractive innovation centres will have either administrative or R & D activities.

The other end of regional specialisation or the spatial division of labour — *routine manufacturing* — *has been largely freed from locational constraints of earlier eras.* This impact of technological change is responsible for the internationalisation of manufacturing, but in a North American context much routine manufacturing is located in peripheral regions where the combination of labour and other costs is competitive with foreign production. The growth of manufacturing employment and population in small towns is the spatial impact of this corporate decision. This occurs in some sectors more than others, especially those requiring little skill or training of employees. For the most part, neither the American nor the Canadian government attempts to alter significantly the locational preferences or decisions of firms. In fact, in the US, state and local governments compete in attempting to attract firms to their favourable 'business climate', which is often a euphemism for low-cost labour (Cobb 1982:226-7).

The urban-regional impact of technological change that is perhaps most pervasive, then, is *a polarisation of the labour force, both locationally and organisationally.* Technological changes allow production to be deskilled in order to be lower in cost and less constrained by location (Friedrichs and Schaff 1982). At the same time, a growing gap has appeared between workers whose skills are sought-after and well-rewarded, and those whose jobs are uncertain even in the short run. In major urban regions both types of jobs are found, while in rural areas only routine production jobs are available (Harrison 1982; Stanback and Noyelle 1982).

Challenges for Planning

Despite the pervasiveness of technological change in modern society, it remains poorly understood at the urban and regional scale. The urban-regional context of technological change is more poorly understood than the international-national scale or the urban and sub-urban scale. The international context into which nations fit has received ample attention from many quarters in recent years as some nations (e.g. Japan) have risen in economic and technological stature, while others have lost ground (e.g. the UK and the USA).[1] National agendas have been proposed that attempt to redress national shortcomings from the standpoint of international competitiveness (e.g. Bluestone and Harrison 1982; Glickman 1981; Reich 1983; Steed 1982). Until five or six years ago, technology was rarely mentioned in national policy debates; now it is raised at every turn despite our incomplete understanding of its mechanisms, catalysts and impacts.

At the other end of the spatial scale, considerable research has addressed urban-level impacts and planning, as exemplified by several of the contributions to this volume (cf. Brotchie *et al.* 1980). On the one hand, urban models are attractively precise because they are based on variables that can be measured relatively easily, such as distance, land values and population. Distance, travel time and travel cost are the principal variables in most such models. Actual people, firms and governments and their decisions rarely enter in. In a sense this doesn't matter, since historically in an urban context population densities and land use have been fairly predictable and have had the greatest impact. But urban models overlook a critical precondition of urban change: the economic base. Whether jobs to support the population actually appear, remain or disappear, however, is of little importance to urban-scale models, because these are determined exogenously.

At the scale of the urban-regional system, it is more difficult to make the assumption that employment is exogenous. Decisions made by firms — about what to produce, how to produce it, and *where* to produce it — determine the type and location of jobs and create the set of regional conditions that are responded to for future decisions (Massey 1979). Because the dominant firms are very large and their impacts are widespread, we do not have good frameworks for dealing with their spatial priorities and impacts (Taylor and Thrift 1979, 1983). Meaningful information is spotty at best for predictions of which cities will benefit from decisions of multinational firms and of the information-financial services that support their activities.

If a region does not have the non-routine activities associated with control, information and innovation, then it also is unlikely to have them on a large scale in the future. Cumulative advantages within firms (Nelson 1981) are also accumulated geographically, but only at some locations.[2] We cannot predict with certainty all of those places, but it would be possible to assign probabilities of future success, based largely on local capabilities and infrastructure for non-routine functions. Success as a production site only is perhaps becoming meaningless as a source of regional growth, unless it is combined with non-routine activities. Chapter 7 represents an attempt to model such growth and change.

One policy approach that is receiving much attention in North America, as well as elsewhere, is a reliance on small firms, many of which tend to be in technology-based industries. However, despite occasional successes of such firms in isolated places or peripheral regions, these locations still fail to possess the full mix of technology, infrastructure and information associated with widespread economic growth. *The greatest likelihood of new firms and their associated economic growth remains in the urban concentrations that appear to receive the bulk of growth in an urban-regional system.*

Technological change has not entered centrally into research on urban and regional change (Malecki 1983). The complexity surrounding its internalisation within large corporations and their strategies poses serious challenges for our understanding. The polarising tendencies of recent technological change within advanced countries such as Canada and the US obviously pale in comparison with the gap within Third World countries and between advanced and underdeveloped nations. These urban and regional issues are likely to grow as technology continues to change in the coming years.

Notes

1. For a discussion of the American context, see Botkin *et al.* (1982); for Canadian views, see Britton and Gilmour (1978) and Steed (1982).
2. This has been modelled by Beckmann and Schramm (1972) in a hierarchical model, and the result of technological change was found to favour the largest cities.

References

Beckmann, M. and Schramm, G. (1972) 'The Impact of Scientific and Technical Change on the Location of Economic Activities', *Regional and Urban Economics, 2*, 159-74

Beyers, W.B. (1979) 'Contemporary Trends in the Regional Economic Development of the United States', *Professional Geographer, 31*, 34-44

Bluestone, B. and Harrison, B. (1982) *The Deindustrialization of America*, Basic Books, New York

Borchert, J.R. (1972) 'America's Changing Metropolitan Regions', *Annals of the Association of American Geographers, 62*, 352-73

Borchert, J.R. (1978) 'Major Control Points in American Economic Geography', *Annals of the Association of American Geographers, 68*, 214-32

Botkin, J., Dimancescu, D. and Strata, R. (1982) *Global Stakes: the Future of High Technology in America*, Ballinger, Cambridge, Massachusetts

Britton, J.N.H. and Gilmour, J.M. (1978) *The Weakest Link: a Technological Perspective on Canadian Industrial Underdevelopment*, Background Study 43, Science Council of Canada, Ottawa.

Brotchie, J.F., Dickey, J.W. and Sharpe, R. (1980) *TOPAZ — General Planning Technique and its Applications at the Regional, Urban, and Facility Planning Levels*, Springer-Verlag, Berlin

Cobb, J.C. (1982) *The Selling of the South: The Southern Crusade for Industrial Development 1936-80*, Louisiana State University Press, Baton Rouge

Freidmann, J. and Wolff, G. (1982) 'World City Formation: an Agenda for Research and Action', *International Journal of Urban and Regional Research, 6*, 307-43

Friedrichs, G. and Schaff, G. (eds) (1982) *Microelectronics and Society: For Better or For Worse*, Pergamon, Oxford

Glickman, N.J. (1981) 'National Urban Policy in an Age of Austerity' in P. Nijkamp and P. Rietveld (eds), *Cities in Transition: Problems and Policies*, Sijthoff and Noordhoff, Rockville, Maryland

Goldberg, M.A. and Mercer, J. (1980) 'Canadian and US Cities: Basic Differences, Possible Explanations, and Their Meaning for Public Policy', *Papers of the Regional Science Association, 45*, 159-83

Harrison, B. (1982) 'The Tendency Toward Instability and Inequality Underlying the "Revival" of New England', *Papers of the Regional Science Association, 50*, 41-65

Hirschhorn, L. (1979) 'The Urban Crisis: A Post-Industrial Perspective', *Journal of Regional Science, 19*, 109-18

Lasuen, J.R. (1973) 'Urbanization and Development: The Temporal Interaction between Geographical and Sectoral Clusters', *Urban Studies, 10*, 163-88

Malecki, E.J. (1983) 'Technology and Regional Development: A Survey', *International Regional Science Review, 8*, 89-125

Massey, D. (1979) 'In What Sense a Regional Problem?', *Regional Studies, 13*, 233-43

Muller, P.O. (1981) *Contemporary Suburban America*, Prentice-Hall, Englewood Cliffs, New Jersey

Nelson, R.R. (1981) 'Research on Productivity Growth and Productivity Differences: Dead Ends and New Departures', *Journal of Economic Literature, 19*, 1029-64

Pred, A.R. (1976) 'The Interurban Transmission of Growth in Advanced Economies: Empirical Findings Versus Regional Planning Assumption', *Regional Studies, 10*, 151-71

Pred, A.R. (1977) *City-Systems in Advanced Economies*, John Wiley, New York

Reich, R. (1983) *The Next American Frontier*, Times Books, New York

Richardson, H.W. (1973) *Regional Growth Theory*, John Wiley, New York

Simmons, J.W. (1976) 'Short-Term Income Growth in the Canadian Urban System', *Canadian Geographer, 20*, 419-31

Stanback, T.M., Bearse, P.J., Noyelle, T.J. and Karasek, R.A. (1981) *Services: The New Economy*, Allanheld, Osmun, Totowa, New Jersey

Stanback, T.M. and Noyelle, T.J. (1982) *Cities in Transition*, Allanheld, Osmun, Totowa, New Jersey

Steed, G.P.F. (1982) *Threshold Firms: Backing Canada's Winners*, Background Study 48, Science Council of Canada, Ottawa

Sternlieb, G. and Hughes, J.W. (1977) 'New Regional and Metropolitan Realities of America', *Journal of the American Institute of Planners, 43*, 227-41

Taylor, M.J. and Thrift, N.J. (1979) 'Guest Editorial', *Environment and Planning A, 11*, 973-5

Taylor, M.J. and Thrift, N.J. (1983) 'Industrial Geography in the 1980s: Entering a Decade of Differences?', *Environment and Planning A, 15*, 1287-91

Ullman, E.L. (1958) 'Regional Development and the Geography of Concentration', *Papers and Proceedings of the Regional Science Association, 4*, 179-98

PART TWO

INDUSTRIAL PERSPECTIVES

4. INDUSTRIAL FUTURES: UK
M. Batty

> The commuting citizens of Prutopia take steam trains to return home to their low-tech villages after a day of work at the data-base complex. They spend their leisure hours restoring relics from the industrial past, such as textile looms and old steam engines, or baking bread. Their lives are monitored at every turn; their health, their social life, driving habits, cooking, central heating, as well as every functioning detail of their workplace. Paper is rarely seen on their twenty-first century daily round. Their non-commuting neighbours earn a living as craftsmen, working with leather, fine metals, porcelain or plastics. This is one of the lucky communities in the employment belt of Britain 2010. (Bellini 1982:89).

Alvin Toffler (1981) calls it *The Third Wave*, the transition from a society based on work and industry to one in which leisure pursuits will dominate. For a generation, thinkers and popularists have referred to it as the coming of the post-industrial society and, apart from some scenarios of the science fiction writers, most have taken an optimistic view. Few have taken to heart what all urbanists know — that development is uneven, and that the post-industrial future is as much likely to be dominated by inequality in a spatial sense as has been the past and is the present. The wave of new technology which is sweeping away our present industrial organisation may be in the vanguard of a 'coming boom', yet the portents in societies such as Britain, where social structure is intimately organised around traditional industry and work, are distinctly bleak. This chapter will attempt to raise some of these issues and speculate on the spatial form and organisation of cities without industry.

What the post-industrial scenarios written a decade or so ago never anticipated was a society dominated by and entirely dependent upon high technology but characterised by unemployment rather than employment, and gross inequality of opportunity. Bellini's (1982) scenario, a little of which is contained in the above quote, although seemingly a science fiction, is built around the economic facts and trends of contemporary Britain, where prospects for the post-industrial society are extremely gloomy. In April 1983 unofficial estimates placed unemployment around 4 million while the number of home computers reached the 1 million mark, the highest per capita of any Western 'industrialised' country. In the same month, the national trading account for manufactured industry (exports less imports of manufactured goods) went into deficit for the first time since the industrial revolution began in the late eighteenth century. In November 1983 statistics revealed that, in traditional areas of manufacturing industry such as the Welsh mining valleys, unemployment among school leavers (or rather school leavers without permanent employ) was greater than 90 per cent, an order of magnitude difference from levels of unemployment reported in the 1930s. The implication of these seeming paradoxes for the future form of urban areas in a Britain with virtually no manufacturing industry, together with the tension caused by the avowed intent of government to disengage from the market place, is hard to predict. Conventional approaches to urban planning and forecasting contain few precedents.

Many of the contributions in this book take a more optimistic view of the impacts of technological change on urban structure, in that technology and employment do not constitute the main focus. Dickey's (Chapter 13) scenario for the electronic village contrasts with that of Bellini's and this comparison serves at the outset to emphasise that the picture of the post-industrial society emerging in Britain and its implications for urban life, may be very different from that of other developed countries. Nevertheless part of our task here is to discuss a range of scenarios and thus provide some explanation of what is likely to happen under different conditions. Moreover linking technological change to current economic change and policy, and particularly to the 'present' recession, also serves to link implications for future urban form to particular economic conditions. In one sense then, the relationship between industry and urban form is of fundamental significance.

Thus this chapter will begin to explore some of the implications for urban form of the collapse of manufacturing industry, the rising level of unemployment and the diffusion of high-technology industry, and will dwell on the medium-term (up to 30 years) significance of these changes. One central theme will be the inability of conventional approaches to the treatment of industrial structure to make much headway in the analysis of implications for urban form, and the need for new approaches will be argued. Traditional approaches to the treatment of industrial structure will be examined, and contemporary approaches involving analysis in terms of institutions and organisations noted. In particular, the treatment of 'industry' as the exogenous component in urban forecasting models will be questioned, in line with Malecki's (Chapter 3) observations, and the need to shift from simple macro models to more micro analyses will be discussed. Some empirical evidence of an entirely anecdotal kind pertaining to spatial development in southern Britain will be described and finally conclusions with regard to research into appropriate forecasting models presented. This paper raises many problems and resolves few. It provides a basis for further discussion and speculates on a possible programme of illustrative work.

The Changing Structure of Industry and Employment

The traditional classification of economic activity is into three industry types, based on the degree to which each is fundamental to the process of producing goods and services. Primary, secondary and tertiary, are the age-old distinctions postulated on the assumption that order implies the stage at which such activities became significant. Contained within this order is also one of precedence. Tertiary depends on secondary which depends on primary, the direction of causation being one-way. This categorisation reflects a very simple, and frequently untenable theory of economic growth and progress, but in many contemporary discussions it has been extended to embrace two additional service-type sectors: quaternary (knowledge-based industries) and quinary (home services) (Jones 1983).

The traditional threefold classification corresponds crudely to Toffler's (1981) three waves, and significantly the growth of each activity and its subsequent decline (in percentage terms of persons employed) provides an historical illustration of this form of wave theory. Toffler's argument suggests that service-based activity will eventually predominate just as manufacturing activity once did, and further elaboration of service into knowledge- and home-based services suggests its growing importance. Despite the limitations posed by such classification, it provides a useful vehicle on which to speculate. Figure 4.1 takes Jones's (1983) fivefold classification and extrapolates service, quaternary and quinary activities forward, providing two of many scenarios: one in which service-based activity will continue to grow as will quaternary and quinary as society demands more organised pursuits, the other in which only quinary activity will dominate in the long term. This second scenario poses the more dramatic change, for in it the distinction between work and non-work in the quinary sector is blurred, heralding a society in which organised work is the exception in contrast to the former scenario in which it is still the rule.

To clarify questions concerning the nature of work and non-work, employment and unemployment, this type of classification is clearly of use, but it is increasingly less useful in an urban context where the influence of spatial constraints decreases, and where the dependence of 'later' sectors (tertiary, quaternary, quinary) on 'earlier' ones (primary, secondary) comes into strong focus. Indeed, it is this dependence, assumed when the classification is used in anything but an historical context, that throws it into doubt. For example, many urban forecasting models partition economic activity into basic and dependent, arguing that basic constitutes the economic motor. Primary and secondary (resource and manufacturing) industry constitute basic, tertiary (service) and so on the dependent industry. Such distinctions lie at the heart of economic base theory and much regional economics. The input-output model, although constituted on a slightly different economic classification into final and intermediate demands for goods, contains a similarly strict distinction consistent with Keynesian economics. Such clear dividing lines between exogenous and endogenous activity are of obvious analytic attraction, but in practice it has never been easy to draw the boundary, and increasingly such distinctions have been in doubt. The mix, for example, of different sectors within the production process has long been a source of difficulty at the operational level, and frequently there are instances where the directional ordering of the dependence chain is clearly reversed.

At one level, the basic-service or basic-dependent industry distinction is useful. Fothergill and Gudgin (1982) show this in their analysis of regional and urban employment change in Britain in the last 30 years. In urban models, such as the Lowry model, it has proved analytically convenient and unproblematic, possibly because service/dependent industry has been spatially correlated with basic employment and/or because of the spatial invariance properties of those models. The distinction too has been reinforced in that regional policy in Britain has been mainly directed at manufacturing industry, although before the demise of such policies during the 1970s some service/government industry was directed through such policies. However most recent analyses of industrial structure have abandoned this traditional ordering or at least have argued that the organisational structure of industry from the production, financial/corporate or political point of view is of greater significance. The issue has been long accepted in that many firms contain both manufacturing and service components when examined using these conventional categories. The development of multinational enterprises, the growth of the corporate state, the increasing flow of international capital in an increasingly complex and

Figure 4.1 Extrapolating Post-industrial Futures

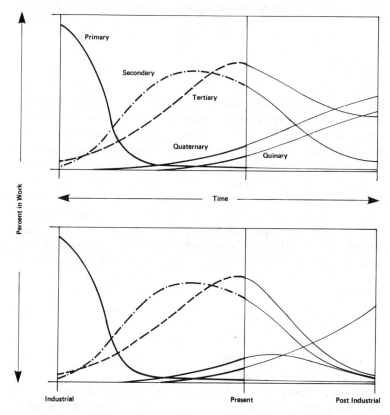

confused world economy, and the burgeoning spatial and international division of labour have led to such distinctions being arbitrary. Their continued use reflects the way data are still collected by agencies as much as any inertia in analytical practice.

It is when high-technology industry is examined in the traditional order that the dilemma becomes clear. High-technology firms manufacture products which can be tailored to a variety of uses in industries across the spectrum from primary to quinary. First, it is clear that a certain level of economic activity is necessary to support the development of high technology, but high technology also changes that base level. Secondly, the level of economic activity is not a sufficient condition for the growth of high technology. There are many advanced industrial societies which have not generated much high technology so far, and there are others where high technology is being stimulated without any massive manufacturing base. Indeed, the assumption that societies had to pass through each of the stages characterising Toffler's three waves appears only of global import and locally, appears to be of less and less significance.

Thirdly, the capital-intensive nature of high technology requires finance that only large agencies like government (or major corporations, see Chapter 8) can mobilise, but such firms by their nature employ small numbers of highly skilled workers. As design and manufacture are closely linked in terms of financing, and as the knowledge base of such industries tends to be related to public institutions such as universities and research councils, the government role is ever present. Indeed, it is increasingly argued that the Japanese economic miracle, of which high technology is a central component, is a consequence of direct government intervention (Vogel 1979). The Japanese fifth-generation computer project has been directly initiated by the Japanese government's MITI, and it is now recognised in a variety of traditional industries, for example aerospace, that a government role is essential because of the finance required. In Britain, the recent Alvey report argues that unless government immediately invests 300 million pounds in information technology to combat the Japanese fifth-generation computer challenge, 1 million jobs in hardware-software related industries will be at risk in the 1990s; this was sufficient to convince government that such a protected programme in high-technology development was essential.

In short, although high-technology industries appear to fall naturally into the quaternary sector, that is towards the end of the traditional industries spectrum, their influence is in all sectors. In this sense their role is central, even basic, rather than one of a dependent-service type function. Moreover, their production processes are like no others in that they have all the characteristics of tertiary-service type industries, and some of those of quaternary industries, yet their processes are never stable. Their rate of innovation sets them apart from other industries. Moreover, it is essential to distinguish the knowledge-based component from the manufacturing process, although this is considerably confused in practice, manufacturing and knowledge-based activities sometimes existing side by side, sometimes on other sides of the world. What is clear however in terms of locational requirements is their link to other knowledge-based industries, and to government resources in the form of grants and contracts. For example, Saxenian (1983) suggests that the genesis and growth of Silicon Valley was strongly influenced by government finance, while Breheny *et al.* (1983) present a similar set of hypotheses for the development of software industries along the M4 corridor in southern England.

The particular characteristics of high-technology industries in Britain, with their link to government, emphasise the role of institutions in generating industrial change. Since the early 1950s the multinational enterprise has also been significant and there is now an extensive literature on the organisation of production processes and the linking of diverse industries across spatial, sectoral and political boundaries. Many case studies show that local factors, at the urban or metropolitan level, play little part in the growth or decline of industries when such industries are an integral part of some supra-local, perhaps non-spatial realm or corporation. In Britain the recent pattern of employment decline on a regional basis is as much a part of the non-regional corporate strategy of the enterprises involved as of structural factors pertaining to the industrial locations in question (Massey and Meegan 1982).

It is easier to explain the decline of manufacturing industry in Britain than the growth of high technology. The conventional wisdom is that Britain has a very high innovative capacity but, because of cultural attitudes and institutional constraints, an inability to follow through. It is rich in software skills as is evidenced by most high-technology locations being close to centres of educational and research expertise. The development of high-technology industries, some manufacturing but mainly software houses, has concentrated in a belt across southern England from Cambridge to Bristol, avoiding London, following the M4 and spilling over into South Wales. Accessibility to London and Heathrow, educational and research expertise, good labour relations, relatively temperate climate and avoidance of central London seem to be the key site factors for location.

Although studies of locational determinants of high-technology industries are at present in progress (Oakey 1982) and in time will shed light on the genesis of location, high-technology industry by its very nature will always remain a very small provider of employment. It seems unnecessary to reinforce the point that, in all advanced post-industrial societies, automation will enable present levels of manufactured outputs to be sustained with employment levels a fraction of what they are now, whether that industry be located in Korea, Japan or Britain. In the British context, the post-industrial society is rapidly becoming one in which there is no manufacturing industry (low or high technology) but there is widespread use and development of high technology at the knowledge-based end of the spectrum. This however will only support a small fraction of the population in work because of the educational skills required.

Contemporary Explanations

Most contemporary explanations of changing industrial structure in spatial terms have moved away from macro-economic explanations phrased in terms of regional economic theory. The increasing complexity of firm structure has focused analysis on the firm or enterprise itself, emphasising the production process and the financial corporate structure of industry in terms of capital accumulation and the profit motive. Structural factors in terms of the performance of the national and world economy when juxtaposed with organisational theories of the enterprise provide a much richer explanation of changes in location.

Massey and Meegan (1982) examine the changing spatial patterns of manufacturing industry in Britain against this backcloth. They show how the national economic crisis and the changing pattern of world markets for goods have led to three processes of de-industrialisation: intensification, i.e. increasing productivity by changes in work practices; technical change involving new investment increasing the capital--to-labour ratio; and rationalisation, i.e. the reduction of surplus capacity. They provide a convincing explanation of the new industrial geography of Britain without recourse to more traditional theories emphasising structural change. In contrast, Fothergill and Gudgin (1982) present an equally convincing conventional analysis which emphasises structural and local factors. In this shift-share analysis, job loss is well-explained in terms of a structural component relating to long-term industrial decline (coal, steel, shipbuilding etc.) while a local component relates to the centre-periphery argument as expressed through inner city decline and rural/ex-urban growth. In this study, the loss of manufacturing industry from the cities is explained by site factors as well as by broader economic ones.

These analyses present a confusing picture, although at one level they are complementary: cities in Britain are losing population to their outer suburbs while peripheral regions are growing. However, it is extremely difficult to generalise these findings to help in predicting future urban form; so many factors other than industrial issues are of importance, although the future pattern of job loss in manufacturing and service activity (which began to decline in 1981) is more predictable than the growth and location of high-technology industries which depend so much on government. The same phenomena of complete decentralisation of urban growth and change at every level has also been detected in the US. Vining and Strauss (1977) argue convincingly that a 'clean break' occurred in urbanisation around 1970, when for the first time the traditional drift to the cities was reversed. It is tempting to see these changes as marking the beginning of the third wave in spatial terms.

High-technology industries in Britain have not in general arisen spontaneously and been sustainable. Those that have, such as Sinclair Research and INMOS, have been aided by government. Even computer firms, such as Acorn who produce the BBC Micro Computer, owe their success to government initiative through the BBC and the Department of Education and Science's schools computer programme. Other high-technology firms have been set up as branch plants of multinationals, such as Sony (but also see Meier, Chapter 6), while the long-awaited decision by Nissan to announce the location of their European car plant shows the critical dependence of new industrial growth on multinationals. Such factors are critical in explaining emergent urban form, and to this end it is clear that the basic distinction between different types of industry is in doubt as both an analytical and explanatory device. If urban areas are to be dominated by high-technology uses with little or no manufacturing industry, the traditional mechanisms for the analysis of urban change are in doubt and many will argue have been for a long time. This raises the need for a new classification of industrial activity more in tune with contemporary explanations.

One possible scheme which would need to be tested in a model-based context might involve classifying industrial uses according to their production processes. The relationship between resources and manufacturing could be seen as a continuum reflecting *materials* (energy) production. In parallel, each enterprise has a continuum reflecting its *information* base, from basic knowledge through to research and development. By emphasising these productive processes which link information to materials, soft to hard, it would be possible to consider the links of any industrial use to other elements of these processes located in other areas. In short, the spatial, information and materials dimensions would serve to classify any industry (from primary through to quinary) and at the same time link uses to the rest of the world through location. It could be argued that the corporate structure of any enterprise might be reflected through this juxtaposition of dimensions. A broader industrial structure would then emerge from the concatenation of the particular profiles and elements of the profile for all industrial uses in the location in question. There would thus be an immediate way of exploring how one industry might be affected by changes in technology, spatial locations elsewhere and the manufacturing process. The scheme would include tertiary-services and other service-type functions. Though it would be difficult to operationalise until information was collected in the given manner, this raises an essential point that until the recent theories of industrial structure are reflected in the way information is assembled, little progress is likely to be made in urban forecasting which involves high-technology industry.

A related issue revolves around the use of such a classification scheme to reclassify different types of urban region. In effecting such a reclassification, it would appear that some means of relating industrial structure to economic change is required. Economic change is clearly affected by spatial scale and thus a distinction between national and regional economic growth would seem crucial. Using those ideas, it would be possible then to consider the impact of industrial change through changes to the materials or information processes under different regimes of economic growth, and to thereby trace these effects on other industries, other regions, and vice versa. The framework would be ambitious. It is a point for argument about the need for new frameworks.

Implications for Future Urban Form

The meaning of high-technology and urban form has been made clear in examples throughout this book. However, it is useful to redefine these terms as their meaning does vary a little between chapters. High-technology industry is used here to refer to electronics, computer, medical based activity, or indeed any activity which is knowledge-based and capital intensive. Such industry tends to confuse the traditional base classifications introduced here and its locational determinants tend not to be those such as transport costs and market access treated in traditional location theory. By urban form, we have in mind the superficial configuration and relation of land uses, and the density/intensity of such forms. It is the thesis of this chapter that such high-technology industries will be the norm in the post-industrial society but that their locational determinants will not be primarily spatially focused, nor will they be large employers of labour. In such a scenario, cities will not be structured in terms of such industries, more likely that telecommunications, leisure habits, amenity factors *as construed from the consumer end will become significant in determining urban form, thus marking the transition from cities determined by producer concerns to those determined by consumer interests.* Traditional location theory and modelling in the classical economics tradition would seem to have little to say about such changes.

To conclude these speculations, it is worth briefly exploring the extent to which traditional and contemporary approaches are able to inform an analysis of emergent urban form. As already mentioned, Britain is now largely in economic decline — with some major exceptions in the form of high-technology industries with both hardware and software orientations and some retailing and office uses. Britain's version of the 'sunbelt' phenomena contains areas where there is growth of high technology. As shown by Massey (1983), these areas are traditionally separate and physically remote from the manufacturing heartland. Of interest is the area of manufacturing closest to the sunbelt in South Wales. Traditionally an area of coal, steel and associated heavy engineering, this base has been declining for 50 years with decline proceeding apace of late. In the last decade, regional policy has brought new light industry to the coastal strip, devolution has brought government functions to Cardiff, and the area has acquired a 'high tech' image in the form of the INMOS plant, the Sony European base, the Ford Engine Plant and such like. All of these locational changes represent decisions made outside the region; and at a local level, the precise locational factors determining development have been subject to local whim.

Forecasting the resultant changes dependent on these industrial decisions seems more certain. The multiplier effects are reasonably tractable although, because the decisions relate to national and multinational interests, they have been smaller than originally anticipated. Much easier to forecast in the traditional way has been the pattern of local decline. Migration out of the region has remained low, thus the use of multiplier techniques to assess decline would appear relevant. More locally, the retailing system in South Wales is exploding as patterns of consumer expenditure adjust to the new network of road and rail routes which has greatly improved accessibility. The housing market is much affected by restrictions on land availability in the areas where demand is greatest.

Putting this picture of emerging urban form together does not give great confidence in the use of conventional modelling and analysis techniques. In particular, institutional and political factors are likely to loom even larger in the future. The proposal to make mining and the rail system profitable within a decade is likely to have a dramatic effect on South Wales as elsewhere in Britain, with a much greater impact on urban form than anything contained in the predictions of service and population uses by current urban models. One area where conventional modelling techniques might apply involves retailing: a ring of hyper-markets is emerging around Cardiff due to changing expenditure levels, accessibility and the economics of retailing. It is possible that the catastrophe/bifurcation theory developed by Wilson amongst others might apply, but at first sight institutional factors relating to land tenure and planning controls also appear significant.

What conventional models have to say about future urban form has limited application, although a good deal of expertise on modelling is available and could be directed to building entirely new forms based on, for example, some of the more appropriate contemporary theories of industrial location and urban change. Two critical issues in the design of such models stand out. First is the notion of a very strong link to the rest of the world especially in terms of the local effects of non-local organisation, private and public. Secondly, there is the notion of change occurring within an urban fabric which adjusts much more slowly physically than in terms of activity use. This suggests that static cross-sectional approaches to technological change are simply in-appropriate (almost by definition), but the presence in appropriate models of a large element of inertia in physical structure seems necessary. More generally, as our techniques are rooted in the second wave, it would appear that they are of limited use in understanding, indeed even detecting, the third. The kind of dramatic transition we are living through is commensurate to a paradigm shift in the social sciences, and this suggests that new techniques and approaches must be evolved to deal with such changes.

An issue which now characterises British cities and is likely to become more significant as the work non-work distinction in the population increases is the increasing spatial distinction found in some American cities between vibrant wealthy havens and run-down, aban-doned areas. This increasing polarisation seems to imply an even greater shift into the hinterland by those who can afford this, although there are countervailing tendencies in terms of transport costs. Indeed Fothergill and Gudgin (1982) conclude that:

looking ahead to the end of the century, a remarkable transformation which began in earnest around 1960 may be nearing completion. To a large extent Britain's cities will have reverted to their traditional medieval role as service centres for their hinterlands, the difference this time being that they will serve hinterlands which are primarily industrial, not agricultural. The 'industrial city' which grew up in the nineteenth and early twentieth centuries, is proving a transient phenomenon.

Vining and Strauss's (1977) 'clean break' hypothesis suggests the same phenomena is occurring in the US. This is consistent with Bellini's scenario and the general idea of this chapter that the analysis of urban form in the post-industrial world should be based on analytical approaches which consider cities without industry.

References

Bellini, J. (1982) *Rule Britannia: A Progress Report for Domesday 1986*, Abacus Books, London

Breheny, M., Cheshire, P. and Langridge, R. (1983) 'The Anatomy of Job Creation? Industrial Change in Britain's M4 Corridor', *Built Environment, 9,* 61-71

Fothergill, S. and Gudgin, G. (1982) *Unequal Growth: Urban and Regional Employment Change in the UK*, Heinemann Educational Books, London

Jones, B. (1983) *Sleepers, Wake!*, Harvester Press, Brighton

Massey, D. (1983) 'The Shape of Things to Come', *Marxism Today*, April, 18-27

Massey, D. and Meegan, R. (1982) *The Anatomy of Job Loss: the How, Why and Where of Employment Decline*, Methuen, London

Oakey, R.P. (1982) *High Technology Industry and Industrial Location*, Gower, Farnborough

Saxenian, A. (1983) 'The Genesis of Silicon Valley', *Built Environment, 9,* 7-17

Toffler, A. (1981) *The Third Wave*, Bantam Books, New York

Vining, D. and Strauss, A. (1977) 'A Demonstration that the Current Deconcentration of Population in the United States is a Clean Break with the Past', *Environment and Planning A, 9,* 751-8

Vogel, E.F. (1979) *Japan as Number One: Lessons for America*, Harper and Row, New York

5. INDUSTRIAL FUTURES: USA
J. Levy

This chapter considers the future quantity, character and location of industrial activity in the US. It begins with a look at 15 factors which may influence the scale and location of this industrial activity and then proceeds to consider two contrasting scenarios for the industrial future of the nation. This is followed by a brief concluding section. The time horizon is roughly the next two decades.

Factors Influencing the Future of US Manufacturing

Openness to World Trade

Exports and imports, as a proportion of US GNP, have at least doubled in the last two decades. There are now increasing and understandable political pressures for a more protectionist policy; witness the push for domestic content legislation in the early 1980s. However, the international political costs and economic risks of a highly protectionist policy are so great that any responsible administration will probably attempt to resist the temptation. A number of domestic interests would strongly oppose a protectionist policy. Among these would be labour and capital in major export industries, US banks which hold a great deal of foreign debt, and firms with major overseas investments or joint venture agreements. Finally, that abstract creature, the consumer, might well be opposed for evident reasons.

It seems more likely that organised reaction to the threat of foreign competition will take forms other than the building of tariff walls. One form might be intra-industry co-operation such as the recent formation of the Micro-electronics and Computer Technology Corporation, a consortium of computer manufacturers. Another might be increased government-industry co-operation to accelerate research and development and investment in promising areas. Some long-held anti-trust views and practices in the US are likely to be early victims of the pressures of international competition, but for working purposes it is assumed that US openness to world trade will continue.

Computing Cost and Power

There seems little reason to doubt that past trends will continue with the costs of processing and transmitting information falling and the power and friendliness of software increasing. Continuing growth in the capacity of memory chips, the combination of fibre optics, laser and computer technology, progress towards molecular switching devices, and continuing development of artificial intelligence and robotics are all examples of these trends.

Real Per Capita GNP

On the future of per capita income there is a wide range of viewpoints, though some convergence is now occurring. Rejecting the very pessimistic view, it is assumed here that, in the absence of unique and unpredictable events, real per capita GNP will continue its long term upward trend. The case for pessimism — the 'age of limits' view — rests on three general assumptions about the future: (1) anticipation of a generalised resource shortage; (2) anticipation of the emergence of overwhelmingly powerful environmental constraints; and (3) belief that growth is now concentrated in those sectors of the economy where the sorts of productivity improvement which have been achieved in manufacturing, agriculture, mining and the like will not be available.

All of these assumptions seem unconvincing for the US in the next two decades. World commodity prices, petroleum excepted, have been relatively stable in real terms for the last two decades or so (US Bureau of the Census). If there is a general resource shortage looming, prices are not signalling it. Perhaps optimism on this point is also tied to a faith in the price mechanism and our ingenuity in finding substitutes, the 'technological fix'.

The argument with regard to environmental constraints is somewhat the same. The empirical evidence that the US is choking on its own effluent to the point that it will voluntarily accept a major reduction in economic activity does not seem convincing. The continuing increase in US life expectancy (three years in the last decade alone) is a powerful piece of contrary evidence. Where serious and sustained efforts to reduce pollution have been made, some absolute decreases in pollution levels in the face of increases in total activity have been achieved. Air quality is perhaps the most important case in point (EPA 1983).

On the third point, it is likely that very large increases in productivity will be forthcoming in a wide range of service and administrative activities as it is learnt how to integrate people and computers effectively (Giuliano 1982). Given the newness of the requisite technology it seems reasonable to believe that industry is still at a very early stage on the learning curve as regards the automation of office and service activity.

Telecommuting

There seems to be every reason for believing that this will increase very rapidly in the next decade or two, making Toffler's (1981) 'electronic cottage' commonplace. The requisite hardware and software have been getting better and cheaper at a rapid pace. Equally important, the number of people capable of using such technology is growing steadily. The increase in single-parent families and high female labour-force participation rates may also favour telecommuting because it permits remunerative work and childcare to go on simultaneously. Firms will be strongly motivated to accept telecommuting because they will be able to capture, in the form of lower wages, some of the commuting cost and time-savings it offers to employees. Having fewer workers on site will also enable firms to save on overhead costs.

The Dispersal of Population and Personal Income

All available evidence suggests that the dispersal of population and personal income continued and may even have accelerated during the 1970s. There is no doubt that the gentrification phenomenon is real, but in purely numerical terms it is a small countercurrent (Kasarda 1980). Net in-migration into non-metropolitan areas, a phenomenon which began in the early 1970s after decades of net out-migration, appears to be continuing. These population trends are consistent with the results of opinion survey data which show that if the population of the US were distributed in accordance with people's expressed preferences, sub-urban and small-town populations would be larger and central city populations considerably smaller than is now the case (Elgin *et al.* 1974).

As was suggested some years ago, growth in real income is perhaps the most powerful and general dispersing force for it enables more to be spent on transportation and on structures (Mills 1972). If the previous speculations on the growth in real income are correct, it seems reasonable to expect dispersal to continue. Telecommuting and the continuing development of electronic technologies generally should facilitate dispersal.

Employment in Manufacturing

Manufacturing employment in the US, cyclical fluctuations excepted, has grown slowly in absolute terms since the end of the Second World War. In percentage terms it has fallen from 33 per cent of total employment in 1940 to 20 per cent in 1980. Essentially all growth has been in non-production employment. Production employment has held steady in the 12-14 million range from the late 1940s through to 1980. Thus on the basis of past experience there is not much evidence to argue for an absolute decrease in manufacturing employment in the next decade or two. However, this appears to be a case where past performance is likely to be a very poor predictor of future events.

The view that manufacturing employment will fall sharply is based on the expectation of massive increases in output per worker from widespread application of computer and related technology. This would apply to the production process itself, to design, and to management of the entire manufacturing process (Gunn 1972). All of the appropriate technologies are fairly new. Numerically controlled machining appeared a little more than two decades ago. Computer-aided manufacturing (CAM), a system in which many numerically controlled machines are linked to a central computer, is little more than a decade old and still not in widespread use. The next step, the flexible manufacturing system (FMS), which combines CAM with computer-controlled inventory, work scheduling and materials transfer, is more recent and in even less frequent use.

Where FMS has been installed the results have been impressive indeed. For example Fanuc Ltd, Japan's largest producer of industrial robots, maintains a manufacturing facility of 5400 square metres with a workforce of 100. The facility operates continuously. At night it operates with a staff of one. If part of the operation breaks down, work is simply rerouted. The company estimates that a conventional facility with comparable output would have a staff of 1000 (Bylinsky 1983).

Implementing CAM and FMS involves a great deal of flexibility and technical sophistication on the part of management and great adaptability on the part of labour. It can also involve very large capital costs. Hence it is not surprising that widespread adoption meets resistance and takes time.

The adoption of new technologies and new products often follows, very roughly, a Gompertz or Logistic time path (Martino 1975). Quite possibly, this will prove to be true for the adoption of CAM and FMS. The technology is here and steadily improving and there are a number of successful applications now in operation. For the US economy a driving force in the form of openness to world trade is clearly visible. The US manufacturer faces competition from places like Hong Kong, where manufacturing may not be highly computerised but labour costs are drastically lower. He also faces competition from Japan where labour costs are not vastly lower than in the US, but where computerisation is proceeding at a very rapid pace. Between the two it is hard to see any way out other than a rapid and massive move into computerisation.

The idea of a sharp break in the manufacturing production-employment trend line has an analogy in agricultural employment. For several decades up until the end of the Second World War US agricultural employment declined rather slowly (Figure 5.1). Adoption of labour saving technology such as the tractor and combine proceeded at a modest pace. In the 1940s a variety of factors, foremost of which was higher labour costs, produced tremendous acceleration in mechanisation and a spectacular drop in agricultural employment. Processes like sugar beet harvesting and tomato picking went from being primarily hand operations to being primarily machine operations in a single decade (Rasmussen 1982). From 1950 to 1970 agricultural employment fell by over 50 per cent even though production rose substantially. No trend-line analysis done in, say, the late 1930s could have predicted what was to happen a decade or two later.

If the above view on the computerisation of manufacturing is correct, a reasonable scenario for those manufacturing activities the US will retain and those it will lose can be constructed. At one end of the scale the US will keep producing those products which, for reasons of low value by weight or perishability, cannot be imported. This is a diverse group including such items as cement, newspapers and bakery products. At the other extreme the US has a good chance of keeping much high-technology activity. It also seems likely that it will be able to retain much activity which involves very large capital expenditures and large economies of scale. Finally, it seems likely that the US will be able to do well in or perhaps remain dominant in fields in which governmental (often military) purchases have built expertise and pushed the industry into an efficient scale of production. In many areas where the US is a major exporter the past or present role of government purchases in building the industry is clear. Two contemporary examples are computers and aircraft. If manufacturing in a gravity-free environment becomes a major commercial activity, public investment in the space shuttle may well have given the country an enormous lead which could last for decades. The recent placement in orbit, for a price, of a communications satellite for the government of Indonesia may be a harbinger of the commercialisation of the nation's lead in space technology.

The US is most likely to lose the manufacturing of products which can be imported and whose manufacture is not economically or technically amenable to computerisation. It seems likely that, on an

Figure 5.1 An Analogy Between Agricultural and
Manufacturing Employment, United States
(Source: Bureau of Census, *Statistical Abstract of
the US* and *Historical Statistics of the US: From
Colonial Times to 1957,* and Bureau of Economic
Analysis, *Survey of Current Business,* 1982)

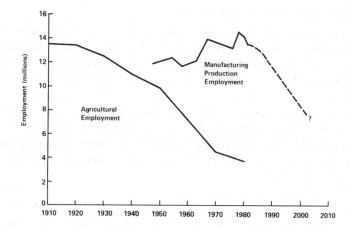

international level, labour costs will continue to vary far more widely
than capital costs. If this is true and the US continues to be a relatively
high labour-cost nation, the last conclusion seems hard to resist. In fact,
it represents just an extension or perhaps an acceleration of present
trends.

The Role of Heavy Industry

It seems likely that heavy industry will decline as a proportion of total
industrial activity and employment. This impression is gained simply by
looking at recent experience. Slow growth, no growth or shrinkage
seems to be the rule in heavy industry. For example steel production
measured in tons showed very little change from 1960 to 1980. Nor was
this stagnation purely the result of increased steel imports. Steel
consumption, regardless of source, grew at only one-third the rate of
real GNP.

Capital Intensity of Manufacturing Processes

Capital per worker has been rising for many decades, roughly doubling in real terms in the last 20 years (about US$20,000 per worker in 1980). The general expectation is that very large increases are in store for the remainder of the century because investment per worker in CAM and FMS facilities may run to several hundred thousand dollars (Bylinsky 1983).

The Size of Manufacturing Facilities

There is reason to believe that in some industries FMS will destroy much of the advantage of very large plants. In conventional manufacturing processes large runs on each product are necessary in order to keep machinery dedicated to that product running for a large number of hours during the course of the year. With FMS the same machine tool, for example, may be used on a number of products during the course of a single day. Thus much smaller runs on a given product become economical. In fact, the phrase 'economy of scope' in contrast to 'economy of scale' has been used to describe the effect upon production of the advent of FMS.

Another factor which may predispose toward physically smaller facilities is the highly capital-intensive nature of CAM and FMS. This will push more industries into round-the-clock operation. Thus a given amount of output can come from much smaller floor space and land area than is now the case.

Changing Labour-Force Needs in Manufacturing

The advent of the computer in its various manifestations probably will shift the desired skill mix away from manual attributes towards cerebral ones. The replacement of the machinist and welder by workers whose skills lie in programming and computer repair are common examples of this. On the office side of manufacturing an analogous replacement seems to be occurring — witness the displacement of the draftsman by computerised drafting systems. If the process of computerisation goes far enough there is likely to be a blurring of the line between production and non-production workers. How does one classify the worker with a degree in electrical engineering who spends half of his or her time at a drafting board (electronic, of course) or computer terminal and half on the production floor? The line between labour and management may blur as the educational gap between labour and management narrows.

Female Labour-Force Participation Rates

Female participation rates have risen sharply since the 1950s. In fact, just the change in female labour-force participation rates from 1970 to 1980 added about 6 million workers to the labour force of the US. Whether this is approaching some sort of upper limit remains to be seen. For working purposes let us assume that female labour force rates will remain relatively high without speculating on the precise direction in which they will move.

Energy Costs

It is easy to over-estimate the influence of energy prices. In 1980, after the second major rise in oil prices, about 6 per cent of US GNP was spent on energy. Given the fall in real energy costs since then and the rising figure for real GNP per unit of energy, the figure would be somewhat lower today. It seems reasonable to believe that the most significant way in which energy costs will affect location is through transportation costs. Note that only about one-quarter of total energy was used for transportation of all sorts.

A look at an input-output table for the US shows a wide range of industries in which transportation amounts to perhaps 4-8 per cent of total inputs (Ritz 1979). About one-fifth of US GNP is devoted to transportation and from the previous paragraph perhaps 2 per cent of GNP goes for energy for transportation. Thus, as a very rough approximation, perhaps one-tenth of all expenditures on transportation are for energy. This suggests that, for a wide range of industry, energy for transportation accounts for 1 per cent or less of total cost. This, in turn, suggests that very large changes in real energy costs would be necessary to have radical effects on the location of most industries. On the matter of bringing the worker to his or her job, if figures are adjusted for inflation and increased fuel efficiency there has been very little change since 1973 in the real cost of the energy required to drive a set distance. Certainly, as far as personal transportation goes, there is still a great deal of room for adaptation in both vehicle design and behaviour patterns before total driving costs would rise enough to force major changes in residential patterns. This would seem to be the main weight of the evidence since 1973.

The locational patterns which would result from major increases in the real cost of travel are far from clear. There are three quite different possibilities: (1) the dense monocentred city which relies heavily on energy efficient fixed route public transportation (see Figure 1.3, point

A); (2) a multi-nodal pattern in which private transportation is dominant and in which savings are achieved by shortened average trip lengths; and (3) an amorphous pattern in which residential, industrial and commercial uses are mixed at a very fine grain permitting short trips, many by foot or bicycle (Figure 1.3, point C).

For many firms sharp rises in energy costs might provoke conflicting motivations. A firm might want to move centrally to avail itself of rail access and public transportation. It might also want to move peripherally to take advantage of wind or solar energy or construct an energy-efficient earth-sheltered building. Thus there may be a certain amount of cancelling out among the various effects of energy price rises.

The way locations are affected by major energy cost increases will be very much influenced by the particular technological response. A major turning towards soft-path technology, probably solar, should favour low-density locations to minimise interference effects. Even here, the results may be somewhat different depending on technical details. For example, on-site generation is likely to be more decentralising than generation in large solar 'farms' with distribution through the grid.

On the other hand if the main response to rising oil costs is heavier reliance on coal and nuclear power, the generating technology may be locationally neutral at the intra-regional level. At the regional level it might tend to favour those regions with large reserves of exploitable coal deposits and/or a willingness of the body politic to make its peace with nuclear power. The latter characteristic seems to vary widely from one section of the country to another in relation to a region's willingness to sacrifice environmental for economic goals (Garreaux 1982).

On the subject of the future of energy costs it is possible to find a highly qualified source to support almost any position. One likely possibility is that if the cost of liquid petroleum moves upward significantly, total energy supplies will prove to be quite elastic. This is because the US seems to be reasonably close to the threshold prices for a number of alternate energy technologies. For example, there was major interest in US shale oil deposits around 1980. When oil prices softened, interest faded. Apparently present prices are close to the threshold for the large scale extraction of oil from the massive shale reserves. With variations this is true for other fossil fuel technologies such as tar sands and coal liquification or gasification.

Soft-path technologies would also tend to make the total energy-supply curve a good deal more elastic. Both active and passive solar heating are becoming more common and their rate of adoption could accelerate sharply if energy prices were to resume the upward trend of the 1970s.

Photovoltaic power has dropped in price from about US$2,000 per peak hour watt in the late 1950s to $5 to $20 per peak hour watt at present (Solomon 1982). It is widely believed that prices of $1 to $2 per peak hour watt will be feasible within the next several years (*Chemical Week* 1982). At such prices, thin film photovoltaic power would be competitive in a wide range of uses and substantial increases in the scale of production might occur.

Value-to-Weight Ratios in Manufacturing

It seems likely that value-to-weight ratios of manufactured products and the factors which go into them will rise. Despite a lack of hard evidence that this is happening, there is suggestive evidence in the fact that growth in inter-city freight haulage has lagged growth in real GNP. One suspects that, in some types of product, increases in value take the form of increases in quality rather than increases in weight. Electronic equipment is an obvious case in point but there are more prosaic examples. For example, the average bicycle manufactured today is a good deal more complicated and sophisticated than its predecessor of two decades ago but, if anything, it has lost some weight. High-strength plastics, filament-reinforced materials and the like appear to be displacing heavier materials like cast iron and steel in many products.

Crime and Disorder

The crystal ball, somewhat clouded on other issues, appears totally opaque on this one. It is generally understood that crime and civic disorder tend to drive manufacturing out of urban areas. They raise the cost of insurance, if it can be obtained at all; they make personnel recruitment more difficult; and they increase security costs and losses from theft and vandalism. But whether crime in urban areas will increase or decrease seems unknowable. It has been argued that the ageing of the population itself will produce lower rates of violent crime. However, a long period in which the economy cannot create jobs rapidly enough may produce a large, permanent urban underclass with very high crime rates. No doubt, many would argue that the US is already well down that path.

It is possible that the coming of computer technology will create increased disparities in income and social status on the basis of possession or non-possession of computer skills. If this happens, those who are left behind may act out their frustration in socially disruptive and criminal behaviour. It has been suggested that a major problem with the automation of industry will be finding a way to share the fruits of automation with those displaced by it (Leontief 1982). There seems little doubt that the US can do this financially if it so chooses. Whether it will choose to is uncertain, as is whether such redistribution would work out in a desirable manner. The psychological and sociological implications of providing large numbers of people with a decent income, but not with the opportunity to do what is commonly defined as useful work, are far from clear.

Whether technology will provide new techniques for moderating violent behaviour is also unknowable. How could one have foreseen in the 1950s that an array of then unknown psychoactive drugs would be emptying out psychiatric institutions a decade or two later? Technology has a way of producing corners around which even the cleverest of us cannot see.

National Policy

In indirect and generally unintended ways federal policy exerts powerful spatial effects. For example, investment of federal funds in irrigation projects clearly had the effect of moving population and economic activity westward. It has been argued that the pattern of federal taxation and expenditure in effect transfers income from some states to other groups and thus alters the patterns of regional growth. Income transfers, now about one eighth of personal income, have encouraged both decentralisation within regions and migration to regions considered to be high in residential amenities, notably the south-east and south-west. The favourable tax treatment accorded home-owners (tax expenditures now estimated in the US$30 billion per year range) and the creation of secondary markets for mortgages have been powerfully decentralising forces.

By contrast, as a matter of explicit national policy, it is difficult for the federal government to systematically favour one type of area over another. This is because of the geographic dispersion of political power within the Congress. As an illustration of this point, the odds of being able to throw a dart at a map of the US and hit a county which is not or has not recently been eligible for some type of federal economic development aid are quite small.

As a working assumption it seems likely that at least some of these inadvertently decentralising policies, particularly income transfers and home-owner tax treatment, will continue. On the other hand, explicit federal policy which strongly, systematically, and continuously favours central cities seems unlikely.

Two Scenarios

How might the above variables play out when combined? Consider this scenario. Continuing pressure from world trade forces US manufacturers into computerisation at a rapid pace. Much of that manufacturing activity which cannot be readily automated but can be imported is lost. The industrial labour force contracts very rapidly, as did the agricultural labour force two or three decades earlier. Continuing growth in real per capita GNP and telecommunications combined with moderate energy cost increases permit a continuing peripheral movement of population and personal income.

In many industries, particularly growth industries such as genetic engineering (discussed in more detail in Chapter 8), the ability to recruit a small, highly educated, highly paid labour force will become critical to corporate success.

At the same time, traditional considerations of rail and water access and the presence of a mass industrial labour force will lose much of their importance. The result is that firms will tend to follow their labour forces, or at least the more elite and less ubiquitous elements of that labour force, wherever necessary.

To a large degree, the traditional pattern of industrial location will be reversed. In the past, places such as Pittsburgh developed as industrial centres because of access to raw materials and transportation. The mass labour force then accumulated because the jobs were there. In the new scenario, manufacturing location will largely be driven by the residential choices of workers. Thus more and more manufacturing activity (in percentage terms) will be drawn into high-amenity areas. In a few cases these may be urban areas but more often they will be suburban or exurban areas. The process of industrial decentralisation will be facilitated by the smaller size of producing units and their relative cleanness of operation. Though much alarm will be expressed over the loss of manufacturing employment by urban areas, it will not be possible to implement effective federal policy to counter the trend.

Coastal areas will often be favoured because of more moderate climates and more recreational amenities. In a few cases, Denver as an example, inland areas which have particular natural attractions may be favoured. The rise of residential amenities as a major locational consideration will continue to pull manufacturing activity out of much of the north-east and north-central area into areas which are, if nothing else, warmer. Some parts of New England which seem to be generally regarded as high amenity areas may prove exceptions to this trend.

The flight of industry to rural locations will slow or stop. A major driving force in that flight was the lure of a non-metropolitan labour force which is less militant, less organised and willing to work for lower wages (Thompson 1975). As industry becomes more capital intensive and skill requirements for its smaller labour force rise, the lure of cheap but not especially skilled manpower will shrink. The firm which has migrated from metropolitan to non-metropolitan America in search of cheaper and more docile labour and which finds it cannot automate is likely either to succumb to foreign competition or to go overseas itself.

In industries where technological change is rapid and failure to remain at the edge of technology is fatal, there will be clustering to take advantage of a shared resource — knowledge and brain power. Also there will be, most probably, a strong tendency toward high-amenity areas to facilitate the recruitment of mobile, highly educated and highly skilled key personnel. This sort of pattern is clear in the computer industry with the well known Route 128 (around Boston) and 'Silicon Valley' complexes. It is rapidly manifesting itself in the emerging genetic engineering industry. This has formed itself into several diffuse clusters, one in the Boston area centred on Harvard and MIT, another in the San Francisco Bay area, clearly attracted by the presence of Stanford and the University of California, a third in the Rockville-Bethesda area of Maryland in proximity to the National Institutes of Health (Levy 1984, see also Chapter 8). While many industries have been born in cities and then moved outward as the scale of operations increased, the genetic engineering industry appears to be going through the birth process largely outside the city. But since the shared resource is a dispersed suburban or exurban labour force, the clustering may be rather diffuse. Thus the industry in question might sprawl in scattered locations over many hundreds of square kilometres.

The industrial district will be a less prominent feature of the landscape. Industry will be far more diffused and more thoroughly intermixed with other land uses than is now the case. Given the decrease in industrial employment, the greater productivity of computer-aided processes and the greater propensity to round-the-clock operations, the total amount of floor space and land area devoted to industrial activity will shrink. In most central cities little manufacturing other than that tied to local markets will survive. Manufacturing will constitute a major share of the export base of only a few central cities.

Is there a reverse scenario which would increase manufacturing employment (or at least prevent a decrease) and concentrate that activity in central or traditional areas? Consider the following. A labour-capital coalition forces a highly protectionist policy upon the administration. Strangely, such a policy triggers little international reaction. The 'age of limits' people prove to be fundamentally correct and real per capita income falls somewhat. As a result, residential construction slows and the dispersal of population likewise slows, perhaps halts entirely. Petroleum prices rise sharply and one substitute technology after another (solar, wind, geothermal, shale oil, tar sands, coal liquification, nuclear, etc.) either fails technically or proves to be environmentally intolerable. A broad range of manufacturing activity proves to be a good deal less amenable to automation than had been anticipated, with the result that the expected substitution of computer technology for the human hand and mind fails to materialise. Given the very high level of energy costs public transportation makes substantial gains at the expense of private automotive transportation. At the same time, and for the same reasons, rail- and water-accessible sites increase dramatically in attractiveness and intense competition develops for them. The retrofitting of old industrial buildings in central locations becomes a major activity. Putting all of the above together, industrial employment remains at the present level and the outflow of industrial activity from urbanised areas is halted. In fact, a good deal of industrial activity which had been lost to rural areas when diesel fuel for trucks was cheap comes back to central places. As manufacturing jobs return to central places, the urban working class grows and much of the urban underclass is absorbed into it. Crime rates decline and crime ceases to be a force pushing economic activity out of central places.

This second scenario is possible, though rather unlikely.

Conclusion

If the general argument of this paper is correct and the first scenario presented above is reasonably accurate, then the prospect is for much smaller total employment in manufacturing and for manufacturing to play a much smaller role in the life of cities on any dimension we care to mention.

The effect of declining manufacturing employment on urban land use patterns is not likely to be large. As of mid-1973 manufacturing production employment in the US was in the 13-million range. Of that, it is doubtful that more than one-third was in central cities. Loss of half of that employment would mean perhaps 2 million jobs. Assume a rule of thumb of 50 square metres of floor space per job and a ratio of about

4 to 1 (site to floor space) for single-storey industrial-park development, with urban sites assumed to be somewhat denser. That translates into something of the order of 250 square kilometres of industrial land. In fact, the actual withdrawal of land from industrial uses might be smaller, for some of the job loss will probably be manifest in lower employee densities rather than conversion to other types of land uses. Spread through several hundred central cities the immediate effects of manufacturing job losses on urban form should be minor. For the city which sees other uses for land once used for manufacturing, whether those uses be residential, commercial or recreational, the prospect of loss of industrial activity may be attractive. The city of Vancouver has actually encouraged the movement out of industrial activity for just such reasons.

However, for the majority of cities the prospect is threatening in terms of tax base, labour force participation rates and unemployment rates. By far the most serious aspect of manufacturing job loss is long-term structural unemployment. For those who fear the development of a large, permanent urban underclass whose numbers are swelled by urban structural unemployment, the more probable scenario is very discouraging. From the national perspective the argument of this paper bears upon the wisdom of strategies designed to retain industry in urban areas. It lends weight to the 'people' side of the 'people versus places' controversy. The US might be better advised to put public monies into job training, education and migration assistance than into grants and tax expenditures designed to favour industrial location in urban areas.

Note

Where not otherwise indicated, statistics are from the *Statistical Abstract of the US* (1981 and earlier editions).

References

Bylinsky, G. (1983) 'The Race to the Automated Factory', *Fortune,* 21 February, p. 52
Chemical Week (1982) 'Photovoltaics: a Multimegawatt Look'
Elgin, D. *et al.* (1974) *City Size and the Quality of Life,* Stanford Research Institute, Menlo Park
Environmental Protection Agency (1983) *National Air Quality and Emission Trends Report, 1981,* Washington, DC
Garreaux, J. (1982) *The Nine Nations of North America,* Avon, New York

Giuliano, V.E. (1982) 'The Mechanization of Office Work', *Scientific American*, September

Gunn, T.G. (1972) 'The Mechanization of Design and Manufacturing', *Scientific American*, October

Kasarda, J.D. (1980) 'The Implications of Contemporary Redistribution Trends for National Urban Policy', *Social Science Quarterly*, December, 373

Leontief, W. (1982) 'The Distribution of Work and Income', *Scientific American*, September

Levy, J.M. (1984) Unpublished research by author

Martino, J.P. (1975) *Technological Forecasting for Decisionmaking*, American Elsevier Publishing Co., New York

Mills, E.S. (1972) *Studies in the Structure of the Urban Economy*, Johns Hopkins, Baltimore

Rasmussen, W.D. (1982) 'The Mechanization of Agriculture', *Scientific American*, September, 77

Ritz, P.M. (1979) 'The Input-Output Structure of the US Economy, 1972', *Survey of Current Business*

Solomon, B. (1982) 'Will Solar Sell', *Science*, April

Thompson, W. (1975) 'Economic Processes and Employment Problems in Declining Metropolitan Areas', in G. Sternlieb and J.W. Hughes (eds) *Post Industrial America: Metropolitan Decline and inter-Regional Job Shifts*, New Jersey

US Bureau of the Census, *Producer Price Indexes*, various years

6. HIGH TECH AND URBAN SETTLEMENT
R. Meier

California of the 1980s has seen a flowering of human settlements based upon the newest wave of forced draft technological innovation. Tumbling on top of predecessors were aerospace equipment, advanced system engineering, computing, telecommunications and software synthesis. They interacted with a regional culture that had accumulated per capita more years of education and moved about on a greater concentration of automotive vehicles than any other. It is a relatively young society, and exceedingly open to new fashions and curious fads.

I serve here as a reporter-interpreter, rather than analyst. Much of the evidence presented in this chapter was assembled from a wide range of trade and commercial publications and by personal communications from consultants. My efforts in the 1950s and the 1960s leading to forecasts of the urban impacts of telecommunications and computing had sensitised me to the issues, so it was possible to frame pointed questions when in contact with the best-informed people. Development stimulated by growth in the quaternary and quinary (knowledge production, home services) sectors cannot yet be represented in a manner equivalent to the widely circulated publications on transportation and land use.

A kind of megalopolis evolved in the 1960s when a string of urban centres was linked by eight-lane freeways and frequent air service. (Bullet trains and Metroliners could not be supported by its 10 — now 18 — million of urbanites.) These improved transport links generated some new services that catered to the expanding technological elite. Specialty breads and fresh fish, for example, could be supplied along the corridor due to 'same day delivery' potentials. The technical maintenance of relatively uncommon digitised instruments could be expedited by the same kinds of vehicles and highway networks. These distribution patterns began to reorganise as soon as a WATS (Wide Area Telephone Service) line became available, with some scattering and others centralising.

Then came SPRINT, a high-capacity channel for packaging telecommunications promoted by the Southern Pacific Railway (a major incentive is that it remains active in real estate) which reduced the cost of interaction along the urban corridor. The impact of SPRINT and its competitors has been diluted by parallel growth in the use of communications satellites, which have brought world cities much closer together, thus virtually annihilating the friction of space. Microwave relay routes and jetport improvements built up transactional activity in a half dozen centres and sub-centres.

With enhanced capacity and reduced cost of communication, the financial markets have proliferated, with many new kinds of services exploiting the potentials. Banking and real-estate intermediaries first went megalopolitan, as quickly as permitted by the regulatory agencies. The latter were forced to relax their oversight, because events began to move too quickly. Most recently New York, British and Japanese banks bought up middle-sized banks. Bigness in banking is no longer a threat to the public interest because customers can be served in many more ways than ever before, competition has increased notably, and enhanced information flow makes equilibration of supply and demand easier to achieve.

A new institution, the metropolitan business weekly, emerged to inform decision-makers about the details of this extraordinary expansion. It used regionwide investigative reporting to dig out the background for change. Interestingly, the three largest metropolitan areas were covered by the same newspaper chain. After a few years of independent operation the management discovered an overlap in advertising, reader interest and company connections, so the reporting has now been merged. These metropolitan business weeklies are often months ahead of other business periodicals in pointing out new niches forming in business, construction and services. A 'high tech' firm with a few million sales is given the same attention as old-line corporations with billions. Thus they serve as amplifiers of change phenomena, noise and all.

At the beginning of the decade these sources revealed the findings of a survey showing that insurance could decentralise to the metropolitan periphery because its daily decisions were very largely dependent upon documents, whereas banking, which seems to be doing much the same kind of paper work, cannot safely move out to the low rent areas on the periphery, because basically its important transactions depend upon trust, and trust arises from face-to-face interaction. Very often quick responses are required to maintain that trust, so most of the banking operations remain anchored in the central business district. Their massive computing, however, moved to suburban centres.

Later it became evident that software firms servicing these large units could accumulate hundreds of personnel. Their operations were held close to the centre of computer design and use, although the 'genius types' in the software business could apparently function almost anywhere. Not a few opted for the open spaces next to the mountains where they could depend upon telephone lines and limit visits to the city to only a few days per month. Practitioners of systems science and the software arts in California seem to hold a very strong preference for untamed greenery and for architectural styles with clean, sharp lines.

Social and Economic Responses

In Silicon Valley, and to a somewhat lesser extent Orange County and San Diego, the social networks of individual participants in the industry have become highly evolved, almost always crossing company boundaries. This condition, combined with a large proportion of new entries, encourages job jumping, because people with hiring authority prefer to work with friends. In Silicon Valley itself turnover is reported to be 90 per cent in the first year of operation of a new facility. Similarly, prime land has been bid up; a typical price for industrial land is $130 per square metre in the estates founded a few years ago.

A common reaction of the companies to this buildup in costs of production is quite classical. Tight-knit prestige groups in the established firms are sent out to colonise environmentally desirable university towns in Colorado, Oregon, New Mexico and elsewhere. Decent public schools for the children are assured there, and weekend mountaineering is convenient. These teams are charged with pushing the technology several years ahead of the competition and are expected then to launch prototype engineering and manufacturing nearby (but see Feldman, Chapter 8).

Profitability in larger-scale technology development is extremely sensitive to the quality of management, the best of which refuses to leave the hurly-burly of Santa Clara and Orange Counties. Therefore the prototype manufacturing plants are settling on the periphery of these clusters, up to about 100 minutes away by automobile — the best sites being accessible to mountain leisure activity. Land cost there drops to US$50 per square metre, new housing for workers costs 40 per cent less, and turnover after startup is very low (5-10 per cent per year). However workers' commute distances become considerably longer and unexpected traffic jams arise within a less-developed road network.

Coincident with the boom some categories, such as semi-conductors, following the economy as a whole, suffered severely from the deep recession of 1981-82. The reaction in firms which were badly hit was the same as that of other larger organisations in the metropolitan regions

— the bosses were dropped in even larger proportions than the assembly ·workers. As Herbert Simon predicted in his speeches 20 years ago, the computer makes the middle manager highly dispensible, because it can supervise inventory control, undertake small-scale optimisation and then report, without standing in the way of rapid adaptive change in the organisation. Therefore the number of early retirements of managers (in the 50-60 year range) has been most extraordinary. Most of them move out of the suburbs to the small market towns, resuscitated villages and rural non-farm districts of the hilly Mother Lode country three hours to the east where they can get boating on the reservoirs together with cabins in the pine forests. An alternative is to go to the vineyard and redwood areas the same distance to the north.

Retired managers are joined by the cases of 'burnout'. These refugees from communications stress are most commonly encountered in the public services where transmitted demands overwhelm the capacity to respond appropriately. The stress felt by the more sensitive individuals builds up to a decision to abandon a promising career, and a nice house in the suburbs, in order to find a simple place with peace and quiet.

Thus the rural counties with wilderness not too far from the metropolis are booming. Without visible means of support for residents, the housing stock is expanding 7-10 per cent per year. The turnaround of the rural areas from secular decline was first noted in 1975-76, and it has been accelerating ever since. Although back in 1959 communications stress was forecast for this area before the end of the century (on the basis of experiments with human subjects), this edge-of-the-forest flight phenomenon is rarely associated with the buildup of metropolitan communications in current reports, but encountered repeatedly in interviews.

Another impact is not visible in California at all. When cost-cutting becomes necessary, a small team is sent overseas to set up and manage components factories there. Local entrepreneurs soon emerge who take on the most standard products. In East Asia outside of Japan there are at least a dozen cities with more than 10,000 workers in the computer, electronics and telecommunications manufacturing industries, and there are others in Ireland and the West Indies. A huge air-freight industry has grown up for moving special commodities, components and sub-assemblies to California and on out to the markets. As the overall industry expands it is expected that this overseas share will increase. Cities in Sri Lanka, Malaysia, Bangladesh and China are busily preparing modern industrial estates in the hope of attracting some of this growth. A disproportionate share of the worker demand in such places is for young women with middle school education, some of whom have also acquired basic English. After the factories open up, special dormitories usually become necessary. So far however, relatively few changes in urban structure have been induced outside the servicing of the industrial park that supports these new industries. If any should appear in the future in places like Korea or Taiwan, they are expected to be very different from California or Japan.

Transformations Inside the Metropolis

Two puzzles in urban dynamics have been encountered which are likely to be reproduced in other metropolises very shortly, if they have not already occurred without public recognition by the urban development professionals. They have been noted at the frontier of development by urban planners in California.

The first of these responds to the observation that the floorspace in the central business districts of the pace-making metropolises has been rapidly expanding at a time when downtown residential population has been constant or declining, so that walking to work has not become a more popular activity. The doubling or trebling of office space is matched by only a 10-20 per cent increase in commuting. Some designers and developers serving commuters working in the newest structures have been embarrassed by bankruptcies of firms they thought had an inside track to commercial success. What has changed? It appears that the old urban designers's formula, which allocated 25 square metres of floor space for each new worker, is obsolete. When looking at specific cases we see a compromise with the advertised office-of-the-future (it is not yet deliverable). Space is dedicated to various machines, some of them microcomputers and telecommunications, but others are processing paper intended for internal consumption and the highly differentiated and updated mailing lists. Machines are pushing people out of fully rented buildings. Machines do not buy lunches or purchase sundries.

We also see a much more carefully planned contact area where the organisation meets its clientele. The front room of the downtown organisation must have an atmosphere that engenders trust and also minimises costly mistakes. Extra space is needed to prevent situations which cause strong protests, vandalism and litigation.

The other puzzle is a response to a continuing urge within each parliamentary body to simplify by decentralisation. Executives are often sympathetic, but the much larger populations of managers and administrators argue otherwise. A plethora of small 'factories' have been moving out to the vicinity of the international airport. Their fronts are neat and very simple; their trademarks and logos are modestly displayed. A critical component or sub-assembly arrives by air freight, or the market is served by that mode of transport. The airports also attract hotels, restaurants, recreational facilities, luxury retailing, vehicle rentals, and unpretentious office buildings sheltering a great variety of services. Altogether this agglomeration of activity is becoming another metro centre competitive with the central business district for carrying out the tasks of organisations.

The premium regional shopping centre (with four department stores as anchors) is producing another competitor. A more diverse stock is now maintained outside the downtown area. Doctors, dentists, psychologists, music teachers, business consultants and other professionals cluster there. Churches and recreational organisations move in to use the huge parking areas in off-peak periods. A new population of urban services is finding a niche there; it is particularly effective in the distribution and maintenance of the new product lines in consumer electronics.

A third kind of metropolitan centre evolves around cultural activities which are predominantly guided by such non-market considerations as music, the fine arts, athletics, cinema production, libraries, publishing of specialised books and journals, research institutes, consulting firms, and smaller laboratories. The seed around which these activities crystallise is the major urban university. The opera and the symphony continue to perform downtown, often to full houses, but the number of events in the emerging metropolitan cultural centre is likely to be 10 to 30 times those in the original central district that includes the classic 'civic centre'.

Thus the large metropolis in a future dominated by quinary and quaternary activities seems destined to become polynucleated. The nuclei would exhibit complementary specialties, but they would compete strongly for the siting of the much more numerous quaternary service activities.

PART THREE

INNOVATION AND DEVELOPMENT

7. URBAN DYNAMICS
P. Nijkamp and U. Schubert

Large-scale urbanisation has become a world-wide phenomenon. In some Third World countries, the rate of this concentration process has accelerated. Within a few decades, new megalopolises have formed. In the industrialised world, a deconcentration process can be observed with people and jobs moving away from the large agglomerations. Is urbanisation, hence, to be considered as an entirely heterogeneous process?

It appears that there is a lifecycle of urban development (see van den Berg *et al.* 1982; Hall and Hay 1980), which seems to occur almost independently of the political and cultural systems within which urbanisation takes place. This lifecycle can best be described by distinguishing discrete phases of urban development: *urbanisation*, characterised by rapid expansion of urban areas and depopulation of rural areas; *suburbanisation*, when population and jobs move to the periphery of a city; *deurbanisation*, when the whole agglomeration loses jobs and population; and *reurbanisation*, when the core of an urban area begins to grow again. The empirical evidence (van den Berg *et al.* 1982; Bradbury *et al.* 1982; Drewett and Rossi 1984; Drewett and Schubert 1983) on which the hypothesis of a wave dynamics of urban development is based, uses population and employment figures most frequently, as these are generally available for longer periods of time.

An important result of this type of research is that there seems to be a strong link between the stages of urban development defined in terms of population and jobs and economic development. The early urban concentration phase can usually be observed together with an early industrialisation phase, where people and jobs concentrate in the already existing urban areas, characterised by the best infrastructure available at the time. As industrialisation proceeds and per capita incomes rise, the demand for new housing as well as for private gardens and so forth leads to suburbanisation. As the network of public and private infrastructure increasingly covers the whole country, urban areas appear to lose their comparative economic advantages and jobs begin to decentralise. In the post-industrial society deurbanisation seems to become a widespread phenomenon.

If the lifecycle hypothesis were a valid concept, then the deurbanisation phase should be followed by reurbanisation, a trend which cannot yet be firmly established statistically, although there are some signals in this direction. Urban renewal in the old centres already leads to increases in the population of some of the old city centres (gentrification) in the economically most advanced countries. Besides these waves of urbanisation, concomitant usually with waves of migration, urban dynamics can exhibit very irregular features. Examples include complete and enduring stagnation, sudden rises or falls, and irregular national patterns — such as the sudden upsurge of a spontaneous growth pole in a phase of general urban decline. What are the factors causing these dynamics?

In the following section a very brief outline of some approaches to this problem will be given. The present contribution is based on the conviction, corroborated by the above mentioned link between urban and economic development, that innovation and technical progress have to be considered as among the more important driving forces in this process. A later section reports a first attempt to model innovation and economic development, defined as the total volume of goods and services produced in an urban economy. It is suggested that the structure of production and its relation to R & D (research and development) indicate the possibility of structural dynamics in an urban system in all its variants.

Theories of Urban Dynamics

In the past decades, several theories have emerged that aim to explain the background of structural urban dynamics in the Western world. In this section, seven major contributions in this field are briefly reviewed.

Cumulative and Circular Feedback Processes

Pred (1977) claims that growth patterns of (mainly industrial) cities can be explained as cumulative and circular feedback processes (see also Baumol 1967). Industrial growth and population growth in cities are mutually reinforcing. Technological progress triggers urban economic development, favoured by economic base multipliers and agglomeration economies. Adoption and diffusion of innovation are hence of paramount importance for urban growth. Pred tested his theory on the basis of data on industrial evolution and urban growth patterns in Western Europe. His multiple nuclei approach may be regarded as a meaningful conceptual framework for explaining spatial-urban growth processes, based on claims that spatial interaction patterns develop due to innovation diffusion and communication infrastructure.

This analysis has some drawbacks: it is mainly a growth theory that fails when urban decline is to be explained; it mainly pays attention to product innovations and neglects process and intellectual innovations; it also neglects the role of urban-regional-national policies in urban dynamics.

Long-wave Migration Patterns

Thomas (1972) attempted to identify urban development waves, similar to Schumpeter's economic development waves (see also Pedersen 1978). His analysis is focused on the impacts of migration to cities. He was able to demonstrate the existence of a wave-like urban growth pattern of US cities prior to the Second World War. These migration patterns he claims had a direct effect on construction and housing activities, thus establishing the existence of a link between urban change and economic growth patterns. After 1945 such urban development waves could no longer be identified, due to the restrictive immigration laws in that country.

Thomas's analysis has a few drawbacks: it fails to explain post-1945 deurbanisation processes and it neglects endogenous urban change.

Functional Diversity and Urban Change

Jacobs (1977) considers urban cyclical processes to be caused by the diversity of urban functions (for instance, living, working, shopping, recreation) in a city. The concept of 'optimal urban diversity' is introduced, characterised by a variety of functions, a stratified age structure of buildings, an accessibility of urban facilities, and a sufficient concentration of urban population. The optimal mix of all these characteristics guarantees an optimal use of urban facilities. Analogously, a lack of diversity may lead to a downward movement of cities. On the other hand, in the case of too many attractive functions of a city, a self-destruction of diversity may take place leading to congestion, land-use competition and environmental decay.

Jacobs's analysis clearly has some limitations: external influences on the city are not considered; it does not explain the similar development patterns of market-oriented as well as planned cities; and the behaviour of urban actors is not taken into account explicitly.

Urban Design and Spatial Organisation

Norton (1979) analyses city lifecycles in the US. He shows that especially older cities are suffering from stagnation and decline due to their compact lay-out, urban segregation and inadequate tax base (due to the flight to suburbs by wealthier people: see also Lynch 1982). Newer cities on the other hand are more spacious and have a more satisfactory tax base. Older cities were structured during the industrialisation that took place in the last century. Due to the now observable transition to the tertiary and quaternary sectors, these cities cannot compete with newer urban places and suburbs having a more flexible economic structure which is more innovation-oriented.

The following critical remarks could be made regarding Norton's analysis: the motives of innovation are not dealt with; specific bottleneck factors in previously established cities are not identified; the role of exogenous factors in urban lifecycles (e.g. the role of urban government) is not acknowledged.

Urban Life Cycles and the Stages of Development

Van den Berg *et al*. (1982) report the results of several investigations into urban development patterns in 14 European countries. The empirical analysis is mainly on population and employment figures. To facilitate the analysis, two discrete urban zones are distinguished, namely core and ring. Urban development stages can be identified by the evolution of both core and ring, in terms of their growth (or decline) rates. On this basis the following phases of urban development are distinguished: urbanisation, suburbanisation, deurbanisation and reurbanisation (see also Drewett and Schubert 1983; Bradbury *et al*. 1982; and Hall, Chapter 2).

This analysis has some limitations: the 'phase hypothesis' is empirically tested by means of macro data, while the behavioural theory is not sufficiently empirically validated; the role of innovation in urban development is not included; the settlement system aspect (i.e. the evolution of an urban system as a whole) has not received sufficient attention.

Cities as Self-organising Systems

Allen *et al*. (1982) have developed a set of dynamic models of urban settlement and structure. These models are mainly theoretical in nature and serve to represent urban systems analytically as dynamic, non-linear entities. Several versions have been developed with a special emphasis on the role of transportation in the processes of spatial and economic self structuring. In addition, spatially relevant decision-making, behavioural spatial patterns and hierarchical interactions were taken into account. Simulation experiments recreated the economic resurgence and the dynamic evolution (including cyclical processes) of cities. In these simulation models, the interactions between employment patterns, residential choice processes, development of the tertiary sector, and impacts of the transportation sector were emphasised. The model itself was based on a simple non-linear dynamic relationship including attractiveness and bottleneck factors.

The limitations of this analysis are: no attention is paid to the spatial and economic effects of innovation-oriented enterpreneurial behaviour; it does not contain sufficient policy-control variables; and it neglects the role of the housing market (and other social infrastructure categories) in the dynamic evolution of an urban system.

Urban Change and the Product Cycle

In this theoretical work (see Vernon 1966), stages in the development of a product from its invention to its obsolescence are linked to urban development (see also below). In each phase, the optimal location of production changes, thus causing a chain of effects via labour demand, migration and so forth.

The drawbacks of this theory are: the production of ideas and basic inventions is entirely exogenous; as many products are simultaneously in different stages of the product cycle, it must be the specific mix of products that causes urban change, yet this 'mix' is not explained; many other factors of change are not taken into account.

Summary Remarks

Some of these theories demonstrate quite clearly the importance of technological progress and innovation in urban life cycles (especially the contributions of Pred, Thomas, Norton and Vernon). The existence of such cycles has been studied by Thomas, Jacobs, and van den Berg *et al*. The importance of bottleneck factors is also emphasised by several authors (especially Thomas, Jacobs, van den Berg *et al*, and Allen *et al.*).

Despite relevant partial contributions, a unifying theory for urban evolution patterns is still lacking. It has been suggested by some authors that technological progress and innovation may be important determinants of dynamics though little attempt has been made to include innovation as an endogenous impulse in the analysis of urban growth patterns.

It is worth noting that the theories just mentioned are based on the assumption that endogenous urban processes lead to the observed dynamics. However, many shocks that have caused disturbances in urban development are caused by exogenous events. A very recent example was the sudden change in the relative (and absolute) costs of transportation as a consequence of the oil price shock.

The approach adopted in this chapter considers, in principle, an endogenous model of urban change, which is, however, influenced by exogenous factors as well. A sketch of such a model follows in the next section.

Towards a Model of Innovation

Some Basic Postulates for a Model of Urban Change and Innovation

Economic growth theory, especially of the neoclassical type, considers the growth of productivity (in a point-economy, of course) as the centrepiece of interest. The change in productivity in an economy, so it is argued, is steered by two elements: first, capital accumulation and factor substitution (an endogenous process) via saving and investment; and secondly, technical progress (an exogenous process) — which has to be 'embodied' in the factors of production, predominantly via investment.

It is argued that the rate of saving does have an impact upon the rate of per-capita income growth, but that its influence tends to fade as the steady-state growth path is approached. At this point, per-capita economic growth is due only to technical progress (see, Solow 1960), as long as investment is still positive. This technical progress is 'manna from heaven', its 'production' is not explained further. Other theories have attempted to remove this assumption (e.g. Arrow 1962: 'learning by doing'), but some part of technical progress always remains unexplained. The central theme, which forms an essential feature of a model of urban development, is the proposition that economic growth (in per-capita income terms) is increasingly determined by technical progress in the course of economic development.

The exogenous component of technological progress to be kept as such will be referred to as 'basic inventions' (see Mensch 1979). These represent technological breakthroughs, which consequently need to be made operational by means of R & D activities. These basic inventions occur more or less randomly over time, although it is sometimes claimed that in times of strong demand for radical technological change they are more likely to occur. What counts, however, is the time of the utilisation of a 'blueprint', which may be quite some time after its conception. This point in time, it is suggested, depends on the demand for a new 'technological paradigm'.

Figure 7.1 The Sequence of Basic Inventions and Their
Utilisation by R & D Investment

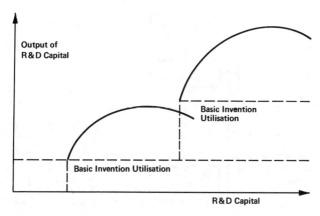

It is further assumed that R & D investment, which starts from a
'basic invention', generally follows the well-known economic law of
'falling marginal productivity', so that after some time the demand for
new basic inventions becomes urgent (see Mensch's 'depression trigger
hypotheses': 1979). This need may be due to the operation of a
'bottleneck factor', which makes the continued use of a basic technology no longer feasible (the necessary raw materials for its use become too
scarce, the externalities created by its use become prohibitive, etc.).
Figure 7.1 illustrates the shifting production functions of innovations by
means of R & D investment. The falling marginal products of
investment in R & D capital after a certain point are assumed to be
caused by the bottleneck factors mentioned.

Besides physical and R & D capital, production of goods and services
requires other production factors as well, such as labour, infrastructure
capital, energy, raw materials, and so on. A macro-economic scheme
showing the basic structure of production and its use is presented in
Figure 7.2.

*A Tentative Model of Urban Economic Growth and Innovation in a
Closed System*

A first mathematical representation of the driving forces of a system as
just described can be found in Nijkamp (1983). Some further developments are considered here. The analysis assumes that an urban system
may be considered in the same way as one of its industries (after Biehl

Figure 7.2 A Macro-economic Scheme of Production

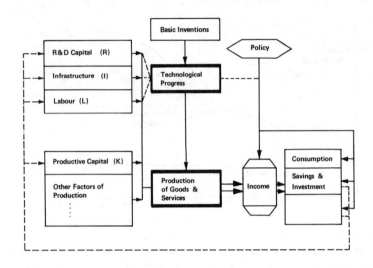

1980; Nijkamp 1982). This means that its total production Y is related to its total factors of production, namely productive capital stock K, labour L, technical infrastructure I, and stock of technological knowledge R, by a production function, which is assumed here to be of the Cobb Douglas form

$$Y = \alpha K^{\beta} L^{\gamma} I^{\delta} R^{\varepsilon} \tag{1}$$

The parameters β, γ, δ and ε represent the production elasticities (of the production factors) and are considered to be positive only over a given range (Y^{min}, Y^{max}) of production.

Urban systems, it is hypothesised, are characterised by:

thresholds — i.e. a certain minimum size the urban system has to reach to benefit from agglomeration economies. Below these levels a marginal increase of a production factor does not lead to increased production.

bottlenecks — i.e. constraints to the expansion of production factors, the increase of which leads to no increase, or even a decrease of production. Among these factors are congestion, pollution and so forth.

The growth rate y_t of production is obtained in terms of growth rates k_t, l_t, i_t and r_t of the factors of production (by differentiation of equation (1)) to give

$$y_t = \beta k_t + \gamma l_t + \delta i_t + \varepsilon r_t \tag{2}$$

where the arguments may be written as relative changes in the original variables viz:

$$y_t = (Y - Y_{t-1})/Y_{t-1}, \quad k_t = (K_t - K_{t-1})/K_{t-1} \text{ etc.}$$

Within the range (Y^{min}, Y^{max}), the urban system will display a stable growth pattern. This growth may be stopped because of two causes: external — scarcity of production factors or lack of demand; or internal — emergence of congestion effects leading to negative marginal products. External factors imply that the system will tend towards an upper limit set by the respective constraints. Internal factors, however, could lead to perturbations and qualitative changes in the behaviour of the system. A congestion effect, such as that caused by too high a concentration of capital in an urban agglomeration, implies that each additional increase in productive capital will have a negative impact on the urban production level. Let us formulate this bottleneck effect by the following linear relations:

$$\beta_t = \hat{\beta}\left(1 - \varkappa \frac{Y_{t-1}}{Y^{max}}\right) \tag{3}$$

Observe that the production elasticity has become a time-dependent variable now. Analogous relationships indicating a negative marginal product may be formalised for the remaining production factors. Substitution of all these relationships into (3) leads to the following adjusted dynamic urban production function:

$$y_t = (\hat{\beta} k_t + \hat{\gamma} l_t + \hat{\delta} i_t + \hat{\varepsilon} r_t + \ldots)\left(1 - \varkappa \frac{Y_{t-1}}{Y^{max}}\right)$$

which may be written:

$$y_t = v_t\left(1 - \varkappa \frac{Y_{t-1}}{Y^{max}}\right) \tag{4}$$

in which

$$v_t = \hat{\beta}k_t + \hat{\gamma}l_t + \hat{\delta}i_t + \hat{\epsilon}r_t$$

What are the stability properties and trajectories produced by equation (4)? The development it describes corresponds to a standard formulation used in the analysis of population dynamics. One common application of this model is the relationship between predator and prey in population biology (see Goh and Jennings 1977; Jeffries 1979; Pimm 1982; Wilson 1981). A logistic evolutionary pattern can be approximated by a Ricker curve (May 1974), which is similar to the above-mentioned specification. A difference equation approach as applied above (pioneered by May 1974, and later Li and York 1975) was applied to spatial dynamics by Brouwer and Nijkamp (1983) and Dendrinos and Mullally (1983).

The results of the investigation of the dynamic properties of (4), on the basis of numerical experiments (May 1974), indicate that a wide variety of trajectories may be derived from this specification. It was demonstrated that the following possibilities exist: stable cyclical oscillations; stable cycles; stable equilibrium points; and chaotic behaviour, including aperiodic, bounded fluctuations.

What determines the pattern of urban economic development in this model? The two important determinants are the initial values of Y and v, the intrinsic growth rate of the urban system. Simulation experiments (May 1974) demonstrated that, as is to be expected, the growth rate v is the influential factor in the long run. A stable equilibrium is likely to occur if the growth rate v is positive and does not exceed a value of 2. In all other cases either cyclical fluctuations or chaotic behaviour may result. The long-term waves shown to exist in urban development after the Second World War are hence a case compatible with the model outlined, although only a specific one.

Note, however, that the model specified above is of a more-or-less tautological nature. The various growth rates determining v in (4) are assumed to be (provisionally) exogenous. In the framework of this contribution we are especially interested in the R & D sector of the urban economy. As a next step a first attempt will be made to formulate an endogenous specification of R & D investment. More specifically, we have to formulate a hypothesis of how the growth rate r in (4) is determined via the decisions by investors.

The starting point of the analysis is the above-mentioned 'depression trigger' hypothesis. R & D investors in principle, it is argued, attempt to remove productivity bottlenecks stifling the rates of return on capital in the urban system. The central information on which their decisions are based is the gap between actual production in the previous period (Y_{t-1}) and the capacity limit Y^{max}. On this basis the following model can be formulated:

$$r_t = \lambda(\frac{Y_{t-1}}{Y^{max}}) - \pi) \tag{5}$$

The parameter π reflects, among others, an uncertainty factor about the level of Y^{max}, as well as the relative weight investors attribute to the level of Y^{max} (from equation 5). The parameter λ indicates the speed of adjustment in reaction to the perceived gap. (This formulation is akin to the 'stock adjustment' principle used by Hahn and Matthews 1964.)

Relation (5) defines a set of simultaneous difference equations, which could be tested in terms of econometric analysis. A reduced form of (4) and (5) leads to a 'nested dynamics' formulation of urban economic growth.

$$y_t = \{\bar{v}_t + \hat{\eta}\lambda(Y_{t-1}/Y^{max} - \pi)\}(1 - \varkappa Y_{t-1}/Y^{max}) \tag{6}$$

It is proposed here that this dynamic simultaneous equation system exhibits similar stability properties to the simple formulation outlined above. Further work is required, however, to investigate the dynamic properties of this model in more detail. It should also be obvious that further extensions in the direction of making the other components of (4) endogenous are feasible within this framework. As no analytical solution to the stability question is available, numerical experiments are required to assess the dynamic properties. In addition, of course, econometric work is necessary to test the validity of the claimed behavioural relations as, for example, in (5).

The disadvantage of working with a one-point urban system remains. A tentative suggestion to remove this deficiency is outlined below.

The Product Cycle Hypothesis and the Change in the Distribution of People and Jobs Over Space

The product cycle theory (Vernon 1966) states that there are four phases of a product cycle (see Deubner *et al.* 1979) from invention to obsolescence:

1. invention and introduction of the product — R & D investment is the driving force;

2. expansion of production by means of 'capital widening' — investment in the productive capital stock is the driving force;
3. maturity — investment is mostly spent for replacement and modernisation to save production cost — 'capital deepening';
4. stagnation and final obsolescence.

It has been argued that these product cycle phases have an effect on the spatial distribution of jobs. The basic assumption behind this argument is that each stage of the cycle has its specific set of locational requirements (Stohr and Schubert 1984).

As is evident from this overview, the optimal location of a firm changes over the cycle, so it can be expected that a movement of jobs will follow. This is, of course, a continuous, overlapping process, as the stages of the cycle do not occur simultaneously for all products. If we apply the same logic to the stages a basic invention goes through until it becomes obsolete, one of the determinants of urban development life cycles may become clear.

In the period of the introduction of a new basic invention, and the ensuing intensive R & D phase to utilise it industrially, urban areas with all the advantages of existing infrastructure (particularly in the form of universities) and low cost face-to-face contacts are the starting point of the industrial activity. Bottleneck factors such as land, capital and labour are not yet operative and industrial growth is feasible. The rising activity rate, however, tends to move urban industries towards these limiting factors. These bottlenecks, plus the fact that face-to-face contacts are becoming less important in the following phases of the maturation of the basic invention, mean that suburban locations offer the best investment and growth opportunities. As marginal returns to the basic invention decrease even further (plus all other factors making life difficult for the entrepreneur utilising a now widely available and refined technology), locations away from the large agglomeration, where especially the production factors of land and labour tend to be cheaper, become the best locations. A new basic invention could then again trigger growth in the large urban areas, where meanwhile residential as well as industrial density has declined to a point where bottlenecks no longer exist.

The scenario just described represents a diffusion process of economic activities, which is seen to be the motor behind urban development cycles. It is as such a supply-side, economy oriented chain of reasoning which still contains many blanks. The role of demand factors, for example, is not taken into account at all, and one might very well tell the whole story from the perspective of the hierarchy and time sequence of human needs. Furthermore, the argument that basic inventions are more likely to occur in an urban climate is plausible, but does not always hold. A closer investigation of this point seems warranted (see Malecki 1979; also Meier, Chapter 6, and Feldman, Chapter 8).

The diffusion process outlined above needs to be more rigorously formulated and must be allowed to interact with the point-economy production model of the preceding section to check its mutual consistency and compatibility. Last but not least, empirical tests of all the claims made would be highly beneficial.

References

Allen, P.M., Sanglier, M., Boon, F., Deneubourg, J.L. and de Palma, A. (1982) *Models of Urban Settlements and Structure of Dynamic Self-Organizing System*, US Dept of Transportation, Washington, DC

Arrow, K.J. (1962) 'The Economic Implications of Learning by Doing', *Review of Economic Studies, 29,* 155-73

Baumol W. (1967) 'Macroeconomics of Unbalanced Growth: The Anatomy of Urban Crisis', *American Economic Review, 57,* 415-26

Berg, L. van den, Drewett, R., Klaassen, L.H., Rossi, A. and Vijverberg, C.H.T. (1982) *Urban Europe: A Study of Growth and Decline*, Pergamon Press, Oxford

Biehl, D., (1980) 'Determinants of Regional Disparities and the Role of Public Finance', *Public Finance, 35,* 44-71

Bradbury, K.L., Downs, A. and Small, K.A. (1982) *Urban Decline and the Future of American Cities*, The Brookings Institution, Washington, DC

Brouwer, F. and Nijkamp, P. (1983) 'Qualitative Structure Analysis of Complex Systems', in P. Nijkamp, H. Leitner and N. Wrigley (eds) *Measuring the Unmeasurable; Analysis of Qualitative Spatial Data*, Martinus Nijhoff, The Hague

Dendrinos, D.A. and Mullally, H. (1983) 'Empirical Evidence of Volterra-Lotka Dynamics in United States Metropolitan Areas: 1940-1977', in D.A. Griffith and T. Lea (eds) *Evolving Geographical Structures*, Martinus Nijhoff, The Hague

Deubner, C., Rehfeldt, U., Schlupp, F. and Ziebara, G., (1979) *Die Internationaliserung des Kapitals-Neue Theorien in der internationalen Duskussion*, Campus, Frankfurt

Drewett, R. and Rossi, A. (1984) *Urban Europe: Settlement Structure and Change 1959-1980*, Gower, Aldershot

Drewett, R. and Schubert, U. (1983) 'The Macro Dynamics of Urban Population Change and the Micro Decision Background', in C.W. Matthiessen (ed.) *Urban Policy and Urban Development in the Eighties*, Report 16, Department of Geography, University of Copernhagen

Goh, B.S., and Jennings, L.S. (1977) 'Feasibility and Stability in Randomly Assembled Lotka-Volterra Models', *Ecological Modelling, 3,* 63-71

Hahn, F.H. and Matthews, R.C.D. (1964) 'The Theory of Economic growth: A Survey', *Economic Journal,* December

Hall, P. and Hay, D. (1980) *Growth Centres in the European Urban System*, Heinemann Educational Books, London

Jacobs, J. (1977) *The Death and Life of Great American Cities*, Vintage Books, New York

Jeffries, C. (1979) 'Qualitative Stability and Digraphs in Model Ecosystems', *Ecology*, 55, 1415-19

Li, T. and York, J.A. (1975) 'Period Three Implies Chaos', *American Mathematical Monthly*, 82, 985-92

Lynch, K. (1982) *A Theory of Good City Form*, The MIT Press, Cambridge, Massachusetts

Malecki, E.J. (1979) 'Locational Trends in R and D by Large U.S. Corporations, 1965-1977', *Economic Geography*, 55, 309-23

May, R.S. (1974) 'Biological Populations with Nonoverlapping Generations', *Science*, No. 186, 645-7

Mensch, G. (1979) *Stalemate in Technology*, Ballinger, Cambridge, Massachusetts

Nijkamp, P. (1982) 'A Multidimensional Analysis of Regional Infrastructure and Economic Development', in A. Andersson and T. Puu (eds) *Structural Economic Analysis and Planning in Time and Space*, North-Holland Publishing Co., Amsterdam

Nijkamp, P. (1983) 'Technological Change, Policy Response and Spatial Dynamics', in D.A. Griffith and T. Lea (eds) *Evolving Geographical Structures*, Martinus Nijhoff, The Hague

Norton, R.D. (1979) *City Life Cycles and American Urban Policy*, Academic Press, New York

Pederson, P.O. (1978) 'Interaction between Short- and Long-Run Development in Regions — The Case of Denmark', *Regional Studies*, 12, 683-700

Pimm, S.L. (1982) *Food Webs*, Chapman and Hall, London

Pred, A. (1977) *City-Systems in Advanced Economies, Past Growth, Present Processes and Future Development Options*, Hutchinson, London

Solow, R.M. (1960) 'Investment and Technical Progress' in K. Arrow, S. Karlin and P. Suppes (eds) *Mathematical Methods in the Social Sciences*, Stanford University Press, Menlo Park

Stohr, W. and Schubert, U. (1984) 'Ansaetze fuer eine Koordinierte Wirtschaftspolitik in der Landerregion Ost, in W. Blaas, G. Ruesch and W. Schoenbaeck (eds) *Regionaloe-Okonomische Analysen fure Oesterreich*, Orac, Vienna

Thomas, B. (1972) *Migration and Urban Development*, Methuen, London

Vernon, R. (1966) 'International Investment and International Trade in the Product Cycle', *Quarterly Journal of Economics*, 80, 190-207

Wilson, A.G. (1981) *Catastrophe Theory and Bifurcation*, Croom Helm, London

8. PATTERNS OF BIOTECHNOLOGY DEVELOPMENT
M. Feldman

The young field of biotechnology is predicted to grow into a multi-billion dollar 'industry' over the next decade.[1] Undoubtedly, a change of this magnitude will have major impacts on the geographic pattern of economic activity. The purpose of this chapter is to examine the industry as it now exists and sketch out what seem to be the major determinants of location over the foreseeable future.

The chapter begins with a description of the technology itself and its implications for location and land use. This is followed by a discussion of the current pattern of capital formation in the industry. This pattern has important implications for the location of production facilities as the technology moves out of the laboratory and into actual production. A third section reports on current location patterns within the industry. This section includes data on the entire US as well as data obtained from key informants within California biotechnology firms. The final section ties this together by drawing some implications for industrial location theory and policy.

The Technology and its Implications for Location

Genetic engineering involves altering the genetic make-up of micro-organisms. In industrial processes these micro-organisms reproduce themselves in fermentation. The altered micro-organisms may themselves be useful or their fermentation may produce useful by-products such as enzymes. Today, genetic engineering is concerned with 'designing' genes for micro-organisms and refining fermentation processes for large-scale production. As the technology matures, large-scale fermentation will become more common.

Fermentation is therefore the key process in actual production. Fermentation involves growing large numbers of cells with uniform characteristics under carefully controlled conditions, and modern, sophisticated fermentors use computer-monitored sensors to control the process. A major productivity goal of fermentation technology is to increase the amount of product produced with given inputs (micro-organisms, nutrients, and other inputs used to control the environment) per unit time.

There are two kinds of industrial fermentors — batch and continuous.

Batch fermentors mix the micro-organism and its nutrients together. The micro-organism reproduces itself until the nutrient is used up and the mixture is transformed. The fermentor must then be emptied, cleaned and reloaded. The product taken from the fermentor is processed further (separated into its components and so forth). Industrial batch fermentors can have capacities of over 200,000 litres.

Continuous fermentors transform their inputs without reloading. Computers can monitor the fermentor, introduce new inputs and control temperature and other processes as needed. The micro-organisms in continuous fermentors are immobilised, so separation is not a necessary part of the process. Continuous fermentors are therefore potentially more economical than batch fermentors, but continuous fermentation is relatively new and requires considerable development before it is competitive for most products.

The bulk of actual production will centre around fermentation but, because of the variation in fermentation technologies and the requirements of different products, it is difficult to generalise from current technology to future employment trends. None the less, fermentation technology is not very labour intensive. A report on batch fermentation at Genentech anticipates between 10 and 15 per cent of the total workforce will ever be involved in fermentation operations (Elliot 1980b). Another study indicates that fewer than six persons are necessary to operate a 1,000-litre batch fermentor (Elliot 1980a).

As continuous fermentors become competitive and other improvements are made, employment potential will be even less. For example, the malt beverage industry, which uses fermentation technology, experienced a 32 per cent increase in physical productivity per production worker between 1972 and 1977; and even though value added more than doubled, production workers declined by 25 per cent between 1963 and 1977 (Feldman and O'Malley 1982:76). The mix of potential products from genetic engineering includes several whose markets are already quite competitive, and this competition should foster accelerated productivity increases which will be generalised and applied to other products. So the production process will not be very labour intensive.

The implications are twofold. First, the technology will require relatively large plants to house large-scale fermentors. Batch fermentors are likely to be more 'vertical' than continuous fermentors are (the batch vats must be very large to be economical), but the potential advantages of continuous fermentation will preclude a plant being designed with no possibility of conversion to continuous fermentation. Furthermore, the rapid growth of the industry will require the availability of adjacent land for expansion. But the high value per unit weight and the possible perishability of products will make location near major airports a necessity. Hence location outside metropolitan areas is unlikely. It is more likely facilities will be located near major airports and in suburban fringes where land assembly costs are low.

Secondly, labour will not be a major constraint on location. The production process is not labour intensive nor does it require particularly skilled labour. In order to construct and maintain production facilities, workers skilled in the fabrication of industrial plumbing (boilermakers, welders, etc.) will be necessary. But, as evidenced by the ubiquity of the malt beverage industry, these skills are available in most metropolitan areas. Hence the technology does not place severe constraints on industrial location, and the industry may be expected to be quite footloose.

Furthermore, the technology is less hazardous than originally perceived and is not likely to experience a repulsive push away from populated areas. Because living organisms are involved, fermentation processes tend to be less hazardous than alternative technologies which use dangerous chemicals or life-threatening pressures and temperatures. In spite of widespread public concern, the micro-organisms themselves are relatively safe. Those currently used cannot survive outside carefully controlled, artificial environments. Hence the danger of a malevolent micro-organism escaping and causing health problems seems unfounded. This might change if new products require more hearty micro-organisms; and public perceptions, however unfounded, may still keep production away from metropolitan areas.

Capital Formation

It is a mistake to view a new technology as strictly a technical issue. Production processes and their technologies are necessarily socio-technical systems, and an analysis of a technology must look at both technical and social sides. At this early date there is little actual production using the new technology, so social relations of production are difficult to decipher. But the current pattern of capital formation in the industry may indicate its future organisation, and this has strong implications for the location of facilities.

Because the technology is so new, most firms engaged in genetic engineering are focused on R & D (research and development);

commercial products are still quite rare. The firms undertaking R & D tend to be small and, because they do not have any marketable products as yet, have virtually no internal sources of funds. They therefore must rely on outside funding.

There are four common ways genetic engineering firms raise capital: debt, public stock offerings, venture capital and joint research agreements. Because of the long lead time in R & D before production, the first two sources have not been very attractive, and firms have turned to venture capitalists and joint research ventures. These two sources are similar except that venture capitalists acquire ownership of a portion of the entire firm, whereas joint ventures give the partner rights only to the venture itself.

There are basically three kinds of venture capitalists: individuals, venture capital firms and corporations. Because of the large sums of money involved, venture capital in the industry tends to be directly or indirectly tied into large corporations (Feldman 1982). This not only provides the genetic engineering firm with funds, it also provides technical and managerial expertise, established marketing organisations, legal assistance, supplies and enhanced credibility with other investors (Rosene 1980).

Large corporations are prone to invest in external R & D ventures for a number of reasons. Smaller firms are more flexible, and this gives them an advantage in recruiting top-level scientific personnel. US tax laws also favour external ventures over internal R & D. External ventures also allow a firm to 'hedge its bets' by tying itself to several external organisations. For example, Monsanto has simultaneously held major ownership portions in at least four competing R & D firms. While the firms might compete among themselves, Monsanto is assured of owning a portion of whatever the four competitors may produce. Because R & D firms do research in a wide variety of applications, this strategy also allows large corporations to diversify and move into industries outside their 'home' industry.

As a result of this pattern, virtually all genetic engineering firms are tied to a complex web of large, usually multinational, corporations. The R & D firms' smallness is misleading. They are actually part of a much larger corporate network, and this has important implications for location of production facilities. It may be that initial 'scale up' will be located close to research labs so that research scientists can monitor the process. But once the process is 'debugged' the location of the research firm will cease to be a factor, if it ever was, and the concerns of the corporate partner will take over.

The example of human insulin, the first recombinant DNA (rDNA) product to come to market, is illuminating. This product was developed by Genentech under contract to Eli Lilly. Although Genentech is located in California, production of the new product is being undertaken in Indiana and Britain. Lilly already controls 80 per cent of the US market, and rDNA insulin is primarily a strategy to break into the European market. The Indiana plant is part of a defensive strategy to protect against retaliation by European firms (*Business Week* 1982).

In this example, market competition dictates location and the location of the R & D firm is quite irrelevant. All it takes is a hotel and an airport to bring in the outside expert, and market considerations play the dominant role in determining location as a *social*, rather than *technical*, process. Given the current pattern of capital formation in biotechnology R & D, this example may very well be typical of what is to come. It is therefore necessary to treat R & D separately from actual production.

Location of Biotechnology Firms

The spatial pattern of R & D firms reveals a number of things about what determines their location. Two sources of information are used here to examine the current pattern. One consists of a list of about 160 firms throughout the US and abroad. Financial, locational and other information on these firms was taken from trade publications, the national business media and other sources. The other data source is the Biotechnology Industry Survey (BIS) conducted for the California Commission on Industrial Innovation (CCII). This survey involves interviews with key informants at ten firms selected at random from all biotechnology firms within the state.[2]

Aggregate Patterns

Three indices are used in this analysis: number of firms, employment and revenue. The number of firms is most reliable, but it may be misleading because many firms are very small. Employment is a better indicator, but the data on employment are incomplete. For example, employment data are available on less than 50 per cent of synthetic genetic firms. For revenues, this problem is even worse — data are available for roughly 30 per cent of all firms. Hence, this analysis must be seen as only a rough approximation.

Table 8.1 shows the location of genetic engineering firms. A high degree of spatial concentration is readily apparent. Half the firms are

Table 8.1 Location of Biotechnology Firms by State and
Region: Synthetic Genetics

LOCATION	Firms No.	%	Employment No.	%	Annual Revenues ($MM)	%
New England						
Connecticut	6	5	91	3	4.5	3
Massachusetts	18	16	175	5	3.0	2
Middle Atlantic						
Delaware	1	1	—	—	—	—
New Jersey	4	4	51	2	—	—
New York	12	11	110	3	1.8	1
Pennsylvania	2	2	35	1	0.2	0
South Atlantic						
Florida	3	3	185	6	3.9	2
Georgia	1	1	—	—	—	—
Maryland	5	4	470	14	11.6	7
Virginia	1	1	—	—	—	—
East North Central						
Illinois	2	2	—	—	—	—
Indiana	2	2	9,200[a]	—	686.1[a]	—
Michigan	1	1	5	0		
Wisconsin	1	1	15	0	0.5	0
West North Central						
Kansas	1	1	315	10	27.5	17
Minnesota	1	1	35	1	1	1
Nebraska	1	1				
West South Central						
Louisiana	1	1	—	—	—	—
Texas	1	1	—	—	—	—
Mountain						
Colorado	4	4	656	20	85	52
Montana	1	1	5	0	—	—
Utah	1	1	85	2	2.6	2
Pacific						
California	39	34	1,030	31	21.6	13
Washington	4	4	15	0	—	—
Total	113	103	3,278	100	162.1	100

Note: a. This figure is for Miles Laboratory and excluded from
         computations.
Source: Feldman and O'Malley (1982).

located in just two states, California and Massachusetts, and an
additional 20 per cent of all firms are located in three others: New
York, Connecticut and Maryland. Jobs are similarly concentrated.
Again, California is a clear leader with 31 per cent of all jobs, and over
86 per cent of all employment is concentrated in six states (California,
Colorado, Maryland, Kansas, Florida and Massachusetts). Revenues

Table 8.2   Location of Biotechnology Firms by State and
Region: Supply and Support

LOCATION	Firms No.	%	Employment No.	%	Annual Revenues ($MM)	%
New England						
Connecticut	1	2	—	—	—	—
Massachusetts	10	24	5,445	21	351.5	25
New Hampshire	1	2	43	0	2	0
Middle Atlantic						
New Jersey	3	7	293	1	16.5	1
New York	4	10	—	—	8	0
Pennsylvania	3	7	4,015	15	351	25
South Atlantic						
Florida	1	2	350	1	12	1
Maryland	2	5	10	0	—	—
Virginia	1	2	1,600	6	102	7
East North Central						
Wisconsin	1	2	—	—	—	—
West North Central						
Minnesota	1	2	—	—	—	—
Missouri	1	2	1,400	5	68	5
Mountain						
Arizona	1	2	—	—	2.5	0
Pacific						
California	11	27	13,120	50	473.1	34
Total	41	100	26,276	100	1,386.6	100

are even more concentrated; fully 80 per cent of reported revenues are concentrated in three states! But revenues are a poor indicator of activity because few firms market anything, and the data are very skimpy.

The location of biotechnology supply and support firms is given in Table 8.2. Concentration of firms engaged in biotechnology supply and support is even greater than that of firms engaged in synthetic genetics. Again, two states, Massachusetts and California, have over 50 per cent of all firms, but in this case California's share is somewhat lower than before. In terms of employment, however, California by itself accounts for about 50 per cent of all employment nationwide! This exceptionally high figure is primarily due to the contribution of one firm, Beckman Instruments, and since Beckman is diversified, not all this employment is related to biotechnology. But it is impossible to disaggregate Beckman employment by using the available data. Supply and support firms also tend to have larger operations than firms specialising in synthetic genetics. The most likely reason for this is a

Table 8.3 Location of Biotechnology Firms Within California

Area		Synthetic Genetics				Supply & Support				Total			
		Firms		Empl't		Firms		Empl't		Firms		Empl't	
Zip	Description	N	%	N	%	N	%	N	%	N	%	N	%
900	Los Angeles	0	0	0	0	1	9	—	—	—	—	—	—
904	Santa Monica	1	2	—	—	0	0	0	0	1	2	0	0
911	Pasadena	1	2	12	1	0	0	0	0	1	2	12	0
913	Newbury Park	1	2	10	1	0	0	0	0	1	2	10	0
917-8	Alhambra	2	5	—	—	0	0	0	0	2	4	0	0
920-1	San Diego	8	20	61	5	0	0	0	0	8	15	61	0
926	Santa Ana	2	5	—	—	1	11	12,400	94	4	8	12,400	87
933	Bakersfield	1	2	—	—	0	0	0	0	1	2	0	0
940-4	San Francisco	13	32	656	55	4	44	2	0	19	36	658	4
945-8	Oakland	7	18	430	36	2	22	720	5	9	17	1,150	8
949	San Rafael	1	2	—	—	1	11	—	—	2	4	—	—
950	Santa Clara	1	2	—	—	0	0	0	0	1	2	0	0
956	Davis	2	5	17	1	0	0	0	0	3	6	17	0
	Total	40	100	1,186	100	9	100	13,122	100	52	100	14,308	100

greater degree of horizontal integration and diversification among supply and support firms. Moreover, their products may be put to a variety of different uses. In other words, the outputs of supply and support firms form the inputs for several industries, biotechnology being just one of these.

Location Within California

Table 8.3 shows the distribution of 52 firms within California according to three-digit zip codes. Some care must be taken in interpreting this table because employment figures are not available for most firms. Firms whose employment levels are unknown are omitted from the computations for employment but included in the overall counts. Furthermore, in some cases it is not possible to classify a firm as either supply and support or synthetic genetics, so figures for the totals are not necessarily equal to the sum of the synthetic genetic and supply and support columns. Finally, one supplier, Beckman Instruments, has a disproportionate share of employment. Since much of this is in non-biotechnology production, the data greatly overstate Beckman's share of the total. The table should therefore be interpreted accordingly.

The most striking feature of Table 8.3 is the extremely high degree of concentration in the San Francisco-Oakland area. Almost half (20) of California's biotechnology firms are located in this area. Even more striking is the fact that, if Beckman Instruments is omitted, 95 per cent of the state's total biotechnology employment is located there. Over 91 per cent of all synthetic genetics employment is in this area, as is all supply and support employment other than Beckman.

San Diego is the major centre in Southern California; 20 per cent of all synthetic genetic firms are located in the San Diego area. In addition, most of the firms in Santa Ana are located in Newport Beach — an area rather close to San Diego. Significantly, the firms that are located in Newport Beach are synthetic genetic firms, whereas the lone firm outside Newport Beach is a supplier: Beckman Instruments in Fullerton. Other centres are to the north of San Francisco-Oakland: Davis and San Rafael.

Determinants of Location

Perhaps the most obvious determinant of location for biotechnology firms is proximity to major university research centres performing rDNA research. This accounts for the locations of the two areas with the most biotechnology firms: the San Francisco Bay Area and the Boston area. Many of the firms in these areas locate there because either the firms were founded by former faculty members from nearby universities, or members of the firms' research staff desire to continue their academic activities by teaching and participating in research activity at nearby universities (*New York Times* 1981).

It is difficult to define precisely a 'major university research centre'. There is a problem in ranking universities according to their research, and a university with strong overall research may be weak in microbiology. One indication that only the leading research centres have attracted biotechnology firms is the fact that only three (Berkeley, San Francisco and San Diego) out of the nine University of California campuses have the majority of firms near them.

The BIS has an entire section devoted to the determinants of location. One question asks firms to assess the importance of a wide variety of location factors, both in terms of general importance and with respect to the particular site of the firm. In general, the latter results are identical with the former and provide a check on the reliability of this question, so only the former are discussed here. Although these results must be treated with care because of the sample size, the uniformity of responses to key questions suggests results can be generalised.

The two most important locational factors are *proximity to major reseach centres* and *quality of residential life*. *All* respondents rank these two factors as either 'important' or 'very important'. Several respondents indicate that local amenities are important for their corporations. Quality of life, especially residential life, appears to be a major attraction of California — particularly in the Bay Area. Environmental questions such as open space and air quality are considered to be key factors in location decisions. On the other hand, the high cost of housing and poor public transport are mentioned as deterrents to locating in the Bay Area. Air transportation is generally considered to be important because future products may be perishable. In contrast, rail and mass transit are not uniformly considered to be important. Both space for physical expansion and availability of skilled labour are fairly important; for example, about 70 per cent list space for expansion as either important or very important.

Several other factors are uniformly ranked as being of 'minor importance' or 'not important': proximity to markets, availability of low-cost labour, availability of reliable energy, proximity to major suppliers, availability of utilities, and proximity to major competitors. Availability of business services, level of taxes and highway transportation are of moderate importance to most respondents.

In light of recent attempts to target subsidies at biotechnology, the low esteem in which firms hold such subsidies is enlightening. All respondents rank 'government incentives' as being either 'not important' or only of 'minor importance'. The response to questions on the BIS on perceived need for government aid for bioindustry development is remarkably uniform. Respondents were asked to rate the impacts of different public policies: biotechnology foundations to fund basic research, increased training in genetics and fermentation technology, tax abatement, land assembly programmes, loans, and any other policies the respondent wished to add. All respondents agreed that research and training are likely to enhance the industry's growth in California. But there is little or no interest in other public policies. At best, some respondents think some of these would 'possibly' enhance industry growth, and many think they are 'unlikely' to do so. Perhaps this reflects the entrepreneurial qualities of early entrants into the field, or perhaps it reflects a recent near-scandal associated with an attempt to establish a biotechnology research park in California. Only one company interviewed indicated that it had ever sought government help; that was from the Small Business Administration, and the company did not get the help.

This pattern continues on subsequent questions. In general, the two most important factors are access to universities (for their research libraries, graduates and academic staff) and the potential for growth (space for physical expansion, transportation facilities, etc.). One problem that is mentioned frequently in the San Francisco Bay Area is the high cost of employee housing. Other site location problems mentioned are: distance from the major population and academic centres in the country (specifically, the north-east), poor ground access, land costs, lack of proximity to field sites, taxes and red tape in state agencies.

When asked if they would consider moving, several firms respond that they either would consider moving or already had moved. These firms almost uniformly say they would (had) move(d) because they needed more space for expansion, but all of these firms say they would (had) move(d) within their present region. Three firms mention that they would consider opening facilities outside the area. In one case, the reason for doing so would be closer proximity to markets (once production of marketable products began). Another firm mentions opening a branch in Europe in order to tap into new markets and networks of biotechnology researchers. Another response along these lines is a firm that says it would consider opening a facility outside the area in order to enter into a joint venture with another biotechnology firm.

In sum, the major positive factors influencing location are proximity to major research centres, residential quality of life, and potential for expansion. The first of these restricts the general region in which firms locate, while the other two influence where firms locate within the region. In general, areal considerations are very important in the decision to open new facilities. There is a certain attraction for locating outside the present region in order to tap into different networks of researchers and new markets. The response to this section of the BIS are perhaps best summarised by one company president who gestured to the green hills visible from his office window and asked, 'Where else could I get all this?'

Implications for Theory and Policy

Industrial location theory points to a wide variety of factors that can influence location decisions. These factors range from the distinction between material and market orientations to the attraction managers and technicians have for urbane, if not urban, lifestyles (Alonso 1975). In spite of the variety of potential factors given in the literature, it appears that biotechnology firms do not conform to any of the more common patterns. Instead, biotechnology R & D firms might best be described as 'amenity-oriented' (Ullman 1954; Stanback and Knight 1970): they locate in areas that will help to attract and retain highly skilled, specialised workers.

It might seem that two commonly mentioned location factors, information and labour, are applicable to the case of biotechnology. This is true only if these two factors are given very unusual interpretations, and then they are incomplete explanations at best. Biotechnology firms do locate near major research universities in order to avail themselves of the latest scientific information, but this is only part of the story. Universities also help firms attract scientific personnel by satisfying desires for intellectual stimulation (Levy, Chapter 5). Also, while universities do supply a certain stratum of workers in the form of graduate students and the like, the key labour input is high-level scientists. There is no one location with an adequate supply of such labour, and so firms adopt the strategy of trying to attract scientists from other locations. Not only universities, but also housing, air quality and the attractiveness of an area are used as lures. Furthermore, the temptation to treat biotechnology as an example of the 'seedbed' function of information flows in urban areas should be resisted. Unless one is willing to call areas such as Madison, Wisconsin, and the research triangle of North Carolina 'urban', any correlation between urbanisation and biotechnology's need for information must be seen as spurious. Rather than locate near potential labour pools, firms locate where they will attract labour from around the world.

In terms of traditional location theory, this can be seen as a process of attempting to capture external economies. A location can offer a mixture of natural and human-made amenities, and biotechnology firms attempt to benefit from these by using them to attract labour. Given a separation of land uses into residential and other uses, a firm may be able to avoid paying a premium, in the form of ground rent, for amenities. If, on the other hand, in-migration raises the bid price of residential land, housing costs may become excessively high and hinder a firm's ability to attract research scientists. It is therefore not surprising that one of the more commonly voiced complaints in the BIS is the high cost of housing in the Bay Area, nor is it surprising that regional housing costs have been given special attention by corporations with highly skilled labour forces.

An orientation towards amenities may lead firms to attempt to influence public policy in the provision of 'collective consumption' goods and services. There is already evidence of public entities adopting such strategies. But localities must be very careful in doing so.

As discussed above, biotechnology firms appear to be small and independent, but actually they are linked by a complex web of financial and other ties to large, multinational corporations. These ties render biotechnology quite footloose when it comes to the location of actual production (as opposed to research) facilities. Any locality subsidising biotechnology as a way to create jobs is taking a substantial risk. Firms may locate in the subsidising community. But, unless the local residents are high-level scientists, it is likely the desirable, newly created jobs will go to persons from outside the area. And, after the technology matures and the subsidised firms begin production, there is no guarantee that production will be located in the subsidising community. In fact, given the complex ties to large corporations and the uncertainty of R & D outcomes, it is more likely production will move elsewhere.

The pattern of biotechnology capital formation may portend a new relation between regional growth and the product cycle. The product cycle is sometimes described as 'the law of industrial growth' and is based on seminal studies by Burns (1934) and Kuznets (1930). The 'law' basically states that products go through four stages: (1) experimentation, (2) rapid growth, (3) maturity, and (4) stability or decline. There may be some question as to how applicable this 'law' is to biotechnology because it is really a technology rather than an industry, but there are several new biotechnology products which would come under this 'law'.

Several authors have argued that industries in their early stages require external economies and undergo a period of rapid growth in close proximity to the innovative 'seedbed' of the space economy (cf. Norton and Rees 1979). As industries mature, the pace of innovation slackens, products and production processes improve, costs go down, and markets expand. Mature industries therefore 'spread out to lower-cost locations ... [and] "decompose" their process ... to transfer some of them'. 'Decomposition' is facilitated by new technologies 'but one can only guess at the speed of these processes of birth and maturity and technological shifts' (Vernon 1960:109).

It appears that biotechnology is 'short-circuiting' the growth stage of the product cycle. Low communications costs and the adaptation of 'mature' technologies, such as computerised production control, allow *initial* production to take place far from the R & D 'seedbed'. In addition, ties to multinational corporations allow biotechnology firms to tap into ready-made marketing organisations and markets on an international scale. Multinational corporations are relatively flexible in their location requirements and may locate more for strategic reasons than for increased rates of return (Yannopoulos and Dunning 1976). It is therefore unlikely that the spatial pattern of biotechnology growth will conform to those of older industries.

In view of the potential mobility of production, the best public strategy for attracting biotechnology firms may be investment in amenities serving the local population. At the very worst, such investment could benefit local residents; at best, it will attract firms, create jobs, and improve the overall standard of living. But care must be taken to ensure that such investment benefits local residents — it is all too easy for rapidly rising property values to force out local residents in a process of gentrification. Indeed if high technology represents the wave of the future, conflict over who benefits from the provision of amenities may colour the urban political landscape for some time to come.

Notes

1. Congress of the US, Office of Technology Assessment (1981), Saltus (1981). The term 'biotechnology' can refer to several distinct technologies, but here the term is used interchangeably with 'genetic engineering'. This technology can be applied to many different products and production processes, so it is a bit misleading to view it as a single industry.
2. See Feldman and O'Malley (1982) for details. Note that the ten firms make up roughly 25 per cent of the population. Also, with there being at most a few hundred firms worldwide, these ten make up a substantial portion of the international industry.

References

Alonso, W. (1975) 'Industrial Location and Regional Policy in Economic Development' in J. Friedmann and W. Alonso (eds) *Regional Policy: Readings in Theory and Applications*. The MIT Press, Cambridge, Massachusetts

Burns, A.F. (1934) *Production Trends in the United States*, National Bureau of Economic Research, New York

Business Week (1982) 'A Market Face-off for Two Insulin Pioneers', 1 November, 31-2

Congress of the United States, Office of Technology Assessment (1981) *Impacts of Applied Genetics: Micro-organisms, Plants, and Animals, Government Printing Office*, Washington, DC

Elliot, L. (1980a), *Industrial Hygiene Survey of the Burns Biotech Facility, Omaha, Nebraska*, National Institute for Occupational Safety and Health, Cincinnati

Elliot, L. (1980b) *Walkthrough Survey of Genentech, Inc.*, National Institute for Occupational Safety and Health, Cincinatti

Feldman, M.M.A. (1982) 'Capital Formation and Spatial Location in California Biotechnology: A Case Study', paper presented at the Twenty-Ninth American Meeting of the Regional Science Association, Pittsburgh, Pennsylvania, November

Feldman, M.M.A. and O'Malley, E.P. (1982) *The Biotechnology Industry in California*, California Commission on Industrial Innovation, Sacramento

Kuznets, S.S. (1930) *Secular Movements in Production and Prices: Their Nature and their Bearing upon Cyclical Fluctuations*, Houghton Mifflin Company, Boston

New York Times (1981) 'Genetic Engineering Thrives in Boston Area', 26 February

Norton, R.D. and Rees, J. (1979) 'The Product Cycle and the Spatial Decentralization of American Manufacturing', *Regional Studies*, *13*, 141-51

Rosene, M. (1980) 'Why Corporations Back Entrepreneurs', *Venture*, May, 34-9

Saltus, R. (1981) 'Genetics Industry: Great Impact Seen, but Not Overnight; $15 Billion Industry Foreseen', *San Francisco Examiner and Chronicle*, 26 April

Stanback, T.M. and Knight, R.V. (1970) *The Metropolitan Economy*, Columbia University Press, New York

Ullman, E. (1954) 'Amenities as a Factor in Regional Growth', *Geographical Review*, *44*, January, 119-32

Vernon, R. (1960) *Metropolis 1985, An Interpretation of the Findings of the New York Metropolitan Regional Study*, Harvard University Press, Cambridge, Massachusetts

Yannopoulos, G.N. and Dunning, J.H. (1976) 'Multinational Enterprises and Regional Development: An Exploratory Paper', *Regional Studies*, *10*, 389-99

PART FOUR

COMMUNICATIONS AND TRANSPORT

9. TELECOMMUNICATIONS AND URBAN DEVELOPMENT
R. Meier

Acceleration Potentials Inherent in the Telephone

Ever since urban planners and managers have been faced with an energy crisis, the potential of using telecommunications and computing services for saving energy has come to their attention. Messages conveyed by channels in the electromagnetic spectrum overcome the friction of space for a tiny fraction of the energy applied in transport. Therefore the established practice of moving people and paper about to get the business of the city done is questioned. Moreover, it has been discovered that energy conservation in buildings and factories requires paying attention to a great deal more detail — a task that should be delegated to instruments, telecommunications channels and computers, because these systems are much faster than clerical workers, and eventually make fewer errors (Goddard 1980).

These concerns raise some questions. What is the place of the telephone, of television, of data transmission, and of computers in the present and future metropolis? What is their contribution to development as a whole? Surprisingly, except for the observations and insights of Jean Gottmann (1970, 1982, 1983a, 1983b), nothing significant is found in the literature except the promotional blurbs for new technology and some forecasting of new markets for the innovations, despite the economic, social, and cultural importance of person-to-person communications. Is this evidence that the communications environment is taken for granted, much as a fish might regard the water in which it swims? As compared to all other major urban infrastructure investments, the telephone impact is the least documented, even though it is just about the oldest and the most familiar.

Two decades ago it was possible to arrive at a series of strong conjectures about telecommunications in cities (Meier 1962). In this perspective the city is a busy message exchange — a promoter of transactions — and a home for organisations that promote specialised transactions. The actors are individuals, households and organisations, each intending to maintain or improve its position in the community (Figure 9.1a). Telecommunications greatly reduce the unit cost of messages as measured in terms of time, money, attention, energy, materials and space.

Figure 9.1 Factors in the Generation of Transactions

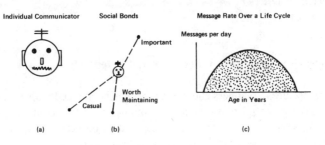

The first of the telecommunications media, the telegraph, evolved as a substitute for overworked couriers and their horses, so it remained primarily institutional. The telephone, when it arrived three decades later, was instantly recognised as an extension of the person, allowing distance to be overcome, so it had a private function (Aronson 1971). Though it is a tool accessible to the pre-literate and the illiterate, massive, sophisticated use is highly correlated with educational achievement. The evidence for this is found in every telephone book.

Communication of extraordinary demands to 'gatekeepers' of organisations, especially those with strictly prescribed resources, can result in *stress* felt first by the individuals receiving the messages and then by the organisation itself. Reduced costs in communication result in increased volume, which can lead to overload at some sensitive points. Temporary paralysis follows, especially when members facing the public have concerns for those not served (Meier 1972). They will invent fair procedures by queuing, priority assignments, combining similar demands, dismissing the trivial, systems analysis, automation, reduction of service standards to conserve resources, and — when morale is low — 'working to rule'. If these policies do not seem to work, the people overloaded by communications often become physiologically sick; they suffer from a severe case of 'burnout'. Many escape responsibilities by moving to the edge of the forest or to the sea. Once the phenomenon comes to be recognised, organisations are forced to change procedures to prevent burnout, but it will be encountered repeatedly in smaller voluntary groups (Paine 1982).

Social Networks Maintained by Telephone

A series of transactions between A and B usually results in an interdependency — a social bond — between them (Figure 9.1b). As

Figure 9.2 The Allocation of Social Bonding (Affiliation)

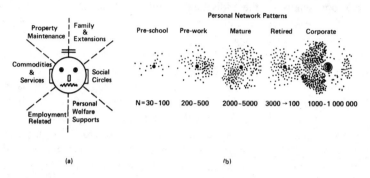

(a)   (b)

the aggregate of messages in a city increases, the greater is the number of transactions, and the number of social bonds rises soon afterward. The individual with more social bonds is alerted to more opportunities and is better secured against disaster (Figure 9.1c).

People evolve their own methods for taking advantage of the potentials of the telephone. What each has in common is a list of important numbers which can be called at liberty. This list can be ranked by the person who maintains it in order of respective import- ance. The functions of the address being called suggest the kind of contribution that is likely to be made to the life of the caller (Figure 9.2a). In a developed metropolis this list of telephone numbers and addresses constitutes almost the whole of an individual's 'social network'. If we say that an important relationship should be designated 'close', and a marginal relationship 'distant', a convenient pattern of affiliation emerges that fits the individual like a fingerprint. The typical life cycle in an urban environment will start accumulating this network even before entering school; it matures at an age range of 30-50 years, and declines thereafter at an accelerating rate (Figure 9.2b).

An ill person will usually have a network size that is subnormal; poverty has the same effect. Indeed, according to the Research Institute of Telecommunications and Economics (Tokyo), the single measure that brought the greatest improvement in the quality of life was a free 'welfare' telephone for the elderly. With it they were able to maintain their networks, sharing each others', without taking to the streets where they were required to depend upon public transport (Takasaki 1977). *The size of the network is a good indicator of human wellbeing; balance in the network provides security for the long run.* These indexes encompass non-market interaction potentials along with income- and expenditure-based transaction opportunities in a way that closely fits the needs and wants of the individual members of society. Very large networks are associated with special social roles, for example, politicians, salesmen and teachers.

What happens in a poor urban settlement when telephones are introduced? By now even the most isolated cities have acquired telephone exchanges, so we are reduced to observing market towns in the Himalayas or in Africa. There the largest networks are sustained with the aid of couriers carrying both written and spoken messages. The first to get telephones when service is introduced, are (1) high-status government officials at work and at home, (2) merchants, traders and dealers making frequent contacts with the outside world, (3) public services, especially police and transport, (4) doctors, lawyers, accountants and other fee professionals, and (5) owners of property. This pattern can still be seen in Burma and in isolated cities of many developing countries.

As outside lines become available the general public gets an opportunity to use telephones, because they are put into kiosks, gatehouses and foyers. Most of the user's network have no household number at which they can be called, but each can be reached in an emergency by messages relayed from a number. Shanghai is now at this level.

Once the elite achieves comprehensive service, the social uses of the telephone expand greatly. Families call each other routinely. Adolescents will play games with the aid of the telephone, acquire assistance in their studies, and conduct courtships. As the number of telephones supplied multiplies, the use patterns established by the elite diffuse into the growing middle class and eventually into regularly employed working class — a condition already reached in Hong Kong and Singapore, while Seoul and Taipei are almost at this stage. In these latter metropolises a telephone can be obtained within a few weeks after ordering, and without paying bribes, whereas a few years ago installations lagged for months, even years. Since neither wealth, clout, nor patience are required to enter the system, we see the channel used for exploration, for fun and for the trivial.

Media Integration

Television fills a prodigious hole in the urban time budget — periods when nothing much is happening. In those societies where government does not monopolise propaganda, or strictly censor the arts, viewing time reaches two to three hours per day per capita. Television can be extremely popular — though it has been introduced more recently than the telephone in most places of the world, it reaches saturation levels sooner. Television makes possible the marketing of *images* which are associated with products, institutions and personalities. Its impacts can be assessed by measuring enhancement in the repertory of images a person can recognise. Relevance to the networks of individuals and organisations illustrated above is small and indirect (*Business Week* 29 November 1982).

Television and telephone are in conflict with each other. Television addicts possess stunted networks, while extensive telephone users find their attention to programmes is interrupted too frequently to follow the story line closely. However, a linkup with radio has occurred over the past few decades; the disc jockey and the call-in talk show resulted from this integration. When audiences are small, and the transmitters are less likely to be overwhelmed by feedback from telephoning listeners, television channels with feedback may be expected to follow the path of radio. As television audiences are fragmented by cable technologies and interactive community systems, we see customers influencing programme scheduling by voting through telephone or sending requests by mail.

The medium of electronic recording, although suddenly ubiquitous throughout the world, is only beginning to interact with the telephone. The boom in tapes conveys mostly American, English and Japanese pop music; it has penetrated far into the back country, way beyond the end of the power line. Tapes are pirated, bootlegged and smuggled into areas where authorities frown upon the decadence of Western culture. Local artists rush in to fill the vacuum, first with imitations, then hybrids (like the steel bands of the Carribean), but already totally novel local syntheses are beginning to appear. TV tapes are following audio, but the admission that almost half of those sold in America are pornographic indicates the kind of difficulties encountered in instituting controls or collecting data. Tapes were used to develop underground support for Khomeini before the toppling of the Shah; they serve the orthodox as well as the profane.

Data processing and computing are rapidly invading the intercity long lines and the regional networks of telephone exchanges. Multinational firms and syndicates, with the aid of communications satellites, are breaking down the sovereignty of nations with respect to the flow of information (*Business Week* November 1982). Portable terminals and microcomputers are more and more connecting individuals to central mainframes through telephone exchanges; the growth rate in data processing and small scale computing has been running 30-40 per cent

Figure 9.3 Social Network of a Typical Person-Computer
Dyad Linked with Data Source
(The bonds are distributed by function about the
centre — origin as before)

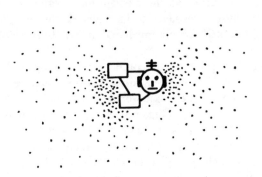

per year in Japan and North America. Voice-operated computers seem
to be just on the edge of commercial feasibility; when they become
available at a competitive price, a new level of integration of media will
emerge. The continuing trend makes it likely that more telephone calls
will be made by machines communicating to machines than humans
interacting with humans before the end of the century, as seemed
possible when the basic science came into being in the 1950s (Meier
1956).

Current observations of the behaviour of young people suggest that
the network patterns described above are changing quite significantly.
At the nucleus we will have a binary (participant-computer) bonding,
with the computer-telephone combination providing links to one or
more 'conferences' which introduce preferential bonds. So far these
conferences have been work-related, or fun-and-games, so they do not
affect many categories of human bonding relationships. For completely
independent demographic reasons, family ties are rapidly diminishing.
Thus the expected network — a pattern which should diffuse to Third
World metropolitan centres within a decade — looks like Figure 9.3
(the extra small square represents a major data source).

The economic impact of data processing and computing will be
difficult to judge because it is the *quality* of products and services in the
mix presently distributed that is primarily affected. After the initial
perturbations have been damped, a greatly enhanced information flow
should (1) reduce error frequency, (2) reduce risk from well-known

sources of loss, (3) quicken response time, and (4) conserve scarce resources. It will also assure a continuing high rate of obsolescence (which people complain about), and open up huge potentials for social and cultural innovation (which is usually appreciated). With the aid of data transmitted by communications satellites, multinational firms and syndicates are undermining national sovereignty almost completely in their attempts to control data transmission — an outcome which may contribute greatly to world peace since isolationist nationalism is at the root of many wars.

Social Engineering

The true value of a communications medium is revealed when it can be mobilised for the solution of a pressing social problem. If a major deficiency of fuel should exist for the short run, the telephone is used to discover where the available stock is held so the owner of a vehicle can arrange for a private supply. Radio and television are likely to broadcast the official description of the situation, but a personal social network is used to make contact with informal sources of supply. This behaviour forces fuel rationing to institute tight controls starting from the refinery and proceeding to retail distribution. A small ration combined with scarcity on the 'grey' market can persuade people to visit by telephone as a substitute for a trip. However, the savings are small in scale, because the bulk of the liquid fuel is spent on the daily commute to work. Commuting by bus or train can be effectively substituted by quite large amounts of telecommunications and computing , so they are able to claim control over a number of channels in the electromagnetic spectrum for exclusive use. In practice, therefore, fuel conservation in cities will remain a conscious, calculated effort that adjusts the habits of workers and the requirements of installed equipment simultaneously.

A new challenge is due to appear on the metropolitan scene very soon. Portable telephones linked to 'cellular' solid-state electronic exchanges will almost surely become more economical to install and operate than additions to existing systems (Wellman 1977, 1983; National Bureau of Standards 1981; Fischer 1982; Marsden and Nan Lin 1982; McPherson 1983). A person with a telephone on the wrist is not held to an office desk. People can move freely while still participating in a tight-knit, fast-paced organisation, so co-ordination with the field — almost always weak heretofore — can be very much improved. This innovation can accelerate both the growth in numbers of sets and an improvement in the quality of service. With the new communications satellites global transactions, so necessary for community balance, can be facilitated.

Relationships Based upon Trust

Telecommunications constitute the fundamental technology of the oncoming post-industrial city. Initially fossil fuel-based technologies were labour intensive and therefore supported heavy immigration into industrial regions. Since then manufacturing has been eliminating the most tedious human operations; instrumented machines, even robots, do more of the work. Also, large quantities of precise information need to be transmitted back to the designers responsible for differentiating the product or service. We should anticipate therefore that the future urban labour force engaged in manufacturing will remain about 10 per cent of the whole, and of these workers many will spend their time overseeing instruments. Cities like Cairo, Manila, Jakarta and Bangkok will bypass most of the previously expected industrial expansion, the ageing of those factories as in Britain and New England, and their replacement with other kinds of work. Instead people will be employed in the distribution of goods, public utilities, maintenance of facilities, banking, insurance, education, medicine, police and security, recreation and cultural activities. These are the primary concerns of the 'service society' now coming into being, even in the Third World.

Telecommunications systems are socio-economic instruments, similar in many ways to money and negotiable securities, but they are more recent and more flexible. They have yet to be fully fitted into the trusting relationships maintained between people and their organisations. Complete dependence upon artifacts is also often referred to as a 'trusting relationship'. Telephones are obviously trusted when clinching a business deal, arranging vehicular repair, dealing in finance, accepting a medical opinion, or reaching a political agreement, but certainly not in all instances. Each of these transactions involves trust in much the same sense that we trust paper currency, but the medium has become electronic. The issue of trust or, to use the double negative, 'prevention of cheating', has greatly delayed the acceptance of electronic banking, for example.

Trust in television depends upon credibility. Popular serial dramas (called 'soap opera' in America because they are sponsored by makers of detergents and toothpastes) have become particularly important to families caught in the transition between tradition and modernism. With the aid of TV people can live many fictional lives in addition to their own; if the portrayal seems 'real', the vicarious experience influences commitments. All societies censor the mass media, but if prohibitions are mild, and the rules are known, people will believe that little of significance is being withheld; so most of the programme content can be trusted. Under those conditions urban viewing can reach the practical limit of 2-3 hours per day per capita.

Tapes and recordings have become a potent new medium for the youth. Their messages infiltrate political boundaries which attempt to censor the messages. The music and themes are appreciated by those who hope to join a larger community much more interesting than the community into which they were born. Trust goes out to those whose taste in popular culture is understandable, but is likely to be limited to only a few spheres of behaviour.

This need to generate trust within a city emphasises the tremendous significance of governmental regulation. Too little invites chaos; too much causes suspicion and distrust. Most countries err on the side of over-regulation, so the accelerators of social, economic and political development inherent in telecommunications are strongly inhibited (see Wegener, Chapter 16). If a city is to prosper its markets must be expedited with regulation that stimulates the flow of messages carried by telephones, telex and computer. Efficiency in pricing and delivering commodities, standardising consumer goods, and promoting securities attracts economic activity from the outside world where wage costs are higher or insecurity worse. Hong Kong, Singapore and Sao Paulo have been exploring the ways to best regulate markets, hoping to catch up with New York, Tokyo and London. Other cities now starting commodities and securities markets must have a much better communications infrastructure than a generation ago.

Conclusion: How to Plan with and for the Telephone

When a major instrument for social development like the telephone is known so widely, but studied so little, the best strategy for planning telecommunications development is 'learning by doing' — a kind of groping in the dark that takes advantage of local indicators. If major investments are to be made (US$500-1,000 for adding a telephone, as compared to $500 for equipping an extra household with television, $100 with tape recorder, and perhaps $50 with radio), they should be made as sequential as possible, with the timing of each new addition justified from current data about performance and market. Regulatory change would similarly be based upon well-founded prospects for improving overall performance. However, all this implies that evidence will be collected — expressions about popular satisfaction, purposes of calling, volume of successful calls by district, daily, weekly and yearly patterns and cycles, frequency of various kinds of faults and failures, lags in installation of new equipment, and amounts of new accessory equipment (like modems) being added.

Trends in the use of the respective channels must obviously be followed closely, but they are not enough for the planner. Acceleration induced in the transaction rates, market and non-market, is more important for the developmental decisions. Are transactions being converted into bonds (affiliations) and then into viable organisations?

Progress with social and economic development is stimulated by a (1) significant reduction in errors in micro decisions, (2) successful aversion of hazards, (3) speeding up the adaptive response to contingencies, (4) the elimination of unnecessary losses and waste, and (5) speeding the acceptance of productive ideas. We can then argue quite persuasively the following propositions, using both logic and observation.

First, social bond creation is a clear indication of the formation of trusting relationships — person-person, person-machine, person-organisation, and then organisation-organisation. Very likely regular sample surveys of social networks will be needed; they can be taken in the manner that many economic indicators are produced today. Some innovatory methods will be needed to estimate the contribution of the informal sector.

Secondly, if the planning strategy is to produce clusters of organisations on industrial estates, or in especially promising activities, telephone service is as important as credit. As organisations become increasingly interdependent, the messages between them are multiplied so as to incorporate many details: these bits of evidence often take the form of data, which in turn proliferate so as to require computing. Therefore the telephone nowadays prepares the way for the computer. This heralding is most evident around the largest marketplaces, the military, insurance offices, transport scheduling, large payrolls and so forth.

Thirdly, successful use of the computer will require prior investment in knowledge importation (licensces, consultation,training) and in knowledge dissemination (intermediate training, publications, advertising). Here we note a distinct need for long range planning —

if the telephone channels are to result in the high payout we expect from modern technology.

Finally, at each stage in this analysis the telephone is revealed as a behind-the-scenes accelerator of the pace of development. It can also be a relatively automatic balancer between market and non-market, official and unofficial, personal and organisational uses. It hastens the appearance of the 'information society'.

Note

This Chapter is developed from a paper by R.L. Meier, 'Telecommunications and Urban Development', *Ekistics*, 202, 1983, 363-68.

References

Aronson, S.A. (1971) 'The Sociology of the Telephone', *International Journal of Comparative Sociology, 12*, 153-67

Business Week (1982) 'Data Could Spark Trade War', 29 November, 100

Fischer, C.S. (1982) *To Dwell Among Friends: Personal Networks in Town and City*, University of Chicago Press, Chicago

Goddard, J.B. (1980) 'Technology Forecasting in a Spatial Context', *Futures, 12*, 90-105

Gottmann, J. (1970) 'Urban Centrality and the Interweaving of Quaternary Activities', *Ekistics*, no. 174, 322-31

Gottmann, J. (1982) 'The Metamorphosis of the Modern Metropolis', *Ekistics*, no. 292, 7-11

Gottmann, J. (1983a) 'Capital Cities', *Ekistics*, no. 299, 88-93

Gottmann, J. (1983b) *The Coming of the Transactional City*, University of Maryland, Institute of Urban Studies, College Park

Marsden, P.V. and Nan Lin (1982) *Social Structure and Network Analysis*, Sage, Beverly Hills

McPherson, M. (1983) 'An Ecology of Affiliation', *American Sociology Review, 48*, 519-32

Meier, R.L. (1956) 'Communications and Social Change', *Behavioural Science, 1*, 43-58

Meier, R.L. (1962)/*A Communications Theory of Urban Growth*, The MIT Press, Cambridge, Massachusetts

Meier, R.L. (1972) 'Communications Stress', *Annual Review of Ecology and Systematics, 3*, 289-313

National Bureau of Standards (1981) *Proceedings, Computer Networking Symposium*, Gaithersburg, Maryland, December

Paine, W.S. (ed.)(1982) *Job Stress and Burnout*, Sage, Beverly Hills

Takasaki, N. (1977) *Quality of Life and the Contribution of Telecommunications'*, Research Institute for Telecommunications and Economics, Tokyo

Wellman, B. (1977) *Networks and Places*, Free Press, New York

Wellman, B. (1983) 'Network Analysis: From Metaphor and Method to Theory and Substance' in R. Collins (ed.) *Sociological Theory*, Jossey-Bass, San Francisco

10. SURFACE TRANSPORT
P. Bly

The Past

The impact of transport innovations on city development is well documented. Indeed, by the turn of the century, when urban tramways and railways were expanding rapidly, it can hardly have needed academic analysis to illustrate the close connection between the outwards movement of new transport services and the springing up of serried rows of suburban housing. It was axiomatic that, once the new rail lines were laid, development and 'progress' would follow automatically.

Before the development of the steam engine, transport had changed hardly at all for millennia, and even the greatest cities were still gauged by distances which could be comfortably walked. The advent of steam locomotion was dramatic, not merely for the sheer spectacle of such unnatural speeds but also, if less immediately, for the great social changes it wrought. In 'Sybil', Disraeli has Lord de Mowbray say of the railway, 'I fear it has a dangerous tendency to equality'. So it had, eventually, and its successor, the private motor car, much more so.

Yet the first impact of steam power and industrial mechanisation was to make the cities much less desirable places to live. The new industries employed labour on a much larger scale than previously, and they tended to congregate together to share the advantages of proximity to one another, to the sources of raw materials and energy, to the shipping of their products and materials through coastal or inland ports, and to large pools of labour. To keep their workers within acceptable walking distance of the factories, housing was provided at such high densities that, even by the standards of the time, living conditions for industrial workers in the largest cities were exceptionally squalid and unhealthy.

Faster transport was able to release some of the pressure towards excessively high densities, by enabling workers to live further from the factories. Of course, in some cities horse-bus and horse-tram services were carrying substantial numbers of people to work well before urban steam-train services began to have a major impact on city development. The horse-drawn vehicles were little faster than walking though, and until the use of larger vehicles in the latter part of the nineteenth century brought fares down, they could only be afforded by the more affluent. These services did facilitate some middle-class suburban development, but it was the coming of commuter services on the steam railways in mid-century, and in Britain the introduction by Act of Parliament of cheap workmen's fares (from 1864 onwards), which finally permitted the dispersion of the tightly packed populations of the inner areas. It might be noted that the railways initially added to the misery of the living conditions in these areas, since their construction often involved the demolition of considerable stretches of housing, in preference to the more valuable and better defended land occupied by factories, yet the railways needed large quantities of workers who could be housed only by overcrowding the houses which were left (Bagwell 1974). A further significant expansion of the cities occurred when electrically powered local rail services were introduced, either in the form of underground or elevated railways in the great cities, or more generally as street tramways, providing quick access because of their closely spaced stops and rapid travel over relatively short distances.

The progression in urban development which accompanied these improvements in transport is clearly visible if density is plotted against distance and time (Bussiere 1975). The decline in population density outwards from the centre of a city can be approximated by a negative exponential function (Figure 10.1 plots city centre density, A, against rate, B, of decline of density with distance, for London and Paris). In the cases of both London and Paris (and in all other cities of the Western world) densities have declined as the cities have spread to cover a larger area. For London, where the census data exist from 1801, the first half of the nineteenth century saw an increase in densities as workers migrated to the city from rural areas faster than the city could grow outwards, constrained as it was by the need to keep its residents within walking distance of their work. Even so, in an age when it was impractical to build higher than three or four storeys, the pressures on housing produced a city of diameter considerably larger than was typical of previous ages, and where the distances involved were inconveniently large to cover on foot. The impact of steam railways (both surface and underground lines) is seen from mid-century onwards as density falls, and the further acceleration around the turn of the century due to electric tramways and underground rail (the first London Underground electric line started in 1890) is also clearly marked. The data from Paris begin later in time, but the impact of the Metro underground rail (the first line opened in 1900) is seen to be very similar.

If road and rail public transport gave a quantum leap to travel speeds when compared with walking, it is to be expected that mass car

Figure 10.1 Trends in Population Density in London and Paris
(Variation of the parameters in the negative
exponential distribution of population density:
Density = Aexp(– br) Source: International
Collaborative Study of the Factors Affecting
Public Transport Patronage, 1980)

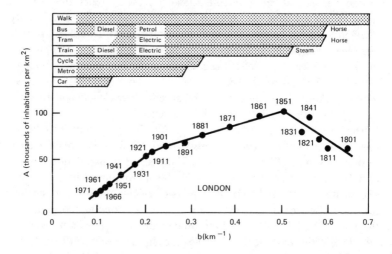

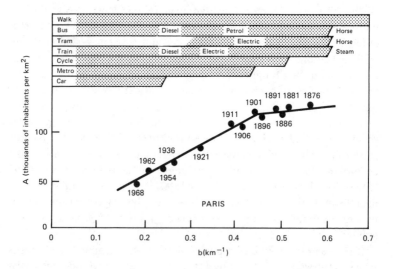

ownership would do at least as much again. There is, however, no dramatic change of direction in the density trends of Figure 10.1 following the rapid growth of car ownership in Europe in the 1950s and 1960s (though the data exclude much of the development which has sprung up outside the metropolitan areas proper in the last two or three decades). It might seem that the private car has merely extended a process which was already well entrenched by the previous spread of public transport. Yet the changes brought about by the private car are not merely the result of an increase in travel speed beyond that afforded by public transport, but also a result of its ability to take its owner anywhere, and directly. Public transport is most effective where people are concentrated along particular corridors, and where the destinations are grouped into well-defined areas. The private car has released its owners from the need to congregate in this way, so that housing has infilled the spaces between the transit corridors, and has sprawled at lower densities into ever more peripheral areas. It has also allowed changes in location of employment, services and facilities which do not necessarily gain best advantage from a central city location. The dominance of road-based freight transport over rail has greatly widened the choice of location for factories and supply depots. Thus road transport and the road network have not merely enlarged the scale of distance which governs our lives, but they have also greatly diminished the importance of specific geographical centres: for those with a car, the difference in accessibility between one place and another is generally small. For those without a car, of course, the more dispersed pattern of destinations and the consolidation of small local shops and facilities into large, well-spaced suburban centres merely add to the damage the 'car habit' has inflicted on public transport services in general.

The Future

The past is well-documented, at least, though even then it is frustratingly difficult to identify and disentangle the various interactions which exist between transport, travel and urban development. We can chart our course into the future only in so far as we can understand quantitatively the mechanisms involved, and can extrapolate the forces acting on those mechanisms. On either count, in this particular field, it must be admitted that our knowledge is woefully inadequate. But here we are charged to go further, to consider the likely effects of forces which are altogether new. At this point, it is tempting to throw off scientific caution and yield to the attractions of science fiction. There are numerous examples of visionaries who have predicted fairly accurately the impact of new inventions long before the technology required was available. The much larger group of visionaries who were wrong has left no lasting memorial, however, so it is perhaps more instructive, if less entertaining, to restrict attention only to those innovations for which the technology is already available, even if the details still need refining.

Even with this cautious approach, our time scale must still be long. The seer who predicts what our cities will look like in the year 2000 can expect little attention, since over 80 per cent of the infrastructure of those cities is already in place. Changes in vehicles could take place on a fairly short time scale, but developments in either urban or transport infrastructure will take many decades to work through.

Before considering possible effects on urban form, it will be useful to review the various technical innovations which are likely to affect vehicles and the road and rail networks. The technology required is already here: inevitably, it depends on the power of the microchip to assemble and act on information in a way which was not previously possible. It is convenient to consider the developments under three headings: (1) in-vehicle communication, (2) vehicle monitoring and control, and (3) automatically guided vehicles. In all three categories, prototype versions of the innovations exist. Whether they will achieve the impact which seems possible depends of course on whether the perceived advantages justify the costs (and in some cases there is a considerable threshold to be overcome since advantage is to be gained only if the new systems are employed on a large scale) but, recessions permitting, it is likely that in future the costs will diminish in comparison with the advantages.

In-vehicle Communication

Now that most road vehicles are fitted with a radio, in-vehicle communication is already well established, with many radio stations providing occasional information to motorists on road conditions, delays, accidents, etc. This type of information is necessarily very limited, and there have been many proposals for more specialised forms of broadcasting. Germany already operates ARI (Autofahrer Rundfunk Information), a system of VHF transmitters providing local traffic information, and special decoders attached to a car radio can automatically tune to the strongest ARI transmitter and interrupt a radio programme being received from a non-ARI station to announce the ARI traffic message. Such systems (including CARFAX in the UK; *Report of the Working Group on the Broadcasting of Traffic Information* 1979) can only deliver very general information, though, because each transmitter must cover a relatively large area (of the order of 40 to 70 km). A more specific system (AWARE), which uses short range transmitters to provide visual messages on dashboard displays to vehicles travelling along a particular road, has been developed at TRRL (Lines and Hodge 1977). This can warn of hazards or delays a specified distance ahead, give an estimate of the delay and indicate diversion routes, the lane to be taken or any speed restriction.

Much more elaborate information systems have been proposed to provide the motorist with route guidance. These again depend on transmitters at road junctions (either buried induction loops or micro-wave) and special in-vehicle decoders, but for this application the in-vehicle equipment has to 'talk to' the roadside equipment. The motorist sets his or her receiver for the required destination (perhaps a six-digit code), and at each road junction the vehicle interrogates the roadside equipment and receives instructions on which exit to take. The best route is then displayed on the vehicle dashboard. Such systems are already technically feasible, and prototype versions have been demons-trated in Germany (Bragas 1979) and Japan (Japanese Ministry of International Trade and Industry 1975). Studies of the potential value of such systems suggest that, even though the saving in vehicle-kilometres driven because of more efficient routing would probably represent no more than 2 per cent of the total, the benefit would still amount to some three times the costs involved (Armstrong 1977; Jeffery 1981), and of course with such a comprehensive system installed the additional benefits of hazard and delay avoidance, at which the simpler systems described above were aimed, could be gained with relatively little additional cost. Although the value of all these systems can only be realised when a substantial proportion of vehicles and roads carry the equipment, it seems inevitable that this type of communication between road and vehicle will eventually be introduced.

Vehicle Monitoring and Control

The benefits of the automatic routing systems described above will be greatest on long journeys rather than the fairly short journeys which account for most urban travel. But once a comprehensive system is available, the potential applications in congested urban areas are obvious. At the simplest level, the motorist could be advised on the best route through congested urban areas, taking account of the levels of congestion prevailing at the time. This would not only save the motorist delays, but would avoid adding further to the most congested parts of the network. Further, traffic-light control systems could enable more efficient use of the available road capacity if signal control could be linked to direct monitoring and regulation of the traffic. Vehicles could also be directed, on request, to parking facilities with the assurance that there would be space available. In these ways, some of the irritations of urban driving could be reduced.

However, once vehicles are equipped to interrogate, and be interrogated by, the road system, it becomes possible to regulate, rather than merely advise, the road users by requiring the vehicle equipment to identify itself uniquely to the road-based equipment. This step is likely to raise important questions of social acceptability if the monitoring of individual vehicle movements were to be done over wide areas, but it is interesting to see that Hong Kong is embarking on a fairly large-scale testing of a system for true road pricing (Dawson 1983). With this type of system it becomes possible to charge for the use of roads at rates which reflect the amount of congestion, or perhaps the environmental cost, of each section of route. Various theoretical studies suggest that considerable benefits could be gained from this type of restraint in some urban areas (for a summary, see Webster and Bly 1980), but understandably up to now traffic restraint has relied on much simpler forms of regulation, by area licensing in a few cases and, commonly, by parking charges and parking restrictions. Road pricing would be much more flexible, however, and charges could be tailored to respond to changes in demand on different parts of the road network in quite a detailed way, with drivers being informed how much the choices of route open to them were likely to cost. If the vehicles are already being billed for road use, parking could be charged automatically in the same way (in any case, the displacement of hard cash by 'electronic money' is going to open up many new possibilities, so that for example the vehicle could also be billed for fuel automatically). More controversially, the system of identification of vehicles could be used to facilitate enforcement of traffic laws, with any violation of parking regulations or bus priority measures being met with an instant automatic fine. The same system would also help in tracing stolen vehicles.

Automatic identification of buses is already fairly widespread: in 1980 there were some two dozen active systems involving 3,000 instrumented vehicles (Britton 1980). Using various detection mechanisms, vehicles are identified at certain points on their route and their location displayed in a central control room. Drivers can be instructed to take corrective action to improve service timing or regularity if necessary. The same monitoring systems could also be used to provide passengers with information both on and off the bus. A bus stop which advertised the expected time to the next bus, and its destination, could be a great help, especially where services have a reputation for unreliability. This type of system has already been installed in Osaka, for example (Amano and Toda 1983). As the necessary electronics and computer power become cheaper, such systems will become more worthwhile, particularly since in some aspects they can be traded off against labour costs. Fare collection is also becoming increasingly automated. Similarly, electronic communications systems are becoming more important on the railways, and much of the present trackside signalling and control equipment is likely to be replaced by communications equipment inside the vehicle cabs. All these developments will either save costs in the provision of public transport or improve the service offered, but in general the advantages are likely to be fairly marginal so that the attractiveness of transit *vis-à-vis* private transport, in particular, is unlikely to be greatly affected.

In a different vein, microelectronics installed in individual vehicles will increasingly be used to monitor and control their mechanical performance. Continuous recording in each vehicle of the output from such devices, as in a 'black box' recorder on aircraft, could contribute valuable information on road accidents and lead to worthwhile improvements in safety and perhaps, at a detailed level, to improved design of road layout and junctions.

Automatically-guided Vehicles

Automatically-guided road vehicles have been suggested and even constructed on several occasions already, with the justification being that this would increase road capacities and reduce accidents (Penoyre 1971). Automatic guidance is obviously far from being a practical proposition, even on special motorways which could be isolated rigorously from pedestrians or other intruders, yet the problems could doubtless be solved by relatively straightforward developments of existing technology, if the returns were judged to justify the considerable cost and effort involved. The threshold for implementation will be especially large because it would not be worthwhile for individuals to purchase the automatic vehicles unless a considerable number of guided roadways were available. It seems likely that many decades must pass before technology lowers the costs and/or society becomes sufficiently affluent to afford it.

More specialised applications of automatically guided road vehicles may be useful in the more immediate future, though, and various systems have been developed to guide buses along special segregated tracks. The Daimler-Benz 'O-Bahn' system is already in service over 3.8 km of guideway in Essen, and operation in a 1.6 km tunnel under the city centre is planned for Regensburg (*Automotive Engineering* 1982). In Australia, 13 km of guideway are being laid in Adelaide as a demonstration project for 'O-Bahn'. The usefulness is seen not so much in the saving of drivers on the automated sections (generally, the drivers remain aboard their vehicles) but in the guidance provision which would make it possible to run buses at speed along narrow rights-of-way and through tunnels. The system has been suggested as ideal for bus services running partly on routes which have been converted from former railway or tram lines. Thus the heavily trafficked part of the network may be automated and operated free of congestion while the flexibility of driver control is maintained where traffic is lighter.

Where vehicles can be specialised so that they are restricted to segregated tracks and have no need to mix with normal traffic, it makes sense to put them on rails (whether steel or concrete), and automatic control becomes an easy proposition. Many of the urban rail systems installed in the past couple of decades were designed to run under automatic control, though it is interesting to note that in all cases the trains retain at least one crew member, because of labour agreements, in case the automatic control fails (though the designs are 'fail-safe'), or for security reasons. Still, it seems that people may be more willing to accept automatically controlled vehicles on systems which are obviously 'new technology', since small-scale 'people movers' have been working satisfactorily for many years now in exhibitions, fairgrounds and recreation parks of one sort or another. The term 'people mover' is generally taken to refer to relatively small and light vehicles travelling on an exclusive guideway and stopping automatically at stations. At their simplest they may provide a shuttle service along a track without any junctions, or more complicated systems may route the vehicles automatically to destinations over an entire network. 'Network cabs' or 'personal rapid transit' would provide small vehicles (carrying perhaps six people) making non-stop journeys to the selected destination station (stops would be made in stations set to one side of the main guideway to avoid delaying following vehicles). 'Minitrams' or 'group rapid transit' provide larger vehicles (seating perhaps 15 to 30 people) on a service with intermediate stops. Some 'people movers' provide trains of quite large vehicles and are distinguishable from tramways only in their

automation and futuristic appearance (elevated guideways, and sometimes monorails, are preferred).

In the early 1970s there was widespread enthusiasm for people
movers, and in the USA, UMTA initiated a Downtown People Mover
Project which funded feasibility studies in several different cities
(UMTA 1977). The only system which was constructed under this
project, and which remains the best-known of all people movers, is a
5.3 km line connecting two campuses of the University of West
Virginia with downtown Morgantown. This now carries 3 million
passengers per year, using 21-seater vehicles operating between five
stations. The initial enthusiasm for such systems has waned in the face
of the very large capital costs involved for any serious urban network
(ranging from US$5 to $25 millions per one-way kilometre of guide,
including stations and vehicles). In the UK, studies of hypothetical
'Cabtrack' (i.e. personal rapid transit) services over extensive networks
in London and Birmingham gave way to more realistic proposals for
much simpler Minitram systems operating on a few lines (Mitchell
1972), and ultimately to advanced planning studies for a Minitram
service connecting the rather dispersed shopping area of Sheffield. This
latter scheme was ultimately abandoned partly, it is interesting to note,
because of aesthetic objections to the elevated structure running across
the city centre.

It is clear that the widespread adoption of people mover systems
envisaged for the end of the century by enthusiasts of the early 1970s is
not going to happen, just as the proponents of automatic guidance for
road vehicles (and much other new technology) have underestimated the
time scale needed for its adoption. But even in the present harsh
economic climate, a few new people movers are being installed. Eight
systems came into service in 1981-82, and several more are under
construction (Fabian 1983). The great majority of these installations are
in places such as airports or recreational areas where the most economic
way of carrying people from one place to another is not the dominant
factor, but truly public systems have been installed or are under
construction in Lille (France), Kobe, Osaka and Tokyo (Japan), and in
Vancouver and Toronto (Canada). However, these latter systems are in
all cases of the automated tramway or metro type; systems using small
vehicles, and particularly personal rapid transit systems, are making
little headway.

An alternative to automatically controlled vehicles is to have an
automatically moving road. Of course, it has not been seriously
suggested that such a system might transport general traffic, though

there have been various proposals for automatic systems to move trains of pallets which would collect private vehicles from the road network and move them quickly on a heavily used line-haul into the central city. A similar theme is that private vehicles should be designed so that they can be coupled together to form trains for line-haul on a road rather than on rails, but the practicality or value of such schemes has yet to be demonstrated. For pedestrians, however, moving pavements are becoming increasingly common for transport over short distances, again especially in airports where the appearance of 'new technology' is important. In fact this particular technology is fairly old: the Chicago exhibition of 1893 had a passenger conveyor, and the Paris exhibition of 1900 had one over 3 km in length. The practicality of conveyors or 'travelators' running at above walking speed is only now being demonstrated and there remain problems with such systems which are connected with their safety, the space taken up by the accelerator systems which provide access to them, and the relative inflexibility with which they can be aligned (Naysmith 1978). Currently, a pavement moving at 12 km/h is being installed in a 175 metre connecting tunnel at the Les Invalides interchange of the Paris Metro.

Freight

The control and despatching of freight vehicles, and the organisation of loads and routing for maximum utilisation of vehicles (in the United Kingdom at least, about a third of freight vehicles on the road are running empty), will all benefit from the continuing improvement in and reducing costs of communications and computing. More automation of loading and transhipment, and more containerisation, may make it relatively more economic to ship freight by rail, but on the whole it seems that road freight will remain the mainstay of freight movement. Vehicles for longer-distance freight transport may carry still heavier payloads (though improved design is likely to make them quieter, and less damaging to the road surface, than present vehicles) and of course road freight will benefit from the information systems for general road traffic described in previous sections. With larger line-haul vehicles the problems of transhipment become more important, but although there have been proposals for combining sets of small freight vehicles, which could be used independently for local distribution, into larger units for bulk line-haul, these are purely speculative and seem unlikely to be superior to some form of containerisation.

Pipelines may also play a larger role in freight transport. Of course, considerable volumes of liquids (and gas) are already carried immense distances by pipeline, but pipelines can also carry bulk solids such as rock aggregate and coal, and work has been done to assess the feasibility of transporting general goods inside capsules along a pneumatic pipeline (for a review, see James 1980). Various installations already exist for specialised transport within individual firms, sometimes with several kilometres of pipeline. However to justify the heavy capital investment required for a system carrying general deliveries to (or from) households, it would have to be used for a wide range of goods, and it is likely to require fairly high residential densities. No such systems exist yet, though various proposals have been made: for example, over a decade ago quite detailed proposals were made for an elaborate pneumatic system to deliver goods to households in Etarea, a new satellite town outside Prague (Celechovsky 1972).

Implications for Urban Form

Most of the innovations described above already exist, even if only in prototype form. Given a sufficiently long time-scale, it seems likely that they will find niches in the overall transport system. In some cases, such as 'people movers' and pedestrian conveyors, the systems offer new opportunities for planning and the design of buildings at a detailed level. For others, such as vehicle control and guidance, the changes in travel patterns will be at a broader level and the implications are more for the general development of cities, and the balance between urban and suburban development, than for their detailed appearance.

Towards Centralisation

Most of these innovations could potentially ease movement within cities, making most effective use of the space available for transport, and so permitting a relatively greater concentration of activities within the city centre. The traffic advice and control systems have the obvious capability of distributing traffic coming into the centre in such a way as to ease congestion and minimise average travel times. It may be that, to do this, charges will have to be imposed for road use or parking which will discourage some people from using the private car altogether. Given the great attachment most people have to the private car this will obviously encourage some people to switch to other destinations where possible, and will therefore provide an impetus for peripheral or out-of-town development. This is a potential problem with traffic restraint measures, because they can only be tuned in the light of observations of their short-term effect, and it is always possible that the long-term effects may run counter to the original aims of the policy in a way which cannot later be rectified. Naturally, the extent of diversion from the city centre will depend upon the attraction of the centre relative to peripheral development, but it is already clear in many cities that, even in the absence of any positive policy for restraint, suburban shopping centres and hypermarkets are springing up and prospering because they can offer much easier access by car users than can the city centre. But if the transport planners can get it right, there will certainly be more scope to organise traffic in such a way that the maximum number of people are attracted to, and can be absorbed by, the centre, if that were considered to be a desirable objective.

To the extent that improvements in public transport could attract people from private cars, or encourage people to shop in the city centre instead of walking to the local shops, the importance of the centre would be strengthened. A new city-centre rail link in Munich has been credited with strengthening the CBD for both employment and shopping (at the expense of local centres, of course) and similarly in Glasgow a cross-centre link between two rail termini has helped stem the decline of the central shopping area (Gentleman *et al.* 1983). However, the Munich urban rail system is said to have encouraged some migration of more affluent citizens to the outer areas of the city, leaving the poorer concentrated in the inner city areas which were not well served by the new rail system, and less well by bus than previously because the bus services had been rationalised to fit the rail system (Kreibich 1978). This does no more than illustrate the very complicated interactive nature of transport and land use, but this segregation of different social groups has important implications for the way different parts of a city are likely to develop, especially in view of the concern expressed in other chapters in this collection that social divisions may widen because of the growing importance of technological skills (see Chapter 23).

Guided bus systems and automatic tramways may play some role in providing improved public transport into cities. In principle, automation will become more worthwhile as society grows more affluent and labour becomes more expensive relative to capital, though the extent to which these more complex systems will actually save labour costs remains to be seen (they may substitute high-cost technical manpower for lower-cost semi-skilled labour). Certainly the capital costs can be formidable, and it will take high passenger flows to justify them. All in all, the improvements in mass transit of this kind from new technology are likely to be modest, rather than revolutionary. In many cities where transit is losing custom to the private car, they may be overwhelmed in the general decline of transit.

The smaller public transport systems such as minitram, and particularly personal rapid transit, would make a much more radical impact if they could be justified economically. Even on a limited scale they could provide very good access to facilities fairly widely dispersed across a city's central area, so that it would become easier to restrict private traffic to the fringes of the area without reducing accessibility to the extent that decentralisation is encouraged. Because of the physically small scale of the guideways and vehicles, and their tight turning circles, it becomes possible to design this type of system at above-street level directly into buildings in a way which would allow transport to enhance, rather than detract from, the urban scene. On the other hand, even though they are small, the overhead guideways are difficult to integrate into existing streets and buildings without creating an eyesore. Much the same applies to pedestrian conveyors. For this reason alone the case for all systems based on overhead track will be stronger where substantial new development is proposed, but in any case the infrastructure costs are likely to be less when they can be installed during construction of the surrounding buildings. Tunnelling is also becoming cheaper as it becomes more automated, and there will also be increasing scope for providing public transport services, and possibly road space for general traffic, below ground level. Ventilation is a problem if the vehicles are not electric, however, though the Daimler-Benz guided bus system, with its standardised vehicles, uses an ingenious system to collect exhaust gases in special ducting. Subterranean transport routes would become more convenient if buildings are also developed to include extensive underground facilities, as in Montreal or Stockholm for example. Distribution of goods by pipeline would also help to separate the traffic from the people, but it is only likely to be justifiable where buildings are at fairly high densities. As a choice for public transport, it seems that unless the passenger flows are very high it would be difficult to justify (by applying normal cost-benefit techniques) these more high-technology systems in comparison with standard bus services, but less tangible benefits may still warrant their use.

Automatic guidance of road traffic, should it come about, would also tend to bolster the importance of existing urban centres, since initially at least guidance would be provided on the major roads which tend to focus on these centres. If, like many existing motorway systems, they stop on the periphery or skirt the city rather than continuing into the centre, they may encourage peripheral development in the most accessible areas, just as motorways themselves have already done (Parker 1974). In particular, freight-handling depots are likely to spring up in these locations. Automatic guidance has so far been considered more with a view to increasing road capacities and improving safety than with the aim of increasing speeds. In principle, it could be used to increase road speeds, though probably not drastically. On rail we are already seeing considerable increases in speed, and this trend will no doubt continue: in some cases steel rail may give way to special guideways for magnetically supported vehicles or air-cushion vehicles. New rail systems offering fast line-haul can compete with air over medium distances, but although they would certainly help to sustain the importance of the cities they serve they are unlikely to have a major impact on settlement patterns.

Towards Dispersion

Any system which increases the speed of travel, or reduces its cost, is likely to encourage people to live further away from their jobs or the other places they wish to visit fairly frequently, as was illustrated in the introduction. Provided these improvements are only available on a limited network focused on a city centre, as would be the case with either guided road systems or enhanced public transport, the jobs and facilities themselves are likely to remain concentrated in the centre.

By contrast, improvements in accessibility which are not locationally tied, so that city centres are no more favoured than other places, tend to encourage dispersion of both homes and other activities. It is this ubiquity which has made the private car such a powerful force for dispersion; other chapters in this collection will show that telecommunications are likely to speed this process for jobs and services. Previous sections have discussed several innovations which will make motoring easier and the private car still more attractive (to its individual users at least — the environmental and safety problems which stem from the automobile will grow with car ownership). Electronic monitoring systems will make vehicles more reliable mechanically, and the trend to turn them into mobile entertainment cabinets is already well advanced.

There remains the possibility, however, that we shall be unable to afford to run them. The 1970s saw a spate of naive claims that, with oil running out, the private car was doomed and that the future must lie in a resurgent public transport. In the present situation of oil surplus these views are no longer fashionable, though concern about oil-based fuels remains just as valid in any long-term assessment. But the problem is one of transition to other types of fuel, possibly electricity or more probably liquid synthetics of one sort or another. These are likely to be more expensive than present fuels, but not absurdly so (Armstrong 1980) and industrialised societies will continue to afford them. Fuel costs account for a quarter to a third of the total operating costs of a private car (and in many countries much of this cost is taxation); moreover the additional costs could be offset considerably by the development and marketing of more fuel-efficient vehicles. Since it seems that car use is fairly inelastic to fuel price, it would require improbably high energy costs to force most car users, in most urban conditions, to flock to public transport (even where it is readily accessible). A more realistic forecast would seem to be one which assumes that some form of private transport will be with us into the foreseeable future.

All the systems described previously as having the potential for sustaining a high concentration of activities in large city centres may have little role to play because the growth of cities is opposed by a very powerful force indeed. The dispersion of homes away from the cities into low-density suburban development is long established in many Western countries, and becoming much more visible even in those European countries with a long tradition of high-density apartment living and planning policies which oppose dispersion. Certainly, the increasing complexity of society has tended to centralise many administrative and commercial functions, so that in many respects the spheres of influence of the major cities are wider than they used to be, but this is no longer reflected in contiguous physical development of the land surrounding them. Accessibility for those who depend on the car is sufficient for them to live well away from the city, preferring as they do to live in more rural surroundings, or perhaps for convenience in a much smaller town. This growth of small and medium-sized towns while large cities decline is marked in both Europe and North America (see Hall, Chapter 2).

The process is not in equilibrium, of course, because it takes decades for land-use patterns to respond to changing circumstances. Even if car ownership grew no more, the process of dispersion would continue for many decades. By the same token, the process is unlikely to be accelerated appreciably even if technology can speed up travel. The private car offers such a large speed advantage over other modes for most travel purposes (averaged over all travel, the age of public transport probably doubled door-to-door speeds compared with walking, while the private car has doubled them again) that further speed increases are likely to have relatively little effect on the choice of home or job, because such improvements will be available only on some routes and for a small proportion of all travel. Although developments such as guided road vehicles might be able to increase speeds, it is hard to see any road-based system offering much of an increase on the speeds currently attainable on the motorways of most countries. It would take the ultimate science fiction development, with everyone taking to the air or, better still, being transmitted instantaneously, to radically alter the pace or pattern of dispersion.

It is instructive to ask what land-use patterns we might adopt if car ownership were universal and we were building from scratch. What sort of cities would we need to put together, and how large would they be? The advantages of such large concentrations of development must be much less clear now than they used to be. For many people there is an inherent advantage in having in one area a large collection of shops, services, entertainment and other facilities, offering a wide choice and the opportunity to combine many different activities. The transport systems discussed above could make this more accessible and therefore more attractive, yet it might be doubted whether we would need the concentrations of activities found in the largest cities. Certainly it seems unlikely that we would cluster homes around them in quite the same way, and most workplaces could also be dispersed. Even concern to limit the amount of land given over to housing will not necessarily oppose dispersion, since the dispersed housing need not occupy more land than if it were all contained in contiguous development around cities, though there may be pressure to cluster it in sizeable developments, perhaps on land not well-suited to agriculture. Of course, such hypothetical discussion begs the question, since future development depends very strongly on the present pattern, but it serves to indicate the way things are likely to change.

Conclusion

It seems that the difficulty with speculation of this kind is that it is easier to say what will become possible in the future than to guess what use, if any, will be made of the new opportunities. Even before the mechanisation of transport, traffic congestion was a problem in large cities. Technological advances will provide some opportunity for easing or controlling this, since in-vehicle information, vehicle monitoring and automatic charging, will enable traffic to be routed and parked more efficiently and, if necessary, some traffic to be priced out of the congested areas altogether. Similarly, the provision of more convenient kinds of public transport such as minitram or network cabs, or for short distances high-speed pedestrian conveyors, will make city centres more attractive and more accessible if private traffic has to be excluded from the central area, and improvements in longer-distance public transport services might encourage some transfer from private car for travel into the centre.

Yet the impact this technology will have on urban form will depend on the extent to which people will still need to visit city centres to work or for services, and on how well the centres are able to compete with more peripheral collections of shops, services or employment. Doubtless science-fiction authors are right in that monolithic, vertical cities, or cities with their own carefully controlled environment enclosed within some plastic bubble, or cities burrowed underground, will all become technologically feasible, but unless tastes change drastically, and barring some global catastrophe, who will want to live there?

As technology makes centres more attractive and city transport less onerous, it will also be making the private car still more desirable and low-density living more available. There is no sign that our love affair with the car is over: more than ever, in the Western world new generations seem to accept it as an unquestioned necessity of life. It may cause various environmental and safety problems to others, but it is only congestion and parking problems which limit its use, and for these it seems set to find its own solution. The accessibility it provides frees its owners to move out to more rural surroundings away from congested streets, and many city-centre facilities will follow them. *There seems no reason to expect any change in the prevailing trend for dispersion and a relative decline in the activity of major city centres.*

In view of all the new technology available, this conclusion must be an anticlimax. Any reviewer of tomorrow's world who can see no reason why things should not go on much the same as they are at the moment might justifiably be accused of lacking imagination. But here we are looking at the broad outlines of what people will do, rather than the details. Of course the details will change. The appearance of vehicles will be very different, the facilities they offer and the convenience of travel will improve, there will be more scope for integrating transport more closely into new city-centre development, and the engineering and architectural details will change. But at a broader level, what people want out of life does not change. People have always had to trade off their desire for personal space and privacy, in so far as they can afford it, against their need to contact other people and to have easy access to a variety of goods and services. For most purposes it seems that the growth of mechanised transport, and especially the availability of the private car, has removed most of the constraints imposed by transport, and land-use patterns must shift to accommodate this. The adjustment is still far from complete, of course, but it seems unlikely that its momentum will be greatly affected by the new transport technology.

References

Amano, K. and Toda, T. (1983) 'A Review of New Urban Transport Innovations in Japan', paper presented to the Conference on Passenger Transport Planning, Management and Policy in Japan, Oxford, June

Armstrong, B.D. (1977) *The Need for Route Guidance*, TRRL Report SR 330, Transport and Road Research Laboratory, Crowthorne, UK

Armstrong, B.D. (1980) *The Allocation of Transport Fuels to Minimise Costs*, TRRL Report LR 956, Transport and Road Reseach Laboratory, Crowthorne, UK

Automotive Engineering (1982) 'Track-guided buses as train substitutes', *90*, 80

Bagwell, P.S. (1974) *The Transport Revolution from 1770*, Batsford, London

Bragas, P. (1979) 'Field Testing of a Route Guidance and Information System for Drivers (ALI)', *Proceedings of International Symposium on Traffic and Transportation Technologies*, Hamburg, June

Britton, F.E.K. (1980) 'Where is that Bus Going?' *Mass Transit, 7,* 92

Bussiere, R. (1975) 'Urban Interactions — the C.R.U. Model (Interactions urbanies — le modele de CRU)', *CRU Annales*, Centre de Recherche d'Urbanisme, Paris

Celechovsky, G. (1972) 'Goods Transport in Etarea', *Transportation, 1,* 151-76

Dawson, J.A.L. (1983) 'Electronic Road Pricing in Hong Kong: the Pilot Stage', *Traffic Engineering and Control, 24,* 372-4

Fabian, L.J. (1983) 'People Movers: from Semi-public to Public Transit', *Transportation Quarterly, 37,* 85

Gentleman, H., Mitchell, C.G.B., Wicks, J. and Walmsley, D.A. (1983) *The Glasgow Rail Impact Study: Summary Report*, TRRL Report SR 800, Transport and Road Research Laboratory, Crowthorne, UK

James, J.G. (1980) *Pipelines Considered as a Mode of Freight Transport: a Review of Current and Possible Future Uses*, TRRL Report SR 592, Transport and Road Research Laboratory, Crowthorne, UK

Japanese Ministry of International Trade and Industry (1975) *Comprehensive Automatic Control System*, Preliminary report, Tokyo

Jeffery, D.J. (1981) *Ways and Means for Improving Driver Route Guidance*, TRRL Report LR 1016, Transport and Road Research Laboratory, Crowthorne, UK

Kreibich, V. (1978) *The Successful Transportation System and the Regional Planning Problem*, Paper L22, Planning and Transportation Research and Computation, London

Lines, C.J. and Hodge, A.R. (1977) *'AWARE': an In-Vehicle Visual Communication System for Drivers*, TRRL Report SR 286, Transport and Road Research Laboratory, Crowthorne, UK

Mitchell, C.G.B. (1972) 'New Technology in Urban Transport', *Proceedings of the Institution of Civil Engineers* (London), *52,* 127

Naysmith, A. (1978) *High-speed Pedestrian Conveyors — a Review*, TRRL Report LR 862, Transport and Road Research Laboratory, Crowthorne, UK

Parker, G.J. (1974) *Can Land Use Management Reduce Energy Consumption for Transportation?* Rand Corporation Report P-5241, Rand Corporation, Santa Monica, California.

Penoyre, S. (1971) 'A Robot in the Driver's Seat', *New Scientist*, 13 May, 371

Report of the Working Group on the Broadcasting of Traffic Information, TRRL Report SR 506, Transport and Road Research Laboratory, Crowthorne, UK

Urban Mass Transportation Administration (1977) *People Mover Profile*, Department of Transportation, Washington DC

Webster, F.V. and Bly, P.H. (eds) (1980) *International Collaborative Study of the Factors Affecting Public Transport Patronage, The Demand for Public Transport*, Transport and Road Research Laboratory, Crowthorne, UK

11. TRANSPORT-COMMUNICATION INTERACTIONS
M. Wigan

The increasing importance of communications and information technology (IT) is beginning to make a major impact on transport and communications, and on expenditures of time and money at the personal and business levels. The impacts on land use and urban form are less apparent at this stage, due to the longer time lags involved in the decision chain before action occurs on the ground.

This chapter identifies a number of places where transport, land use and urban form and information technology have major potential interactions, and draws out the present evidence on the rates at which these should occur. The changing balance of household expenditures and industrial output in various components of communications and transport are presented using both Australian and UK data. The structure of this chapter is as follows. First the impacts of the rapidly decreasing costs in data acquisition, processing and access are reviewed. Secondly, available numerical evidence of change in terms of family expenditures, industrial output, taxation revenues and subsidies is considered for the UK and Australia.

A major conclusion is that the overall importance of transport expenditures in the economy is remaining fairly stable, while communications expenditures are increasing. The two types of industry are now approaching comparable size, and will — when parity occurs — force changes which will amount to substitution and competition. Similar findings also apply to household expenditures, with the exception that at lower levels of income the relative expenditures on communications and transport were already comparable in 1980 in the UK, and thus products in the information technology area which are priced to be attractive to below-average income households will make significant impacts. This has been confirmed for the UK by the combination of very cheap home computers allied to cheap modems, as with the current MicroNET 800 service on Prestel. The speed of the onset of the impacts of information technology on urban form will be determined by the rates at which people and businesses gain access to the networks which can carry the new information technology-based services.

The time lags in behavioural adaption to such access will compete with the location and business provision demands for land use and physical communications so that the urban form aspects of these impacts will be as dependent on access to the services as on the rate of technical advances in the field.

The discussion will concentrate initially on the transport and communication aspects, with an increasing emphasis through the text on the land use and urban form effects that can be deduced from present trends.

Transport has frequently been bracketed with communications in professional and public debate, but recent changes in the means of accessing and processing information have begun to make widespread impacts on both transport technology and user demands. These issues have the shortest lead times to visible and tangible effects, and in general will substantially precede changes to land use and urban form.

The lags in terms of behavioural or other observable effects will vary from immediate — in the case of an online retrieval of an item without the need to travel to a library to search — to long term, as different areas of a city change character due to altered relative advantage in terms of cost, travel and amenity.

Some of the key factors in the early impact areas can be expressed in terms of information acquisition and use as: data acquisition cost reductions (leading to major advances in the amount of vehicle movement data which can be obtained and handled); data processing cost reductions (leading to a quantum advance in the economics of vehicle control, user charging, and vehicle identification); and data access cost reductions (which are beginning to deliver a vastly important quantity and quality of information for both transport services themselves and their marketing, and for the ranges and quality of alternative end user services which would otherwise have required travel by the end user to obtain; shopping being only one of these).

The overall impact of the convergence of communications and transport through the stimulus of computer and telecommunications technology advances also has broader effects at the regional (Wigan 1983a, 1983b) and international levels. The transport-specific issues at an (implied) sub-national level are given primary place in the present chapter, and factual data on the trends in industrial output and household expenditure in Australia and the UK are presented to provide a numerate basis for consideration. The urban form implications are considered as delayed consequences of the changes indicated by household and industrial shifts in expenditure and output.

The changing importance of the industrial output aspects of these two major and closely complementary industries is illustrated in Figure

Figure 11.1 Trends in Industrial Output of UK Transport and Communications Industries

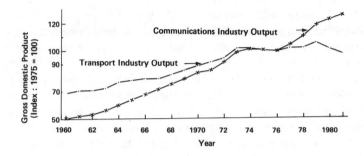

11.1, where the development of the output of the UK transport and communications industries are shown over time.

The output of the transport industry has risen by about 30 per cent since 1960, while the output of the communications industry has increased by about 150 per cent. This tells only a small part of the story, as the consumer expenditures and other aspects of the transport and communications markets have a great deal more to say about the nature of the changes taking place. The fact remains that the rate of growth of the communications industry in the UK has now firmly overtaken the transport industry. As the absolute gap between transport and communications narrows, communications can be expected to catch up with and overtake the transport industries. These changes in emphasis on the physical movement and movement of information aspects of communications are now being reflected in the public and industrial attention devoted to telecommunications.

The underlying forces driving the impacts of information technology can be usefully reviewed by examining how the reductions in cost (and increases in capability) are inducing and making way for change. Cost reductions in data aquisition, reduction and access are now considered in turn.

Data Acquisition Cost Reductions

The implications in transport terms of data acquisition cost reductions are that dynamic road user congestion charging and routing information has now jumped the barrier previously set by the enormous cost of equipping all vehicles with the intelligence to handle and display such information. The microprocessor controlled instrumentation system for cars is emerging piecemeal in the market place, and is rapidly turning the road-user charging/information/vehicle-identification question from one of expensive, solely hardware additions to eventually one of (far cheaper) software changes: a genuinely economic proposition. The capability to inform users dynamically of the congestion price that they are (or would be) incurring was for a long time the major cost bottleneck strangling the most practical (and economically effective) selective area policy option for effective road utilisation and environmental protection (Wigan 1978; Department of the Environment 1977).

For such a policy to be effective, both parking charges and area licence charges were needed — and the information context of the road use congestion charges was the largest single contribution to the economic benefit. The major costs were concerned with licence-issuing, enforcement and monetary transfers. The microprocessor-oriented active instrumentation systems now emerging offer the opportunity to achieve all of the 'information' benefits — without the monetary transfers or the enforcement superstructure.

The land-use implications of such a road pricing scheme have been a major concern to retailers and planners in city centres for nearly two decades. One of the effects pointed out during the early (1969-72) work carried out at the TRRL was that road pricing would make overt some of the implied subsidies to city centre retailers provided by the shoppers and the community bearing the costs of the congestion and time delays associated with many of the prime retail locations. These effects are significant, as the surcharges often levied by hauliers required to operate in major congested areas (such as central London) can be significant. The net effect of the expected reductions in net freight costs and the increased perception of customer travel costs will determine the net effect on retail location. Increased cost pressures for out-of-hours delivery are likely to be resisted and passed on to customers in the form of higher prices (Greater London Council 1976).

The networks of data links now becoming a widespread reality are beginning to offer not only high-speed data paths from many points to many others, with full public access, but even video bandwidth two-way linkages are close to the same takeoff point. This means that the opportunities for distributed road pricing, road-user advice, and communications have now converged to make effective use of the road system an economic and practical proposition within a short handful of years. The considerable increase in the adoption of microprocessor-controlled distributed instrumentation systems for ordinary cars is now providing the only missing link in this network of interrelated influences. The adoption of this latter type of system could have a substantial impact on urban network utilisation.

If monetary transfers are regarded as essential, permanent transponder systems in the roads or on the near side of the road are then needed together with vehicle identification. The emergent attitudes towards data privacy are likely to inhibit, if not prohibit, this. Who would like to have detailed (urban) movements continuously recorded — apart from enforcement officers and vehicle fleet operators of all types? The initial reactions to the first such systems will have a long-lasting influence on the acceptability — and therefore introduction — of future innovations in this area.

This discussion has up to this point been restricted to the private passenger vehicle in its emphasis. This is misleading, as the far smaller fleets of freight and passenger service vehicles have in general a much higher value, and can justify investments in vehicle electronics and communication systems at a considerably earlier point in the development of this applied field, and before mass-market prices (or mass-market acceptance) could be expected for the larger private passenger-vehicle fleet. This has substantial importance to the public sector, as the key determining factor in road structural design expenditures is the need to sustain the substantial axle loads applied by trucks. Small increases in the load carried above the legally permitted limits (to which designers perforce must look when designing the road itself) have a very large effect on the remaining life of the part of the road in question, as the damage potential of an axle varies approximately with the fourth power of the loading. When axle loads of 8-12 tonnes are in question — and overloading is common in Australia to up to about 50 per cent above these permitted limits — the importance of surveillance is evident.

Here, too, information technology is bringing into existence a complete framework of detection, enforcement, and even possible taxation. The ability of the microprocessor-based dynamic weighing systems to accurately assess axle loads on a continuous basis is at present limited to speeds of about 4-6 km/h versions in the offing, although operational highwayspeed weighing has operated for some time. However, the implications for road user damage cost recovery are apparent, in the context set out for private passenger vehicles, but must await an accurate highway-speed data acquisition system. This will not be long delayed.

The combination of such a system (developed to a stage where the dynamic axle loads can be picked up automatically on each lane of the road), with vehicle identification number picked up from an interrogation signal from the monitoring system so triggered, and an automatic transfer of a fine (perhaps we should call it a tax?) on to the ledger of the licenced operator, could become entirely automatic in countries with a greater density of data communication networks and population than those of Australia. Such methods will also permit infrequently travelled roads to be monitored continuously and effectively.

Similarly, automation and continuous central acquisition of vehicle movement data at marginal cost (another side effect of the trends specified above) provide an economic means of continuously monitoring flows and their composition — something that labour costs have precluded for some decades. The age of the automated helot is now arriving, and here is one application (to classified vehicle monitoring) where it will be greatly appreciated.

It is important to note that these options are technically feasible now, but that the inertia of political and investment processes means that implementation — even if it were considered by some to be desirable or urgent — must be viewed as requiring at least a decade. The promulgation of innovation through the vehicle fleet requires this order of delay, although the usage patterns of older vehicles indicate that an effective on-the-road impact could be achieved in rather less time if such measures as on-road tonne/km were to be taken to be the sole criteria (Thoreson and Wigan 1980).

Data Processing Cost Reductions

The control and adaptive response possibilities of the advances listed above are already apparent from microcomputer-based dynamic traffic control systems such as SCOOT and SCAT (Robertson 1982). The transfer of control application to a wider scope depends only on the increasing quantities of relevant information acquisition and processing systems which will increase very much faster than the technology, as the various control implications are linked together.

The impact of the ability to set such systems to pick out specific vehicles or locations of special interest would swiftly become a major political issue. The heavy — and increasing — use made of video monitors may become a matter for greater concern when image-processing and recognition systems become economic for such applications. The UK Home Office has been reported to have already tested an automatic vehicle number plate detection system, linked to a 'wanted vehicle' file. This level of monitoring and response capability will ease the impact of the suspected intrusiveness of vehicle identification and charging systems, such that the accountability of such a public and large scale system may become politically and publicly preferable to the unpredictable tracing that would arise if the potential capabilities were realised by Police and other official bodies simply as a surveillance and enforcement tool.

Data Access Cost Reductions

The complementary issue to the effects on vehicles and vehicle movements concerns the effects of higher quality and quantity of information on those who use the vehicles. The freight transport system is less affected by this class of question, as the decision to travel is one set by the need to move a physical item from one place to another. However, one of the key costs in road (and other) freight operations of any complexity is the documentation costs and delays. These arise in a visible manner more commonly in international trade, but they are still a major cost at any scale of consolidation of freight movements.

The areas of greatest vulnerability are those where 'search' behaviour is required by individuals looking for the best price in a set of near-substitutable items. The range and quality of information available on public transport services have been demonstrated to have some effect on usage, while fare and service structures restructured with better marketing have had far more. In this case the movement possibilities have been the subject of attention. In future the destination possibilities will become of far greater importance.

Evidence is building up from studies of time allocation trends by age, lifecycle stage, and vehicle access to identify these markets, especially for recreation and personal business. It is apparent that a slight change of emphasis in the treatment of travel time as just one of the activities in which people spend time over that day is emerging from transport studies (Wigan 1981,1983c). The current 1983 data collection in the irregular series of time use surveys carried out by the British Broadcasting Corporation (BBC 1975) includes time spent on personal computers, video recorders and video games. As television watching is a large part of the day for many people, the enhanced services now becoming available on the same medium will lead both to greater freedom of choice and to more competition for time on the dedicated communication channels.

The effects of greater reliance on communication channels can already be seen in the transport field, where car usage and access have become the prime determinant of activity location and participation for many — or the car purchase decision has been dependent on the wish to increase unconstrained accessibility for the members of the household. The permanently engaged telephone carrying adolescent voices will be — and is being — replaced by the permanently engaged telephone with the warble of modem tones (see Meier, Chapter 9)! The amount of information required to maintain effective search, exchange and decision processes through such a digital link is very substantial, and can only be made an adequate substitute for direct verbal or visual exchanges if the content is carefully constructed, if assistance for the construction of efficient queries is provided, and if the communication overload potential of computer-assisted communications is not to become a major problem.

Computer-aided conferencing and extensive electronic mail systems provide many of these support tools — and still hit the communications overload problem for the user. The ability to scan quickly and cheaply becomes degraded as packet switched networks — the carriers of such services — charge distance and time independent tariffs and thus push the price of such searches steadily higher as the information access quality improves. For closely defined objectives, and for well-defined groups of people, such tools are highly effective in increasing social networks to a truly global span. Computer Utility companies (such as the SOURCE based in Maclean, Virginia, and CompuServe in Columbus, Ohio) carry such services (and provide the medium for an increasing number of added value services to boot).

Computer conferencing within NASA achieved a 25 per cent reduction in travel for the Apollo project (Fordyce 1974). The economics of such special-purpose long-range business co-ordination have improved significantly since then, and the necessary public-access packet switched data networks have emerged to make the network infrastructure enjoyed by NASA in the 1960s and 1970s available to all. The effects of these developments can be expected to impinge mainly on the long-distance travel market, at least at first, and thus influence travel rather than land-use location at a more local level. Expanded audio conference links can have a similar effect in expanding activity, locational and personal links over an area. This is currently being studied by Telecom Australia and Macquarie University in central Victoria, Australia (Galloway and Albertson 1982).

A central problem in assessing the probable growth in usage and influence on locational behaviour of information technology based service innovations is that the equipment required to access the emergent systems (which subsume VideoTex and responsive cable vision) is still expensive, and still requires more than merely software changes (which usually can be economically and readily retrofitted to an existing piece of household equipment).

The essential problem of road-pricing encountered in the late 1960s was that of the cost of the single-purpose add-on hardware, which overwhelmed the cost/benefit case for an intelligent system at that time. It is even now not very different for many terminal dependent services, and is one cause of the initially slow rate of penetration of Prestel in UK homes. Business organisations are, however, very rapidly becoming terminal oriented for a variety of reasons. Consequently the business impact of Prestel (and internal dedicated VideoTex-systems such as IVSs AREGON) has been much more marked.

The key finding to date from UK Prestel experiences is that enhancing interactive capabilities (such as travel bookings at a high-street travel agent) has cut internal (and public) costs of obtaining and locating volatile competitive services such as ferry seats. The most recent development in this line is the provision of a two-way link through Prestel directly into the PanAmerican Airlines main booking computers in New York, with other airlines set to follow. The transport industry shares the volatility of seat (and cargo) capacity utilisation with the entertainment industry, and similar moves by the entertainment industry are now taking place.

This enrichment of choice, and increased efficiency of utilisation, is but a harbinger of the future. The impressive intercontinental linkages of packet switched networks, Gateway systems on the British Telecom Prestel service computers, and support in two continents are brought simply to the desk of a travel agent.

This push from business for internal costing reasons will first be integrated with personal business. Banking and EFT (electronic funds transfers) are responding to the poor accessibility to such service now available to many people (due to the mis-match between opening hours, location, and the times at which people can get to these services).

This thrust (from the banking side for cost reasons) is likely to be effective for the same reasons that the UK Prestel travel booking services have worked out. The provision of 'teleshopping' has not yet been very effective as access instruments in the home are essential, and until this has been corrected will probably continue to be the case. The French are taking large scale action to replace the telephone directory service by placing terminals in most homes to access a suitable computer based service. This will, at a stroke, place 'telematique' in the same category as the microprocessor equipped car: that is, awaiting only software (and data communications network support) to be exploitable for a wide range of uses.

In the case of home access to information services, one segment of the workforce is already responding. Large firms such as Xerox now have the key members of their staff working from home terminals, thereby breaking the 'necessary' link between presence at workplace and communication with colleagues. It is particularly important to note that this initiative (in the case of Xerox) is specifically linked with new centres for innovative business, and to small scale initiatives where the executives concerned are freed to build up businesses on their 'own' account — while still executing substantive and often senior tasks in Xerox. The breaking of the time and location nexus for such duties is the key item to observe, and the message for transport and communication planning is abundantly clear.

The many experiments with visual, aural and computer text-based conferencing have shown that it is social and not technical and cost factors which have slowed penetration. The key change will come when terminals (under various guises: home computers, enhanced video games, 'smart' telephones or VideoTex adaptors for TV sets) become commonplace in every home. The 'cost reduction' applications already seen to be effective and economic in business applications of VideoTex will then be possible, but may result in a similar level of trip making albeit to more satisfactory destinations. One might hypothesise that the time spent at given activity destinations might lengthen, and the ratio of activity to travel time increase as a result.

The 'journey to work' and 'in course of work' have been found by some workers (Harkness 1973) to be the most energy intensive (and thus in absolute terms, under the most pressure from alternatives), and the increasing emphasis on service industries and on information-oriented products leads to the conclusion that these types of journey are the most likely to be reduced (or at least affected). The time profiles of involvement in various activities then become valuable tools, and some are given in Wigan (1983d).

The freight system will also be affected by the enhanced ability to allow 'search' for consumer products to be done with less travel (as discount warehouses already illustrate), and to permit direct delivery from factory or warehouse to purchaser. This has already happened to some extent, and it is the extension of price competition to a far wider catchment that will have the impact. This has already been seen in US recruitment for 'home-based' skilled workers, and in the UK in the almost exclusively home-based female professional workforce of the 600+ strong F-International Systems Consulting Group.

Countervailing reactions are now emerging, as less sophisticated 'home terminal workers' have been finding (in the UK) that their pay rates are remaining the same as for office attendance — but the firms are now saving substantial sums in office overheads, which are not being passed on. The increased control of their output (as it is simple to use the host computer to monitor them on an automatic and continuous basis) and the reduced personal interaction due to lack of the office social contact framework are both unwelcome.

If the home workers fail to obtain some part of the cost reduction gains that their employers are now enjoying, then the impetus for changes in location of such business activities will build up swiftly. If on the other hand the home workers extract a price for their more cost-effective performance, such changes would be unlikely to gain much momentum over the next few years. A substantial shift to home working is perhaps the most significant trend to watch for in a land use or urban form framework.

At an international — or continent-wide — level, the increasing importance of travel costs (and time) in what is now becoming a global market for most products will force much of the underlying growth in demand for travel into other channels. This will be due not only to price relativities, but to the elapsed time and quality of the telecommunications products.

It is therefore of crucial importance that transport and telecommunications planners get together with social planners and ensure that the huge capital investments now being progressively committed within the communications sector are brought into the most effective employment at a social and national level. This is just as important for recreational and social interchange as it is for freight movement, aircraft service provision and business communications.

The convergence in transport and telecommunications technologies has not to date been matched by any significant convergence in the medium- and long-range planning goals of the major disciplines involved. Too much time and effort have been spent on the chimera of 'transport substitution', and not enough on the common determinants of the markets for movement and communication services. Transport substitution will continue to occur, but the major impacts will be in the alterations in the timing and location of activities that people choose to

Figure 11.2 Australian Household Expenditures on
Transport and Communication, 1974-75

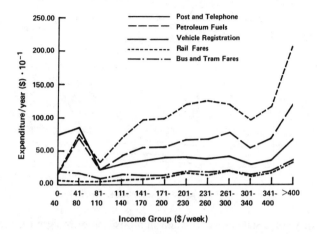

engage in, as the constraints of time, space and timing (Wigan and Morris 1980) are progressively loosened by improved services provided through information technology changes.

Communications Costs at Present: Some Australian and UK Data

The basic trends in expenditures on transport have already shown signs of change. This section covers some of the practical perspectives which can be derived from data available today. Much of this information is necessarily some years old. The Australian material is based on the 1974-75 Household Expenditure Survey, and the next is not due until 1984. This makes comparisons with the annual publication of detailed UK Family Expenditure Survey data rather difficult. However, the patterns of household expenditure in Australia already contained a number of important indicators. Figure 11.2 shows the weekly dollar expenditure of households at different income levels on a range of commodities including postage, telephone and transport elements.

A surprising observation can be drawn from Figure 11.2: the very lowest income household groups spent more per week on communications than even the highest-income household groups. The substantial elderly population in Australia has largely arranged its affairs to minimise income and maximise capital holdings in their retirement so as

Figure 11.3 Australian Household Expenditures (%), 1974-75

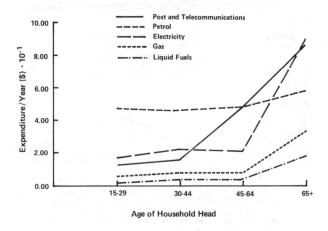

to qualify for a state pension when in a position of modest (or greater) wealth, and this has some effect. The influence of unemployed households, with low car ownership, would dilute these results: however, Australia in 1974-75 had a historically low unemployment rate. The results of the 1984 Household Expenditure Survey will show a much greater influence by unemployed households. Even allowing for this distorting influence, the importance of communications relative to some of the transport expenditures was considerable even in 1974-75. The comparatively low levels of petroleum prices in Australia at that time (and subsequently, though modified to a degree in the last few years through the 'import parity pricing' policy), also work to elevate the communications expenditures in the family budget.

Figure 11.3 expresses the communications and energy aspects of the family budget as percentage shares for households of different ages. The results already discussed are amply supported by the rapid climb in the importance of communications expenditures as the age of the household head increases. The importance of all forms of energy consumption as a proportion of the family budget follows much the same trends.

The picture in Australia in 1974-75 is therefore one of low-income older households as the greatest (relative) users of communications. Much has happened since then. The adoption of the world parity pricing policy for domestically produced oil and a marked change in the overall economic and employment outlook have both raised pressures to encourage the incipient trends just discussed.

In order to obtain a time series view it is necessary to return to UK data. The Central Statistical Office (1982) provides a useful basis for examining the overall trend patterns for the primary transport and communication consumer expenditure headings. Figure 11.1 showed how the underlying trends of industrial output have progressively moved against growth in the transport industries, and in favour of growth in the communications industries. Industrial output is only a fairly small part of this overall change, and some results are now given to assess this. Examining consumer expenditure between 1971-81 (indexed in terms of constant 1975 UK pounds) reveals that expenditure on railway travel has remained quite stable over the whole period, while air travel has more than doubled in real terms. Some — if not most — of this growth is due to the development of the holiday travel market into a mass market product. This is significant, as the consumer impacts of information technology are focusing increasing pressure on leisure expenditure and leisure time. The impacts on time use are the subject of separate investigation, and are covered by the 1983 BBC Time Use and Activity Survey as a result of the emergent competition between viewing and video/computer/games time. Viewing time is for many people second only to work and sleep in terms of the numbers of hours spent (BBC 1975).

Similar competitive trends in expenditures are apparent within both transport and communication sectors. Postal expenditures have remained stable, in the face of rapid growth in expenditures on telephones, telegrams, and radio and TV rental. The growth in expenditure on telephone use is consistent with that in other countries, but the growth in telegram expenditure is not: Telecom Australia has recently effectively discontinued this service. The close match between telephone usage expenditure and radio and TV rentals is more than an accident due to the complementary nature of increases in real income with increases in leisure equipment.

The overall pattern of UK expenditures by household income are given in Figure 11.4 for 1980. The longitudinal patterns are placed in a clearer perspective by the patterns of expenditure across different income levels. Expenditure on communication headings may very well have risen by a considerable amount in real terms since 1971 — but it is still not a very important part of the household transport/communications budget for high-income households.

In 1980, the average UK household income was at roughly the point where the car and motorcycle purchase expenditure curves cross the communication expenditures line. This suggests that the functional role

Figure 11.4 Weekly Expenditure on Selected Commodities by Income Class, UK, 1980

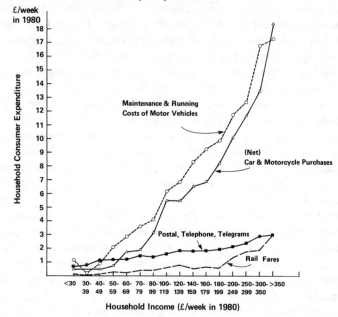

Figure 11.5 Motor Vehicle Components of UK Household Expenditure, 1980

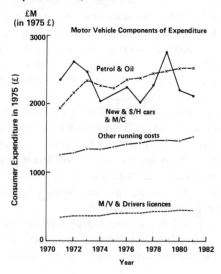

of postage and telephone expenditures is increasingly important for a growing proportion of UK households, and the 1974-75 Australian observation that communications costs can exceed at least a number of transport expenditure components is more than confirmed, as for the lowest income levels communications expenditure exceeded the total expenditures on motor vehicles.

The sheer size of the budget share spent on motor vehicles suggests that a little more detail on the time trends would be useful here. Figure 11.5 contains this data for the major components of motor-vehicle expenditure. The generally stable trend of most of these components belies the large changes observed in the UK car market over the decade. The sums involved are large by national budgetry standards, and 'comparative' stability in household expenditures at this scale still has substantial impact. These figures demonstrate that the general trends in industrial output are being reflected in household expenditure patterns.

The overall comparative stability of the transport expenditure headings and the aggressive growth in the communication expenditures mean that, if present trends continue, the absolute size of the communications share of the household budget must soon begin to affect the transport expenditures. The relative scales of expenditure demonstrated in Figure 11.4 indicate that products in the competitive overlap area between transport and communications should start to be able to make a competitive impression on both if the pricing places the relevant product or service within the financial resources of the average household.

Practical confirmation of this observation has very recently been obtained from the MicroNet 800 Prestel service aimed at the estimated 1+ million home computer owners in the UK. This service has just been launched, and appears to be priced in the right zone: in a few months it has increased the numbers of home based Prestel access systems by over 30 times.

These comments should be taken in conjunction with those at the end of the last section, where the complementary nature of most of the transport/communication innovations was identified: such observations must be qualified once the budget shares of the two types of partially substitutable product become of comparable size. Entertainment and educational activities are likely to react first, for different reasons. Common to both is that the activity involved is the objective of the exercise, and the location at which it may be carried out is quite unimportant if the entertainment/educational goal is met.

The massive cross substitution which took place in the 1960s and 1970s between the cinema and television as entertainment media not

Figure 11.6 UK Communications and Transport Subsidies
and Taxation Revenues

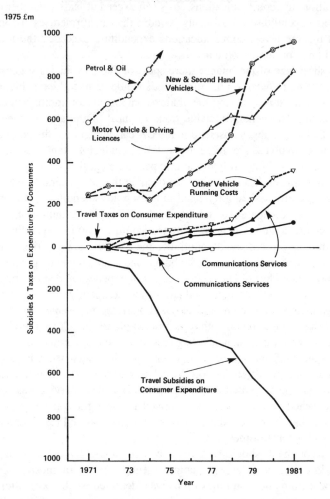

only showed one style of entertainment losing a competitive fight
(Smith 1978), but demonstrated a clear destination substitution effect.
People stayed at home instead of travelling. Future competition between
transport and communications is therefore probable on the basis of the
interaction between time and money budget constraints.

Just as transport has a large place in household budgets, it also has a
large place in public expenditure. Public transport is very expensive to

provide, and motor vehicles are costly to operate and own. Equally, the inelastic response to petrol-pricing leads Treasuries to raise substantial sums of revenue from private transport ownership and use. This would suggest that communications of other varieties will become of progressively greater interest for their revenue raising power (as well as their capital hunger).

Figure 11.6 shows the recent history of this aspect of transport and communications as revenue sources — and sinks. The lines above the median division refer to areas where the UK Treasury is gaining revenue from the nominated sources, while below the line are the subsidies. Communications services figured briefly on the subsidy side of the UK ledger in the mid-1970s: at present they are producing revenue, at an increasing rate. For a period there were (unspecified) subsidies and revenues from telecommunications, and thus two lines entitled 'communications' in Figure 11.6. The overwhelming importance of private transport expenditures and less of public transport subsidies is all too clear.

Conclusion

Different aspects of transport, information technology, data and communications have been considered, and a few of the links drawn between new capabilities and linkages and the transport interactions. To provide a perspective on the importance of present levels of communications and transport expenditures, detailed Family Expenditure, National Accounts and other data from both Australia and the UK have been considered. The overall conclusions are that the present complementarity between transport and communications expenditures and usage is at least in part due to the small relative size of the communications aspects — but that as communications output and expenditure are both growing swiftly while transport output and expenditure are both static, this may not remain true for very long.

The influences on urban form and land use are now becoming visible, but will be critically dependent on the social reactions to the changes in overhead costs and productivity of home workers. Information technology changes can be expected to influence longer distance travel considerably earlier than urban movements, although the density of interactions between individuals increases sharply with physical proximity, even for telephone contact.

The simultaneous expansion of the ability to search for contacts and information on a world-wide scale and the accelerating usage of the international networks to broaden the personal community of knowledge based workers has led to a reduction in general usage of printed media for publication.

This has reduced the ability of many to link up with the current state of the art in knowledge-based systems through the conventional routes, although it has increased the effectiveness of intercommunication between those 'on the net'. This is an example of the 'information rich elite' which many have expected to emerge, and the increased travel which will now be needed for others outside these golden circles to make the personal and professional contacts needed to join these world-wide online communities (the invisible colleges of the past) will be repeated many times.

The functions of the central city meeting place for knowledge-based workers will therefore be reinforced for some time, until universal access (in terms of both physical and monetary constraints) is available for all.

The increased ability to monitor both detailed land parcels and the activities taking place on each parcel will considerably improve the ability of regional authorities to determine what is actually happening on the ground — but politics rather than technical capabilities are likely to continue to determine the land use influences actually emergent from such systems for monitoring and control.

References

British Broadcasting Corporation (1975) *The People's Activities and the Use of Time*, BBC, London

Central Statistical Office (1982) *National Accounts*, HMSO, London

Department of Employment (1980) *Family Expenditure Survey 1980*, HMSO, London

Department of the Environment (1977) *A Study of Some Methods of Traffic Restraint*, HMSO, London

Fordyce, S.W. (1974) *Telecommunications as a Substitute for Transport*, NASA, Washington, DC

Galloway, J.J. and Albertson, L.A. (1982) *Diffusion of Teleconference Facilities*, Report 1, Planning, Telecom Australia, Clayton, Victoria

Greater London Council (1976) Background Papers, London Freight Conference, Freight Unit, London

Harkness, R.C. (1973) 'Telecommunications Substitutes for Travel: a Preliminary Assessment of Their Potential for Reducing Urban Transport Costs by Altering Office Location Patterns', PhD Thesis, University of Washington

Robertson, D.I. (1982) 'Research on Strategies for Traffic Control and Management', *Proceedings of the Eleventh Australian Road Research Board Conference*, **11**, 83-90

Smith, R. (1978) 'Telecommunications Technology: Current Trends', in *Importance of Telecommunications on Planning and Transport*, Research Report 24, Department of Environment and Transport, London

Thoreson, T. and Wigan, M.R. (1980) 'Vehicle Population Dynamics: Tracing, Forecasting and Assessing Changing Population Characteristics', *Proceedings of the Tenth Australian Road Research Board Conference*, **10**, 206-34

Wigan, M.R. (1978) 'A Comparison of the Costs and Environmental Impacts for Transport Policy Assessment', *Environment and Planning A*, **8**, 125-47

Wigan, M.R. (1981) *Lifestyle Impact of Changes in Real Transport Costs*, Internal Report AIR 380-1, Australian Road Research Board, Vermont, Victoria

Wigan, M.R. (1983a) *Information Technology and Transport: What Research Needs to be Started Now?*, Technical Note TN110, Institute for Transport Studies, Leeds University

Wigan, M.R. (1983b) 'Information Technology and Integrated Regional Development', in P. Nijkamp (ed.) *Information Systems for Regional Planning*, North-Holland Publishing Co., Amsterdam, (in press)

Wigan, M.R. (1983c) 'The Travel and Activity Structure of Australian Cities: Perspectives from Transport Planning Surveys', *Proceedings of the Eighth Australian Transport Research Forum*, **8**, 360-85

Wigan, M.R. (1983d) *The Effects on Transport Demand of Increased and Economic Access to Information*, Internal Report AIR 1118-2, Australian Road Research Board, Vermont, Victoria

Wigan, M.R. and Morris, J.M.M. (1980) 'The Transport Implications of Activity and Time Budget Constraints', *Transportation Research A*, **15**, 66-86

12. TRANSPORT-ENERGY INTERACTIONS
L. Klaassen

The study of the role that energy and energy prices play in urban development raises a remarkable question, which is not answered in the same way the world over. That question is: does a rise in transportation costs to the level they have attained, for instance in continental Europe, invariably have only negative implications, or are there also effects on the volume and structure of traffic as well as on the physical structure of the town that are beneficial to town life? One basic principle of road-pricing is that road users have to pay more, the more they make use of roads with high traffic intensity. Through such road-pricing, traffic will tend to redistribute itself to less occupied routes or less occupied hours. In that way, some say, not only traffic structure but also, in the longer run, the location patterns of households and companies will be affected favourably. Higher fuel costs may have similar if not identical effects, as may become evident from what follows.

To the extent that this is true, many governments, in particular local governments, may have welcomed the oil crisis as an effective means to create a more habitable town. Road-pricing, however,much as it might have contributed to an improved urban environment, invokes so many objections of a technical, organisational as well as political nature, that the decision taken by OPEC-countries to raise the price of oil, in two instances most drastically, may really be considered a blessing from the point of view of traffic development.

Ten years have elapsed since the first oil price increase and car makers in the meantime have done what they could to produce more efficient cars, largely offsetting the price rise and thus reducing its effects on traffic volume. On the other hand, the oil crisis had its effect on the general economic level, and has been one cause of the present economic recession in the early 1980s. The resulting contraction of many household budgets may well have an even greater effect on car use than the oil price could have brought about directly.

Not only families but also (and in particular) governments have fallen into difficulties owing to the economic recession, especially in the countries of continental Europe with very advanced systems of social security. Such systems imply high taxes, and these have largely been imposed on fuels needed for traffic. Unlike other taxes, those on fuel are simple to levy and raise the government's revenues from the very day they are introduced. Such a tax policy, working towards the effective control of car traffic that all citizens in their hearts want and approve, can be implemented without much difficulty. Regular tax increases in many countries on the European continent have offset the effect of more economical car engines on the kilometre cost of transportation.

Here there appears to be an essential difference between the US, or perhaps the Anglo-Saxon world, on the one hand, and continental Europe and most other countries on the other. In the US, a policy of urban concentration — reanimation of town centres, measures against traffic, pedestrian zones and so forth — will not touch a responsive chord with many citizens, while in Europe such matters predominate urban policy. The reason is not clear but presumably cultural factors play an important role (see Pressman 1981). What matters is that such differences exist and that measures and developments in the field of traffic quite acceptable in one area may be not so, or less so, in the other.

In what follows the significance of high transportation costs (due either to the high energy prices we shall have to accept also for the future, or to other factors, such as road-pricing, taxes on gasoline) for urban development is discussed. We shall see that the social and physical reorientation brought about by high transport costs may once more lead to a 'human' town. The necessary adjustment processes will be painful to some and unacceptable to others, according to the kind of town they would consider 'desirable'. If Europe and the US have different ideas on that score, Europeans tending to prefer human, green, compact structures and Americans spacious, efficient structures giving priority to motorised traffic, that makes research into both structures all the more imperative. Only in this way can we weigh carefully the advantages and disadvantages of either, and get to know what weights to attribute to the differences in opinion.

In the following sections some relevant aspects of the problems raised will be considered. The question to be answered is: what is the influence of a very high fuel price on urban structures, and how should that influence be evaluated? No need to mention that the author is a continental European.

The Past

Some important trends, characteristic of the post-1945 period, can be considered the *causae ultima* of the recent developments in transportation. These trends were continuous and strong increase in real income per capita; increase in leisure time; persistent low price of oil; full employment with a strong tendency to shift from manufacturing to services; steady decrease in the average size of households and corresponding heavy increase in the demand for dwellings; increasing number of foreign workers; progressive sensitivity to environmental factors; and the increasing criminality. Let us consider these trends.

Obviously, these trends are not independent. Full employment alone would never have resulted in the large number of foreign workers now present in Western Europe, nor would income have risen so steeply, had employment remained largely oriented to manufacturing. There is not much point in going into these relationships here; interesting though they are, they do not bear on the subject at hand. Instead let us consider for a few moments the question of to what extent the trends mentioned above are indeed the *causae ultima* of recent developments of transportation.

An increase in income results from an increase in productivity, such as has manifested itself very strongly in car manufacturing. Indeed, car prices have risen less than the general price level; cars have become relatively cheaper over time. With real income steadily increasing, people had more disposable income than before, and they spent it on cars. More people became car owners, and car owners used their cars for more frequent and longer trips. When cars became cheap enough for persons in the lower income brackets, much more heavily populated than the higher ones, car ownership soared.

The intensive use of cars, already boosted by the income rise, was further stimulated by the accompanying progressive shortening of working hours and the introduction of the free Saturday. Low petrol prices, improved infrastructure, and reasonably economic cars all helped to keep the cost of intensified car use at an affordable level.

People were not slow to profit from the possibility of intensive interaction, making more trips and travelling farther. Nor did they limit themselves to the use of the car. Three 'means of interaction' reached almost equal densities in the Netherlands in 1979: cars (288 for every 1,000 inhabitants), telephones (306 for every 1,000) and television (288 sets per 1,000 inhabitants). Other means of interaction stayed way behind. Motor cycles, railway carriages and autocars had the same density in 1978 as in 1938.

The traffic produced by the different means of transportation surged upwards too. We find that the total number of passenger kilometres travelled in the Netherlands increased from 41.4×10^9 in 1960 to 135.4

x 10^9 in 1978, the latter figure corresponding to 10,000 km a year per capita. The number of passenger kilometres by car rose in the same period from 15.9 x 10^9 to 112.3 x 10^9, an increase of roughly 96 x 10^9 passenger kilometres by car out of a total of 99 x 10^9. The simple conclusion is that the increase in passenger kilometres is due to the introduction of the car. The use of public transport rose from 18.2 to 19.9 x 10^9 passenger kilometres, that of the motor-assisted bicycle decreased from 5.9 to 2.2 x 10^9.

Such developments naturally had consequences for spatial location and activity patterns. Living away from one's workplace became a normal phenomenon. When transportation costs were high, people had to live near their place of work, but as cars became common, that became less and less important. Within wide limits both the residence and the working place could be chosen at will. Commuting distances increased as a result, and city limits became more and more difficult to define as nuclei at some distance from the central city of the agglomeration actually became part of the agglomeration.

The shrinking of households accelerated the process of urban sprawl. The process of urbanisation passed into a process of suburbanisation, a process that was actively promoted by local governments.

It is easy to see that these developments rendered the position of public transport very uncomfortable. As cities thinned out and the pattern of settlement became spatially dispersed, with ever decreasing building densities and even faster decreasing population densities, the costs of a passenger kilometre by public transport rose sky-high. In the Netherlands they finally reached the level where local governments could no longer finance their own public transport, and the central government was called upon to make up the deficits. That is the prevailing situation.

A change in the structure of employment contributed to the present difficult position of public transport. When service firms came to replace manufacturing industries as employers, at first they seemed to consider the inner cities of large agglomerations the only possible locations for their offices. Office space was created at the expense of housing lots, and more people were driven from the inner cities, already much diluted by the tendency towards smaller households. Again, work places and residences were separated, and commuting became the normal pattern for many citizens. Commuting means traffic; large one-sided flows of traffic towards the city centre in the morning peak, and equally large ones from the centre to the outskirts in the evening rush hours. Public transport, already hard put to make ends meet, now began to resemble a factory which, working at 50 per cent of its capacity for four hours a day, is still expected to be viable. With public transport tariffs being determined by political rather than economic considerations, the revenues obviously failed to meet the costs.

An additional cause of structural change in the inner cities was the shifting composition of the population. Sensibly or not, the shortage of Dutch labour in the 1960s and early 1970s was made up by a rapidly increasing army of foreign workers, who tended to settle in the cheaper parts of town centres. The somewhat delicate question whether or not the inflow of foreigners has accelerated the outflow of the domestic population must probably be answered in the affirmative.

The conclusion may be that post-1945 developments have led to dispersed spatial patterns and disintegrated urban structures, as a result of which society also started to disintegrate.

The Present

Spatial units and spatial social structures are built up gradually, as the result of a long societal development process. By the same token, such structures cannot readily be changed. Of course, society has its own way of dealing with the disadvantages of a given spatial structure. In response to environmental factors, congestion and increasing criminality, to which people are becoming more and more sensitive, people will emigrate from, or stop migrating into, the larger agglomerations. The rural and smaller urban areas of the so-called Emanation Zone of the Randstad and the rural periphery of the Netherlands have felt the effects as an accelerated growth of their population. Another effect is that middle-sized urban areas are beginning to show the signs of the very developments that the larger cities went through earlier, giving rise to the expectation that in a decade or two they will be exactly where their larger sisters are now. Indeed, urban decline is contagious (see van den Berg and Klaassen 1980).

The sharp increase in oil prices of 1973, entailing corresponding rises in the cost of petrol, diesel oil and electricity, introduced a new factor into spatial developments, namely, transportation costs of an unheard-of magnitude. Indeed, such high transportation costs as we now have and are likely to incur for several decades to come, through high energy prices and increased tax levels or decreased subsidies, are anomalous to the dispersed society we have developed. Long distances between workplaces and residences, shopping centres far from the city, holidays in far-away countries, friends and acquaintances living hundreds of kilometres away, are phenomena fitting a world of cheap transport. Now that travelling has become an expensive luxury once more, there is tension between people's desire to go on living as they are, and their disposable budget, which tends to shrink as prices rise faster than nominal incomes. With the price of oil and other energy sources continuing to rise, an ever-increasing proportion of disposable income goes to the gas and electricity, and a host of other energy-intensive products.

Our car-based society is in jeopardy, and with it, the way of life we have become used to. Of course, there are other ways of getting around; we could ride our bicycle, or Shanks' pony. The point is, however, that though they would suit our money budget, they would strain our time budget. At an average walking speed of 5 km an hour, we should have to walk for 5.5 hours each day to cover the same distances we now cover by car; the bicycle is faster, but still we would have spent three times as many hours travelling as we did by car in 1978. Not a very realistic proposition!

Could public transport offer a solution? We have already seen that from various causes the deficits of public transport have become gigantic. Admittedly the public has recently shown a heightened interest in buses, trams and trains, and revenues have risen accordingly. Unfortunately, the additional demand is concentrated in peak hours, when the marginal costs of a passenger kilometre exceed by far the 'reasonable' price that passengers can be asked to pay. Indeed, carriages being more than full during peak hours, any additional demand creates the need for capacity expansion, as recent experiences with the Netherlands Railways have shown. So, more passengers just mean greater deficits for public transport. Now that would not be so bad if the central governments had the means to pay the deficits, but the precarious state of the Exchequer, likely to last for at least several years, prevents that. A drastic increase in the price of bus and rail tickets seems inevitable, and we shall have to face the unpalatable truth we have tried to ignore so far, namely, that we no longer have unlimited access to everything and everybody. We shall have to adjust to the new circumstances.

Let us consider a few possible adjustments. One of the most crowded roads in the Netherlands is motorway A 13 between Rotterdam and The Hague. In the morning rush hours thousands of people living in Rotterdam drive to their work in The Hague, and many others drive from The Hague to reach their workplace in busy Rotterdam. If 10,000 of them decided no longer to drive their 10,000 cars from Rotterdam to The Hague and back or vice versa — a total distance of 50 km — on 200 workdays a year, at US$0.20 p. km, but instead find a house near their place of work, they would in one year save, in money alone, an amount of, say, 40 x 0.20 x 10,000 x 200 = US$16 million. The thought that only 72 per cent of that sum is a real cost saving, 28 per cent being tax savings, would probably not bother them much, but to the government, already in a financial fix, such a drastic fall in the demand for petrol would spell a corresponding loss of income. That consequence tends to be overlooked, also by those who urge car drivers to shift to public transport. Indeed, such a transfer makes the government bleed twice: increased ridership means increased public transport deficits, and a diminishing demand for petrol means shrinking revenues.

But let us go back to our main theme, and consider another solution to the distance problem. Instead of moving house, commuters could change jobs — a medium-term but by no means unthinkable solution. If by changing jobs they could save $1,600 a year — which in the Netherlands corresponds to at least $3,200 gross income — they might be content with a less well-paid new job, and still save on time and energy. What the prospects are on that score depends in our example — on the structure of employment in Rotterdam and The Hague — but they do exist.

A change in shopping habits is another possibility. In 1972, roughly one in three of all passenger kilometres was produced in commuting trips (covering an average distance of 13.4 km), which makes commuting the most important travel purpose. One in ten passenger kilometres is taken up in shopping trips, covering an average distance of 4.8 km. Savings could be achieved by shopping closer to home; in that way one would at the same time give much-needed support to the small shops on the corner (at the expense of the larger hypermarkets 'in the green', of course).

Curtailing social traffic would be another suggestion. This traffic accounts for one in four passenger kilometres, and the average distance per trip is the longest of all, viz. 14.5 km. A 1 per cent cut would save an annual $68 million in the whole of the Netherlands. But would it be easy to break up social ties, replacing far friends with near neighbours?

In short, there are possibilities, amounting to what we might call a *social reorientation* in society, a new orientation on closer destinations. Such social reorientation could be stimulated by changing the use of certain buildings. In the past, the increasing demand for office space in city centres has led, among other things, to old, often impressive residences being transformed into offices. With increasing congestion, offices in their turn have begun to take to the suburbs. If that movement could be stimulated, for instance, as is done in Rotterdam, by offering attractive alternative locations in secondary centres, perhaps these fine residences could be restored to their original function, preferably for those who work in the inner city. Relocation of offices in secondary centres could also help to shorten commuter distances for those who work in these offices and live in the suburbs (a move towards the point C in Figure 1.3).

The Future

Looking into the future is essentially impossible; however, we have become used to the idea, arguing that planning is necessary, and we cannot plan without a vision of the future. Let us accept that phony argument, and consider what may be in store for us in the long run. The theorem is that after the short-term social reorientation, *physical reorientation* will follow and densities will increase. Physical urban structures cannot change overnight, but may be transformed in the longer run in two stages. The first adjustment could be to prevent current rules for urban design being applied in the future. New constructions could at least be adapted to the present high transportation costs. The second adjustment would be to increase existing densities. One way to do so would be to build up empty places (there are far more of those than is commonly realised), another to decrease the volume of traffic.

There are very real possibilities of building houses in city centres. In the city centre of The Hague alone there are some 35 ha that can be considered unused open space and which could easily accommodate 7,000 people (Hengel 1980). In the centre of Rotterdam large numbers of dwellings have been constructed leading to a surprising intensification of land use.

To decrease the traffic volume, particularly during rush hours, one could try to turn one-sided traffic flows into two-sided ones. To achieve this, one would have to strengthen the residential function of the inner city while creating secondary centres at places within the agglomeration that are readily accessible to public and private transport. To that end, the first thing to do is to stop building offices in the city centre for uses with a low ratio between visitors and workers; the next step would be to promote the movement of such offices to the secondary centres; the final stage would be to stimulate housing projects, in various rent classes, in and near the city centre. Obviously, renovation of the older quarters in central cities fits into that kind of reurbanisation policy. All the elements mentioned are instruments of a policy of physical reorientation, a reorientation with respect to such interrelated activities as living and working, living and shopping. In Chapter 24 more will be said about these aspects of the role of transportation in urban areas and their influence on the 'quality' of the urban area.

The philosophy behind the reorientation policy is that we should not, as we have done too often in the past, create physical structures with total disregard for the volume and structure of traffic (and the inherent cost) they generate. Our proposal is to design physical structures that implicitly minimise total generalised transportation costs for the city as a whole. Such a policy recalls the policies that were pursued in former periods of high transportation costs in relation to disposable income, policies that resulted in the very dense urban structures to be observed in European inner cities. In the US, too, the influence of high transportation costs becomes clear when we compare a compact city like Pittsburgh with cities built for the car, like San Diego and parts of Los Angeles. European cities also reflect the decrease in transportation costs through time in the difference between a central centre and its suburbs. The central city was designed in a period with high transportation costs, the suburbs when their importance was rapidly dwindling. The norms of urban design shifted in the course of time to lower and lower densities, reflecting more than anything how people were able and willing to cover longer and longer distances for almost any transport purpose.

Science

Under the influence of a continuous decrease in transportation costs, European society has moved towards more and more spatial disintegration — in the sense that travel resistance diminished to the point where there was no longer any need to locate residence, workplace, shopping and leisure facilities in one locality. Diffusion came to be the basic characteristic. Companies, institutions and residences became more and more 'footloose', and city planners and architects felt free to design structures without giving a thought to their transportation effects. That freedom, for the time being at least, is now a thing of the past. Transportation will be an important concern in future designs, which means that city planners will have to co-operate more than ever with traffic engineers and transportation economists to arrive at sensible new structures. The less diffuse society to which we are once more moving, calls for integrated city planning, which might well make for new cities that are better to live in than they have been for a long time. And that is the essence of a policy of reurbanisation.

References

Berg, L. van den and Klaassen, L.H. (1980) 'The Contagiousness of Urban Decline', *Foundations of Empirical Economic Research*, **6**, Netherlands Economic Institute

Hengel, A. van. (1980) *Om de Kwaliteit Van Het Ruimtelijk Beheer in Den Haag, Maken we er wat Van?* Kamer van Koophandel en Fabrieken voor's-Gravenhage

Pressman, N.E.P. (ed.) (1981) *Creating Livable Cities*, University of Waterloo, Waterloo

PART FIVE

INFORMATION SYSTEMS IMPACTS

13. URBAN IMPACTS OF INFORMATION TECHNOLOGY
J. Dickey

Presented here are some thoughts on changes in information technologies and their impact on urban form. This is very difficult to assess since, as we all know, information technologies have altered drastically in the last decade and are bound to change even more in the near future. As soon as we obtain some insight into the topic, and particularly the emergent technologies, some unexpected new innovation appears and forces some rearrangement and reconceptualisation. Longer-term (10-20 year horizon) technological changes and their impacts are particularly difficult to imagine, much less predict.

To make matters worse, information is as basic to life as, say, energy. Since it pervades almost all transactions in society, analysts of its impacts have to think comprehensively indeed. Moreover, it appears that most scientists and prognosticators have treated information as an unsullied 'good'. All additional data simply add to our storehouse and enrich our lives (see, for example, the large number of books and papers on information entropy theory). This view is in stark contrast to many occurrences in the real world where *mis*information (lies, distortions, withholdings and so on; Webber 1982) abounds and where information overload (and thus negative marginal utility) is epidemic.

Neither do many prognosticators want to focus on the 'quality' of the information stored and purveyed. The 'seamier' aspects particularly are avoided. Few want to notice that more of cable TV's programming is becoming X-rated (as are some of the video casettes, videodiscs, and software for microcomputers) or that information systems can be and certainly are being set up to advance power enhancing and freedom-suppressing activities (also see Wegener, Chapter 16).

The task proposed here of delving into the mysterious connections between technological developments in information systems and urban change is thus extremely difficult, and only a few glimpses of (hopefully) significant features can be indicated. Since information has to be communicated to be of any value, we necessarily must touch on that area of technology also (as well as on the use of computers in making these communications; see Chapter 11).

The focus of this chapter is on urban change in the developed, capitalist countries since this is where the new technologies are most likely to make their first impact. We do not consider, however, many international interrelationships (or lack thereof) which could have a bearing on information technologies in particular developed countries. Examples here would be technological transfer through multinational corporations, patent protection, and embargoes in one country against products from another. Finally, we do not emphasise review of the vast literature on the overall topic, as this would be rather overwhelming, but instead try to bring out ideas that could spur further useful discussion.

The discussion begins by exploring the characteristics of several prominent (or possibly prominent) technologies and then highlights how these help people rise in their hierarchy of goals. Since people seem to depend on more information as they mature, economic demand naturally increases. We examine this phenomenon, as well the supply (production) side, paying particular attention to the impacts of technology on information overload. We then explore the implications for urban form, in part through the use of a model for integrating trends.

Potential Technologies

As mentioned above, it is almost impossible to foresee the kinds of information technologies that may evolve 10 to 20 years from now. Some ideas can be traced from those currently coming on the market, however, which is where we will start. Our concern is for the collection (or monitoring), storage and transmission of information.

Most of us are familiar with data base management systems (DBMSs). Data are organised into various fields, which subsequently allow for search, sorting, mathematical operations and display. Systems will be available shortly where DBMSs are just one part of an overall package which starts with collection or transmission (for example, from other DBMSs), modelling (with Visicalc for instance) and graphical presentation of the results. These results can become part of 'standardised' reports, aided in their creation by integrated word processing and report generation programmes.

On the immediate horizon are voice recognition programmes which can be translated in a variety of ways through natural language processing (NLP). Videotext and other similar systems will eventually supplement these by adding the visual dimension. Two-way cable TV and teleconferencing already are in operation.

Eventually, broader use can be made of all the human senses in collecting data. This includes touch and smell. Somehow these will be employed in concert in an 'integrated sensor machine' that enables collection and storage of sights, smells, words, sounds, touches and so on. These will be 'animated' in the sense they each will have a time dimension. Transmission of these then might be done by various types of holography. The implications for entertainment here are immense, and perhaps close to Aldous Huxley's (1932) visions of 'feelies' in *Brave New World*.

Gathering, storing and transmitting information somehow is technologically much easier than *using* it productively. This is demonstrated by our current capability to transmit up to 6 megabytes of data per second, but with few people knowing what to do with such a load when they are the recipients. Part of the answer apparently lies in new techniques for discriminant analysis (in the broad, not only statistical sense) and in decision support systems (DSS) aided by expert systems (or computer consulting systems — CCSs: Dickey 1983). The principle here is to set up procedures that help decision-makers wade through vast stores of information, pick out what is relevant to their situation, and use it effectively. A CCS, for instance, helps to show chains of logic (as well as associated probabilities) connecting decisions and external events to goals, so that the likelihood of the latter can be maximised. In this process, much reliance is placed on the knowledge of 'experts' who have had similar (but not necessarily identical) experiences.

In 10 to 20 years we would envisage that the vast 'gut' knowledge of experts (which includes any individual, since a person usually is most expert about his own life) will be tapped systematically by computer. This will enable individual decision-makers to draw future scenarios, evaluate these scenarios, and come to more-informed decisions as to which directions to take.[1]

It is unlikely information technologies will enable us to understand a larger *proportion* of happenings in the world. They will increase our absolute knowledge rather rapidly, but meanwhile cumulative knowledge will be growing (in absolute terms) even faster. This is demonstrated in part by a very perceptive relationship, proposed by Brotchie *et al.* (1979), where total utility, U, of goods and services, depends on the variety, S, of offerings of goods and services, the amount of variation, $(1/\lambda)$, in individual utilities, and the initial level of utility, $\bar{U}$:
$$U = S (1/\lambda) + \bar{U}.$$
From this it can be seen that it is in the interest of suppliers of goods and services (particularly of information technologies themselves) to increase S so as to raise consumers' overall utility, U. In other words, variety is the spice of life and much effort will be made to induce this variety at an increasing rate.

Life Goals and Resultant Demands

The psychologist, Abraham Maslow, is famous for proposing a five-level hierarchy of human goals that builds on the utility idea suggested above (Maslow 1970). Man generally starts by wanting to fulfill his basic needs — primarily the physiological ones of food and shelter — and then works up the ladder to safety, affiliation and eventually to esteem and self-actualisation. Some have surmised that Maslow would have proposed a sixth level of 'transcendentalism', where a person spends most of his time stepping outside and looking back at himself as well as at his relationships with others (see Clark 1979). Notice that the degree of consumption and communication of information increases markedly as a person goes up Maslow's hierarchy. In fact, the 'transcendental' level is in one sense the ultimate in information flow.

Maslow's hierarchy and its meaning can be debated, but it is fairly clear that most countries and cities are evolving through similar stages over long periods of time. Jones (1982) has given persuasive evidence that Australia (along with other advanced industrial societies) has gone through at least two phases, where primary industry (particularly agriculture) has become very small (in terms of employment), secondary industry (manufacturing) is losing employment rapidly, and even tertiary employment (e.g. retail) may have reached its apex. To follow, claims Jones, are increases in quaternary (information, analysis) and quinary sector (home personal services) employment. The point here is that urban areas are evolving roughly along Maslow's hierarchy and that this evolution will involve more and more information intensity (and subsequent demand).

Information in Production

No matter what the evolutionary stage, goods and services must be produced to meet demands (including the increased demand for information services themselves, as noted above). In the past economists have represented this supply facility through production functions involving components of land, labour and capital. It has been assumed that there is decreasing marginal productivity for increasing levels of inputs of each of these three factors of production (Samuelson 1973), as indicated in Figure 13.1.

This type of production function is inadequate for our analyses here

Figure 13.1 Standard Production Function

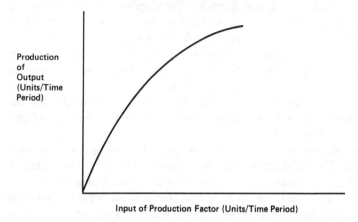

Figure 13.2 Revised Production Function

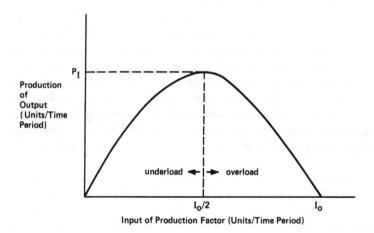

for two reasons. First, information in itself is not seen as a factor of production, when it obviously is an important input (as is expendable material). Secondly, the function displayed in Figure 13.1 allows us no absolute *decrease* in production if there is overabundance of an input factor (e.g. if labourers get in each other's way or if too much information is provided).

In an attempt to overcome these two problems we have examined a variety of new production functions. For simplicity of presentation, we have elected to employ the symmetric, parabolic form displayed in Figure 13.2 (for more sophisticated and theoretically acceptable versions, see the discussion in Chapter 7 by Nijkamp and Schubert). In our relationship, I_o is the 'crush' level of input where nothing is produced because of input overload. If we now take the four factors of production of land (L), labour (W), capital (C), and information (I), we can develop an *overall* production function which is a multiple of one shown in Figure 13.2.

No pretence is made that this imagined function gives an accurate portrayal of individual production processes, but it does help us identify some general results which occur when different types of information technologies come into effect. Special attention can be paid to situations which push the production function into the 'overload' area (past $I_o/2$ in Figure 13.2). As an example, an information technology (as, say, for traffic monitoring) that contributes mainly to the information gathering process (increases I) may increase productivity up to the point where I exceeds $I_o/2$. Thereafter productivity decreases.

Offsetting this, a data base management system (DBMS) or an enhanced graphics system mainly helps to increase I_o. In other words, while they might not add much to maximum productivity (P_I), they do allow us to absorb more information, thereby stretching out Figure 13.2 to the right. If we were in a situation where information overload were serious (Figure 13.3), we then might be able to drop back to the point where we were near the maximum productivity point (thereby increasing actual productivity). On the other hand, the DBMS actually might make us less productive if, for instance, we were on the underload side of the curve.

In a similar vein, an information system that adds considerably to our understanding of the information and therefore its more efficient utilisation should increase P_I (Figure 13.4) and be beneficial to production no matter the side of the curve (under or overload) on which we are located. An expert system (or CCS) might fall in this category (Dickey 1983).

A crucial aspect of information systems is their impact on other elements of production. If we assume that in the long run the value (price) of a factor reflects its marginal contribution to production, then unit cost coefficients can be obtained from our hypothetical production function. From our manipulations of simple mathematical representations of such functions we have found that information technologies that

Figure 13.3 Change in Production Function with Additional
Information Absorption Capabilities

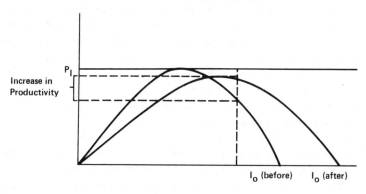

Figure 13.4 Change in Production Function with Additional
Maximum Productivity Capabilities

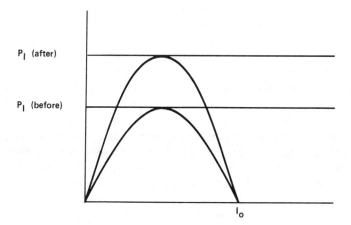

increase P_I, I, and I_o all tend to *increase* the value of labour. This is true
only, however, if $I \leq I_o/2$. If I goes into the overload range, say through
some overzealous information-gathering process using highly sophisticated technology, then wages for workers in the associated industry will
tend to fall (all other things being equal). Similar conclusions would
hold for the value (price) of land (particularly in urban areas). Note that
the unit price of labour is increased with technologies that increase P_I no
matter what the values of I and I_o.

Similar kinds of manipulation have helped us find that the unit price of labour, for instance, tends to increase as the unit cost of information increases, again up to the point where information overload takes place. Then there is a drop. Information technologies leading to overloads thus can have fairly disastrous effects on the prices of land, labour and capital and on productivity if they create excessive burdens on the production and decision-making process.

Implications for Urban Form

The preceding discussion on demand and supply now enables us to try to bring these concepts together to help identify a rough long-term equilibrium of consumption and values (prices). This conjoint has many implications for urban form, only some of which can be imagined, much less presented here.

If people do use information technologies to progress up Maslow's hierarchy and if these same technologies keep them out of overload realms in production, then we foresee a world much more attuned to self-gratification, sensualism and sensationalism. We also see an urban world that, because of the utility of greater variety, is much more dispersed than at present.

On a broader level, information technologies should help to spread the interconnections *between* cities (and nations). This would mean that many more of the factors which influence growth and change in cities will come not from within but from without. Decisions which affect, say, Toronto's future will come from offices in Calgary, San Francisco and Hong Kong, rather than from Toronto itself and Ottawa. The implications of this for local governance are, of course, serious. Local land use policies and controls like zoning, for instance, will be less likely to stand up against outside forces and therefore have less effect on the use of land.[2] Moreover, interactive TV will allow for much more local participation in decision-making processes (but with even less influence on the outcome).

On a suburban level, we see many more entertainment recreation areas, catering to the variety and sensualism suggested above. These 'erotic zones' also will provide some dwelling units for a number of individual and (increasingly) small family units seeking a widening spectrum of alternative life styles. Sports, particularly of the more violent type, will continue to increase in entertainment value, and more land will be set aside for these near the 'erotic zones'. Politics also will become more like entertainment, and less productive.

Since work in most cases will not involve physical labour, most will be performed in information handling and personal services. A large part, we feel, will be in providing personal contact in the inevitable large number of situations where computers (in particular, their programmers) have messed up and/or failed to communicate. This will happen more frequently because, in an attempt to increase utility through variety, manufacturers will increase the diversity of their information/computer technologies and actually make it *more* difficult to make them compatible.

'Work', meanwhile, will take on a somewhat different definition, with many people paid to create variety in information or, on the other hand, to try to understand it and make it compatible. Some of this 'work' will be done in the 'erotic zones' since the 'information' will be of the 'touch, feel, smell, hear, see' type (mostly with a lot of sex and violence). The 'erotic zones' thus will be new nuclei of entertainment and sports areas, with some work and dwelling sites intermixed. Much of the remaining information work will be done at home. This will increase social isolation because impersonal information networks obviously will be highly expanded. Moreover, because impersonality breeds violence, which will be further aggravated by the new heights of exotic violence portrayed in the 'erotic zones', small clusters of highly protected housing blocks will evolve. These will be something like feudal villages, built for security and privacy, with the exception that they will be able to keep contact with the whole world through computer information and communications technologies. Perhaps they also will harbour a hierarchy of 'lords' of information, served by 'uninformed' (but protected) local serfs.

Because of fuel-saving technologies, increased individual quests for variety, and lingering dissatisfaction with information technologies in reproducing 'reality' within the home, there will be a continuing increase in travel. Most, however, will be to far-away places rather than those nearby in the city, since these already would have been explored. This means that there will be little tradeoff between communication and transportation, but rather increases in both. In fact, rises in capabilities for communication and transportation will allow the start of sizeable extraterrestial colonies. Even now, there are serious proposals for small stations for manufacturing in space. In 10 to 20 years we may see the beginning of small cities in space — the ultimate variety in urban living.

Some Model Investigations

The preceding discussion represents only one scenario. Several others have been developed by Newton and Taylor (see Chapter 23) and employed to help explore the impact of various technologies on selected urban conditions such as activity dispersion, residential density, leisure space and traffic congestion. Their schematic for a major portion of the model is presented in Figure 23.4.

The assumption is made that the rate of change in an internal factor (one influenced by another, i.e. having an in-arrow) in any time period depends on: (1) rates of change of other internal influencing factors in the preceding time interval; (2) rates of change of external influencing factors in the current time interval; and (3) rates of change in the unique factor for the internal factor. The unique factor is analogous to an error term in regression, representing all other influencing factors not directly specified. This type of general model was run recursively for a 17-year time horizon (1983-2000) for conditions felt to be relevant to Melbourne.

As can be seen in Figure 23.4, information technology (near the lower right hand corner) is seen as directly influencing employment in tertiary and quaternary industries and subsequently through the chain of interconnections to urban activities and their space usage. Each factor is taken to start off at an index value of 100 and progress up or down from that level until the horizon year (2000).

From the results presented in Table 13.1 we can see that information technologies by themselves seem to have the largest impacts on spatial segregation, leisure space and population polarisation. The last is aspatial, referring to income and employment groups. The implications of this have been suggested by many people before; namely, that the gap will widen between the information 'haves' and 'havenots' and that this will be reflected in income and jobs. Spatial segregation (the second characteristic) subsequently should increase (as it does) since each social group will become more and more introverted as the members will have less in common with those in other groups. This will lead to the feudal 'information villages' alluded to earlier.

The significant *decrease* in leisure space may at first seem surprising. While the space does include the 'erotic zones' mentioned previously as well as outdoor recreation areas, we must realise that more *local* leisure will occur in the home or in the smaller 'erotic zones'. Spectators at sporting events like football, for instance, will take less space even though there will be more games being played. Most of the spectators

Table 13.1 Approximate Change[a] Brought About in Six Urban Characteristics by Technologies

Urban characteristic	Technology			
	Information	Computer	Telecom-munications	Fuel
Dispersion of activities	5	5	-15	-5
Spatial segregation	35	15	20	0
Residential density	-10	-5	20	5
Leisure space	-35	15	0	10
Traffic congestion	-5	-5	-75	-30
Polarisation of population	65	30	35	-5

Note: a. Expressed as % increase or decrease to the year 2000 from a base level of 100 in 1983.

will be at home or even in other countries. Crowd reactions, as incentives to players, will come mostly through remote interaction (such as two-way TV) which will be 'canned' and broadcast to players.

The large impact of telecommunications technologies on traffic congestion, with almost zero impact of information technologies, is particularly curious. One explanation, which fits with previously expressed ideas, is that telecommunications technologies will vastly increase *inter* city travel as people quest for a wider range of experiences, but that the time spent in these activities will be taken from that of *intra* city travel (thus decreasing urban congestion). Similarly, since more of the work and shopping will be done at home, with telecommunications providing the connections to the rest of the world, intracity trips will be less frequent and at more varied hours, again decreasing urban congestion.

Conclusions

The preceding results from the modelling effort seem to add weight to the evidence of the scenario suggested earlier in the paper. Basically, we see urban areas as becoming much more nodal; much more segregated between the information 'haves' and 'have nots'; much more attuned to the value of information-related goals in life (knowledge, wisdom); and as a result much more subject to 'information overload' as a prime health hazard. In fact, as a result, we envision mental health clinics and hospitals as rapidly replacing those for physical health.

This scenario does not take into account possible massive governmental interventions, however. Two would appear to be of great importance. They concern employment and income (and wealth) redistribution. The need for the former will come when the inevitable attempts to displace workers (including managerial) with technologies arise. Some employees will be absorbed into the information 'haves', but many others cannot. The question then is whether to create 'make work' or alternately allow the workers to simply spend their life finding various means of entertainment (in the erotic zones for example). The former alternate is simply one means of redistribution. If the latter action is taken, however, the question of redistribution will become more directly important. If none is carried out, polarisation might increase even more vigorously than we have suggested in this paper. The result could be a harmful political/social backlash or even revolution. On the other hand, if redistribution is great, the information 'haves' may revolt in protest over their lack of reward for their contribution to production (primarily of information).

Samuelson (1973) presents an interesting observation that may bear on this age-old dilemma. He has found that over the last 100 years or so (as far back as data allow), technology has had the impact of adjusting for those prices of factors of production which become exorbitant. For instance, if land becomes very expensive relative to labour, then landsaving technologies tend to evolve and be employed rapidly.[3] In this way the path of economic production is smoothed appreciably. Could it be that, likewise, information technologies will contribute to an equivalent 'smoothing' over time, resulting in more 'productive' life for us, as measured say, in progress up Maslow's hierarchy? We can only be hopeful.

Notes

1. Since such systems could be very personal, the likelihood of invasion of privacy could be increased substantially, possibly creating a whole new level of regulatory action.

2. These situations also point to the need for urban models which focus more on external (to the area under study) factors than on internal ones.

3. Samuelson (1973) even states, surprisingly, that land saving technologies have been such that land worldwide is not much of a consideration in production.

References

Brotchie, J.F., Lesse, P.F. and Roy, J.R. (1979) 'Entropy, Utility and Planning Models', *Sistemi Urbani*, 3:33-53

Clark, B. (1979) *Growing Up Gifted*, Charles Merrill Inc., Columbus, Ohio

Dickey, J.W. (1983) 'Computer Consultant Systems', paper for the International Conference on New Directions in Urban Modelling, Waterloo, Canada, July

Huxley, A. (1932) *Brave New World*, Harper and Row, New York

Jones, B. (1982) *Sleepers, Wake!, Technology and the Future of Work*, Oxford University Press, Melbourne

Maslow, A.H. (1970) *Motivation and Personality*, Harper and Row, London

Masuda, Y. (1983) *The Information Society as Post-Industrial Society*, World Future Society, Bethesda, Maryland

Samuelson, P.J. (1973) *Economics* (9th edn), McGraw Hill, New York

Webber, M.J. (1982) *Information Theory and Urban Spatial Structure*, Croom Helm, London

14. TELESHOPPING AND RETAIL LOCATION
R. Sharpe and J. Roy

The likely impacts of technological change, especially electronic information systems, on retailing have aroused widespread interest and speculation. The technological change expected to have the greatest impact on the location and form of retail stores is so-called electronic shopping.

Electronic shopping has existed in a primitive way for some time in the form of radio and TV advertising of merchandise coupled with telephone ordering. It is part of a segment of the market called non-store retailing (NSR) which also includes the long-established mail-ordering systems, home inspection systems and door-to-door sales. A research executive of a large department store chain has estimated that 15-20 per cent of purchases in Australia will be by NSR by 1990 and that half of this will be by electronic NSR. Consumers are expected to have unprecedented quantities of up-to-date information available to guide their product selection, for example, price, specifications, availability and consumer reports on performance. Home computers may be programmed to sort through the data to suit personal needs.

Home shopping is expected to reduce both customer and store labour involved in obtaining low-interest standard items such as food and groceries. The effort of searching supermarket aisles, reading the labels on prepackaged goods, making selections, waiting in check-out queues and driving to and from the store might be replaced by use of home video and computer-based information systems, and electronic payment. This would also reduce the need for goods display in stores and the labour involved in maintaining such displays.

More costly consumer durables such as white goods, clothing, cars, furniture and even housing, might be sought and evaluated via the same system, before making visits to stores or showrooms for a final check. As the quality of electronic information systems improve, travel to shops is expected to decline unless shopping centres take on other functions, such as entertainment which is occurring in North America. One example of home shopping that has already become well established is shopping for travel and some recreation. It is relatively easy now to book extensive travel, holiday and entertainment packages without visiting a travel or booking agent. The introduction of the Prestel teletext system in the UK has proved popular for this purpose.

Historical Perspective

This section considers how traditional forces acting on retail stores have shaped their location patterns, and then estimates the impacts of technological change.

In early towns a central market-place provided urban dwellers with one-stop shopping convenience and an ability to compare similar goods by different sellers in close proximity. As cities have grown, outer consumers have shown a preference for decentralised shopping by trading-off travel costs against range of goods. Firms have been able to partially offset their increased transport costs from the central market by reduced location rents in outer areas. Warehouses have increasingly moved outwards.

In addition to providing benefits of one-stop convenience and comparison of goods, clustering of shops has also tended to occur at points of high accessibility (for example, at transport nodes). As transport technology has changed over time, from pedestrian, horse and cart, rail and finally to private car, the transport nodes and associated commercial clusters have also changed character and location.

Over the last 30 years some significant changes have occurred in the location and form of urban retail outlets (Berry 1980). In the 1950s, the rapid outward residential growth moved the focus of market demand away from traditional CBD (Central Business District) centres. As retailing and employment followed residential movement, the CBD centres suffered a dramatic decline in market share. Berry (1980) summarises the developments that occurred in the US:

> First came the planned shopping centre, an architecturally unified development with off-street parking, owned and managed as a unit, to replace the individual business establishment as the development entity. These were rapidly differentiated by size of market into neighbourhood, community, and regional types standardized by major chains and franchisers, and then differentiated again by market segment into discounters, theme centres, and the like. Since the mid-1960s has come yet another technological innovation, that of the 1 million square foot (100,000 square metre) leaseable area regional mall offering an enclosed environment for shopping, entertainment and recreation — a distinctively American piazza.

However, Berry sees that the future is against further development of these superregional malls in the US, where their costs have escalated due to building delays arising from adverse environmental and political impacts. Instead the focus is now on smaller centres and stores which are better integrated into urban development. These include redevelopment projects with mixed shopping and other uses, such as commercial, recreational, residential, convention, entertainment, and tourism developments. Many of these are occurring in CBD (downtown) areas.

In Australia a similar pattern of retail suburbanisation and regional shopping centres has emerged (Edgington 1982; Jenkin 1981) although the pace and scale of development have been less than in North America. There has also been a recent backlash against large shopping centres, and the latest planning policy is to integrate shopping into the urban fabric to maximise total community benefits in terms of economic efficiency, energy, equity, environment, employment, land-use infrastructure and transport (*Report of the Technical Advisory Committee on Retailing*, 1980). The large regional shopping centres cannot meet many of these criteria, especially with regard to energy efficiency and equity of access, as these shopping centres are oriented towards automobile owners and generally discriminate against public transport and pedestrian access. Hence there is some move back towards more localised centres with good public transport access, and low infrastructure requirements, but higher land rents.

In the UK the pattern of new retailing development has mainly been sited in traditional town-centre locations since the outward forces favouring suburbanisation of retailing have been strongly resisted (Bennison and Davies 1980). However, much debate has occurred about the benefits of out-of-town schemes, as the town-centre developments have had some adverse environmental and economic impacts. Pacione (1979) reviews these arguments in some depth and concludes that in-town hypermarket developments, especially if located in redevelopment areas, could have higher net positive benefits compared with out-of-town developments. Bennison and Davies conclude that while it is difficult to predict the next ten to fifteen years, they think that any future changes will only tend to reinforce the role of traditional town centre retail areas.

Comparison Shopping and Clustering

Hotelling (1929) examined the clustering of two homogenous firms in a linear market (such as two ice-cream sellers on a beach). The equilibrium solution occurs when the two sellers set up together at the centre of the beach. Hotelling considered this wasteful since a socially optimal solution in terms of minimising consumer travel costs would occur if the sellers set up separately at the quarter points. However from a seller's profit-maximising point of view this would be unstable since each could increase their market share by moving towards the centre (assuming that consumer demand was inelastic to transport cost changes).

Subsequent researchers, including Eaton and Lipsey (1979), have indicated that clustering is not as socially wasteful as claimed by Hotelling if there is some variation in price or quality requiring consumers to make comparisons between goods offered by different firms. In the example above, the total travel would increase if the ice-cream consumers wished to compare goods offered by the two sellers located at points other than the centre.

Eaton and Lipsey have examined the case of a linear market with N stores where the number of stores, S. visited by customers before a purchase is made is greater than one. They present results for the case S=2 and indicate that these results extend in a direct and obvious way to cases where S>2. Their basic model assumes the following:

a linear market of length one unit;
customers are spread along the market at uniform density;
all customers purchase an identical quantity of goods and wish to minimise their total distance travelled;
after sampling two stores the customer returns to his base and costlessly orders and receives his chosen good;
the probability that a customer who samples any store actually makes a purchase from that store is one-half;
all stores have the same cost function made up of a constant fixed cost, K, and a variable cost of v per unit output TC = K + v Q v<1;
all stores charge the same exogenously imposed price, although comparison shopping for price is shown to be easily accommodated (the fixed-price assumption allows the model to concentrate on the locational aspect and to neglect non-price factors (e.g. quality of goods, delivery and servicing arrangements) of competition between firms);
each firm owns only one store;
stores are separated at least by a small arbitrary distance, δ;
in choosing its location, each firm assumes that others will not move except after a long time lag, if at all;
firms seek to maximise their expected profits, that is, to maximise their sales. The second and fifth assumptions imply that sales are maximised by maximising the length of the market segment over which customers sample the firm.

Figure 14.1 Equilibrium Store Configurations in a Uniform
Linear Market (a) two-store search before
purchase (after Eaton and Lipsey), (b) single store
search before purchase

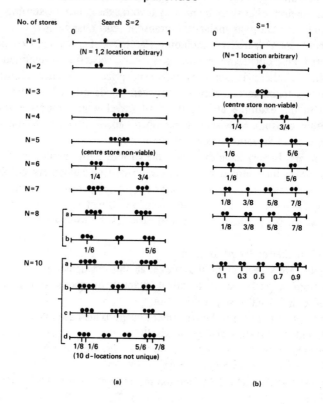

(a)   (b)

Eaton and Lipsey then show that under equilibrium conditions, where
no firm can unilaterally relocate to increase its profits (a Nash
equilibrium):

peripheral firms must be grouped in at least a triplet;
no single grouping contains more than four firms;
no firm can be unpaired;
the market area of each grouping extends half the distance to the
neighbouring group on either side;
no firm's whole-market segment can be less than any other firm's half-
market segment;

the location of triplets and quartets is uniquely determined at the midpoints of the market they serve;
the location of any pair that is neither the second nor the penultimate group is not unique within its interval.

Figure 14.1a shows the configurations thus derived for different numbers of firms from $N=1$ to $N=8$ and $N=10$. The configurations are unique for $N<8$ and non-unique for $N \geq 8$ (e.g. $N=8$ has 2 while $N=10$ has 4). The last configuration in the $N=10$ case also has non-unique locations for the triplets within the ranges 1/8 to 1/6, 5/6 to 7/8, and for the pairs within 1/6 to 1/2, 1/2 to 5/6. An interesting case is $N=5$ where the centre store is non-viable, so that a jump should occur from $N=4$ to $N=6$.

Eaton and Lipsey state that as δ approaches its minimum value for triplets, the centre store has twice the custom of each of its flanking stores. This implies that there is a continuing incentive for the outer stores of a cluster to move into the central position. Once the stores have moved as close as *physically* possible, they could be *perceived* by the customers as *indistinguishable* in accessibility properties, particularly if the average distance to the shops from residences is several orders of magnitude greater than δ. In this case, the custom would be equally divided between the members of any cluster. This situation would imply, for instance, that for $N=3$ and $N=4$, the position of the clusters would be arbitrary (as for $N=2$), unless the stores are also selling some goods for which comparison is not required, that is $S=1$, in which case they would move to the centre. Also, it would allow the $N=5$ case to become viable. Note also that once δ reduced to the point that adjacent stores are indistinguishable in location by customers, the market shares would *suddenly* become equal. This cluster would also be *stable*, as any store moving unilaterally out beyond this δ threshold would suddenly have its profits reduced.

Optimality

Eaton and Lipsey state that a socially optimal distribution of firms in an $S=2$ comparison shopping model, that is, the one which minimises the total cost of travel between customers and firms, would result if firms were grouped into pairs (similar to the even-numbered configurations in Figure 14.1b, or pairs plus one triplet in odd-numbered configurations). While the equilibrium configurations shown in Figure 14.1a are not socially optimal, they are more optimal for $S=2$ than a configuration of single firms spaced equally except in the cases of $N=1$ and $N=2$ if the

Table 14.1 Clustering of Stores in Melbourne into Suburban Groups

	Supermarkets			Department Stores		
	No. groups	No. stores	%	No. groups	No. stores	%
Quartets	4	16	9	3	12	12
Triplets	10	30	17	8	24	24
Pairs	33	66	38	13	26	26
Singles	62	62	36	38	38	38
Totals	109	174	100	62	100	100

Source: Melbourne Telephone Directory 1983

stores are not centrally located. It is also interesting to note that the least desirable solution, i.e. the one which maximises customer travel costs, occurs when the number of groups is minimised.

Shopping Centres

The configurations derived in Figure 14.1a occur when firms act as individuals in the market without co-operative behaviour. Eaton and Lipsey point out that it is in the interests of individual firms to set up in pairs to maximise their profits for a given location, and this typically occurs in the development of shopping centres under the control of a single firm. It is common in these cases for the first store to positively encourage competitors (often of varying sizes) to set up in the same centre. The number of competitors ideally should be matched to the search value S, in order to avoid excess capacity and inefficiency.

Empirical Evidence

As a test of the above theory, a brief examination of clustering of supermarkets and department stores in the Melbourne area was made from telephone directory information and yielded the suburban groupings shown in Table 14.1.

While these figures are only approximate due to definitional problems and incomplete telephone listings, they lend support to the Eaton and Lipsey model as more than 60 per cent of stores in each case were grouped, and no grouping greater than four was detected. It is also interesting to note that these market equilibrium solutions show a strong preference for pairs (33 and 13 groups) ahead of quartets (4,3) and triplets (10, 8) indicating that these markets tend to be at the socially optimal end of the spectrum of possible configurations (cf. Figure 14.1a).

Dynamics

Figure 14.1a implies an interesting dynamic growth pattern for a small town growing into a large city. A town could be seen to start with a centrally located single store which is joined by competitors as the town grows. Initially we could consider the town to have a fixed unit length with growth reflected in increasing population density, and the number of stores being proportional to that population density. After N=4, a split into two centres appears appropriate. However it is unlikely that the existing centre will suddenly disappear as depicted in Figure 14.1a. Due to high relocation costs, one alternative is that the original centre would remain and a new centre will be formed on the dominant growth side.

A second alternative is that the old centre declines while two new centres spring up either side if population growth is symmetric. This may be likened to the 'doughnut' growth characteristic of cities in the US and also to a lesser extent of cities in other developed countries.

After further growth (N≥8) the new centres might be seen as growing outwards towards the periphery (from 1/4 to 1/6 to 1/8 positions). Also newer in-between growth would occur (N=8b; N=10a, 10b, 10c). In the case of the previous 'doughnut' alternative, this in-between growth might be a redevelopment of the original centre.

These dynamics may appear artificial, since the length of the market is assumed constant and the population density uniform. However, if the length of the market is allowed to grow with population and store growth, then the configurations produced will be similar. The assumption of constant population density may also be relaxed by applying a transformation (linear or exponential) to the horizontal scale.

Extensions to the Eaton-Lipsey Model

Technological Change

The introduction of electronic shopping is expected to have two major impacts. First it will partly reduce the need for physical inspection of goods where superior information on the goods can be obtained electronically. Secondly, it will expand the quantity and variety of goods available to customers since they may search through large electronic inventories more conveniently than physically searching through a store.

The first impact will reduce the number of store visits required per item. The second impact has a less clear outcome since, like the introduction of the telephone, it may entice the customer to search for a more diverse set of goods in more distant places. In this case the shopping may contain an element of entertainment. However the overall trend is expected to be one of reducing the number of store visits for each item being purchased.

It is then interesting to look at the cases of $S=1$ and $S=0$. Figure 14.1b is developed for the case $S=1$ using the simple Hotelling approach and shows that equilibrium configurations now include only singles and pairs, with single stores only appearing when N is odd, and then only once. In this case ($S=1$) and for $N>1$ the social inefficiency of the system is quite clear as customers must now travel twice as far on average than if the stores were evenly spaced. It is interesting to note that the even numbered $S=1$ solutions are socially optimal for the $S=2$ case as discussed earlier. At $N=3$, the centre store is non-viable according to Eaton and Lipsey for the same reason in the $N=5$, $S=2$ case. However it becomes viable if at $\delta=0$ the market is shared equally by the stores in the triplet.

At $S=0$, there are no customer store visits, and hence store locations will be decided by other factors such as delivery-to-customer costs, site rental costs, economies of scale and delivery-from-wholesaler costs. If delivery-to-customer costs were dominant, then the stores would be evenly spaced (which is the social optimum for $S=1$).

Ring Markets

The homogeneous line market assumption is only realistic in the case of a linear city. A first step in relaxing this assumption is to consider the case of a ring market, with customers only wishing to travel circumferentially and not radially. This scenario might be seen as a simplification of an automobile dominated city with a relatively uncongested ring road and highly congested radial routes.

A city might be considered as composed of a concentric set of independent rings with the CBD being the ring of smallest diameter. A feature of the ring system is that there is no peripheral market along the ring, unlike the linear case. Hence the condition for peripheral triplets disappears.

Figure 14.2 shows the set of configurations generated for $S=2$ and different numbers of stores. Here the alternative market equilibrium

Figure 14.2 Equilibrium and Social Optimum Store
Configurations for a Ring Market with Two
Searches Before Purchase (S=2)
(Maximum customer return trip distance =
Max.)
(Average customer return trip distance = Av.)
(Length of circumference = 1)

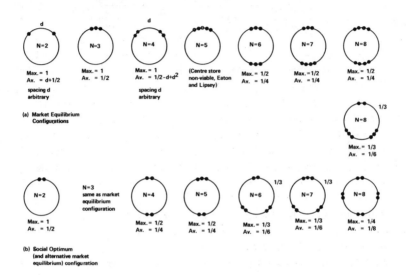

configurations are shown in (a) and (b), with (b) also representing social
optimum solutions. Important features are as follows:

all socially optimum solutions are also market equilibrium solutions,
unlike the linear market case;
at N=2, single stores are viable, with store owners being indifferent to
location while customers benefit most when they are located together;
at N=3 and N=5 there is only one market equilibrium solution which is
socially optimum;
N=4 is a paired version of the N=2 case;
at N=6,7 there are only 2 possible market solutions;
N≥8 there are more than 2 solutions possible;
social optimum solutions give greatest market equity to store owners,
and as in the linear case will only contain pairs in even-numbered cases,
or pairs plus one triplet in odd-numbered cases;

Figure 14.3 Ring Market Equilibrium Configurations for S=1
(Social optimum solutions occur when stores are
equally spaced)

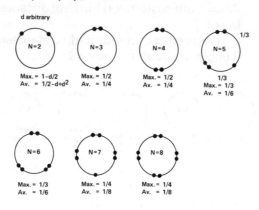

the ring market prediction of a greater predominance of pairs than the linear market is more in line with the empirical evidence shown in Table 14.1. For example, the following percentages are obtained for the linear and ring markets by aggregating solutions over the range N=2 to N=8:

Linear market   0 singles   11 pairs   47 triplets   42 quartets
Ring market   0 singles   75 pairs   25 triplets   0 quartets
(social optimum only)
Ring market   3 singles   46 pairs   39 triplets   12 quartets
(all solutions)

Figure 14.3 illustrates the market equilibrium solutions for S=1. Here there is only one configuration for each N case, and these will be different to the social optimum solutions except when d=1/2 for N=2.

Planning Implications

The implications of the configurations shown in the figures are significant from a planning viewpoint:

First, S=2. In the linear case, the market solutions are not socially optimal except for N=3 and perhaps for N≤2. Hence planning authorities would need to manipulate the market, for example, through planning controls and incentives, to force a socially optimal solution.

Table 14.2 Minimum Number of Store Relocations Required
for Technological Change in Form of Progressive
Reduction of S=2 to S=1 to S=0

| | Linear market | | Ring market | |
	S=2→1	S=1→0	S=2→1	S=1→0
N=2	0	2	0	0
N=3	0	2	1	2
N=4	4	4	0	2
N=5	5	4	3	4
N=6	6	6	0	3
N=7	7	7	5	6
N=8	8	8	0	4
Total	30	33	9	21

On the other hand, the ring market gives socially optimal solutions which are also market equilibrium solutions. Some minimal planning intervention may still be required to ensure stores select a socially optimal configuration in each case. The latter is achieved without any loss to individual stores if custom is equally shared in each cluster. Hence for $S=2$, ring solutions are preferable to linear solutions.

Secondly, $S=1$. Both the linear and ring market equilibrium configurations are different to the social optimum configurations in each case, with neither form showing any advantage over the other (except for minor differences at $N \leqslant 3$). For $N>3$ the ring configurations are the same as those obtained if the linear market was converted into a ring.

Progressive Technological Change

If we assume that electronic comparison of goods gradually takes over from physical inspection so that the value of S progressively reduces from $S=2$ to $S=1$ and then to $S=0$, the minimum relocations that would be required are shown in Table 14.2.

In this case the ring market is the more robust to technological change in the form proposed, especially from $S=2$ to $S=1$ which is likely to be the dominant change in the medium term. This also provides a good starting point from a planning viewpoint, as it would enable planners who had complete control over the entry and location of stores into the market to set up an optimum final configuration.

The introduction of more complex behaviour on the part of stores and individuals, coupled with dynamics of growth, will most probably lead to models which may be analytically intractable, and could only be solved by computer simulation (as Eaton and Lipsey have stressed in their paper).

Two-Dimensional Cities

While the above discussion is limited to a study of linear and ring cities, it is interesting to extend it to two-dimensional cities with transport networks as depicted in the examples shown in Figure 14.4.

Radial Cities

The linear model extends readily to the radial case (Figure 14.4a) when the number of radial spokes is even and the customer density is inversely proportional to distance from the centre (Figure 14.5). In this case, each pair of adjacent arcs may be regarded as an independent linear market with a bend in the centre (Figure 14.5). Hence the configurations shown in Figure 14.1 may be transformed into the patterns shown in Figure 14.6 for the case of four radial arcs. In the case of $N=10$ and $S=2$, the two centre stores on the inside of the triplets will only be viable if the Eaton and Lipsey assumptions are relaxed, as discussed earlier. The radial solutions now produce clusters with greater than four stores in the case of $S=2$, and this is at variance with the earlier empirical evidence, and our intuition. In reality, congestion may rule against clusters containing more than four stores, and hence it might be necessary to include congestion in a more realistic model. Once again the store relocations that would be required for a technological change that reduced $S=2$ to $S=1$ can be seen.

Multi-ring Cities

In this case the stores have freedom to move between the rings as well as around the rings. It is assumed that customers only travel around their closest ring, and do not move between rings. The first step of the analysis is to assume that the stores apportion themselves between the rings to obtain an equal market share. Then the procedure shown in Figures 14.2 and 14.3 can be used to determine store locations around each ring.

Multi-centred Cities

If the linkages between the centres are relatively weak, then each centre may be treated in isolation and analysed according to its particular transport network pattern, for example, radial or ring, as above. If the

Figure 14.4 Other City Shapes to Which Analysis May be Extended

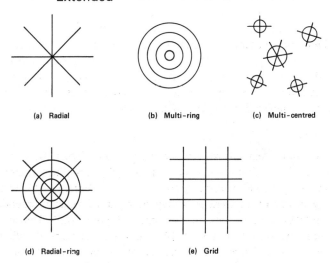

(a) Radial   (b) Multi-ring   (c) Multi-centred

(d) Radial-ring   (e) Grid

linkages between centres are not weak, then computer simulation may be necessary, with the 'weak linkage' analysis in the preceding case providing a good starting solution.

Radial-ring and Grid Cities

Once again these may be approximated in terms of the radial and ring configurations above. Nodes in these gridded networks might be assumed to have independent behaviour as in the multi-centred city if the grid spacing is sufficiently large. The number of stores apportioned to each node would be proportional to the market share in the region of each node. The detailed location in the vicinity of each node would then be undertaken using procedures outlined in radial and multi-ring city types. If the nodes on the grid are not relatively independent, then it may be necessary to use a simulation model, possibly including a hierarchy of nodes, store types and roads.

Other Aspects of Technological Change

The impact of technological change on the distribution of goods may also affect the location of production centres, distribution networks and

Figure 14.5 Symmetrical Radial Markets
      (a) may be split into independent linear market
          with a bend at the centre
      (b) customer density is assumed inversely
          proportional to distance from centre, thus
          giving a constant number of customers per
          unit length of market

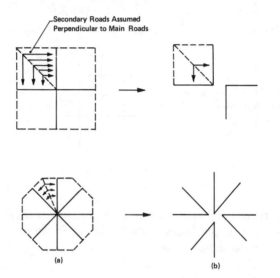

(a)

(b)

Figure 14.6 Examples of a Radial Market for Searches of
            S=2 and S=1

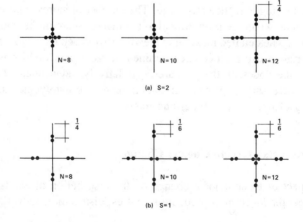

consumer location. In a recent report on the likely impact of videotext and teletext, Tydeman *et al.* (1982) conclude that:

> since production may be triggered electronically [as a result of consumer demand], geographic location becomes irrelevant at the time of the choice of purchase [unless the transportation costs and time delays for receipt of product are significant] . . . New demands will be placed on the efficiency and timeliness of the delivery system.

Tydeman *et al.* also forecast a return of home delivery with intelligent home computers taking over the role of looking after family needs. Home computers might be preprogrammed to monitor household stock levels and family preferences for different items, and then to scan the available outlets for the 'best buys', making an order, arranging delivery and electronic payment. The mail service (the only remaining widespread home delivery service) might be expanded to become a delivery vehicle for other products. However, they conclude that the shopping centre will not necessarily disappear. Instead it may take on a more diverse mix of services including entertainment and recreational services, and the purchase of non-routine goods which will be displayed physically, electronically or both.

Wigan (Chapter 11) examines the interaction of transport and communications from a household expenditure viewpoint. He concludes that for Australia and the UK, transport is remaining static in terms of the percentage of household expenditure in time and money, whereas communication is rapidly increasing in both modes. While the two modes are at present complementary, it is expected that they will become more competitive in terms of household expenditure in time and money as they become more nearly equal. It is not clear at this stage whether the two modes will compete for a fixed or variable share of the household budget. This is an area that requires further research.

The variation in the number of comparisons, S, with the diversity of the goods required is another interesting area for further study. Simple homogenous goods, such as milk, require little comparison (S small). More complex or diverse goods such as durables require additional comparison or a potentially larger value of S. Increasing diversity of goods and services requires increasing quantities of information for adequate comparison. However, electronic information systems appear to provide the means for achieving this comparison while the number S of stores actually visited is reduced.

Discussion

The above approach is very useful in providing insight into the general nature of expected locational adjustments to various technological and other changes. In an actual planning context, one will often be confronted with less uniform locational patterns, different types of externalities and uncertainties about firms' perceptions of their own best actions in relation to uncertainty in the expected behaviour of their rivals. Thus, there exists a need for further models which incorporate these factors, but at the same time allow an interface with policy decisions required to permit the market to operate more efficiently and equitably. An early attempt to develop models to consider some of these factors is contained in the work of Harris and Wilson (1978). Recently, Roy *et al.* (1983) have made further progress in this area.

The features which such models are attempting to cover include: external factors such as the utilisation of public infrastructure, and income distribution; uncertainty due to lack of information on future market growth and competition; inertia in customer, competitor and developer response; behavioural effects such as preference of customers for different attributes of centres, and changes in these preferences with time and technological change; and differing objectives of the various parties involved including the community. In order to forecast the effects of technological and other changes, and to plan for their effects, these various factors must be taken into account.

References

Bennison, D.J. and Davies, R.L. (1980) 'The Legacy of Town Centre Shopping Schemes in Britain', Proceedings of the Planning and Transport Research and Computation Annual Summer Meeting, P190, 75-85

Berry, B.J.L. (1980) 'Forces Reshaping the Settlement System' in H.J. Bryce (ed) *Cities and Firms*, Lexington, Massachusetts

Eaton, B.C. and Lipsey, R.G. (1979) 'Comparison Shopping and Clustering of Homogeneous Firms', *Journal of Regional Science*, **19**, 421-35

Edgington, D.W. (1982) 'Organizational and Technological Change and the Future Role of the Central Business District: An Australian Example', *Urban Studies*, **19**, 281-92

Harris, B. and Wilson, A.G. (1978) 'Equilibrium Values and Dynamics of Attractiveness Terms in Production-constrained Spatial Interaction Models', *Environment and Planning A*, **10**, 371-88

Hotelling, J. (1929) 'Stability in Competition', *Economic Journal*, **39**, 41-57

Jenkin, D.H. (1981) 'Information Technology in Retailing' in A.W. Godsworthy (ed.) *Technological Change — Impact on Information Technology*, AGPS Canberra

Pacione, M. (1979) 'The In-Town Hypermarket: An Innovation in the Geography of Retailing', *Regional Studies*, **13**, 15-24

Report of the Technical Advisory Committee on Retailing 1980 (1983) A Report submitted to the Victorian Government and the Melbourne Metropolitan Board of Works, Government Printer, Melbourne

Roy, J.R., Johansson, B. and Leonardi, G. (1983) 'Some Equilibria in Location of Retail Facilities with Uncertain Demand', paper presented at 8th Pacific Regional Science Council Meeting, Tokyo, August

Tydeman, J., Lipinski, H., Adler, R.P., Nyham, M., and Zwimpfer, L. (1982) *Teletext and Videotext in the United States*, McGraw-Hill, New York

15. INFORMATION TECHNOLOGY AND URBAN PLANNING
P. Nijkamp

Spatial Dynamics

Cities and regions have never exhibited a static pattern, but have always been in a state of flux (cf. Robson 1973). In the past decade however, spatial dynamics has shown an acceleration due to the impact of new technology. Rapid transit systems, microelectronics, telecommunications and energy-saving measures have had profound consequences for the spatial organisation of our world.

Whereas conventional spatial analysis has been concerned primarily with *location*, modern spatial analysis has increasingly addressed *movement* or *allocation* questions (see also Lowe and Moryades 1975), with the analysis of dynamic spatial processes clearly coming to the fore.

Current spatial dynamics does not display one unambiguous spatial and urban pattern however. Contrasting developments take place, varying between continuing suburbanisation and increasing popularity of compact city patterns. These diffuse spatial changes involve many conflicting issues in urban planning and policy (cf. Nijkamp and Rietveld 1981). Examples include: socio-psychological benefits of a dispersed settlement pattern versus increased interaction costs (due to increases in transportation and energy costs); frictions between various kinds of land use inside and outside the city (e.g. residential land use, recreation, industry); social and economic disintegration of the urban space (segregation, separation of working and residential places); disequilibrium tendencies in the urban housing and labour market; and new emphasis on industrial redevelopment versus a rapid increase of the quaternary sector.

Technology seems to stimulate many of these drastic spatial changes, but has not yet provided the means to tackle the resultant problems. This situation is likely to intensify in the years to come, as modern technology is very much oriented towards interaction and (tele-)communication (see Pred 1977; also Meier, Chapters 6, 9) and where major spatial shifts may be expected from the modern microelectronics revolution. This development forces spatial analysis to move to another phase, one concerned with *interaction* and *communication*.

Though in many cases social and face-to-face contacts are still necessary, it is also evident that an avalanche of information and communication systems is emerging that will have a profound impact on spatial mobility patterns. First signs of such spatial impacts can already be observed in multi-plant companies, and shifts in settlement and mobility patterns in other parts of society are expected to emerge.

Identification of key factors in such trends is difficult. Sometimes urban change processes may be determined by general technological factors (e.g. automation), but in other cases urban forms may be affected by specific urban technologies (e.g. underground rapid transit systems). Clearly, the resulting urban pattern is a multi faceted phenomenon, as it is simultaneously co-determined by industrial, residential, transportation, architectural, recreational and institutional factors. It is no surprise that urban planning has great difficulty in keeping pace with all these diverse developments.

Urban Planning and Information Systems

Urban planning may be regarded as any public activity (or set of activities) that aims at achieving certain — often pre-specified — goals for a city or a system of cities. In this broad context, urban planning may encompass various components such as: economic and industrial planning; land use planning; manpower and labour market planning; housing planning; transportation planning; infrastructure planning; financial planning; environmental planning; energy planning; social planning; facilities planning; and technology planning.

It is evident, especially in a era of transition and drastic change, that urban planning has to be supported by adequate *information systems*. Modern technology (computer hardware and software, microelectronics, videosystems, telecommunications systems and the like) has led to an information explosion and has offered great potential for handling information in a logical and well-structured way (see also Burch *et al.* 1979; Debons and Larson 1983).

The need for proper information emerged from the lack of insight into complex dynamic spatial processes, the social costs incurred by ineffective public decisions, the interest conflicts among decision agencies ('information is power'), the enormous data production by many statistical offices (both private and public), the increased use of econometric and statistical techniques in planning and policy-making, and the accessibility of modern computer equipment.

Until very recently, however, many information systems were global in nature, for example, by focusing attention on national levels of information or specific sectors of the economy (such as housing or labour markets). Local and urban information systems have been developed in various cities and regions, but many of these systems are partial and do not present a coherent and integrated picture of a local or urban system. It is important to pay more explicit attention to (urban) information systems for two reasons. First, cities display a dynamic pattern that is co-determined by modern (information) technology, while at the same time urban dynamics has various impacts on modern (information) technology. Secondly, modern (information) technology is providing the tools for understanding urban dynamics in a more appropriate manner (for instance, by means of adaptive computerised information systems, computer consulting systems).

An urban information system is a set of data structured (for instance, by way of modelling, organising or converting data) so as to increase the insight or level of knowledge regarding the spatial dimensions of urban phenomena, especially from the viewpoint of forecasting and influencing urban structures and processes. The present chapter emphasises the significance of such information systems for urban planning and policy-making in an era of transition.

Urban information systems can be developed in urban planning and policy-making for three purposes: description, impact analysis and evaluation (Nijkamp and Rietveld 1984). *Description* is a systematic analysis and representation of the characteristics of a spatial system based, for instance, on a multi-dimensional profile representation in a systems analytic approach (Nijkamp 1979); a clear typology of targets, instruments and predetermined variables has to be made. An example of a computerised information system can be found in Peters (1981).

Impact analysis is a systematic assessment of foreseeable and expected consequences of changes in exogenous circumstances (e.g. technological change) or of policy measures for the state of the urban system (e.g. environmental management); impact analysis may be useful for making (conditional) forecasts of the endogenous development of an urban system.

Evaluation is a systematic investigation of alternative policy plans, proposals or projects with the aim of identifying their comparative advantages and disadvantages (e.g. by means of programming analysis or multi-criteria analysis), taking into account prevailing external constraints.

The following aspects have an important bearing on urban information systems (cf. Willis 1972): the spatial interactions and spillover effects of a dynamic and open urban system; the spatial scale of measurement of the various variables and profiles included in the information system; the urban problem orientation of the information provided by the system concerned; the connection between urban information systems and urban and regional planning and policy-making; the consequences of various spatial institutional policy levels (e.g. in a hierarchical setting, or in a bottom-up vs top-down structure) for the information system at hand; the consistency and comparability of information systems across multiple cities; the contribution of urban information to integrated urban and regional planning and policy-making; the spatial diffusion patterns through which new technological, social and economic activities evolve; the 'incubation' conditions which stimulate new technologies in the city; the linkages between data selected at different spatial levels, models developed for different spatial levels and policies designed for different spatial levels.

In many studies, a less than satisfactory specification or performance of urban models is ascribed to a *weak data base*. Though unreliable data may affect the quality of the results, it is also true that the structures of many models presuppose a data base that does not fully exist. Model users have to accept a situation of inappropriate information systems and of gaps in statistical data.

In addition the possibilities of incorporating *qualitative* data have to be considered. Qualitative data are measured on a non-metric scale (ordinal or nominal). Too often, such data are left out of consideration, although they may contain substantial pieces of information. Recent developments in the area of qualitative (and fuzzy) spatial data analysis may be the most meaningful way of employing all relevant available information (see Nijkamp *et al*. 1984).

In an ideal situation, one might expect the availability of a large data set for all relevant variables in an urban model. In reality, however, much information is missing. Examples of information often found to be lacking include (see Issaev *et al*. 1982):

economic variables: stocks and flows of wealth, financial assets and liabilities, scale and agglomeration advantages, capacity constraints, and value of public overhead capital, distributional effects;
spatial variables: spatial interactions such as disaggregated commuting and commodity flows, spatial spin-off and spillover patterns;
process and state variables: technical progress, innovation, research and development, infrastructure, communication, energy productivity;

Figure 15.1 Impacts of Technology on Urban System Components

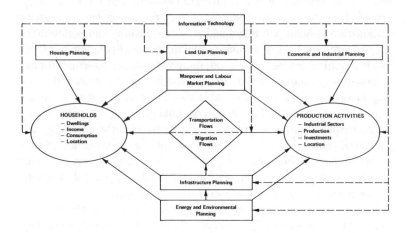

socio-political variables: power groups, segregation patterns, decision structures, interest groups, policy controls;
basic variables: demographic developments, long-run urban life-cycles.

The way in which modern information technology may have an impact on all components of an urban system is represented in Figure 15.1. Clearly, coherence and integration are prerequisites for urban information systems.

Use of Urban Information Systems

An efficient use of urban information systems is far from easy as there are many costs involved, depending on the accuracy, adaptability and availability of necessary information. Moreover, an information system has also to be judged on the basis of its social benefits to improved decision-making (for instance, risk avoidance, higher effectiveness, or multi-purpose use).

The local demand for information may vary, with respect to information content, both between cities and over time within a city. Given the need for coherence of data, one may raise the question whether or not information collection and production should take place at a local level or be centralised.

It should be noted however, that in most countries decentralised and heterogeneous demands for information from local planning levels are increasingly coming to the fore. The need for general information (global trends, sectoral developments and so on) are basically met by a centralised, homogeneous supply. But as the number of decentralised government bodies has multiplied, the need for specific local information has also increased, though this has not been accompanied by a corresponding increase in the number of local information systems and data bases. Thus the use and design of coherent local information systems is still problematic.

When data collected from different sources (different spatial levels, different industrial branches and so forth) are combined, there is a danger that information on individual citizens or firms could be traced, resulting in loss of privacy. Among some nations, US, Japan, Germany and the Netherlands being some of the first, a trend of increasing resistance to government collection of survey data is already apparent (see Chapter 16). Many countries have confidentiality laws that prohibit public release of information on individual units, implying that statistical data cannot be used completely. For example, statistics on the annual profits of firms will normally only be made available in an aggregated form such that no single firm could be identified. This is especially true at local or regional levels of information, where data are presented at a lower level of aggregation and the probability of disclosure is higher. The basic problem here is how confidential information may be used in urban planning without betraying identity.

Several methods have been designed that minimise the information loss and present the data in as informative a way as possible. However, although individual firms generally attach great importance to the confidentiality of data given to statistical offices, usually the same data can be obtained from annual reports of firms, journals and newspapers. Moreover, a good firm always has fairly accurate information about its competitors. Consequently, confidentiality provisions for individual business data may be relaxed without doing any harm. Many discussions on confidentiality of data tend to be more strategic in nature rather than concentrating on necessary statistical confidentiality. Retention and control of information represent a considerable source of power at the disposal of planners, and can increase their bargaining position in negotiations by creating uncertainty or obscuring true motivations. Exchange of information, seen in this light, is less a technical problem than a political matter of power distribution. This may explain why a comprehensive spatial 'supersystem' of data banks is difficult to establish through the exchange of information between different administrations: many agents obtain influence and autonomy from their control over information, and will not readily give it up. Since 'supersystems' would be difficult to control and uneconomical, a decentralised, spatially distributed organisation seems a better alternative.

Several efforts in designing suitable local information systems have been undertaken in the past years. Examples can be found *inter alia* in the Urban Data Management Systems (UDMS) holding annual conferences in the field of urban information systems, and in the international journal *Computers, Environment, and Urban Systems*.

A comprehensive review of computer software for spatially oriented information systems can be found in a study undertaken by the Commission on Geographical Data Sensing and Processing of the International Geographical Union (1980). Beside a systematic presentation of various spatially-oriented information systems (such as full geographic information systems, data manipulation programmes, and computerised cartographic and graphic techniques), an 'ideal' geographic information system is suggested. This system comprises six main components: management, data acquisition, data input and storage (control processes, encoding, filing), data retrieval and analysis (comparative and statistical analysis), information output, and information use (user-expert dialogue, man-machine interaction). This clearly indicates that spatially oriented information systems should act not just as data bank systems, but more as vehicles for planning and policy-making.

The review also shows that there has been progress in advanced local information systems, especially regarding areal unit information, natural topological data, surface information, graphic symbol data, label text information, colour display, choropleth mapping and geocoding systems. The recently developed integrated geocoding systems offer great potential, as they are able to combine the dual aims of appropriate spatial detail with flexibility in spatial aggregation (see Nijkamp and Rietveld 1984). Indeed, spatial scale and aggregation problems make up the heart of spatially oriented information systems analysis.

When statistical information is distributed, it is often of limited use to local planners because the data have been arranged to describe economic variables at the national level or for specific industrial sectors, neglecting the geographic and urban dimension. In addition, discrepancies between administrative and socioeconomic areas often lead to a lack of agreement between the spatial scale on which information is based and the scale appropriate to the planning problem. It also happens that overlapping spatially oriented information systems are set up independently and are difficult to integrate. For example, the land-use recording systems for London, UK, over the last decade were inconsistent between different boroughs. At the same time, the Greater London Council set up a regional accident location data base and several surveys were carried out on regional transportation, housing and recreation — each having a different geographic basis. The integration of such systems has had to await the development of large-scale data base techniques and methods for organising data access.

Spatial referencing of information did not receive the attention it deserved until the late 1970s. Now there are many software packages for management and analysis of geographic data, such as the ODYSSEY package devised by the Harvard Laboratory for Computer Graphics and Spatial Analysis in the US. New methods of geocoding have made it possible to produce maps by computer, doing away with the laborious job of drawing them by hand, and generally making it easier to adapt information systems to the user's requirements. By digitising information on all intersections of the national transport infrastructure, one can define a network of nodes connected by numbered segments.

Such a system, called INSYRON, has been developed by the National Physical Planning Agency in the Netherlands (see Nijkamp and Rietveld 1984). INSYRON not only integrates land-use classifications, dwelling details and public utility access points, but also covers traffic flow, road accidents and other activities. Because the side of the street, for example, can be represented by one segment, encoding of all segments allows one to obtain information on the distribution of shops or car parks, or on relative positions of public facilities. The advantage of storing data at such a level of detail is that it offers flexibility in aggregating data to different scales according to the planner's needs. INSYRON includes a nationwide system based on a grid of 500-metre squares, and an automated cartographic system of basic maps stored in digitised form. The system is able to produce maps containing selected physical elements for a particular region. It is much easier for the planner to see these details on a map than read them from tables. The availability of a coherent set of data such as this has increased the consistency of data use by different government agencies in the Netherlands, so that problems arising from differences in basic information are avoided. However, progress in this field is held up by the unavailability of disaggregated data and by data being available only for particular administrative zones, which prevent the linking of data sources. This is especially true for employment and population data.

With the Dutch system, disaggregated data can be stored in local data bases without overloading the central geographic computer file. Local agencies have the responsibility of maintaining and updating the data bases. Decentralisation guarantees efficiency of information flows and solves the problem of the size of the information system, which normally has to be much bigger and more complex in order to accommodate data on the spatial positions of thematic elements and therefore raises the costs of storage capacity and computer processing. Although no major software packages have yet become general standards for spatial information systems or computerised cartography, this might change soon as sales of hardware and software increase.

At present, urban planning practice in many nations is moving from a 'blueprint' mode, whereby the final conditions are prescribed, to one recognising that planning is a process. This implies less focus on the plans themselves but more on procedures and interactions with the policies of other agencies and on their consequences. An eye is continuously kept on how plans are functioning, via policy instruments and organisational structure, to meet their objectives. The recent preoccupation of planners with this practice of monitoring stems to some degree from the inability of plans to cope with change and uncertainty, and their tendency to obsolescence. That some uncertainty underlies all plans has become more openly acknowledged, and efforts have been made to accommodate this in the planning process, in place of earlier attempts to eliminate it. But not all uncertainty originates from outside the planning and information systems. For instance, aggregation (i.e. compression of data) summarises variables by single measures, which are then used as indicators to influence policy judgements. The uncertainty hidden within these figures is absorbed when inferences are drawn from the body of evidence and the inferences are presented to the decision maker, instead of the evidence itself.

Another approach to handling uncertainty is to construct different scenarios in order to establish the range of futures with which a regional plan may have to contend. This method has been used in South Hampshire, a growth area in south-east England. It was realised that over a 15-year period regional trends could be affected as much by national as by local factors, and similarly that national economics could not be isolated from international trade and politics. Therefore, trends were considered at each of the three levels, taking into account the implications of one for another. Three scenarios were constructed that described possible long-term changes, but in different directions. After making a list of critical areas at the national level, the planners attempted to interpret the effects of the national trends on South Hampshire.

Several kinds of uncertainty in regional planning can also be treated by so-called early warning systems. These were originally designed to aid decision-making in business and have been adapted, using the latest decision support systems, to help in regional planning. The basic stages are to draw up conceptual relationships that define the problem, to collect data from the literature and from experts, to evaluate the data so that projections can be made, and finally to establish thresholds, below which changes in the situation would not significantly affect people's attitudes.

The effectiveness of urban planning is typically measured against standard quantitative indicators, such as employment figures. But there is much skepticism among planners about measuring performance in this way because of the difficulty of separating the effects of policy from influences beyond the planner's control. Even in the plan-making process itself, formal analysis of quantified information is often a minor aspect — negotiations, habit and 'muddling through' have been known to be more persuasive than the results from a computer programme or mathematical model. And because the information needed in monitoring is so diverse in terms of type, source, and spatial and time scales, there is a widely felt need to handle not only numerical information but also qualitative information. It has been said that the hardest of facts are open to varied interpretation, so some would prefer to describe all information as 'squashy' (like a tomato), since it is valuable only if handled with care and not required to support too much.

Qualitative information can be 'hard', such as information on policies approved, planning commitments and events, or 'soft', such as emerging policies, proposals and public opinions. Although it may seem difficult to translate these various kinds of information into policy-relevant form, computer technology is providing increasingly sophisticated means of storing, collating and interrogating combinations of statistical and textual materials, using keywords and strings. Several methods exist for helping the decision-maker evaluate qualitative information where there are problems caused by conflicting objectives and criteria. With the aid of such methods as computer-based decision support systems, complex planning issues are being rationalised through better use of all relevant information, regardless of its nature. The planner interacts with the data base through user-friendly software and hardware support, such as graphics processors and 'natural' computer languages.

Planning of Information

Today's planners are faced with an overabundance of some kinds of data, so the real bottleneck in modern planning is not the supply but the evaluation of information. This is indeed the era of information but, at the same time, the identification of meaningful structures and patterns in the mass of information that confronts us is fraught with many problems. The need for better information for planning has evolved into the need for better planning of information. Clearly there are various institutional and technical reasons why integration of information systems is hard to achieve in current planning practice. Yet lack of integration means an enormous waste of effort. It would be a significant step forward if national or regional bureaux of statistics were authorised to provide uniform rules for data collection and standard classifications for economic activities.

It is clearly more important to increase the speed of response to, or recognition of, conditions that call for planning action, and to broaden the range of variables considered, than to increase the amount of data on each variable. This is especially true, as in the majority of countries urban information systems are not yet fully developed. The potential of modern information technology is much higher than its current use. This may be due to several factors, such as expectation of high costs, lack of insight, institutional rigidity and insufficient co-ordination. However, it should be realised that more adequate design and use of modern information systems for regional planning will lead to better decision making and thus to higher social benefits.

Despite the avalanche of information, one of the major short-comings in many urban information systems is lack of coherence (see also Figure 15.1). However, it is almost impossible and even undesirable to design urban information systems that are both fully integrated and sufficiently detailed regarding all planning components. In regard to this, it may be desirable to design effective urban information systems that fulfill at least three conditions for use in urban planning.

First, one may design an information system that provides a *coherent* pattern of all major urban planning components, so that, at the level of global urban indicators necessary for integrated urban planning, comprehensiveness is guaranteed. Then, at the level of a more *detailed*

Figure 15.2 A Two-Level Representation of an Integrated
Urban Planning Information System

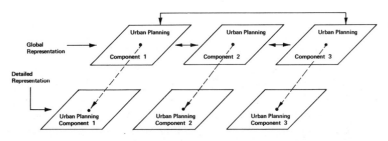

representation of individual planning components, the condition of detailed integration with indicators from other planning components may be abandoned. This two-layer strategy, represented in Figure 15.2, is much easier to handle and less rigid than detailed comprehensive information systems.

In the second place, it may be meaningful to adapt a *problem orientation* regarding a specific urban planning issue to be dealt with by means of an urban information system. Such a problem orientation requires a specific *key factor* approach, in which the driving forces and mechanisms of a planning problem are identified (e.g. demographic processes, ageing of housing stock and so forth). Given these key factors, a *satellite* approach may be used in which the links between these key factors and the urban planning information system (see Figure 15.3) are identified. Given information on the impacts of key factors on successive urban planning components, a satellite structure may be constructed in which the key factors are positioned in the core and the impacts on the various planning components in the periphery (see Figure 15.3).

Finally, if one adopts a procedural view of planning in which decision-making is considered a process, information systems have to be *flexible*, in order to provide planners and decision-makers with specific tailor-made information at any desired moment. In a complex dynamic urban system this leads to the necessity of designing *adaptive* information systems. Due to modern computer technology, these systems have gained much popularity. This tendency runs parallel to the recent interest in interactive user-oriented multiple criteria decision models (see among others Nijkamp 1980 and Rietvald (1981).

In conclusion, modern technology offers much potential for more

Figure 15.3   A Satellite Structure for a Key Factor Approach to
Urban Planning Information Systems

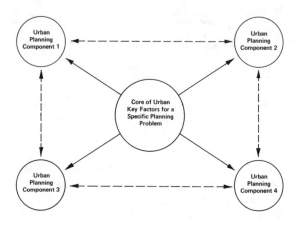

effective urban planning. In regard to this, it is regrettable that in many urban planning situations the use of this (already available) technology is lagging far behind compared to the possibilities offered by this technology. Some explanation of this lag is given in Chapter 16 to follow.

Note

This chapter contains sections taken from a draft article for IIASA's quarterly newsletter 'Options', written by Steven Flitton. The Options article gives a summary of a research project on Integrated Information Systems for Regional Development, undertaken by the Regional and Urban Development Division of the International Institute for Applied Systems Analysis (IIASA), Laxenburg, Austria. A full description of the whole project is contained in Nijkamp and Rietveld (1984).

References

Brown, P. and Masser, I. (1977) *Spatial Representation and Spatial Interaction*, Martinus Nijhoff, The Hague
Burch, J.G., Strater, F.R. and Grudnitski, G. (1979) *Information Systems: Theory and Practice*, John Wiley, New York.

Report on Commission on Geographical Data Sensing and Processing (1980) International-al Geographical Union, Ottawa

Debons, A. and Larson, A.S. (eds.) (1983) *Information Science in Action*, Martinus Nijhoff, The Hague

Issaev, B., Nijkamp, P., Rietveld, P. and Snickars, F. (eds) (1982) *Multi-regional Economic Modelling: Practice and Prospect*, North-Holland Publishing Co., Amsterdam

Lowe, J.C. and Moryades, S. (1975) *The Geography of Movement*, Houghton Mifflin Co., Boston.

Nijkamp, P. (1979) *Multidimensional Spatial Data and Decision Analysis*, John Wiley, Chichester.

Nijkamp, P. (1980) *Environmental Policy Analysis*, John Wiley, Chichester.

Nijkamp, P., Leitner, H. and Wrigley, N. (eds) (1984) *Measuring the Unmeasurable*, Martinus Nijhoff, The Hague

Nijkamp, P. and Rietveld, P. (eds) (1981) *Cities in Transition*, Martinus Nijhoff, The Hague.

Nijkamp, P. and Rietveld, P. (eds) (1984) *Information Systems for Integrated Regional Planning*, North-Holland Publishing Co., Amsterdam

Peters, A. (1981) 'Die Verstatterung in den Neiderlanden nach 1950 und seine Raumordnungspolitischen Implikationen', PhD Thesis, Technical University, Berlin

Pred, A. (1977) *City-Systems in Advanced Economies*, Hutchinson, London

Rietvald, P. (1981) *Multiple Objective Decision Methods and Regional Planning*, North-Holland Publishing Co., Amsterdam

Robson, B.T. (1973) *Urban Growth*, Methuen, London

Willis, J. (1972) *Design Issues for Urban and Regional Information Systems*, Centre for Environmental Studies, London

16. URBAN INFORMATION SYSTEMS AND SOCIETY
M. Wegener

Since 1966, an annual survey has been conducted in the Federal Republic of Germany, in which respondents are asked: 'Do you believe that technology is more blessing than evil?' In 1966, 75 per cent answered 'yes'. In 1982, this had fallen to 30 per cent. The dramatic decline heralds a change in the relationship between man and technology from one of optimism and confidence to that of pessimism and mistrust. It may be less pronounced in countries with a more pragmatic, matter-of-fact attitude towards technological change than Germany, but it has affected all Western industrialised countries to some degree.

The reasons for the disenchantment with technological progress are manyfold. Most technological achievements of the century have failed to be as beneficial as originally expected. The 'green revolution' did relieve the hunger in the Third World, but also led to grave imbalances in the rural ecosystems of developing countries and made them more dependent on fertiliser imports. In industrialised countries, surplus production and mass consumption have been paid for by air pollution, poisoned rivers and dying forests. Modern chemicals have revolution-ised medicine, but have brought new toxic hazards and drug dependency. The private motor car opened a new world of personal mobility, but has nearly choked cities with monstrous expressway structures. Nuclear power, once thought to be a clean and inexhaustible resource of energy, has turned out to be not nearly as safe and economical as envisaged and now, through the arms race, threatens to end human existence on the globe altogether.

Another time-bomb, not as conspicuous but hardly less frightening, may be unharnessed information technology. Large-scale computerisa-tion and more recently the microcomputer revolution are quietly pervading all fields of modern life with deeper impacts on the production and consumption spheres than most technological advances of the past. Automated production lines, decentralised office work and computerised communication systems open new dimensions of work, education and leisure leading to changing patterns of movement, locational choice and eventually urban form (see Dickey, Chapter 13).

The objective of this chapter is to speculate on the Janus-faced character of the information age as it may affect the future city through urban planning and management information systems. Urban information systems of the future, if realised, might be of hitherto unconceived sophistication and comprehensiveness. They might not be novel, in the sense that they use special hardware or software that have been available in other fields of application or even in rudimentary form in many city administrations for quite some time. Their new quality would result from their immense potential to link, merge and combine data files formerly maintained independently and without co-ordination by different agencies or institutions. Now through computer networks, teleprocessing and distributed online access to a multitude of data sources, an enormous gain in efficiency of urban management information systems seems possible: housing policy, traffic operation, environmental protection, social services, medical care and crime prevention might greatly benefit from more up-to-date and detailed information about problems and needs of citizens. However, hand in hand with each advance in these fields, there would be an advance in centralised knowledge and hence potential control on the side of the administration.

The dialectic relationship between centralised control and the public welfare has been a recurrent theme of political theorists from Plato to Campanella, Hobbes, Lenin or more recently Popper (1945), Etzioni (1968) and Friedmann (1973). With the electronic revolution, this relationship may acquire a new, dramatically different quality. What will be the consequences for urban planning? Two basically different positions seem possible, the rational and the critical.

The Rational Position

At the core of the rational position is the dream of rationality as the guiding principle in organising societal matters. Rational decision making requires a comprehensive evaluation of all action alternatives, hence information is central: with the right information at the right time, a rational solution to all societal problems must be possible. Information is therefore beneficial and enlightening.

The rational position has formed the intellectual underpinning of most developments in urban information systems and computer-based planning techniques (see Batty and Hutchinson 1983). When these techniques were adapted from military and business applications to urban planning, they met with great expectations. However, their implementation soon encountered serious difficulties: data were not available, computer technology was still primitive, to produce results took longer than expected. The proponents of the new techniques claimed that the next technological break-through would bring the long-awaited success: interactive computing, computer graphics and most recently microcomputers would eventually firmly establish computer-based information systems in the urban planning process. However, this has not happened to date.

The most important reason for this failure may be that the information contained in the urban information systems was not the kind of information planners really needed. What they needed was informal *ad hoc* information about social, economic and political issues; 'gut knowledge' as Dickey (Chapter 13) calls it — but what they got were elementary statistics and the most routine descriptive data manipulations and presentations in tables, graphs and maps. More ambitious policy-oriented methods such as forecasting, simulation or optimisation models were either nonexistent or (with few exceptions) too costly, too sophisticated or too poorly documented to be understood and appreciated by practising urban planners. In addition, the results of the methods frequently had a distinct technocratic bias suggesting predominantly technical solutions, because they relied exclusively on quantitative information and failed to take account of the more important 'intangibles', that is the social and political environment of the planning problems. Moreover, the results were often outdated and poorly geared to the planning problems at hand, because methods reflected the problem perception at the time and were too inflexible to be adjusted fast enough to changing problem contexts. Large quantities of irrelevant information resulted in information rejection by the planners with the effect that most planners soon returned to more conventional forms of information gathering.

A second major cause for the disappointing performance of urban planning information systems is the change in the style of planning experienced in most Western countries during the last two decades. In the prosperous 1960s, the ideal of 'synoptic' (comprehensive and co-ordinated) planning of all social subsystems seemed achievable, and in fact the concept of the information system itself was inextricably linked to this illusionary belief. With economic decline and shrinking public budgets, the margin for grand designs narrowed and planning became more incremental, local and partisan in its ambitions and clientele. Planning information of the kind produced by the information systems became even more irrelevant or even dysfunctional: planners working for a particular client group could no longer be interested in too much information about the implications of their policies on other groups, because that would weaken their bargaining position.

As a consequence, in most Western countries the rational position has lost most of its adherents in local government and public planning agencies. Instead, a much more cautious, modest and realistic assessment of the usefulness of urban planning information systems has been adopted, over-ambitious schemes for their implementation have been cut back or abandoned, staff and funds for their application have been reduced. Most planning schools no longer emphasise the skills necessary for their application, and this in the long run leads to a further reduction in the demand for their services. In summary, there exists a widening 'application gap' between the technological potential of computerised urban information systems in general, and the minimal actual utilisation of that potential in the urban planning process.

Further advances in information technology notwithstanding, only a renaissance of the rational position in the planning profession and the urban policy-making environment could reverse this present downward trend in the utilisation of information technology for urban planning. However, this seems not at all likely. It is much more realistic to expect that a fundamentally different, critical position towards the use of information for urban planning will become even more prevalent than it is already.

The Critical Position

Where the rational position held that 'information equals enlighten-ment', the critical position believes that 'information equals power and control'. The difference is the small step from Huxley's (1932) *Brave New World* to Orwell's (1949) *Nineteen Eighty-Four*, from a partly alluring, partly chilling perfect utopia to a straight-out nightmare. In this view, information is still central, not in an enlightening, beneficial way, but as an instrument of surveillance, detection and persecution of the disobedient. The followers of the critical position are convinced that this view comes much closer to the reality of the electronic age than the naive optimism of the rationalist.

The important issues here are all related to the growing opposition to computers observable in many countries. It started with the silent penetration of every aspect of daily life by computers. When nearly every transaction and communication was performed by machines, people felt reduced to passive victims; when poorly programmed computers made errors or produced unintelligible printout, they were thought of as being soulless and bureaucratic; when computers began to replace more and more people, they were called job killers. Soon computers became the epitome of everything technocratic and inhumane in modern society.

This position contrasts strangely with the enthusiasm for home computers, video games and other electronic gadgets now in fashion. It is hard to say whether this enthusiasm will be a short-lived fad (because the present small computers do not serve any serious purpose) or whether home computers serving as access nodes to universal communication networks will succeed in transforming their users into the sort of computer-minded customer-consumers the electronic industry envisages (cf. Meier, Chapter 9). At present, aversion to the computer still seems dominant.

The second issue giving momentum to the critical position is the controversy about computers and privacy. In the early days of the computer, nobody seemed to be aware of their potential to manipulate, combine and transmit personal data. However, even in a stand-alone computer it is possible through cross-matching of originally separate files to extract much more information about an individual than would be legitimised by the purposes for which the original data were sought. This dangerous potential multiplies where computers of various agencies and institutions are linked by powerful electronic networks and are not shielded against illegal access by electronic safeguards and strict privacy legislation.

The privacy issue connected with public information systems has been a matter of concern in many countries, but with different intensity. To name just two, in Sweden far-reaching plans of the government to install a nationwide personal data bank have met with only moderate criticism, whereas in the Federal Republic of Germany the opposition against all sorts of public and private information systems has been and still is vehement. Its first targets were the police information systems introduced in the early 1970s, mostly as anti-terrorist information systems. Critics of these systems pointed out that by using information collected at border checkpoints and by traffic patrols 'movement protocols' of practically every citizen could be compiled, and that by accessing files such as the population register in conjunction with other files held by public agencies or private firms, extensive 'personality profiles' of suspected or unsuspected citizens could be assembled. Although a federal law clearly confines the operation of these instruments to criminal prosecution purposes, public confidence in police observance of this is low. The younger generation especially considers the police information system to be among the ugliest and most dangerous products of technological progress, enforcing the power of the state against, not for, the citizens. Other matters of concern are the free and largely uncontrolled access of the secret services to public data banks on all administrative levels, the growing number and perfection of industrial personnel information systems strictly opposed by the trade unions, and the vast number of commercial information systems selling addresses, mail order and credit information to whoever pays the bill.

The most recent manifestation of the strength of the critical position, and one directly pertinent to urban planning, was the opposition against the 1983 West German population and employment census. There has been opposition against censuses in other countries, most notably in the Netherlands in 1971, which led to the abandonment of the census planned for 1981, and in the US in 1980, but nowhere else has anti-census opposition become virtually a mass movement. In West Germany, the last census was conducted in 1970. The next one was first planned for 1975, then 1981, then postponed to 1982 for alleged lack of money, and finally scheduled for 1983. The opposition became more intense as census day came nearer. Critics argued that the government could use census data to update the population register and thereby identify non-registrants, tax or draft evaders or foreigners without permit of residence, in other words, establish a network of surveillance of hitherto unknown dimensions.

Two weeks before the census, by which time 60 million questionnaires had been printed and distributed, the census was cancelled by the Constitutional Court for being, in part, unconstitutional. In its opinion, the Court defined the right of 'informational self-determination' as a right of citizens against being registered by the public authority in all facets of their lives. A new census, if there is to be one at all, will not be held before 1986 and in much reduced format. This means that for urban planning purposes, the 1970 census will for a long time remain the most recent available source of spatially disaggregated household, housing and employment data.

For the critics who fought against the census, urban information systems are no less dangerous than the census, in fact more so because they can always be updated from other files maintained by the city. It is an irony that while the lack of efficiency of present urban information systems was responsible for their failure under the rational position, it is their potential efficiency that makes them unacceptable to those following the critical position. With the critical position still growing in strength, political support for the modernisation and extension of urban planning information systems is not likely to be very strong in the near future.

Conclusions

The above analysis may not be relevant to every country. However, if it has identified the major positions and trends relevant for the future of urban planning in most Western industrialised countries, it can be concluded that further advances in information technology are not likely to have major impacts on the method and style of urban planning in these countries. In the past, urban planning has shown a remarkable resistance to the adoption of computer-based methods and techniques beyond the most elementary. The reasons for this resistance are not technical, but are related to the fundamental socio-political attitudes of people towards the ends and means of planning. The *rational* position, which would support the implementation and use of urban planning information systems, has been too weak to survive in times of economic decline and narrowing decision margins. The *critical* position has become the dominant paradigm but, for it, urban planning information systems are just one more instrument of the state to extend its power and control over its citizens.

What are the likely consequences? The extrapolation of current trends does not point to a pleasant future. First, the data available for urban planning will never be as good as in the recent past, although at the same time information technology will still be vastly improving. Secondly, due to lack of empirical data, urban research will become even more academic and remote from planning practice than it is now. Thirdly, the skills of planners in the application of computer-based planning techniques will be further reduced because of the aversion of the population against being the object of investigation and the disinterest of decision-makers in such investigations. In summary, the application of computerised information systems and methods for this important sector of societal planning will stay where it is, namely close to zero.

This development is regrettable as it is likely to coincide with the rapid proliferation of the most sophisticated information technology in the private domain of corporate planning and decision making, where no reservations against this kind of technology exist. That, however, will further weaken the position of the local planning authorities in negotiations with large firms which, already powerful enough as major tax payers and employers, will use their advanced information to exert an even stronger influence on public planning decisions than in the past.

An alternative to this bleak perspective could come about only through a re-evaluation of the role and proper use of information for societal planning. Unfortunately, computers and computer-based methods have so far been perceived as inseparably linked to technocratic planning. This is a misunderstanding, because there is nothing inherent in this kind of technology that reserves it exclusively for one particular style of planning. On the contrary, advanced communication and information technologies offer a wide variety of concepts and techniques for decentralisation of control, system transformation, conflict resolution and social learning. If the dichotomy between the rational and the critical positions sketched out in this chapter is ever to be resolved, this potential needs to be carefully explored.

References

Batty, M. and Hutchinson, B. (eds) (1983) *Systems Analysis in Urban Policy-Making and Planning*, Plenum Press, New York

Etzioni, A. (1968) *The Active Society: A Theory of Societal and Political Processes*, The Free Press, New York

Friedmann, J. (1973) *Retracking America: A Theory of Transactive Planning*, Anchor Press, New York

Huxley, A. (1932) *Brave New World*, Harper and Row, New York (1981 ed.)

Orwell, G. (1949) *Ninety Eighty-Four*, Penguin, Harmondsworth (1982 ed.)

Popper, K.R. (1945) *The Open Society and Its Enemies*, Routledge and Kegan Paul, London

PART SIX

INSTITUTIONAL INFLUENCES

17. PLANNING AND TECHNOLOGICAL CHANGE
L. Gertler

Common experience as well as sophisticated analysis confirm that this is an age of uncertainty. There is a supreme irony in the inescapable observation that the forces of rationalism and scientific experiment — the legacy of Bacon, Descartes and Spinoza — are now expressed in a world of seemingly irrational turbulence and daunting complexity. The three major symptoms of this are global: the threat of ecological disaster, economic disorder, and the menace of nuclear annihilation (after Bernal 1969).

That this should be our fate in a time of such manifest technological mastery with its extraordinary potential for mobilising information and comprehending complexity is especially paradoxical. And that in the face of these cruel prospects the 'advanced industrial societies' should choose to reject public sector planning appears to be a species of cosmic madness.

We confront today a conjunction of both cyclical and secular upheavals. Decline in the growth rates of critical aggregates like income and employment are complicated by the economic and social reverberations of a technological revolution, of the combined and interactive effects of microelectronics, telecommunications and robotics. Some of the consequences that can be contemplated are jobless growth, the polarisation of the social structure between 'decision-makers and machine-minders', greater spatial segregation of the social classes, and an increasingly precarious social balance (Homenuck and Martin 1982; also see Chapter 23).

But the new technology has decidedly 'two faces'. Along with these disruptive tendencies, there has been a quantum leap in just those capabilities required to forestall the impending crisis: a capacity to assemble comprehensive information quickly, to bring together and relate a great diversity of conditions, to undertake complex analysis, to simulate real world systems and try out policy options, to keep people well informed, and to sustain interactive communication between government and its public and amongst social groups. These powers are latent rather than active. Their use in a purposeful way depends on the kind of constructive initiative, political as much as technical, implied by the concept of planning.

Planning is that social function which links scientific, technical and personal knowledge to organised action. As such it is an important part of that array of institutions — political, legal, economic, sometimes called the 'guidance system' — that steer the processes of change in society. It is a function which has been historically associated with government because some of the most crucial problem areas, environmental and economic, are societal in scope and can only be addressed through institutions that are functionally and territorially broad (Friedmann 1973). Thus the retreat from planning which we witness in the US, Canada and Britain, for instance, appears to be a retreat from the purposeful deployment of contemporary knowledge where it is needed most. In its place, there is an implicit plea to *believe* that the unleashing of the egocentric, self-serving and vested interests in society will somehow eventually work out for the best. Keynes maxim, 'In the long run, we will all be dead', takes on today a particularly ominous note.

We suffer in the Western world from a fixation on the Orwellian nightmare. *Nineteen Eighty-Four* has produced the archetype of the demonic state that uses technology to subjugate its people and pursue its evil designs (see Chapter 16). To be sure, dictatorship is unfortunately still a hazard, but as a guide to the role of technology in Western society, Orwell's (1949) vision is seriously misleading. For it detracts attention from the fact that, in the main, the great enterprise of translating research into development, the fashioning of the tools of oppression or liberation, is in the hands of the large industrial bureaucracies. That this is done effectively in response to corporate goals, be they profit, prestige or aggrandisement, is amply demonstrated. If there are some undesirable externalities, such as chemical and nuclear pollution, the loss of jobs, stressful working conditions, degraded habitats, or disjointed cities, that is not because of some diabolical corporate plot. Rather, it is because we have not found a way to sustain a balance between societal values and the dynamics of commercial enterprise.

Historically, when Western societies have faced crisis, like a depression, or wished to accomplish a transcending social purpose, like post-war reconstruction, they have turned to government. On such occasions, planning has played a critical role. The fact that in these troubled times the trend is reversed, behoves us to raise some searching questions.

The Retreat from Planning

It is probably a safe assumption that the retreat from planning is not a simple matter and to be properly understood requires a multi-dimensional perspective. One view is that it is part of a general disenchantment with interventionist governments. For the Canadian case, readers are directed to such works, to be read interactively, as Terrence Downeys' (1982) account of the increase, commencing in the early 1970s, of public dissatisfaction with all levels of government, and Nigel Richardson's (1981) chronicle of the fate of planning in Canada's heartland which he titled 'Insubstantial pageant: the rise and fall of provincial planning in Ontario'.

One finds a clue to the forces at work in the particular form that government restraint has assumed, namely an attack on human services. The skeptical view is that during a period of about 25 years (1951-75) of buoyant development, government was called upon by business to provide the infrastructure to support economic and urban expansion. This extended from the mundane to the sublime — from sewers to higher education. Now that times have changed, government is again responding to the interests of business by, on the one hand, providing subventions and tax breaks in support of the new technologies, while on the other, eliminating the burden of 'redundant' facilities and social services.[1]

Underlying this view is the concept that government in capitalist industrial societies reflects, mainly, the dominant corporate interests. It is interesting that such an interpretation has been offered in the late 1970s by Charles E. Lindblom, the Yale political economist who in the 1950s and 1960s was one of the high priests of 'disjointed incrementalism': a theory of government by the mutual adjustment of diverse and roughly equal contending interest groups. Lindblom (1977:175) explains 'the privileged position of business' in this way:

> Any government official who understands the requirements of his position and the responsibilities that market-oriented systems throw on businessmen will therefore grant them a privileged position. He does not have to be bribed, duped, or pressured to do so ... He simply understands, as is plain to see, that public affairs in market-oriented systems are in the hands of two groups of leaders, government and business, who must collaborate and that, to make the system work, government leadership must often defer to business

leadership. Collaboration and deference between the two are at the heart of politics in such systems.

If the influence of business was the sole basis for the retreat from planning, it might be regarded as one of those contentious issues which can only be resolved by adversarial struggle in the political arena. But there is more to it than that. One of the ingredients of public disenchantment relates to the trauma of bureaucracy. This, of course, is a feature of all large organisations in industrial societies, but the focus of concern has been on government because of the high rate of expansion during the past 30 years, and because public institutions are much more open to public scrutiny than are private ones.

Today, the restoration of planning as a relatively benign process for addressing the issues of technological and other change depends on coming to terms with bureaucracy. This is very much related to freedom, power and participation in our society. According to the sociologist, John Porter (1979:221-30), unregenerate bureaucracy wherever it exists will eventually meet resistance, unless it provides scope for social participation. As a power instrument, designed to enforce the will of an elite, it goes against the deep-seated urge for freedom: the ability of people to direct their own affairs. The very structure of bureaucracy — a hierarchy, the division of tasks, a system of top-down command — cultivates attitudes of servility and obedience. And it can also produce an intimidated citizenry, with neither the courage nor inclination to participate in broad social development.

From this perspective the reaction against planning associated with big government is a healthy symptom. We are deluded, however, if we think that the automatic result is greater scope for freedom in the sense of a broad-based participation in determining the shape of society's development. Given the nature of Canada's social structure, the retreat of public sector planning allows full sway to planning by a highly centralised private corporate structure. Porter (1979:221) has stated this bluntly:

> The planning is done through the machinery of corporate bureaucracy countered from time to time by the bureaucracies of organised labour and government. The aims of corporate organisation determine the shape of social development. This is the creative role.

To extend the 'creative role' from a strictly private to the public sphere is the central challenge that faces planning institutions today. And this challenge assumes special importance in an era of rapid technological change because we are faced with choices that have farreaching social, economic and environmental consequences as well as opportunities.

Technological Change: Repercussions and Choices

Some of the important questions that arise from the ubiquitous powers of the computer have been incisively identified by Joseph Weizenbaum (1983:60):

> Increasing computerisation may well allow us to increase the productivity of labour indefinitely — but to produce what? More video games and fancier television sets along with 'smarter' weapons? And with people's right to feed their families and themselves largely conditional on their 'working', how do we provide for those whose work has been taken from them by machines? The vision of production with hardly any human effort, of the consumption of every product imaginable, may excite the greed of a society whose appetites are fixed on things. It may be good that in our part of the globe people need no longer sort bank checks or mail by hand, or retype articles ... But how far ought we to extrapolate such 'good' things? At what price? Who stands to gain and who must finally pay? Such considerations ought at least to be part of a debate. Are there really no choices other than that 'we' win or lose?

Against the background of these contextual questions, there are a host of specific choices involved in the application of contemporary technologies to the urban system. The prospect of the wired city has been anticipated. This involves trading off contacts by transportation, as in the journey to work, for contacts by communications via the computer terminal. It also means replacing personal with impersonal interaction. How far should this be pushed? Prospects for the decentralisation of work are increased. What form is preferred, work at home in a kind of 'electronic cottage industry', or the development of community computer centres? What effect would these have on the urban structure? What will be the impact of anticipated changes in the social structure? Will spatial stratification be intensified? Is this dimension amenable to housing and other social policies? In the long run, what choice will be made between the centrifugal bias of communications and the centripetal bias of energy constraints: the regional city vs. the compact city, and so on (see Homenuck and Martin 1982; Pressman, Chapter 25)?

Prospects for Democratic Planning

The foregoing implies the kind of deliberation usually associated with a process of planning. There is an assumption that choices can be made consensually, and through a considered assessment of options, rather than on the basis of the cumulative inadvertence of commercial exploitation. At this juncture when society has to contend with the converging repercussions of several innovations, instead of mere additions of known products and processes, effective planning is very much needed. The challenge, as suggested, is to evolve planning systems which are democratic rather than bureaucratic. This suggests a planning process which, meeting Porter's criteria, would not be the captive of special interests, which would function as much as possible on collegial rather than hierarchical lines, and which would provide an avenue for the vital involvement of would-be beneficiaries. There is an assumption here of dispersion rather than concentration of decision-making power, and with that a broader and freer flow of creative energies. 'Democratically planned societies, even when they are based on large-scale industry', writes Porter (1979:230-8 and 209) 'must solve the dilemma of power by building in mechanisms of achieving political and social consensus which are responsive to human needs as these are expressed by mobilised publics'.

In offering this prescription the author has few illusions concerning the difficulty of moving in the indicated direction. The forces that can work against reform in a planning system have been illuminated in a recent overview of the evolution of Canadian planning (Gunton 1983:27-36).[2] Several points are made. On the issue of bureaucracy, planners have at times been part of the problem rather than the solution, as they take cover behind legal frameworks that tolerate counter-productive and costly regulations. The beginning of wisdom is the recognition that the role of planners is constrained and defined by the social and political context in which they work. But this does not justify a passive and submissive stance. On the contrary, past performance suggests that the most damaging periods have been those of uncritical acquiescence, and the most creative, those of vigorous assertion of professional leadership. The 'destruction of working class neighbourhoods' in the 1960s through to urban renewal is an example of the first. And the establishment of a system of regional planning in Alberta in the 1950s and of enlightened national housing legislation in the early 1970s, an expression of the upbeat.

Reform is not assisted by a posture of professional objectivity and scientific purity. In fact, planning is inescapably involved in the allocation of scarce resources amongst competing interests, and this is a function which is politically highly sensitive. The planner, while not directly involved in these struggles, can contribute to their equitable resolution by incorporating distributional impact statements — 'who gains and who loses' — into his methodology. This approach becomes meaningful when the protagonists in the process, disadvantaged groups in particular, have access to and can act upon the results of such statements.

Finally, a critical appreciation of the history of planning can be most edifying and should be an essential part of the consciousness and strategic sense of the contemporary planner. One of the insights from Canadian experience is the cyclical nature of support for planning, bullish during periods of active development, bearish in the declines. The upswing of the technological revolution may provide one of those rare moments of opportunity.

While this time of turbulent change demands that planners be 'street wise' in the manner indicated, it is important in this kind of discussion to note that innovation in planning processes has implications for learning processes. There is a report to the Club of Rome on this subject that leads into the concluding theme of this chapter (Botkin *et al.* 1979). The point of departure is the *human gap*, the distance between the contemporary cluster of global problems and our ability to deal with them. It is asserted that learning by shock, the historic way of making necessary changes, is in a nuclear age a dangerous game. Given the nature of the world problematique — population, energy, food, war and peace, revolutionary change, the drive for greater equality in the sharing of the world's resources — we dare not lose control over events. This is both for sheer survival, and because the human costs of not preparing options, which with complex technology may require long lead times, are too disturbing to contemplate. And there is a great risk that in the panic of crisis learning and crisis action, the interests of the many will be lost in the shuffle.

It becomes increasingly necessary in our kind of world to build 'fail-safe' features into the framework of learning itself — hence innovative learning, with its two essential, linked concepts of *anticipation* and *participation*. Anticipation is the capacity to face new, possibly unprecedented situations, the ability to deal with change in society, to imagine future events and to evaluate the consequences of current decisions and actions. 'It is not limited simply to encouraging desirable trends and preventing catastrophic ones: it is also the "inventing" or creating of new alternatives where none existed before', and exploring the effects, the advantages and disadvantages of each path. As someone has said, through learning by anticipation 'the future may enter our lives as a friend, not as a burglar' (Botkin *et al.* 1979:12-13).

Participation is no stranger as an idea. It is the involvement of people, individually and as groups, in such a way that whatever the context and the circumstances, those participating feel they have a genuine effect on what happens. It thrives when reinforced by success — the effort makes a difference. It can be a powerful learning process, because there is no substitute for direct experience. It involves dialogue and co-operation, the sharing of perceptions and insights, the broadening of understanding as a basis for effective action.

What is special about innovative learning is the linkage between these two elements. Furthermore, the linkage of anticipation and participation is also a feature of the concept of transactive planning in planning theory — the combining of organised action with two kinds of knowledge, the processed knowledge of the specialist (e.g. the social forecaster) with the personal or gut knowledge of the man or woman on the firing line (Friedmann 1973). The shaping of an effective planning process for these demanding times, one that links technical sophistication with democratic values, will require no less than this kind of consonance between the life of introspection and action.

Notes

1. The alternating stance of business *vis-a`-vis* city governments in Canada is explained by Magnusson 1983:36): 'The economic crisis that began in the 1970s again brought the 'cutters' and 'boosters' to the fore in municipal politics. They could claim that the problem was no longer one of excessive growth, but of declining economic activity. The solutions they suggested were to cut municipal spending (to relieve burdens on ratepayers) and to boost the local economy by stimulating construction and offering incentives to industry and commerce. Boosting and cutting were ever more frequently presented as complementary policies, with broad support from the business community.'

2. With regard to some of the tools of the planning craft, Gunton (1983:33-4) has some provocative observations: 'While spatial and forecasting models appear to be objective techniques for assessing planning policies they are, in fact, empirical descriptions of how metropolitan areas have evolved under certain institutions such as private markets. Any planning proposals which are based on these findings often simply

assume that things ought to evolve the way they have evolved. By implicitly shifting from the empirical observation to prescription, planners have often concealed the normative aspects of their craft under the guise of technical expertise.'

References

Bernal, J.D. (1969) *Science in History, The Scientific and Industrial Revolution*, (3rd edn), Vol. 2, Penguin, Harmondsworth

Botkin, J.W., Elmandjra, M. and Malitza, M. (1979) *No Limits to Learning*, Pergamon Press, Oxford

Downey, T.J. (1982) 'Ontario's Local Governments in the 1980s: a Case for Policy Initiatives', *The Canadian Journal of Regional Science*, 5, 146-54

Friedmann, J. (1973) *Retracking America. A Theory of Transactive Planning*, Anchor Press/Doubleday, Garden City, New York

Gunton, T. (1983) 'Origins of Canadian Urban Planning', *City Magazine, II*, 27-36

Homenuck, P. and Martin, A.P. (1982) 'The Impact of New Technology: New Pressures on Urban and Regional Planning', *The Canadian Journal of Regional Science*, 5, 67-82

Lindblom, C.E. (1977) *Politics and Markets*, Basic Books, New York

Magnusson, W. and Sancton, A. (eds) (1983) *City Politics in Canada*, University of Toronto Press, Toronto

Orwell, G. (1949) *Nineteen Eighty-Four*, Penguin, Harmondsworth, (1983 edn)

Porter, J. (1979) *The Measure of Canadian Society*, Gage Publishing, Toronto

Richardson, N.H. (1981) 'Insubstantial Pageant: the Rise and Fall of Provincial Planning in Ontario', *Canadian Public Administration*, 24, 563-85

Weizenbaum, J. (1983) 'The Fifth Generation by Edward A. Feigenbaum and Pamela McCorduck', *New York Review of Books*, 30, 58-62

18. UNEMPLOYMENT: THE STATE AS A SAFETY NET
M. Kesik

Historically, technological change has had an impact on the nature and number of jobs in an economy. The present high rates of unemployment can thus be related to current or recent technological changes, but these may not be the only factors involved. There is a need to analyse the various causes and effects of present unemployment and to act upon the findings.

Unemployment in Canada, as in many industrialised countries, is a two-sided problem. On the one hand, there is an over supply of labour as expressed in a high rate of unemployment geographically as well as within occupational groups.[1] On the other, there is a lack of skilled labour as identified by the National Training Act (NTA) of 1982 (see later) both geographically and within various occupational groups. This situation threatens to hamper national and regional economic development.

According to the federal Ministry of Employment and Immigration (1983a:4) it is expected that during 'the next few years ... employment growth will lag output growth ... current high levels of unemployment can be expected to come down only slowly over this period [to 1990]'. With this jobless growth scenario in mind, this chapter evaluates the present institutional approach of the Canadian federal government to unemployment.

Employment/Unemployment

Some of the elements underlying long-term unemployment may be demographic shifts, recessions and changes in production systems. The shift in the size and composition of the labour force in Canada after the Second World War was the result of such elements as the 'baby boom', increased immigration as well as urbanisation and a relatively large increase in the labour-force participation rate of women.

This demographic shift was accompanied by a shift in production systems. Historically Canada has had a relatively large reliance on the primary sector. During the 1960s and 1970s a shift took place from primary to secondary and then to the service sector. This shift (see Table 18.1) was accompanied by a decline in employment in the

Table 18.1 Employment by Industry, Canada, 1951-78

	1951	1961	1971	1975	1978
			(per cent)		
Agriculture	18.4	11.2	6.3	5.2	4.7
Forestry	2.3	1.4	0.9	0.6	0.8
Fishing and trapping	0.6	0.3	0.3	0.2	0.2
Mining	1.5	1.3	1.6	1.5	1.6
Manufacturing	26.5	24.0	22.2	20.2	19.6
Construction	6.8	6.2	6.1	6.5	6.3
Transportation, communications and other utilities	8.8	9.3	8.7	8.7	8.6
Trade	14.1	16.9	16.5	17.6	17.4
Finance, insurance and real estate	3.0	3.9	4.8	5.1	5.5
Service	18.0	19.5	26.2	27.1	28.2
Public administration	—	5.9	6.4	7.2	7.1
Total: Per cent	100.0	100.0	100.0	100.0	100.0
Thousands	5,097	6,055	8,078	9,284	9,972

Note: The 1975 and 1978 data are revised annual averages necessitated by the changeover to the 1976 Census of Canada as the base for labour force population projections.

Source: Labour Division, Statistics Canada, unpublished data, Labour Force Annual Average, 1975-78, Catalogue 71-529, taken from Ministry of Supply and Services (1980:92).

primary sector, a slight decrease in secondary-sector employment growth and an increase in service-sector employment growth.

Care should be taken in the interpretation of such employment figures. Massey and Meegan (1982), in their examination of the impact of changes in production on employment in selected industries, suggest that

> the general assumption that the decline of employment is, more or less, equivalent to the decline of an industry is inadequate. Job loss may go along with industrial decline, but it may also be the means of avoiding decline or even be an outcome of the process of growth.

This is particularly relevant at present where there is an inclination to ascribe high rates of unemployment to structural changes only. Structural change alone does not explain job loss: job loss is often a result of and a precondition for shifts in the political economic climate. Further possible causes may be loss of output or changes in productivity (whereby 'increases in output may occur with a much reduced labour force as a result of an even faster growth in labour productivity', Massey and Meegan 1982:18). It is tempting to see technological change as the 'scapegoat' for job loss. According to Malecki (Chapter 3) it is noteworthy that until five or six years ago, technology was rarely mentioned in national policy debates; now it is raised at every turn despite our incomplete understanding of its mechanisms, catalysts and impacts.

Massey and Meegan (1982:18) distinguish three specific forms of production reorganisation that provide *mechanisms* for job loss: intensification, investment and technical change, and rationalisation. These authors define *intensification* as 'being changes designed to increase the productivity of labour but without major new investment or substantial reorganisation of production technique'; *investment and technical change* as a situation where 'job loss occurred in the context of significant investment often related to changes between techniques of production'; and *rationalisation* as a 'simple reduction in total capacity'.

When such mechanisms are combined with increased technological innovation in a constant market condition, an initial loss of employment in less innovative competing industries and job obsolescence in the industry involved may result. Solutions may be sought in market expansion, through increased productivity, increased competition, increased investment for innovation (both in R & D and for diffusion purposes), or an increased number of job creation programmes and programmes for human resource development at the state level. However, the fact remains that no long-term solutions to the present high rates of unemployment have been developed and little is known about future shifts in number and kinds of jobs available. It is certain that the productivity of an economy needs to be balanced with the social needs of its human resources, and production will be increasingly linked to these needs as indicated in Chapters 4 to 8.

The State as a Safety Net

Labour market intervention is not new in Canada. In various forms[2] this has occurred since 1900 (largely in the technical and vocational training area). A change in approach did not take place until 1960. At that time the main characteristics of the Canadian labour market were:

increasing rates of unemployment; major changes in the industrial and occupational composition of the labour force, partly as a result of shifts in the nature of demand and partly as a result of technological change; potential job obsolescence and a subsequent need for a flexible labour force; a labour force whose educational attainment and hence flexibility was below optimum levels; an unprecedented increase in the numbers of persons reaching labour force age and thus creating an 'age bulge' at the point of labour market entry. (Dupre *et al.* 1973:37)

The state's response was the Technical and Vocational Training Assistance Act (TVTA) followed by the Adult Occupational Training Act (AOTA) 1970 (initially introduced in 1968). These Acts recognised that a labour market is not inherently self-adjusting. However, many of the programmes still reflected the notion of 'workers follow jobs' (see Chapter 5), hence assuming a high degree of labour mobility. At the same time both levels of government, but specifically the federal government, concentrated on job creation to lessen the impact on the job market of the unprecedented growth of the Canadian labour force.[3] Most programmes under the AOTA of 1970 reflected skills needed in the service sector. No long-term human resource development occurred, in anticipation of further shifts in production systems.

The state's initial response to the 'employment crisis' of the 1980s has been job creation specifically aimed at the hardest hit groups of youth and long-term unemployed, and to encourage potential growth industries.[4] The job creation section of the National Training Act (NTA) of 1982 consists of several parts: immediate job creation programmes for those 'hardest hit'; and a consolidation of existing job creation programmes (twelve) to 'more clearly meet the needs of labour market stabilisation, employment development in slow growth regions, and human resource development' (Employment and Immigration 1983b:1). The total of new (consolidated) job creation programmes is four.[5] Further objectives of the NTA 1982 are: to provide for occupational training of the labour force to meet the immediate and projected needs of the labour market; to increase the earnings and employability of adults; to serve special interest groups (such as youth, women and handicapped); to stimulate training by employers; and to enhance occupational mobility. The third part is increased funding for R & D in order to, indirectly, stimulate employment growth.

When the Canadian federal government introduced the NTA in 1982 this was done in recognition of the fact that the high rates of unemployment (close to a national average of 13 per cent at the time) showed no signs of decreasing and increased government intervention was considered a necessity. (The NTA replaced the AOTA of 1970 which was no longer deemed adequate.) Increased labour market intervention was seen as needed to ensure national and regional economic development and to reduce rates of unemployment.

As a result of jurisdictional separation, however, there will be a different perception of needs, resources and funding, as well as a different perception of goals and objectives among both levels of government. For example, under the Canadian Constitution, education falls under provincial jurisdiction and training and retraining (viewed as part of economic policy) fall under federal jurisdiction. Most of the human resource development programmes are initiated and funded by the federal government, although most provincial governments have their own manpower training and retraining programme as well.

The NTA 1982 was announced as a major departure from previous approaches toward human resource development. Within its framework (guidelines), the NTA would allow the labour force to adjust to and prepare for technological change; for example, under this Act, 82 skills, for which shortages have been predicted, have been identified, and a Skills Growth Fund has been created. This Fund provides the monies for training and retraining in the identified skill categories.

The NTA 1982 is not as significant a departure from previous federal/provincial approaches to labour market problems as suggested. The high degree of uncertainty of what is to happen in the future, the jobless growth future, is *not* addressed by the NTA. The immediate future, that is present high rates of unemployment, is addressed in the sense that temporary job creation programmes will provide some work for some people for a short time. But what will happen then? There is no doubt that technological change is affecting the kind and the number of jobs needed in the future. We are entering into a new stage of societal development in which the old remedies no longer apply. Major institutional and social changes as well as political and legislative changes will be required as a result. A government approach towards developing human resources should and can reflect this change, considering supplementary mechanisms (to income from employment) for providing access to goods and services, while structural changes occur. That is, there should be a framework in place which will enable people to have access to these goods and services by means other than 'job-money'. (The present upswing in the informal sector of the economy is an indication of this.) Furthermore, the 82 skill areas designated in the Act match, to a large degree, the areas of expected growth, but the rationale for the determination of these skills and areas of employment growth is unclear and appears to be based only on historical trends. And although an 'upward swing [in employment growth] comes with the diffusion of innovations' (Soete 1983), it is clear that there is a great degree of uncertainty with regard to the speed with which this may take place. However there appears to be little uncertainty that it *will* take place (Science Council 1983; Ministry of Employment and Immigration 1983a). If the speed of technological change is as fast as expected, it is not practical to train and retrain people over and over again: not only is training, and retraining, often a lengthy and expensive process, but the skills may be obsolete by the time these people enter or re-enter the labour market.

An institutional change would be for the state to channel a substantial amount of money into providing people with a general education rather than preparing them with specific skills.[6] A general education could increase the flexibility of the labour force and at the same time provide people with better knowledge enabling them to monitor and adapt to technological change. In Canada in particular, this would mean major institutional changes given the previously mentioned constitutional jurisdictions for education and training. The present funding formulae for education and training would need a major overhaul. The implications of such a change could be farreaching for the provincial educational systems (primary, secondary and post-secondary). More fundamentally, it requires an examination of the relationship between human skill and technology and a programme for education which makes best use of both over the longer term.

The need for institutional changes does not go unrecognised by the federal government: 'The challenge to government, employers and individuals will be to maintain a positive attitude to change and to develop more flexible and innovative institutional arrangements' — (Ministry of Employment and Immigration 1983:5).

What is not recognised is the need to *induce* social and institutional change and the role government could play in this. The government may play a role as 'safety net', but continuing research as to the actual strength of such a net and its long-term relevance and effectiveness is needed.

Several other assistance mechanisms are also developing. Some firms are recognising that they have a responsibility in providing for the welfare of employees made redundant by production changes. This assistance can take the form of early retirement benefits such as superannuation lump sum or annuity payments for forced or voluntary retirement, retraining schemes for other employment opportunities within the firm, and various forms of assistance in finding alternative employment (one specialist firm in New York has set up to train redundant employees, in other firms, in how to apply for alternative employment). However, plant closures and layoffs with little or no assistance for the people affected are more common.

The informal sector is also developing, providing a range of goods and services, yielding income or its equivalent in bartered goods and services for those involved (Naisbitt 1982). This informal sector is largely 'low tech' — but can also include software development and utilise information technology in its development and distribution. Self-help networks are developing within this framework. The telephone can be an important component in these networks (see Chapter 6). Other more-localised networks have also formed as subsistence communities or communes sharing rural or urban sites. Self-help networks have developed in such areas as small lot food growing, home building and maintenance, legal aid, conveyancing, bulk purchasing, transport, education, and health care.

Part of this informal sector is transient and will likely exist only during periods of economic downturn or structural change. Some, however, may form the seeds for new industries and services in the conventional secondary and tertiary sectors or in the growth sectors of quaternary-information industries or quinary-home service industries. Whereas the quaternary sector is largely information (technology)-based and highly interconnected, so that entry into it is limited to those with appropriate skills and networks, the quinary sector is based on low technology with minimal network connections and open to a broader, unskilled or partly skilled segment of the population. The provision of home services, whether gardening, house cleaning, meal preparation, laundry, childminding, home health care or care of the elderly, is projected to be a growth industry, catering for that part of the increasingly wide diversity of households which prefer to expend their personal efforts in other ways. According to some estimates, this sector may grow even more quickly than the quaternary sector in the decades ahead. The state may also have an effective role to play in nurturing this growth, thereby reducing its own dependants in the longer term.[7]

Notes

1. Unemployment may be further divided by age, sex and industry.
2. 'Forms' relate to various modes of funding: e.g. on a per capita basis or a matching-basis (between federal and provincial government).

3. In turn, this growth of the labour force was a precondition of allowing the Canadian economy to grow.

4. Employment growth is expected in such areas as the service sectors, specifically for health care personnel and in business services, trade, finance, insurance and real estate (Employment and Immigration 1983a:19). In addition, it is expected that ultimately high technology, especially the information processing industry, through diffusion, will bring about employment growth in other sections.

5. LEAD — Local Employment Assistance and Development Program; JOB CORPS — specific programmes aimed at the disadvantaged (to enter the labour force); CAREER ACCESS — for those interested in continuing employment; CANADA WORKS — for people who are laid-off; for people on unemployment insurance (Ministry of Employment and Immigration 1983c).

6. One of the reasons why government in Canada has often served as a safety net with regard to unemployment is because of the *general versus specific* cost aspect of training and retraining.

7. The Canadian government to some degree encourages employment growth in such areas through financial incentives for small community-based businesses such as under the LEAD scheme (5. above); but quantitative projections of spatial and temporal effects appear to be lacking.

References

Dupre, J.S. *et al.* (1973) *Federalism and Policy Development: The Case of Adult Occupational Training in Ontario*, University of Toronto Press, Toronto

Massey, D. and Meegan, R. (1982) *The Anatomy of Job Loss, the How, Why and Where of Employment Decline*, Methuen, London and New York

Ministry of Employment and Immigration (1983a) *Perspective on Employment: A Labour Market Policy Framework for the 1980s*, Ottawa

Ministry of Employment and Immigration (1983b) *Economic Development: Program Consolidation*, Ottawa

Ministry of Employment and Immigration (1983c) *Government of Canada Job Creation Programs*, Ottawa

Ministry of Supply and Services (1980) *Perspectives Canada III*, Ottawa

Naisbitt, J. (1982) *Megatrends*, Warner, New York

Science Council of Canada (1983) *Prospects for Man: Science, Technology and the Economy*, Conference at York University, Faculty of Science, Toronto

Soete, F. (1983) 'Conference Notes' in Science Council of Canada, *Prospects for Man: Science, Technology and the Economy*, Conference at York University, Faculty of Science, Toronto

PART SEVEN

MODELLING URBAN CHANGE

19. LAND USE-TRANSPORT INTERACTIONS
R. Mackett and A. Lodwick

The objectives of this chapter are to consider how the impact of technological change on urban form can be forecast using a computer model of a city, to demonstrate the use of a particular example to do so, and to assess the results from the exercise.

Forecasting is, by its nature, a difficult process, and requires careful assessment of the assumptions underlying the approach adopted. This is particularly true when the response being predicted may be outside the sphere of past trends. However, if an understanding of the possible impacts of such change is to be gained, then various techniques need to be considered, and it is in this context that this work is presented.

Urban Modelling

A number of urban models have been developed over the past 25 years. A group of these may be characterised as integrated land use transport models. These represent the spatial interrelationships between transport and the location of population, employment, housing and shopping. One such model is the Leeds Integrated Land Use Transport (LILT) model, developed at the Institute for Transport Studies, University of Leeds. The LILT model is described fully elsewhere (Mackett 1979, 1983), so only its basic concepts will be discussed here.

The LILT model, in effect, links the trip distribution and modal split stages of the conventional aggregate transport demand model with a land use model of the Lowry (1964) type, using accessibility factors in the activity location mechanisms. In the model a distinction is made between the urban fabric (represented by housing, jobs and so on) and the activities carried on within it (for example living and working). In essence, the model allocates the exogenously defined total population in each social group, jobs in each industrial sector and new housing to a set of zones, given the cost of travel to work and to shop between all pairs of zones at the point of time being considered, the values of a number of parameters obtained by calibration, and the zonal allocations of all the activities and physical infrastructure at the previous time horizon. The model works over time in intervals of, typically, 5 years. At each time horizon being considered the interzonal generalised costs of travel, the exogenous totals and any zonal values which it is desired to locate exogenously, are input. Initially the overall change in the car ownership level as a function of the relative cost of travel by each mechanised mode, the area of land available for development in each zone, the zonal distribution of housing demolitions and the number of people who have remained in the same home and/or job over the time period, are calculated. Then the spatial distribution of mining and public utilities, which are assumed to be independent of accessibility, are found. Next the secondary economic sectors (for example, manufacturing and transport) are located as functions of the accessibility to labour and economic activity. At this point initial estimates of the location of tertiary economic activity (shops and services) and agriculture and the number of jobs in each zone are found. New dwellings are located as a function of the available land, the existing pattern of housing and accessibility factors. Then people are allocated to houses and jobs, either their existing ones if they have not moved during the preceding time period, or vacant ones if they are relocating. The allocation procedures take into account car ownership, the cost of travel to work, the availability of homes and jobs and the social status of residential areas. The spatial location of population is used to obtain an estimate of the distribution of tertiary activity, which is converted to jobs. A second allocation of secondary activity is obtained using the revised accessibilities to labour and economic activity. From this a new estimate of the housing pattern is made. The cycle of location processes is repeated until equilibrium is established. As well as the spatial distributions of population, housing, jobs and shopping, a range of other indicators are calculated, such as modal splits, the mean distance, time and money spent travelling to work and to shop, and the consumption of energy by transport.

There are a number of potential difficulties in the use of this type of model for examining the impact of technological change:

1. *The structural relationships represented by the model are assumed to be fixed over time.* In fact, technological innovation may lead to completely new relationships between the components of the urban system.
2. *Models are designed to forecast marginal change.* Models are designed on the basis of the range of observed behaviour (or only just outside), yet the response of urban systems may be well beyond what has happened in the past.
3. *The forecasting ability of models is difficult to test.* Given that the changes to be forecast may be outside the range of observable

behaviour, it is difficult to test the capability of models to predict such changes.

4. *Models tend to emphasise allocation.* In most urban models the emphasis is on allocating the growth (or decline) to the spatial system, rather than the estimation of the overall level of activity, yet the latter is likely to be far more critical in terms of the impact on urban systems.

5. *Models tend to contain a limited amount of variety.* By definition models are simplifications of reality, and so do not contain the full complexity of the processes being represented. In fact, some of the processes which are part of the response of urban systems to technological change may be missing.

The Application of the LILT Model

The model has been applied to Leeds, a city in the north of England with a population of about 500,000. It is an industrial city with relatively low car ownership and public transport provided by bus.

The model is used to make conditional predictions by making a 'base' or 'most likely future' forecast using the best estimates of what is expected to occur over the period being considered, and then making a forecast representing the change being considered. The differences between the two sets of results are interpreted as being due to the change being examined.

The forecasts being discussed here have 1971 as a base year and then go forward in 5-yearly intervals to 2001. The technological changes are introduced in the period 1981-2001. In the base forecast, the cost of travel is kept constant in real terms and the total population and number of jobs in each sector in the city is held at the 1981 level.

The five technological change scenarios, and their interpretation for input to the model, are as follows:

1. *Major developments in private transport producing substantial reductions in vehicle operating costs.* This is modelled by reducing the perceived vehicle operating costs of the private mode by 50 per cent and increasing the car ownership rate by an extra 10 per cent during each time period after 1981.

2. *Oil price increase causing the monetary cost of operating private transport to increase, but with subsidies used to reduce public transport fares in real terms.* This is modelled by increasing the

perceived vehicle operating cost of private transport by 50 per cent and reducing public transport fares by 50 per cent in each time period after 1981.

3. *Oil price increase and rises in public transport costs.* This is modelled by increasing the monetary elements of the generalised cost for both mechanised modes by 50 per cent in each time period after 1981.

4. *Shift in the employment structure from the basic to the service sector.* This is modelled by a 20 per cent increase in the level of total employment in each of the five tertiary (shopping and service) sectors, with a decrease in the levels in the other sectors so that the overall number of jobs is constant, in each 5-year period from 1981 onwards.

5. *Increase in labour saving technology.* This is modelled by a 20 per cent reduction in the number of jobs in each sector in each 5-year period after 1981.

In the next section a method for displaying the results from these applications of the model is discussed.

The Urban Technological Triangle

The results from the model can be plotted on the 'urban technological triangle' defined in Chapter 1 (and Fig. 1.3) and illustrated in Figure 19.1, in which the dispersal of interaction between land use and residences in an urban area is plotted against the spatial dispersal of non-residential land uses. The former can be represented by the average distance travelled to work and the latter by the mean distance of employment from the city centre. The points of the triangle correspond with three extremes of urban form: point A representing complete dominance of the central place with economies of scale, served by a radial transport system; point B having dispersed land use with complete interactions between all areas of the city based on a closed fully connected network; and point C corresponding with a dispersed land use with a localised unconnected network, representing a number of self-contained urban settlements.

In this application, point A of the triangle represents the mean journey-to-work distance when non-residential land uses are concentrated at the city centre. By definition, therefore, in the most extreme case possible the mean distance of employment from the city centre is zero. The mean journey to work distance corresponding with this value is given by the mean distance of the residential locations of all

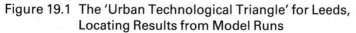

Figure 19.1 The 'Urban Technological Triangle' for Leeds, Locating Results from Model Runs

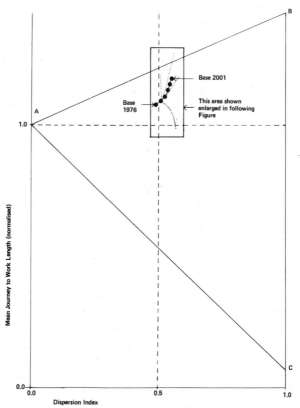

employees from the city centre. In 1971 for Leeds this value was 6.15 km. The line CB represents complete dispersal of non-residential land uses. In the application of LILT to Leeds this is interpreted by locating employment at the centre of each zone in proportion to the number of employed residents living there. At point C, where the deterrence to travel is such that all trips are made to the nearest destination, the mean journey-to-work distance is given by the mean intrazonal distance weighted by the number of employed residents in each zone. In 1971 the value was 0.47 km. At point B where distance has no deterrent effect on travel the mean distance travelled to work was 8.8 km.

These values have been used to define the structure of the triangle shown in Figure 19.1. In fact, the relative positions of the points would

Figure 19.2 The Results from the Model Runs

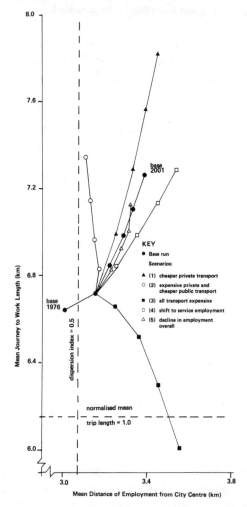

shift over time with changes in the spatial distribution of activities, for example point A would shift upwards as population decentralised. For the sake of clarity the points have been kept at the values derived from the data for the calibration year (1971). In the next section the results of the technological change scenarios will be considered in relation to this triangle.

Figure 19.3 Percentage of Population in Households Owning
One or More Cars in the Base Forecast and Five
Scenarios
(Scenarios 4 and 5 are almost identical to the
base and are omitted from the diagram)

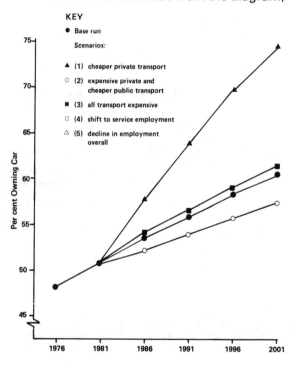

Results

The results predicted by the model for the base forecast and the five
technological change scenarios have been plotted in Figures 19.1 and
19.2. On Figure 19.2 each forecast is shown as a set of points
representing values for the years 1986, 1991, 1996 and 2001, which
have been connected for clarity. The base values for these years and for
1976 and 1981 are also shown.

It will be noted that in one case the results for 2001 lie above the
straight line between A and B. Possible explanations for this are that the
line AB is not, in reality, straight or that the structural dynamics of the
triangle have not been fully represented in the diagram.

Figure 19.4 Percentage Travelling to Work by Car in Leeds Under the Five Scenarios and the Base Forecast (Scenario 5 is almost identical to the base and is omitted from the diagram)

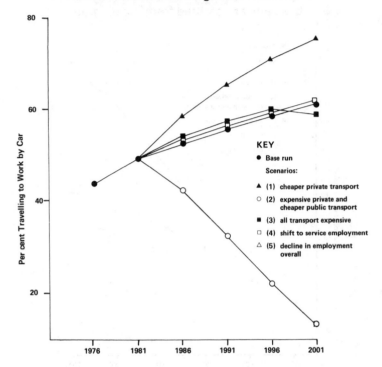

Figures 19.3 to 19.6 illustrate other model outputs which are related to those shown in Figures 19.1 and 19.2. Figure 19.3 shows the percentage of people in households owning one or more cars. Figure 19.4 shows the percentage travelling to work by car at each time point. Figures 19.5 and 19.6 show the percentages of total employment and population respectively that are located in the inner and central areas of Leeds.

In the base forecast, Figure 19.2 shows that the journey-to-work distance increases and that employment becomes more decentralised in each time period to 2001. The increasing mean journey-to-work distance reflects the dispersal of employment and population (Figures 19.5 and 19.6). The latter results from the replacement of demolished homes in the inner city by newly constructed ones on the periphery of

Figure 19.5 Percentage of Employment Located in the City Centre and Inner Suburbs of Leeds in the Base Forecast and Five Scenarios

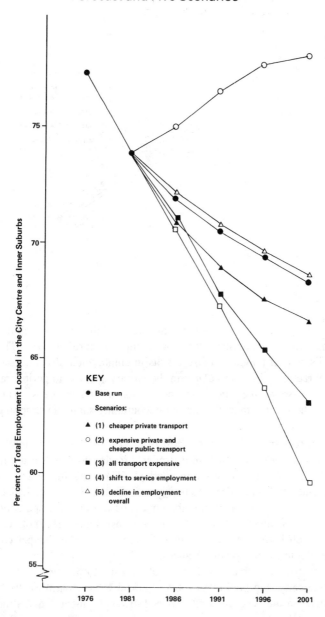

KEY

● Base run

Scenarios:

▲ (1) cheaper private transport

○ (2) expensive private and cheaper public transport

■ (3) all transport expensive

□ (4) shift to service employment

△ (5) decline in employment overall

Figure 19.6 Percentage of Population Located in City Centre and Inner Suburbs of Leeds in the Base Forecast and Five Scenarios

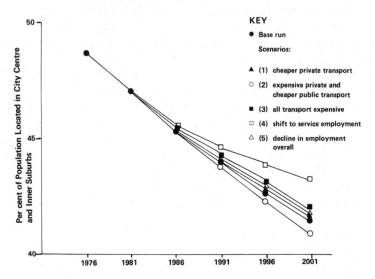

the city. The increase in the distance also reflects the greater mobility stemming from increased car ownership (Figure 19.3). The decentralisation of population also results in employment decentralisation by attracting jobs, particularly in the tertiary sectors, to peripheral locations to serve the additional population in those areas. This reinforces the local authority policy of encouraging suburban shopping centres.

The first scenario, in which the cost of private transport is reduced, results in a trajectory which is in a similar direction to the base but in which the trends are much more marked. Thus the dispersion of employment, and the mean journey-to-work length in particular, increases at a faster rate over time than in the base forecast. Population decentralises less quickly than in the base forecast (Figure 19.6) but car usage is much higher in this scenario (Figure 19.4). The cheaper car travel results in longer travel distances.

When fuel price increases cause private transport operating costs to rise dramatically, but public transport is subsidised (scenario 2), there is a reversal in the base trend of dispersal of employment. This is the only case considered here in which this occurs. It results from a relative increase in the accessibility of the city centre on which the public transport network is focused by a system of radial routes. The reduction in public transport fares leads to a large shift to public transport from both car and walking. Some of those who previously walked can now afford to travel by public transport and have chosen jobs further from their homes, thus increasing the mean distance travelled to work. The net inward movement of employment implies a slight shift towards the left in the technological triangle. In this scenario there is, not surprisingly, a very marked decline in car usage (Figure 19.4). The increase in journey-to-work length (slightly greater than in the base) reflects the fact that the cost of travel becomes very cheap by the (now) most popular mode. An increased decentralisation of population (Figure 19.6) results from the fact that less land is available for new housing in the inner areas of the city because it has been used for economic activity, reflected in the growth of employment there after 1981 (Figure 19.5).

The third scenario results in the reversal of the trend towards greater journey-to-work distances. This is the only case where this occurs. Population decentralises less quickly than in the base (Figure 19.6) while employment exhibits greater decentralisation (Figures 19.2 and 19.5). The effect of this, combined with the fact that all mechanised transport is more expensive, is to shorten the mean journey to work distance considerably. Car usage is little changed from the base (Figure 19.3) as there is little to be gained by transfer to bus, but the diagram conceals a substantial shift from bus travel to walking. Over the last time period even car usage declines.

When there is a major shift to shopping and service employment (scenario 4), the most notable effect is increased decentralisation of employment (Figures 19.2 and 19.5). This is because the location of such employment tends to be highly dependent upon the location of the population it serves. Population decentralises at a slightly slower rate than the base because of the additional land used by service industry on the periphery and the relatively greater availability of land in the centre which affects the location of new housing. The journey-to-work distance increases for the same reasons as in the base.

In the final scenario, in which there is a reduction in the total number of jobs, there is a slight slowing down in the relative growth of both population and employment in the outer areas of the city (Figures 19.5 and 19.6). Because both are less dispersed than in the base forecast, the mean trip distance to work grows less rapidly.

Conclusions

The results discussed in the previous section demonstrate the feasibility of using an urban model to predict the impact of technological change. Any such model could be used for this purpose provided that the technological change can be represented by suitable modifications to the model inputs. The effects on urban form will be based on the mechanisms incorporated within the model. However, as is clear from the examples in this paper, not all the modifications that may follow from such changes are represented within the model. In particular, the first three scenarios, which are transport-oriented, show greater impacts than the last two, whereas it may well be that the decline of the manufacturing base and the further shift to the service sector, and the decline in the number of jobs, have far greater impacts, although not necessarily on urban form in the medium term. It may well be that more sophisticated indicators of change than the ones used here are required if the impact of technological change is to be monitored and predicted.

In terms of the results from LILT, the general trends forecast with constant travel costs in real terms are of increasing dispersal of employment and increasing mean distance to work. Most of the scenarios follow these trends. The two exceptions are more expensive private transport with cheaper public transport fares (scenario 2) which reduces the dispersal of employment, and the increase in the monetary cost of all mechanised modes (scenario 3) which leads to a decrease in the mean trip length to work.

These results are quite plausible. Greater differences between the impacts of the scenarios would appear if some of the other output indicators were considered. The validity of both the methodology and the results is a matter of debate. None the less the use of LILT for forecasting and the technological triangle for displaying the results offers a practical framework for discussion, and that in itself is extremely useful.

References

Lowry, I.S. (1964) *A Model of Metropolis*, Rand Corporation, Santa Monica

Mackett, R.L. (1979) 'A Model of the Relationships Between Transport and Land Use', Working Paper 122, Institute for Transport Studies, University of Leeds

Mackett, R.L. (1983) *The Leeds Integrated Land Use Transport Model (LILT)*, Supplementary Report 805, Transport and Road Research Laboratory, Crowthorne, UK

20. IMPACT OF ENERGY FACTORS ON URBAN FORM
L. Lundqvist

Since the 'energy crisis' of 1973 considerable research effort has been devoted to energy studies of the built environment. In Sweden as much as 55 per cent of total energy use in the mid 1970s could be directly attributed to space heating and transportation. By adding the energy utilised in the production of building materials for physical infra-structures, the total may rise to 60-70 per cent.

In spite of this strong connection, the last half century has seen a gradual decoupling of settlement patterns and industrial locations from the location of energy resources or energy import facilities. The growing market shares of oil and electricity made available high-density energy carriers which were easy to distribute. The urban sprawl phenomena relied on individual transportation and space heating by use of such easily distributed energy forms. In Sweden, a large supply of inexpensive hydropower, the emerging nuclear power production and falling oil prices (in real terms) were all key elements behind the high-growth society of the 1960s.

The sudden shift on the global energy markets during the last decade has not only implied more expensive and more uncertain oil supplies and emphasised escalating costs and safety problems in the nuclear industry; it has also had a profound influence on economic policies in the industrialised countries and it has affected life styles and expectations of large groups of people. The world has only seen the beginning of a long transformation process changing the energy supplies from inexpensive and 'clean' oil and gas to more costly and dirty energy forms. Historically, such transformations have taken 50-100 years (wood coal, coal oil). A similar time period is likely to be valid for the shift from the present use of oil, gas and uranium to sustainable energy systems.

Since energy costs will be higher, it will pay to use energy more efficiently in the future. In the short term, this can be achieved through improved management of energy systems, simple conservation measures in buildings, and better fuel efficiency of new transport vehicles. Behavioural adjustments (e.g. shifts in modal split or lowering of indoor temperatures) can give important contributions. In the longer term, further improvements in energy efficiency can only be gained through more farreaching measures, such as major changes of heating and transport technologies, recycling, and new social and spatial organisations leading to more efficient use of building spaces and transport systems. This mode of *structural conservation* or improvements of *system efficiency* will certainly affect and require support from urban decision-makers.

The Swedish energy situation may turn out as an interesting pilot case for two reasons: (1) a very high initial dependence on oil and nuclear energy (about 75 per cent of total supply); and (2) an ambitious oil reduction policy (50 per cent reduction in ten years) and a parliament decision to abolish the use of nuclear energy in 25 years. Hence the Swedish energy transformation may be farreaching and more rapid than in many other countries. The comparatively high energy efficiency initially suggests that major behavioural or structural adaptations will be required at a relatively early date.

Energy Impacts on Urban Form

There are a number of direct ways in which energy factors influence urban life. Disturbances of oil and electricity supply systems incur drastic restrictions on urban functions. The oil price shocks of the 1970s resulted in modal shifts affecting the capacity utilisation of both private and public transportation. A major reintroduction of coal for urban space heating purposes will require collective heating systems due to modern environmental standards. Land-use requirements of solar collectors and seasonal heat storages will put constraints on urban form (through lower residential densities) if solar heating is going to be a viable future option. An efficient use of biomass technologies for fuel production and space heating will also have implications for urban form and function.

Even if these examples of *direct impacts* on urban land use and transportation are straightforward, the *indirect impacts* through energy interactions with the wider socio-economic environment may turn out to be of at least equal importance. The rising energy prices in the last decade created massive disturbances on the world market. Contractive economic policy actions were taken to restore balance of payments bringing about a long period of low economic growth. The 'stagflation' period has witnessed changes in competitiveness among industries in various parts of the world. Many production units of highly industrialised countries have become obsolete and a major restructuring of production has become necessary with obvious consequences for urban and regional development. Rising energy prices and falling real wages have held back housing demand and car-ownership rates. Extended over longer time periods, even minor changes in housing demand and car ownership rates will heavily influence urban form. There is a range of other important issues concerning labour demand, migration patterns, working hours, public services and technological development in general which may be affected by or may affect energy developments. For an analysis of energy impacts on urban form to be plausible in a long-term perspective, we need to take both direct and indirect impacts into account.

As part of an ambitious energy policy, urban planning may have an important role in the long-term in diversifying energy use and reducing energy vulnerability, and in stretching the limits of energy efficiency through structural conservation by carefully organised urban systems. Also in the short or medium term, urban planning may support energy policy efforts through traffic management and transport pricing, infrastructure policies (efficient use of public facilities), and incentives for efficient use of floor space and transportation (e.g. car pooling).

In the following section three ongoing projects dealing with interdependencies between energy planning on the one hand and urban and regional planning on the other will be briefly summarised. Finally, the emerging structure of a flexible system of models for urban energy impact analyses will be sketched. Throughout the chapter we distinguish between the scenario level and the urban-systems level of energy impacts. Some preliminary results will be presented to illustrate the analyses. However, firm conclusions have to await completion of the projects.

Models for the Analysis of Energy Impacts on Urban Systems

Metropolitan Planning and Future Energy Systems (Stockholm)

The metropolitan area of Stockholm comprises 25 municipalities which are mutually interdependent in terms of labour and housing market, transportation facilities, services and infrastructure. It is therefore natural that some planning functions that normally go with local governments (housing supply, transportation, energy planning) in Stockholm have been taken over by regional authorities. The importance of this metropolitan level is emphasised by the fact that approximately 40 per cent of production, income and floor space occurs in the three main metropolitan regions of Sweden.

Figure 20.1 Stockholm Energy — Urban Planning Model System

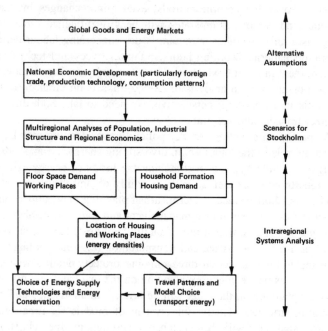

To investigate the mutual interactions between energy systems and urban structure, a multi-level model system has been developed (see Figure 20.1). It starts with an analysis of global energy markets in order to identify likely future energy price ranges and assumptions concerning the development of new energy technologies, including new technologies for space heating, electricity generation and transportation.

Given energy price assumptions and related alternatives for world trade and world market prices, the next step is to study the influences on the national level under various hypotheses concerning the result of economic policies (continuing imbalances, restored economic balance). Here we use a general equilibrium model of the Swedish economy developed at IIASA (Bergman and Por 1980). This model covers price-formation and price-dependent substitution processes in foreign trade, production technology and consumption.

In the multi-regional model step, national and international energy economic scenarios are 'translated' to consequences for the Stockholm region. We have used the multi-regional population projection model developed at IIASA (Willekens and Rogers 1978) for the computation of four quite different population scenarios based on migration patterns observed during the last 15 years. A dynamic multi-regional linear programming model has been developed for analysis of international and inter-regional trade linkages and regional economic development (Lundqvist 1980). By producing complete regional transaction accounts, the model provides information concerning private and public consumption, housing investments, employment by sector and preliminary estimations of energy demand.

The intra-regional part of the model system comprises three major components and two interfaces translating information from the multi-regional analyses to floor space demand for industry and services on the one hand and dwellings on the other hand.

The first major component of the intra-regional step computes Pareto-efficient residential location patterns based on exogenously specified workplace allocations and transportation capacities (Lundqvist and Mattsson 1983). A number of planning indicators reflecting urban planning goals (accessibility, outdoor space per capita, costs) may be used in the generation of efficient alternatives. The outcome of the model can be expressed in terms of energy densities for space heating expressing the demand for useful energy per unit area. These densities are important for determining distribution losses and investment costs in energy distribution systems (electricity, gas, district heating).

The second major component of the intra-regional step starts with information on the need for useful energy by energy density class, the composition of the building stock, costs for energy conservation, present energy supply systems, and costs and availability of potential energy supply technologies. The energy system model (MESSAGE II developed at IIASA) seeks the cost-minimising development of the energy system, energy supply and conservation (Regional Planning Office 1982; and Schrattenholzer 1981).

The third major component of the urban systems analysis estimates the energy use for transportation in future urban structures under alternative assumptions concerning income, fuel prices, public transit policies and so forth. Within the public transport board of the Stockholm County Council, the multi-modal equilibrium model EMME is presently being installed. The model is capable of producing very detailed forecasts of capacity utilisation on network links as a basis for energy accounts (Florian *et al.* 1977).

It should be clear from the above exposition that assumptions concerning the socio-economic development attached to a certain energy scenario (prices, technology) are dealt with quite extensively. Energy impacts on migration, industrial development, income and prices are considered crucial inputs to the intra-regional analyses. Also the competitiveness of urban energy supply options (such as co-production) is closely related to national energy needs.

To illustrate the discussion we will briefly report some examples of early results pertaining to a subset of the model system. These are based on two sets of global/national scenario assumptions:

1. *Economic growth recovered*.
   Slow energy price increases (2 per cent per year)
   Rapid development of net investments (2.25 per cent per year)
   Balance of payments restored 1990
   Low growth of public consumption (+1 per cent per year after 1980);
2. *Continuing Economic Crisis*.
   Rapid energy price increases (5 per cent per year)
   Slow development of net investments (1.5 per cent per year)
   Continuing balance of payment deficits after 1990
   Rapid growth of public consumption (+2.0 per cent per year till 1990, then 1.25 per cent per year).

In later work two additional scenarios have been formulated providing a more complete picture of possible growth conditions and economic policy alternatives. After running the national economic equilibrium model for the years 1990, 2005 and 2020 and the dynamic multi-regional input-output model for the time periods 1975-90, 1990-2005, 2005-20, the following results were obtained for the regional distribution of private consumption (see Figure 20.2).

According to these results, Stockholm will face a very slow and possibly negative long-term development of private consumption. Also the estimated total energy consumption stays well below the development of the national average. For other regions (such as western Sweden) the private consumption level develops faster than the national average in both scenarios. The northern region is well off in the growth case but falls below the national average in the crisis scenario. These patterns are created by a complex multi-regional interplay between final demand and production technologies (national trends from the equilibrium model) in the two cases. We have assumed that the inter-regional trade patterns are stable over time in both scenarios. If better

Figure 20.2 Development of Private Consumption in Two Energy Impact Scenarios

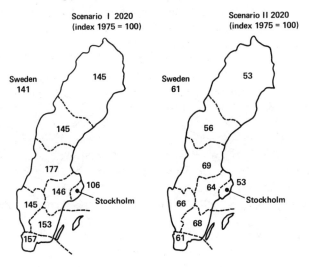

information were available, however, the effects of transport cost changes on inter-regional shipment patterns could be taken into account.

Information concerning income, housing prices (from national equilibrium model) and average age of the population (from IIASA population model) was fed into the housing demand interface and the future development of floor space per capita was computed. The next step was to run the residential location model for the two cases taking the estimated housing demand into account. (In the final round the impacts on car ownership and modal split will be included.) Figure 20.3 shows the housing energy demand under two combinations of scenario assumptions and energy conservation policies. In both cases the results are based on the volume and composition of the housing stock in each municipality according to the model results.

The two urban structures producing the energy demand patterns of Figure 20.3 differ only in terms of the housing demand and the level of energy conservation. The principles behind the urban development (specification of welfare indicators, contact patterns, land-use constraints and so on) are the same in the two cases. By also varying intra-urban priorities and constraints within reasonable limits, an overall set of urban locational structures will emerge reflecting both the

Figure 20.3 Energy Demand for Space Heating of the
Housing Stock 2020, TWh/year
(The Stockholm region is divided into 23
municipalities; 25 from 1983)

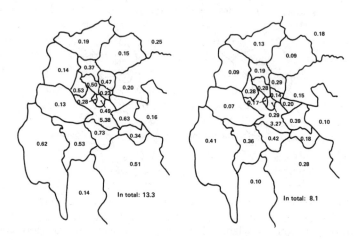

uncertainties at the scenario level and at the urban systems level. Our
two cases result in a total range of 8.1-13.3 TWh per year for the
housing energy demand in 2020. An independent estimation at the
Regional Planning Office, based on many alternatives and detailed
assumptions, arrived at a maximal range of 7.0-13.5 TWh per year.

The energy-demand figures are available on a detailed level of 105
zones. They can be used to compute energy densities as input to the
energy system optimisation. In our first case (Scenario I, no
conservation) about 75 per cent of the dwellings in 2020 are located in
areas with dwelling energy densities above 20 KWh/m^2 which,
according to accepted practice, are feasible for district heating systems.

Finally, we will report on results obtained by the energy system
(MESSAGE II) model. After a large number of computer runs, the
following robust prescriptions were made:

1. reduce the dependence on oil for space heating purposes by at least
   two-thirds during a 10-year period;
2. the share of district heating should not exceed 75 per cent;
3. use the Forsmark nuclear power reactor for electricity production (no
   retro-fitting for heat production);

4. build energy complex for co-production of methanol, heat and gas;
5. large-scale gas introduction is not competitive;
6. the annual use of electricity for space heating should maximally increase by 5 TWh.
7. the use of coal should not exceed 5 TWh/year before the year 2000;
8. conserve 15-20 per cent of the primary energy use for space heating during the 1980s.

These results were taken into account when the Regional Planning Office evaluated a recent proposal by the Greater Stockholm Energy Company to extend the district heating system and feed it by heat from a retro-fitted Forsmark nuclear reactor.

An Alternative Approach to Metropolitan Energy System Modelling (Stockholm)

Energy system models of the MESSAGE II type provide a comprehensive treatment of energy extraction or import, energy conversion, energy transportation, energy conservation and final energy use. However, the comprehensiveness is not complete: (1) regional energy networks have to be specified and treated exogenously; (2) only a small number of production units can be treated as indivisible units which implies that fixed costs are usually linearised; and (3) energy conservation measures are specified as technologies defined for each demand category. Hence, the level of energy conservation is not distinguished by heating technology or geographic location.

For the local optimisation of heating technologies in a given settlement structure, linear programming models have been developed which treat conversions and energy savings as transitions between combined technology/level-of-conservation states. However, these models treat the regional supply systems (electricity, gas, district heating) as given in terms of delivered prices and capacity limits (see Bergman 1976).

In the present study, an alternative approach for energy system modelling is sought which integrates and complements the model types discussed above. Two aims are fundamental to our approach: (1) the distribution networks should be dealt with explicitly and preferably endogenously as should the indivisibilities of heat production units; and (2) the local choices of heating technologies and energy conservation should be viewed as joint decisions which are conditioned by the access to regional energy supply networks. An iterative approach has been

Figure 20.4 Decomposition of Urban Energy System Model

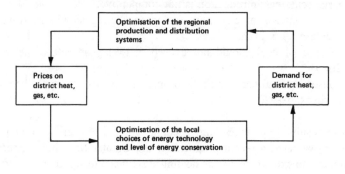

used to reduce the complexity involved by decomposing the total problem into regional and local levels (see Figure 20.4). The improvements with respect to earlier models are gained at the expense of comprehensiveness in the overall system description.

When completed, this approach to energy system modelling will be capable of providing information on how energy prices and new energy technologies affect the distribution of heating costs, energy conservation and the choice of heating technologies in an explicitly spatial setting. By varying the assumptions concerning the distribution network, alternative energy supply strategies may be investigated.

Modelling the Trade-off Between Energy Goals and Urban Planning Goals (Uppsala)

In Uppsala, north of Stockholm, ambitious planning strategies have been developed both in the energy area (energy supply, energy conservation) and for community development in general (housing supply, transportation, social and technical infrastructures). However, the linkage between energy planning and urban development planning at the intra-regional level has not been thoroughly analysed.

We have designed a residential model that is well adapted to the present Uppsala community planning context. It is an optimising model in which feasible allocations of new residences are evaluated in terms of cost and welfare criteria (Figure 20.5). In fact, this model is a slightly generalised version of the Stockholm residential location model used to generate the results in Figure 20.3.

With a base year of 1982, the model has been used to: (1) study goal conflicts and residential allocation for 1982-92 and 1982-2002; (2)

Figure 20.5 Structure of Uppsala Residential Allocation Model

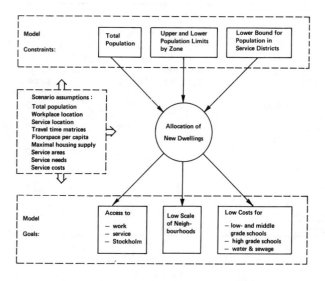

evaluate proposed residential allocations in the municipality programme (three for 1992, five for 2002); and (3) study how short-term residential allocations affect the long-term freedom of action in the three goal dimensions.

We illustrate the model results by showing a payoff table for 1992 outlining how separate optimisation of each goal component affects the other components (Table 20.1).

We observe that investment cost for social and technical infrastructure is very sensitive to the future pattern of residential location. However, cost-efficient compromise solutions are available without giving up too much welfare efficiency. Due to the short time perspective, the constraints exerted by the base-year structure only permit 10-20 per cent variation in the level of the welfare criteria. A more complete discussion of these results can be found in Lundqvist and Barkema (1984).

The five urban structures underlying Table 20.1 are extreme examples of alternatives on the urban systems level that may be generated within each scenario for national/regional socio-economic development. As pointed out in the Stockholm case, only a certain subset of these (efficient) urban structures tend to be reasonable in

Table 20.1 Illustration of Goal Conflicts in Uppsala Community Planning

Minimisation of	Welfare criteria		Cost criteria		
	Average travel time to work and services	Average size of neighbourhoods	School investment costs	Water & sewage investments costs	Total investment costs
Value of					
Travel time index (min.)	34.8	38.4	36.4	36.9	36.2
Size index (1,000 persons)	7.6	5.9	7.0	7.3	7.1
School costs (milj. SW cr)	23.9	40.5	0.0	54.7	0.0
Water & sewage costs (milj. SW cr)	30.6	58.9	35.9	20.6	20.6
Total costs (milj. SW cr)	54.5	99.4	35.9	75.3	20.6

Figure 20.6 An Illustration of 'The Urban Triangle' in the Uppsala Case (*Workplace dispersion* measures the fraction of work and services distributed according to the base year population. The rest is allocated in the CBD area. The *travel time* index measures the average public transit travel time to an opportunity set of workplaces and services defined for each residential location. This opportunity set has been varied between 3 per cent and 97 per cent of all workplaces and services. For each solution, the values of the size and total cost indices are given in parenthesis)

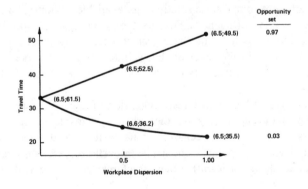

combination with each socio-economic scenario. Hence, the travel time minimising solution is more likely to be related to a high energy price scenario than a low energy price scenario. High space consumption (low neighbourhood size) tends to be linked to high private consumption. Alternative future contact patterns may further complicate these linkages.

A final illustration of the scope of the Uppsala model is provided in Figure 20.6. Here the dispersion of workplaces and the sizes of workplace and service opportunity sets are varied to sketch a picture of 'the urban triangle' proposed in Chapter 1. When the opportunity sets are large, the average travel time index reflects potential contact costs to the regional supply of workplaces and services in Uppsala. When the opportunity sets are small, the average travel time index reflects potential contact costs to the local supply of workplaces and services.

We observe that very different workplace location and contact patterns give rise to fairly small variations in terms of residential location (average neighbourhood size varies between 6,500 and 6,600; the fraction of new dwellings allocated to the central-city area varies between 50 per cent and 64 per cent). This is because we have used the same set of relative weights on travel time, size and cost criteria in all calculations. The resulting urban forms produce quite different average travel times depending on the nature of the future contact pattern. For each set of priorities in the multi-objective residential allocation model, a specific urban triangle may be generated.

We are about to further develop the Uppsala model by also integrating space heating energy considerations. With given district heat production capacities and distribution networks, the local choice of heat technologies will be modelled in a linear programming module which will be linked to the residential location model. Hence, energy planning goals will be introduced as a third major goal dimension beside welfare and cost criteria. The extended model will be able to highlight interdependencies between urban energy planning and urban development planning and how these interactions are affected by changing energy prices and new energy technologies.

Towards a Flexible Model System for Systematic Studies of Energy Impacts on Urban Form

We have presented three different but related approaches to energy analysis in an urban context:

Figure 20.7 A Flexible Model System for Analysing Direct and Indirect Impacts of Energy Factors on Urban Form and Function

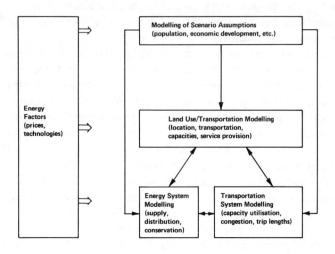

1. one comprehensive model system for metropolitan planning of energy systems and land use;
2. one metropolitan energy system model emphasising the indivisibilities in district heat production, the geographical structure of distribution networks and detailed energy demand calculations on the local level;
3. one multi-criteria model of urban land use energy planning emphasising the interdependencies between urban structure and the achievement of energy objectives.

In the first and third cases, indirect as well as direct impacts of energy factors on urban form are taken into account. The second approach treats direct impacts on the energy system of energy price and technology assumptions. The models discussed in this chapter can be seen as examples of an emerging flexible model system for urban energy impact analyses (see Figure 20.7).

The Uppsala model represents one attempt to extend land use/ transportation models to cover energy aspects. In the Uppsala model, this is done by extending the residential location model to include space heating energy demand. The welfare maximising residential location model by Mattsson (1984) can be seen as an analogous extension towards an explicit modelling of transportation energy demand. We also investigate the possibilities of using detailed energy system and transportation system models to relate space heating and transportation energy demand to simple measures of urban form (accessibility, density). Such 'short cuts' would make our land use/transportation models (see Lundqvist and Mattsson 1983) capable of analysing energy saving urban forms.

We have outlined a research strategy for a systematic treatment of direct and indirect energy impacts on urban form and function. These impacts are both short run and long run. Energy prices as well as costs and availability of new technologies in energy production and energy use are important elements in our analysis. There are very different views on how these key factors will develop in the next few decades. Moreover, the role of energy concerns in the formation of individual behaviour and urban policy making is uncertain: energy is but one factor influencing urban development. Finally, even from a pure energy efficiency point of view, very different urban structures may be optimal depending on the specific socio-economic context in terms of national energy needs, availability of land and local energy sources, level of economic and technological development and so forth. While the compact city may be energy efficient in one situation, a system of decentralised self-sufficient settlements may be energy efficient under other conditions.

Our approach permits a broad analysis of the socio-economic context, the urban space heating system, the urban transportation system and the land use transportation linkages. By covering external uncertainties in terms of scenarios and uncertainties concerning urban values, policies and behaviour in terms of urban system alternatives, we can investigate the nature of robust urban developments preserving good options for future adaptations.

References

Bergman, L. (1976) *An Energy Demand Model for the Swedish Residential Heating Sector*, Document D4:1976, Swedish Council for Building Research

Bergman, L. and Por, A. (1980) 'A Quantitative General Equilibrium Model of Swedish Economy', Working Paper WP-80-4, International Institute for Applied Systems Analysis, Laxenburg

Florian, M., Chapleau, R., Nguyen, S., Achim, C., James, L. and Lefebvre, J. (1977) *EMME: A Planning Method for Multi-Modal Urban Transportation Systems*, Publication No. 62, Centre de Recherche sur les Transports, Universite de Montreal

Lundqvist, L. (1980) *A Dynamic Multiregional Input-output Model for Analysing Regional Development, Employment and Energy Use*, TRITA-MAT-1980-20, Department of Mathematics, Royal Institute of Technology, Stockholm

Lundqvist, L. and Barkema, H. (1984) *A Policy Oriented Model for Residential Location Based on Cost and Welfare Criteria*, Research Group for Urban and Regional Planning, Royal Institute of Technology, Stockholm

Lundqvist, L. and Mattsson, L.-G. (1983) 'Transportation Systems and Residential Location', *European Journal of Operational Research, 12*

Regional Planning Office (1982) *Long Term Energy Supply Strategies for Stockholm County*, Stockholm

Schrattenholzer, L. (1981) *The Energy Supply Model MESSAGE*, RR-81- 31, International Institute for Applied Systems Analysis, Laxenburg

Willekens, F. and Rogers, A. (1978) *Spatial Population Analysis Methods and Computer Programs*, RR-78-18, International Institute for Applied Systems Analysis, Laxenburg

21. MODELLING URBAN DYNAMICS
W. van Lierop and P. Nijkamp

The post-1945 period has demonstrated significant shifts in spatial and urban systems. Although settlement patterns have always been in a state of flux, contemporary changes in cities and in urban systems show transitions which have profound consequences for the spatial organisation of our world. These changes concern both the internal mechanism of the urban system and the position of the city in a total spatial system (see Gauthier 1970; van der Knaap 1980; Korcelli 1980). It should be noted, however, that the urbanisation trend has not demonstrated a uniform pattern within and between nations.

Rapid urban concentration has been associated with many problems: congestion, segregation, decline in quality of life, pollution, unemployment, lack of satisfactory facilities, crime and so forth. Urban problems have been and still are related not only to efficiency questions (for example, devising rules for an optimal allocation of resources), but also to equity questions. Equity problems are not only relevant at the level of interregional inequalities, but also for intra-urban, intra-regional and urban-regional inequalities (for example, unemployment rates in some urban districts are much higher than in peripheral regions and vice-versa). It is no surprise that urban inhabitants have in more recent times made an attempt to avoid the negative externalities of large urban agglomerations by moving to medium-sized and smaller towns or to rural areas. Clearly, this movement was co-determined by shifts in priorities regarding quality of life and leisure time (for elaboration of additional factors see Chapters 2 and 3).

At present three different trends can be identified in spatial and urban systems. The first is one of continued growth for large urban agglomerations (major cities in Eastern and Southern Europe, many urban centres in developing and semi-developed countries — e.g. Napoli, Mexico, Seoul, Bombay — where one often observes an accelerated urban growth). A second trend in many western countries is urban decline, urban sprawl and deurbanisation (e.g. Berlin, Boston; see Chapter 7). The third trend is the more recent re-urbanisation of inner cities which exhibited strong deurbanisation some years ago (e.g. several medium-sized cities in the US or Amsterdam in the Netherlands).

The past decade has been marked by an increasing interest in analysing the structure and development of urban areas (e.g. van den

Berg *et al.* 1982, Bryce 1977, 1979: Nijkamp and Rietveld 1981). Several reasons may explain this phenomenon. First, the (sometimes opposite) shifts in urban systems have led to the need for a more problem-oriented view, compared to previous decades. Secondly, the uncertainty inherent in structural economic change has evoked interest in long-term bottleneck factors associated with urban growth processes. Thirdly, lack of success of conventional models in policy and practice has seen the need for a re-evaluation of existing scientific analytical tools (with a special emphasis on dynamic and multi-disciplinary techniques). And finally, economic stagnation has made the future prospects of cities less favourable, so that instabilities may be expected.

In this chapter strategies for analysing urban/metropolitan developments in a spatial context are considered. Two aspects emerge. First, cities are interacting with more general regional and national systems (a nested structure, either bottom-up or top-down); and secondly, cities may sometimes display highly non-linear dynamic growth patterns (including bifurcation).

Several crucial issues in analysing such developments will be briefly outlined. After some methodological aspects, spatial and dynamic impact patterns of urban and regional processes will be considered. Subsequently, intra-metropolitan structures will be discussed, with special attention to the industrial sector, the housing market and infrastructure. Special emphasis will be placed on the following issues in these dynamic processes: *key factors*, *threshold factors*, *desired developments* and *bottlenecks* (see Chapter 7). The confrontation of these issues leads to an outline of research areas for dynamic urban/ spatial developments. The final part of the chapter deals with the integration of the information from the three sectors into the dynamic framework of the earlier sections.

Methodological Remarks

An adequate study of complex and dynamic urban phenomena requires a conceptual framework characterised by completeness, relevance and a lack of ambiguity (cf. the holistic view in an urban systems approach). Urban processes are complicated multi-dimensional phenomena which can hardly be studied by one separate discipline (see Nijkamp 1979). In general, the complex urban world can be described *inter alia* by means of the following categories of variables:

1. *economic* — stocks and flows of commodities, scale advantages, agglomeration economies, financial variables, employment, growth perspectives, capacity constraints and distributional effects;
2. *spatial* — spatial interactions such as migration flows and commuting flows, spatial spin-off and spill-over effects, spatial distribution of economic activities, congestion;
3. *process* and *state* — technical progress, innovation, management and organisation, suprastructure, communication, energy;
4. *socio-political* — power conflicts, decision structures, interest groups, policy controls;
5. *basic* — demographic structure, consumption and production patterns, long-run dynamics of urban developments.

A comprehensive urban model should try to incorporate all these categories. However, no discipline can guarantee the validity of the complex relationships describing urban structures and processes by means of a wide variety of cross-disciplinary variables. Even a systems approach is not capable of solving this validation problem, although it may provide an integral picture of urban phenomena. Therefore, a holistic view of the pluralist urban reality is problematic (cf. Stewart 1972).

In our opinion, it is worthwhile considering another direction, viz. an economic analysis of urban phenomena which tries to take into account cross-disciplinary relationships in so far as they influence the economic aspects of urban problems. This more restricted approach may have a firmer basis in empirical and theoretical evidence from the existing body of economic knowledge. Clearly, in addition to empirical estimations of structural economic relationships, techniques such as simulation may be used in order to get some information on the behaviour of complex urban systems.

In addition to the five categories of variables above, the *structure* of urban systems (the interactions between components or the causality pattern) deserves closer attention. A simple example of interactions between components can be found in Wilson (1981), who describes the structure of an urban system in terms of population activities, economic activities and communication infrastructure (see Figure 21.1).

Clearly, this structure is rudimentary and requires an extension in several directions. This can be achieved by designing a complete module for each component (e.g. a population activity model). Such a modular design may facilitate the construction of an integrated urban systems model. However, the *dynamics* of such models are a source of

Figure 21.1   Main Structure of an Urban System
(Source: Wilson 1981, p. 265)

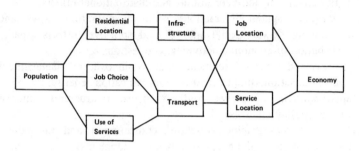

many estimation problems (see Casti 1983; Forrester 1969), while *the scale of analysis* (micro versus macro, or bottom-up versus top-down) leads to many analytical problems.

Usually, a validation of urban economic theories requires the construction of a mathematical model describing all relevant relationships of an urban system. Such a model is partial in character, because only certain aspects (measured by means of variables specific to certain disciplines) are taken into account. Consequently, any validation is only a *partial* test on the reliability of the ingredients in the model.

It may be worthwhile to formulate a set of methodological criteria which have to be fulfilled by urban economic models, so that, apart from the theoretical foundation of the model itself, their structure and results may be validated. Major criteria for urban economic modelling are:

1. An urban system is an *open* system, so that potential spatial interactions and spillover effects are to be taken into account in urban modelling.
2. An urban economic system is an *interwoven* system in which social, political and demographic variables exert a significant influence; thus cross-disciplinary relationships between urban economic variables and other variables should not be neglected.
3. Urban phenomena are sometimes of a *qualitative* nature (e.g. measured by means of ordinal numbers); such qualitative variables may not be left out of consideration, when they are judged to be relevant.
4. Urban phenomena are in general *multidimensional*, so that the attributes of these phenomena are to be measured by means of multidimensional profiles.

5. Urban models may have several functions (illustrative, analytical, explanatory, policy-oriented), but normally a model will be appropriate only for one specific function; the ingredients of a model have to be in agreement with its *specific functions* (e.g. a policy analysis model should incorporate policy actors).

6. Urban phenomena are the result of *human decisions and human behaviour*, so that any urban picture should reflect behavioural relationships or conditions (at either a microscopic or a macroscopic level); sometimes only a probabilistic approach is possible.

7. The *size* of an urban economic model should be in accordance with the aim of the model (e.g. a special interest in only one variable will normally not require the construction of an extensive integrated model); there is usually a declining marginal impact of model size on its effectiveness with regard to a specific variable.

8. Urban phenomena are highly *dynamic* in nature. Hence the *stability* of an urban economic model has to be analysed or tested (e.g. by means of sensitivity analyses, or simulation experiments); there is no need to concentrate only on equilibrium models, because sometimes dis-equilibrium models (e.g. catastrophe-type models) may provide a more reliable picture of urban crises.

9. The urban model at hand should incorporate *crucial key ingredients* such as actors, sectors, distributional aspects, structure patterns and so forth (at least in as far as these elements are necessary for the analysis concerned).

It should be noted that these criteria are fairly general and have to be adjusted for each specific urban problem. For instance, the focus on urban problems has gradually shifted from urban growth and land use problems to problems of intra-urban equity, urban quality-of-life, urban amenities and urban policies. Consequently, the abovementioned criteria are not static, but have to be related to the changes in priority of issues for urban analysis and decision.

An Interdependent Nested Spatial Structure

Urban and metropolitan areas do not display autonomous development processes, but are strongly linked to broader regional, national and international processes (demographic change, international migration, labour market conditions, and so on). Interactions between urban areas (or cities) and regions (or nations) presuppose the existence of a communication sector (transportation, traffic, migration, telephone communication, video systems). Clearly, communication *per se* is a flow, whereas regions and urban areas are stocks, so that they have different dimensions. This situation is similar to the existence of links and nodes in a network. The resulting interactions between links and nodes are represented in Figure 21.2.

This figure displays a nested structure from a spatial point of view, as urban developments are co-determined by developments in regions and in the communication sector. Clearly, such interactions are a result of functional and economic relationships between all components. The interior (dashed) triangle indicates that models, methods and techniques provide an operational tool for analysing such nested development patterns.

In studying these patterns, three important factors have to be considered: *threshold*, *key* and *bottleneck* factors. Threshold factors refer to the necessary conditions before an actual growth process can start (e.g. infrastructure endowments) key factors refer to variables that exert major impacts (e.g. presence of energy resources) on the long-term development of an urban area, and bottleneck factors refer to conditions that hamper a continued growth process (e.g. population density, congestion, environmental pollution). These three factors respectively make up the conditions for, the driving forces of and the constraints on dynamic urban development. They also lead to a logistic growth curve of cities, and are analogous to the phases of economic growth distinguished by Rostow (1978). Clearly, all three elements are of crucial importance in studying urban growth processes.

The S-shaped growth curve of an urban system deserves closer analysis, as there are three additional elements that may affect this logistic growth pattern: *initial values*, *policy controls* and the *possibility frontier* (or development space). The *initial values* of a complex spatial system refer to a compound set of threshold values at the lower part of the S-shaped curve. The various elements of a spatial system may display diverse logistic growth patterns and hence be characterised by synergistic effects. If the system is only driven by a single force and characterised by a single element, the threshold value is uniquely determined. Otherwise, the threshold value is co-determined by the initial values of the remaining variables characterising the state of the system. Such interaction patterns may affect the level at which a dynamic system will operate (see also May 1974).

The abovementioned key factors may have two underlying mechanisms, viz. *exogenous parameters* and *policy controls*. The

Figure 21.2 Metropolitan-Regional Interactions

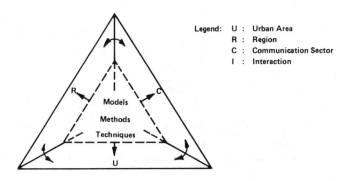

Legend: U : Urban Area
R : Region
C : Communication Sector
I : Interaction

policy controls depend to a large extent on the desired development patterns for the system concerned and are hence co-determined by political priorities, social interests, power conflicts, and so on. Although many urban systems display uncontrolled growth and decline patterns, such policy controls are essential in long-run urban policy analysis.

Finally, the *possibility frontier* or *development space* has to be mentioned; this is the set of feasible solutions (determined *inter alia* by technical, social and financial constraints) within which the actual development (including consequences of policy actions) may take place.

The nested structure becomes more evident if the urban segment (U) from Figure 21.2 is regarded as a projection of a more complex and compound urban system (see for a general exposition of multi-layer projection, Hafkamp 1983). Such an urban system may be composed of at least three major interacting components: the industrial sector I (including employment, technology); the housing sector H (including residential choices, quality of life); and infrastructure N (including roads, facilities). These interactions are represented in Figure 21.3.

The nested structure of urban developments can be illustrated by means of Figure 21.4, which displays a spatially and sectorally interdependent nested structure. Clearly, the I, H and N segments might also be projected on the regional compartment or on the infrastructure compartment. Formally, this would require a fully integrated (top-down and bottom-up) model for a regional urban system.

Figure 21.3 Intra-urban Interactions

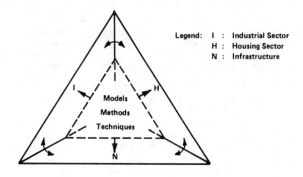

Legend: I : Industrial Sector
         H : Housing Sector
         N : Infrastructure

Figure 21.4 A Nested Structure of Regional-Urban
             Interactions

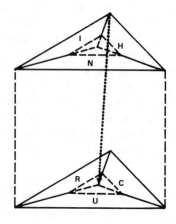

Dynamic Structures

Regional and urban dynamics may display a smooth transition, but also
a fast-changing (sometimes even catastrophic) type of behaviour. The
analysis of these dynamics requires an explanation in terms of
threshold, key and bottleneck factors at the intra-urban, intra-regional
and urban-regional levels. In this regard, the development space of the
urban and regional system, the initial values of the system's elements
and the policy controls also have to be taken into account (including all

Figure 21.5 Structural Dynamics Within an Urban System

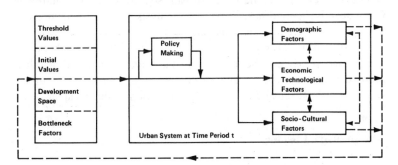

kinds of synergistic effects). Both external and internal conditions may affect the stability of an urban system. The current economic stagnation especially may lead to unstable urban development patterns.

The following causes for structural changes of complex economic systems may be mentioned (see Nijkamp 1982; Nijkamp and Schubert 1983): monetary changes (e.g. the naive quantity theory), resource scarcity (e.g. lack of food), profit behaviours (e.g. acceleration and deceleration of capital accumulation), bottlenecks (e.g. inertia in the primary sector), investment behaviour (e.g. inertia in capital adjustments), systems dynamics (e.g. unco-ordinated feedback mechanisms) and innovations (especially lack of diffusion).

The first four factors do not have a specific urban/regional dimension so that their emergence may have a top-down effect (from the national economy) on an urban system. The next three factors have a clearer spatial dimension, so that they can be used more properly for an *endogenous* explanation of urban/spatial development. These factors may also be important for explaining a wave-like or S-shaped development pattern: each retardation of growth is caused by bottleneck factors, each acceleration implies favourable threshold values and key factors. This is also common to 'demand-pull' versus 'depression-trigger' hypotheses regarding the impacts of industrial innovations.

Long-term driving forces (key factors) for an urban system include demographic developments, economic-technological factors and socio-cultural factors. Their autonomous growth patterns and sometimes drastic changes can be structured or even stimulated by policy-making. Their developments may lead to structural changes in dynamic urban systems (see Figure 21.5).

It should be noted that threshold, key and bottleneck factors may emerge in either of the three urban segments (I, H, and N). Consequently, a solid nested dynamic analysis of such interactions is necessary in order to understand the complex long-term behaviour of such a system. In this regard, qualitative calculus, bifurcation theory or tensor theory may be useful to study the structure and the stability properties of the system. The successive components of the urban system will be discussed in a subsequent section of this Chapter.

The Industrial Sector

Industry and Metropolitan Development

Until recently, urban economic problems were often regarded as a result of spatial maldistribution, marked by sheer concentration of activities. It was widely accepted that these problems could be solved by an intra-metropolitan redistribution of population and activities in a small number of separate suburban locations.

Such ideas were always based on the assumption of metropolitan economic growth. Yet in the last decade urban economic decline became common in big metropolitan areas all over the Western world. A relatively high urban unemployment was accompanied by a high loss rate of urban firms. Technical and organisational factors on the one hand, and the ageing and inflexibility of older 'heavy' industrial areas on the other, caused the traditional locations to lose a great deal of their attractiveness. Heavy industry moved to suburban or even peripheral locations with better infrastructure and good connections with national and international traffic and transportation networks. Many ancillary business firms followed this pattern. Central Business Districts (CBD) became typified by an unbalanced growth of big offices and shopping malls. So, the urban economy extended over a much wider area, creating in this way real metropolitan regions with clear spatial economic *diversification*. The consequence of this diversific-ation was a tension in the labour market concerning a shortage of specific types of jobs in some areas, while an oversupply of labour emerged elsewhere. One of the results was a tremendous traffic problem which made the conditions for location in certain areas worse.

Industrial Key Factors

To a large extent, metropolitan developments are influenced by factors having a key impact on the intra-metropolitan economic growth patterns. Such factors include: agglomeration effects (benefits of scale, location benefits, etc.); decline of industrial sectors which are heavily represented in the metropolitan economy; infrastructural developments; technical developments and innovations (e.g. microelectronics); and changes in available income. Appropriate social overhead capital leading to sufficient urban infrastructure facilities and positive agglomeration effects may transform the city into a centre of new and innovative activity.

Threshold Values

Several threshold values have to be fulfilled to make the key factors stimulate new intra-metropolitan economic growth. The metropolitan system should contain enough capital, land and qualified labour for R & D. It should stimulate the use of direct productive capital and infrastructure capital; and should be able to create a market for new products. The metropolitan structure and production system should not be energy-inefficient, but flexible in the choices of its energy sources. Sufficient attractive housing not far from new industrial settlements should be available, and environmental pollution should be kept within acceptable limits.

Desired Developments and Policy Issues

As a result of the above requirements, the following policy issues related to the industrial sector have emerged: stimulation of a better distribution of employment in metropolitan areas; to encourage integration of working and living within functional urban areas; and to encourage the settlement of technologically oriented companies within the city centres (stimulating growth of the quaternary and R and D sectors).

Bottlenecks

Bottlenecks to the realisation of these desired developments in metropolitan industry include the absence of sufficient capital, land or *skilled* labour to fulfil substantial growth, lack of innovative capacity, and environmental requirements.

Industrial Research Issues

Important research issues include: the relation between technical innovation, employment and metropolitan development; unemployment and intra-metropolitan mobility; the frictions caused by segmented and segregated labour markets; the influence of reduced working hours on metropolitan spatial requirements; and the possibilities of a renewed integration of living and working.

In general, these research items have become increasingly complex. Standard statistical and econometric analytical methods are hardly suitable any longer to cope with them. Disaggregate analysis for specific sub-areas or sub-populations seem more important, combined with qualitative (soft) data techniques or behavioural methods. Also, multidisciplinary approaches and systems analyses seem promising.

The Housing Sector

Housing Sector and Metropolitan Development

Typical of the first stages of post-1945 metropolitan development has been the migration of the urban population to suburban areas at various distances from the city centre with a strict separation between working and living. In this respect the rise in per capita incomes in most western countries after 1945 and the socialisation possibilities provided by the car, offered unprecedented opportunities for the urban population to move into modern dwellings in new and less densely populated areas. Due to the nature of demand (spatial and by dwelling type) and low building prices, the construction of housing was largely concentrated in new suburban areas. The old cities lost many inhabitants (even in an absolute sense) and old inner cities exhibited decay (urban renewal started only much later). Functional metropolitan areas arose with special sections for living (dormitory cities), working (heavy industrial parks), outdoor recreation, and central city services (CBD). An obvious drawback to this development was the increase in distance between all these areas, adding to traffic and transportation congestion problems.

Housing Key Factors

According to the literature, the factors which play a central role in the functioning of the metropolitan housing market include: demographic factors (trends and/or overall changes in household formation, household size, etc.); net migration; cheaper lot prices at increasing distance from the CBD; oversupply of dwellings in relatively remote suburban areas; tension on the housing sub-markets (with better amenity conditions) closer to the CBD; the change of old city neighbourhoods into 'slums'; the creation of facilities like schools, swimming-pools and so forth in new suburbs and the closure (or absence) of these facilities in older city areas; and the fact that people perceive the inner city environment to be unsafe for young children.

Threshold Factors

Threshold factors involved in housing market development include: infrastructure facilities; public building programmes (including financial aspects); restriction in admission to specific housing sub-markets; interest rates; and the availability of sufficient building space.

Desired Developments and Policy Issues

In many Western metropolitan areas some of the following issues concerning the housing sector are becoming important: the creation of new housing areas according to the dwelling preferences of households which are willing to move, but at the same time, intensive conservation of living areas within the old city centres; urban renewal and further increase of density of urban building; revitalisation of city life and absolute growth of population living in inner city neighbourhoods; the creation of a flexible housing market (viz. the housing market should not constrain labour mobility); and where possible, integration of working and living, but strict segregation of living and heavy industry.

Bottlenecks

Bottlenecks to development in the housing sector can be caused by: absence of sufficient public funds; negative expectations of potential movers concerning their future job position and/or income level; interest rates; pollution; and shortage of building space.

Housing Research Issues

These include: changes of housing preferences over time; differences between dwelling preferences and actual demand; supply demand relations per sub-market; relations between dwelling mobility, job mobility and traffic and transportation conditions; the construction of technically new houses; and the influence of various economic circumstances on moving behaviour.

The main body of research on housing has basically been static until now and undertaken with little consideration of the entire set of aspects influencing the housing market (like labour market conditions, environmental circumstances and so forth). Interest seems to be increasing in more in-depth (disaggregate and behavioural) housing studies (focusing on mobility motives as well as location patterns, and including soft data analysis); more dynamic approaches; approaches which connect disaggregate and aggregate analysis; and more integrated (systems) approaches.

Infrastructure

Infrastructure and Metropolitan Development

The tremendous growth of infrastructure during the last 50 years has been a major factor in the development of cities. At the same time lack of integration between various kinds of infrastructure (for instance, of regional with urban infrastructure) started to cause the typical metropolitan congestion of traffic and transportation. To increase mobility, new entrances to the old inner cities had to be created in conjunction with spacious parking facilities; space-consuming traffic and transportation networks were built between the various metropolitan areas (mainly for the private car); and special infrastructure facilities in the new and separated areas were created for heavy industry.

Yet, old inner cities became increasingly less accessible, while external costs of infrastructure and traffic went up tremendously. At the same time, the financial losses of public transport became higher every year. The demand for mobility, however, also kept rising, still causing very large traffic and transportation problems. Even modern sophisticated communication networks have not been able to reduce this need for mobility.

Infrastructure Key Factors

Key factors influencing metropolitan infrastructure include: the functional diversification of metropolitan areas; the supply of relatively cheap and high-quality housing in suburbs at increasing distances from the CBD; changes in the demand for transportation for various reasons (work, social, recreation); the demand for parking space in the CBD and shopping areas; the growth of the (tele)communication sector; and changes in vehicle efficiency.

Threshold Factors

Threshold factors for infrastructure developments include: spatial constraints; availability or shortage of metropolitan capital; energy inefficiency and energy substitution possibilities; planning, environmental and technical constraints; and expected undesired stimulation of mobility.

Desired Developments and Policy Issues

In most metropolitan areas the following infrastructural policy goals are important: better integration of various infrastructure projects; more efficient use of existing infrastructure; reduction in the need of (or demand for) mobility (e.g. by shortening the distances between workplace and dwelling); and rehabilitation of the old centres.

Bottlenecks

The desired infrastructure developments might not materialise due to conflicting political interests; shortage of public funds; or technological difficulties.

Infrastructural Research Issues

Research issues include: cost differences between infrastructure for private and for public transport; energy-efficient traffic and transportation systems; changes in mobility patterns; the relation between car ownership, car use and changing energy supply (or prices); and the mobility consequences of the introduction of new communication systems. In this research there is increasing demand for dynamics studies, behavioural analysis, systems approaches and forecasting oriented techniques.

Conclusion and Research Outlook

How should the information from the above three sectors be integrated into the dynamic systems framework described earlier in the chapter? Can that framework cope with the developments within and between the various urban and regional sectors and developments of the entire system, and deal with cross-disciplinary relationships in this integration process?

For each sector, one may identify a set of policy issues (or key factors) which may have a direct or indirect impact on another sector. For instance, a housing policy may indirectly lead to an increased attractiveness of urban districts, resulting in traffic problems (related to the infrastructure sector).

Instead of a sector-specific policy or focus on one key factor, combinations should also be considered. Such packages are usually described by *scenarios*, representing a consistent set of policy plans (and/or key factors) dealing with various sectors or relations between sectors, or relations between one or more sectors and the entire system

Figure 21.6 A Three-level Impact Matrix

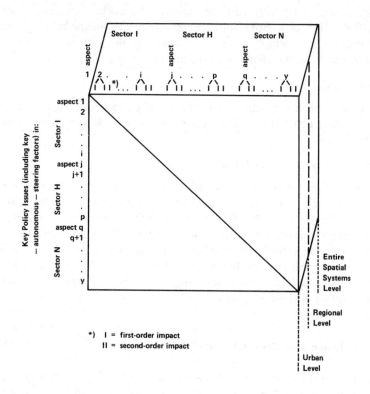

(see Chapter 22). In order to get a systematic overview of key factors and policy issues which may help in the definition of policy plans and/or the description of relevant scenarios, it could be useful to define a three-level impact matrix as presented in Figure 21.6.

Figure 21.6 is nothing more than an extension of economic impact analysis (see e.g. Nijkamp 1983). It aims at gauging all important first-order and second-order impacts that elements of sectors in urban and regional systems exert on each other. The result of such a comprehensive description should be a better understanding, in a dynamic sense, of the systems relations on which more adequate policy making could be based.

For the completion of Figure 21.6, a wide variety of econometric models are currently available. A particular problem in this respect is the availability of data necessary for gauging the (direct and indirect) effects within and between sectors, and concerning the entire system. Many of the effects in Figure 21.6 may be either quantitative or qualitative. It should be noted that qualitative information is by no means *a priori* inferior or irrelevant information. In addition, if no other information is available, qualitative statements are the only relevant ones in a practical situation. Usually in cases where no (or insufficient) quantitative data are available, no operational econometric model exists to describe the relations in specific cells of Figure 21.6. Consequently, it is difficult to make cardinal assessments of the various effects and one has to stick with soft statements.

Promising research is currently being undertaken into new data collection techniques and into qualitative data analysis (see Nijkamp *et al.* 1984). Undoubtedly this will facilitate the completion of impact matrices conforming to Figure 21.6 in an operational and adequate way for systems analysis. In this respect it is worthwhile to mention longitudinal data sampling, economic-psychological group discussion techniques, qualitative calculus, fuzzy set analysis, loglinear modelling and Lisrel techniques.

Another problem in completing Figure 21.6, partly connected with the new developments in qualitative data analysis, is the issue of comprehensiveness. What level of detail is required for this three-level impact matrix? Possible answers to this question are related to two current research approaches. One approach opts for relatively *simple* models in order to get a quick dynamic overview of the entire system (e.g. by means of micro-simulation). The other continuously searches in a *complex* way for more adequate models in order to be able to take into account all details of reality (e.g. by means of disaggregate choice models). In this respect, one can pay much attention to one subsystem (or even one aspect) of an urban and regional system and hardly any attention to the overall structure. Urgent policy questions may not allow detailed analysis, whereas limited research funds and time will usually restrict complex modelling to only parts of the system.

In our view both lines of research are worthwhile, the first assisting policy-making directly, the second developing instruments to aid future policy-making. Urban and regional information systems and models to facilitate policy making are still in a stage of adolescence (cf. Nijkamp and Rietveld 1984), but more mature (both adequate and efficient) methods are rapidly emerging.

References

Berg, L. van den, Drewerr, R., Klaassen, L.H., Rossi, A. and Vijverberg, C.H.T. (1982) *Urban Europe, A Study of Growth and Decline*, Pergamon Press, Oxford

Bryce, H.J. (1977) *Small Cities in Transition*, Ballinger, Cambridge, Massachusetts

Bryce, H.J. (1979) *Revitalizing Cities*, Lexington Books, Cambridge, Massachusetts

Casti, J. (1983) *Topological Methods for Social and Behavioural Systems*, RR-83-3, International Institute for Applied Systems Analysis, Laxenburg

Forrester, J.W. (1969) *Urban Dynamics*, The MIT Press, Cambridge, Massachusetts

Gauthier, H.L. (1970) 'Geography, Transportation and Regional Develoment', *Economic Geography, 46*, 612-19

Hafkamp, W.A. (1983) *Triple-Layer Model*, PhD Dissertation, Department of Economics, Free University, Amsterdam

Knaap, G.A. van der (1980) *Population Growth and Urban Systems Development*, Martinus Nijhoff, Boston/The Hague

Korcelli, P. (1980) 'Urban Change: An Overview of Research and Planning Issues', Working Paper WP-80-30, International Institute for Applied Systems Analysis, Laxenburg

May, R.M. (1974) 'Biological Populations with Nonoverlapping Generations', *Science,* No. 186, 645-7

Nijkamp, P. (1979) *Multidimensional Spatial Data and Decision Analysis*, John Wiley, Chichester/New York

Nijkamp, P. (1982) 'Long Waves or Catastrophes in Regional Development', *Socio-Economic Planning Sciences, 16*, 261-71

Nijkamp, P. (1983) 'Qualitative Impact Assessments of Spatial Policies in Developing Countries', *Regional Development Dialogue, 4*, 44-65

Nijkamp, P., Leitner, H., and Wrigley, N. (eds) (1984) *Measuring the Unmeasurable*, Martinus Nijhoff, The Hague

Nijkamp, P. and Rietveld, P. (1981) *Cities in Transition: Problems and Policies*, Martinus Nijhoff, The Hague

Nijkamp, P. and Rietveld, P. (eds) (1984) *Information Systems for Integrated Regional Planning*, North-Holland Publishing Co., Amsterdam

Nijkamp, P. and Schubert, U. (1983) *Structural Change in Urban Systems*, Collaborative Paper CP-83-57, International Institute for Applied Systems Analysis, Laxenburg

Rostow, W.W. (1978) *The World Economy*, Macmillan, London

Stewart, M. (ed.) (1972) *The City*, Penguin, Harmondsworth

Wilson, A.G. (1981) *Geography and the Environment*, John Wiley, Chichester

22. THE URBAN MODELLING IMPLICATIONS
OF NEW TECHNOLOGY
B. Harris

Modelling as Thinking

The general tenor of the book, and indeed of much of our thinking these days, has been to reflect on the bewildering variety and unpredictability of the changes which are affecting urban life and the environment in which it develops. These reflections are perhaps inevitably both undisciplined and undisciplinary — although more often the latter — and it behoves us to try to see our way through to a better understanding of the complex reality which we face in these circumstances. Certainly, more information will provide us with more enlightenment; but I would add to this the thought that information becomes intelligence only through interpretation. Many of our interpretive capabilities arise out of the same kind of intellectual activity that is employed in the construction and use of models.

In the most general sense models are simply patterns of thought about the real world. In this manner they pursue a certain tendency toward abstraction, but this does not necessarily make them 'abstract' in the usual pejorative way that we use this word. While models and the theories with which they are related remove or disregard details which are irrelevant to a given purpose, they retain the underlying patterns of detail which it is sought to explain, and provide connections with other and possibly causally related detail. The abstraction is made in the same sense that one makes an abstract of a paper, retaining the essentials in compact form.

I have written elsewhere that a model is an experimental design based on a theory. In this slightly eccentric definition, I attempt to make clear that models properly considered are not vacuous but are indeed related to theory. At the same time, the experimental context differentiates the model from 'pure' theory in a very general way. The experiment being considered may be one of many different types: it may be a thought experiment or an experiment in the real world; it may or may not be an experiment designed to test the theory of the model. We can apply a model to a phenomenon or a situation in which not all of the relevant characteristics are well understood, in an exploratory and observational mode. We can use a model as a laboratory tool to create conditions in which to conduct still another paper experiment. Most frequently, we use a model to conduct an action experiment, either on paper or in fact; that is, we assume the model to be correct, and experiment with the outcomes of different policies and plans. Thus we use models to establish connections between putative actions and putative results.

In this context, it should go without saying that models may be of many different types. Most people and most social units, when taking action of any kind, try to connect the actions with their results. Even the simplest mental connection is a model of cause and effect. Such models can be elaborated logically, algorithmically, in a process of debate and discussion, or mathematically — and computers have greatly extended our ability to utilise some of these methods. Indeed, the strong identification of modelling with computers obscures the fact that even the most apparently judgemental decision-making contains, among many operative elements, a mental model connecting the decisions with their outcomes.

Realism in Models

Because models and theories deal with the real world, there is always a need to test their correspondence with this reality. Such reality-testing or verification raises a central problem in the philosophy of science, but I will treat it from a more narrow and perhaps pragmatic point of view.

In the first instance, we must recognise that the students of urban phenomena do not ordinarily engage in experiments; like the perfectly respectable hard sciences of geology and astronomy, we mainly observe. We do not build cities of 20 million people to see how they work, just as geologists do not build volcanoes, and astronomers do not build stars. On the other hand, laboratory sciences like psychology, chemistry and physics can be used in constructing theories in the observational sciences, and nature is constantly providing us with 'experimental' material as we extend the range of our observation. For urban studies this material is particularly rich because society is always performing experiments on itself by creating new social relations, new laws, new customs, and new technological means of dealing with the environment and with itself and its constituent parts.

The carefully designed and expensive experiments which have been conducted in the US about familial and market responses to income maintainence, housing allowances, and variations in the terms of medical insurance are rare and unusual. While the social cost of these experiments is low relative to the very practical value of the knowledge which they generate, there are political and ethical questions (as in medical experiments) which make it seem more expedient to use blunter instruments. Perhaps the enlarged variety of social experiments is one of the more attractive features in the idea of federalism and smaller governmental units.

The observational nature of the social sciences has the enormous consequence that any new full-scale social experiments appear to be a leap in the dark; perhaps as a result of this, the social sciences feel a burden of guilt for not being able to solve social problems in advance. While urban modellers have not laboured heavily under that burden, the topic of the conference and the discussions here demonstrate an increasing awareness of the difficulties in guiding developments which are affected by the rapid technological revolutions surrounding us. At the same time, not only have these changes in technology affected social events, but the ensuing political uncertainties have been exacerbated by the growth of world population and by the inequalities of wealth and power on a national and world basis. Some political outcomes have put in question the willingness of society to consider seriously its own futures.

Model Transferability

We need, therefore, to try to come to grips with this uncertainty, and this leads us into a second set of considerations with respect to our modelling approaches. It would appear that the difficulties of making firm statements about the effects of future actions on still more distant events, occurring in what may be an unstable and unpredictable environment, are virtually insurmountable. I feel that while these difficulties are indeed challenging, they can in part be overcome. We can look for substantial help in the literature of management with regard to decision-making under uncertainty, but I will take that as given and look for answers in our own practice.

Almost all sciences attempt to make statements about phenomena which have not been previously observed. Such statements serve initially to test a theory, when a new effort is made to find a confirming instance of the statement; and as the theory becomes established these statements provide the rationale for the utility of science, leading as they do to suggestions for new technologies and to a broader reach for science itself. The observational social sciences are disadvantaged in these attempts to 'go beyond the data' by their dependence on statistics, which seems in many instances to regard this as a cardinal sin.

One of the most powerful means both for testing the validity of models and for extending their usefulness seems to me to lie in the search for more widely transferable (and hence in some sense more universal) approaches to the construction of theories and their associated models. Transfers across space, economic levels, and political organisation (and occasionally transfers backwards in time) provide us with an easy opportunity to go beyond the data in situations which can be more deeply explored. We need to examine a little more thoroughly the kinds of modelling and modelling assumptions we are talking about.

Essentially, going beyond the data means making some assumptions about constancies in the realm which we are studying. Casting about for an example of extreme assumptions of constancy, it occurred to me that the astrophysicists, in examining the fossil light which reaches us from quasars at the outermost observed edge of the universe, are looking at light which is some 15 billion years old and reaches us from billions of light years away. This light is also shifted toward the red end of the spectrum by the relative motion of these objects, receding at a large fraction of the speed of light. Yet the astronomers have little hesitation in identifying the hydrogen emission spectrum, which has been studied directly only in the laboratory, and which is thus assumed to be essentially unchanged over space, time and the red shift.

In modelling urban systems, we do much the same thing — although in the forward rather than the backward direction. It is not unusual to make a 10-, 20- or 30-year projection of the behaviour of a transportation and land use system, even though we know that the conditions which will obtain at these future times are going to be very different from today. We have assumed constancies of several different kinds — particularly in behaviours and in technology — and hopefully we have projected changes in other circumstances like income levels and family composition. At this point I will focus largely on the behavioural aspects of these assumptions, returning later to others.

We are all too fully aware that some of our constancy assumptions have proved wrong; let us take transport demand planning models as a brief example. These models were developed and successfully applied first in the US, although there were some indications that they were not reliable in all instances. They were transferred almost indiscriminately to Europe and then to many developing counties. The further that conditions in these new countries diverged from those in the US, the worse the models performed. Clearly the models were not transferable. Yet in retrospect it seems obvious that a few changes could have been made (and are now made) which would greatly improve their performance. Most particularly, these models suffered from exclusive emphasis on the automobile mode, neglecting public transit and walking modes among many. Changes such as introducing new modes greatly improved the transferability of the models, and even improved their operation in the country of origin. This provides a crude example of how a model may fail by totally disregarding the simplest behavioural considerations, such as the choices which people are actually forced to make in their daily lives.

The constancies of behaviour on which such models rest are related to the organisation of cities and to the underlying features of familial and individual behaviours. Even at a relatively superficial level, behavioural constancy implies that within the constraints of income, physical capability, energy, tolerance for dissonance and social acceptability, people will secure shelter, travel to work, and leave home to shop, to meet other people, and to secure services and recreation. But the more we expect that social and technological conditions will change drastically, the more we have to seek an underlying level of behavioural constancy, such as the kind of deep structure which Levi-Strauss postulated for kinship systems and Piaget for the learning patterns of children, but which they never explicated.

There does not appear to be any easy way to look for this deep structure, and as has been suggested it may not even be possible to calibrate or statistically fit a model relying on it. We therefore have to look for other ways of testing models and of designing them. In any event, statistical measures of goodness of fit do not tell us much about other aspects of the model, such as its parsimony, elegance, behavioural basis and transferability, and we have to look far beyond what statistics can tell us to judge the quality of the modelling effort.

Credibility

One suggestion in this direction entails the idea of 'credibility,' and this idea can be given both debilitating and useful interpretations. We are apt to be led astray if we take credibility to mean in correspondence with conventional wisdom, and matters are even worse if it merely means reproducing in pseudo-scientific form the decision maker's preconceptions. There are, however, more credible and less credible conceptions of probable behaviours, and it would be foolish to believe that ordinary citizens and decision-makers can never perceive and evaluate these differences. Similarly there are more and less realistic assumptions about the relation of behaviours and their environments, and it is hard to give credit to perverse views such as the assumption in the Lowry model that households choose their place of residence without regard to the quality (or even the existence) of the housing stock. Finally, models are not credible if they produce untrue results, and they gain credibility if they produce results which are strikingly correct and far removed from their assumptions.

All of these aspects of credibility can be regarded as an area of common ground between scientists and citizens. On this ground the former have standing because they look for clarity of expression, for the absence of contradictions, and for deep connections between different aspects of life. The latters' standing arises out of the fact that, as multiple and diverse critics, their knowledge of the nature of behaviours and consequences (but not necessarily of all their connections) is apt to be broad and informative, or at least provocative. It seems probable however that the evaluation by citizens of their own prospective behaviour will frequently prove unreliable, and rather than inquire as to preferences it might be better to examine past behaviour to determine them. At the same time, a citizen may be well situated to comment on the behaviours of others, especially as they impinge upon the self.

There are many dimensions on which we can look at the credibility and operability of models so as to improve their performance. Many of these ideas will prove to be interrelated, and they will lead us back to one another, perhaps in an apparently circular fashion. Exploring others will provide us with a taste of novelty.

We have already touched in a way on the idea of qualitative versus quantitative models, because much conventional wisdom about behaviours and outcomes is qualitative. Realism and credibility are themselves qualitative notions. Nevertheless, we need to be alert to track down the instances when quantitative changes lead to qualitative changes. In the extreme case, these instances might alert us to, or be signalled by, qualitative differences which also seem to be barriers to transferability. Examples might be the differing locations of slums in Latin America and Paris on the one hand and in India and the US on the other, or the shift in patterns of retail trade with the advent of supermarkets.

The identification of qualitative differences provides us with an opportunity to test the transferability of models, and this test often permits us to learn not only more about the models, but also more about the situations in which we apply them. Indeed, our model design might be deeply influenced by our looking ahead to this kind of application.

New Modelling Problems

The scale of technological change and its social impacts tends to lead modellers into situations where, having learned to deal with spatial interactions and arrangements, they are suddenly confronted with the need for non-spatial models, or for mixed ones. The growing concern with matters of health and education foreshadow the introduction of modelling issues which are a new challenge to the profession. These models will be spatially bounded by the extent of local labour markets and health care delivery systems, and important spatial questions of access and discrimination based on location will arise — but major aspects of the modelling will have to deal with novel cultural and environmental issues which are at most only partially spatial in character.

This consideration highlights the influence on urban growth and form of many technological changes which are affecting employment, health and health care, reproduction and population dynamics, communications, and indeed every aspect of urban life. These changes also suggest that we look for new integrative mechanisms as they exist in urban affairs and as they ought to reappear in urban models. We have already built our profession around the integrative nature of transportation. We are beginning to give open recognition to the latent influence of land markets, which underlie much of our thinking. We are perhaps somewhat less able to deal with the interactions of the labour market under the impact of exogenous changes, with the unknown influence of communications as they rapidly expand, and with latent patterns of social and class interaction which have always bedevilled the closure of our modelling efforts.

As we move more deeply into these realms, we also deal more often with the class of infrequently repeated actions. The daily patterns of commuting, shopping and attending school seem to have been relatively easy to predict. The non-repetitive decisions with which we have dealt up to now have been familiar in this context — buying a car and perhaps moving house. Now as we try to catch up with the effect of technology on behaviour, as it affects urban form, we will have to deal with educational decisions, job choices, health patterns, household formation, and many other social and economic phenomena. Unlike many sociologists and economists, we will have to model these things in a spatial context, and in interaction with each other.

One approach which will serve us well in dealing with some of these issues is to recognise that different scales and sectors require different models. Our direct concerns with urban form do not call upon us to model interregional employment shifts induced by changing technologies and resource use. But we find that these things must be modelled in order to provide exogenous inputs for a locational model. Lundqvist has given us a fine example of this style of work (see Chapter 20). Similarly, one might criticise the Lowry model's claims to completeness on the grounds that the location of 'basic' industry must be exogenously given, but perhaps it is better to recognise that we often want to examine a particular issue in isolation — in this case residential and retail development. When we do this we can supply observational data for the sectors and tendencies which we hold fixed or exogenous, or we can model these sectors separately in a serious way, or we can use a variety of descriptive and short-cut models to provide an environment for our more serious modelling efforts.

Scenario Writing

There is naturally a strong drive to reduce the complexity of models and their awkwardness in approaching questions of policy — a drive which is only partially satisfied by truncating models and embedding them in a largely suppositious environment. We ought to think, as Dickey (Chapter 13) has suggested, about more effective means of making quick examinations of problems and phenomena, and this approach is greatly aided by recent advances in computer hardware and software. Since most modelling is surrounded by a great variety of assumptions, an alternative and potentially very productive approach is to reduce the scope of modelling by considering these assumptions in more detail and more systematically. Such a process is called scenario writing, and I propose to examine some of its varied aspects in a slightly expanded form.

In its original form, scenario writing provides the planner and the modeller with a means for coping with the exogenous events which will be the setting for future decisions, some of which must be sketched now, and some of which will be influenced by those which are to be taken most immediately. As we have seen, the alternative choice to scenario writing is to prepare and run models of the larger environment, but there are obvious limits to this. It is virtually certain that such matters as the growth of total and per capita production, the growth and changes of the population, the state of international trade and migration, and the sectoral composition of economic activity, must be handled by assumption. Such a simple statement belies the complexity of the matter.

Obviously, there will be alternative choices regarding the assumptions both individually and collectively and this leads to the question of the number of scenarios which can be adopted for further exploration. When the modelling and planning effort is very large and complex it has been standard practice, on the grounds of economy, to select only one carefully chosen most probable scenario. If we had more effective quick-scanning models, it would probably be rewarding to consider a number of alternative scenarios. We would then look for commonalities and differences in the problems which these scenarios presented, and search for policies and plans which bridged them. This view requires further exploration.

The principal problem with writing multiple scenarios (or even single ones in some cases) is combinatorial complexity. If we were to be considering, say, ten exogenous variables and had to make two, three, or four choices regarding each one, we could generate respectively a thousand, sixty thousand, or a million different scenarios. We would reduce the number of these possibilities, and control our process of search and selection, by introducing ideas of probability and consistency. We would not want to consider highly improbable scenarios unless we were greatly concerned about the most serious worst case, and we would not care to explore scenarios whose assumptions were so inconsistent and conflicting as to reduce their probabilities to zero.

But this line of thought has led us into a contradiction: we cannot seriously consider probabilities and consistency for collections of events without a model of the system in which they occur. We have therefore to recognise that writing scenarios is itself an exercise in modelling, even though the models are very general, and often mental and qualitative. This confronts us, moreover, with the difficulty of enlisting expertise in the fields to be (secretly) modelled, and of ensuring that this expertise considers the problems in a light which is relevant to our actual problems. It is perhaps small wonder that we often substitute our own judgement in these fields.

A special problem in predicting the environment of planning and modelling arises in the case of technology. We have been concerned in this volume most frequently with this problem, recognising as we do that the effects of technology work their way to the level of urban form not only directly as urban technologies, but indirectly through their influences on national policy and on national and regional activity levels and their changes. We are somewhat fortunate in the fact that, as a partial outcome of the findings of basic science, the technology of the immediate future is perhaps somewhat predictable. The scientific basis of much future technology has already been laid. Further, the trends of scientific and technological development can be extrapolated with a good deal of confidence in regard to computing, biological research, and a few other fields. However, the rate of scientific discovery and the rate of its application to and interaction with technology are accelerating, so that the reliability of our projections is impaired. Finally, while we may know for example that the future costs of information and intelligence will be greatly reduced and their availability greatly increased, we probably cannot foresee in any detail either their applications in other economic activities or their impact on the gross behaviours of the population. Even in this volume we have been unable to judge whether better communications will reduce or increase the volume of travel for shopping.

New Types of Scenario

Scenarios which deal in an arbitrary way with the external or exogenous circumstances surrounding a modelling and planning effort are designed to reduce the scope of that effort and thus to make it more effective. These methods deal with uncertainty by making it explicit and exploring alternative futures. In this light, we can think of at least three more types of scenario which take the same general approach but which deal with different issues. These issues are the superordinate policy decisions which control the areas to be explored, the assumptions which are made about the ultimate goals to which the effort is subordinated, and finally the constellations of behaviours which may be expected as a basis for model formulation and use. This last issue is one which has scarcely been thought of as a basis for scenario writing.

Policy scenarios are a necessary part of the first set of scenarios dealing with exogenous events. To project a pattern of employment by sector and region, we must make many implicit and explicit assumptions about the policies as well as about other forces which lie behind it. But at this point, I wish to emphasise the possibility of making both broad-scale scenarios as to policy which will govern many other aspects of scenario writing and, additionally, the need for targeted policy scenarios dealing with the topics being modelled. In the first category we would find policy alternatives on topics like the devolution of governmental powers, the relative emphasis on the private and public sectors, and international trade and national defence. At the other end of the spectrum we would find, for example in a transportation planning effort, that certain decisions would be taken as binding. We might be prohibited from considering the design of toll facilities, the splitting of neighbourhoods with new facilities, or even the construction of certain types of facilities. Budgetary limits are a powerful form of policy statement which among other things greatly modify the application of benefit-cost analysis. In the opposite direction, policy might mandate the achievement of a particular given level of service in a particular domain.

Obviously, policy scenarios may be written on many topics and at many different levels, and at all levels and on all topics there are severe problems of consistency. These problems extend to relations with other types of scenario.

As we turn to the question of values, we note that these are frequently confused with policies. To say that 'our policy is to obtain the greatest good for the greatest number' states a goal, or more than one, but not a policy in any implementable sense. Goals are here understood to be proxies for values, and a scenario about values describes a value system. Once again, enormous problems of consistency arise, as in the foregoing example, and the mutual consistency of value scenarios and those describing policies or exogenous circumstances can ultimately be tested only by some form of modelling. Methods of multicriterion and goal achievement programming attempt to provide simple ways of discovering and displaying these latent conflicts.

Finally, if we are uncertain about the behavioural assumptions of our models, and especially about the persistence of these behaviours into the future, we could generate alternate scenarios about behaviour itself. As a simple example, we might alternately suppose in a period of rising income that a particular income class will have on the one hand the same behavioural patterns that it had at a lower income, or on the other hand the same behaviour as did the class which had previously enjoyed its new income level. In so far as these assumptions cannot in any way be currently proved or disproved, these alternate assumptions about individual behaviours are quite legitimate.

In this context, however, combinatorial problems and difficulties with consistency once again appear in an exacerbated form. In all probability there are constellations of behaviour which are unstable because of their inconsistency, while the patterns of stability and instability may vary under the variation in (assumed) socio-economic policies and conditions. All of this opens up an unexplored area which might repay some serious attention. Systematic speculation in these matters of uncertainty might broaden the discussion and suggest new theories of behaviour and new ways to test them.

Initially, I raised the questions of combinatorial complexity and consistency only with regard to each of the four types of scenarios taken separately. Peter Nijkamp (Chapter 7) points out that these are both compounded when we consider all four together. The combinatorial issues cannot be dealt with in principle but must be tested in a purely artful and arbitrary way with some danger of failure. The consistency problems cannot be dealt with arbitrarily, but raise enormous problems of principle. For example, if a policy oriented to collective action conflicts with a set of individualistic behaviours, must they be harmonised in the scenarios, or can they be expected to create a unique dynamic outcome? And in the latter case, how could we project it?

Technology, Planning and Politics

In this book as well as in my own review of scenarios of values and policies, a number of issues of the greatest societal importance have emerged. Since these issues are brought to the fore by our changing technology, and since they deal with matters of substantive importance to modellers and planners, we will look at them in our concluding discussion.

One central problem always encountered in planning is to determine the right location for the line between individual autonomy and social control. It is not useful here to belabour the substantive arguments on both sides of this question. But it is useful to note that information technology provides not only instruments for planning and modelling, but also for extending the degree of control over individuals and groups in society. For this reason many of the benefits deriving from computers (often hidden from public view) are regarded by some as unimportant in the light of the evils of possible extended control (see Chapter 16).

A related but not identical dilemma affects modellers and planners more directly. Better understanding of our society is, we suggest, based upon a better understanding of behaviours, and this often means that aggregated data cannot be used as pointedly as individual data in which the social and behavioural relationships are preserved in detail. But securing and preserving individual data are often regarded as an invasion of privacy. This preservation may extend the power of the bureaucracy to control and possibly to persecute people, and the purposeful or accidental disclosure of certain information may subject individuals to social pressure and personal harm from other individuals or groups.

In this volume and elsewhere we frequently hear questions in the same vein regarding the possibility of a special form of social control — this time over the social investment in new technology. Here we should recognise that there already is enormous social control through the funding of research, the national control of health insurance, tax laws, trust laws, patent laws, and pollution control. In fact, the most hated and feared forms of technology, atomic energy and atomic bombs, would never have existed except for massive social investments, and their continued threat is a direct result of the social policies of governments with respect to alternative energy sources and armaments.

We are also fearful of the outcomes of biological research and engineering (as well as of the aforementioned consequences of the computer revolution) and here the problem is more complex. Scientific discovery is still socially supported, but the development of new technologies can be undertaken by relatively small enterprises. Given the world scope and diversity of science and industry, it seems unlikely that the flowering of new technologies can be halted or even widely redirected, and it seems unlikely that it would be possible to foresee all of the applications to which any given technology would be put.

Clearly under all of these circumstances, decisions about the uses of technology are political decisions in both good and bad senses. Where politics are corrupt and where nations are fiercely competitive, socially maleficent uses of technology will tend to proliferate. Where politics are truly democratic and where nations co-operate, the application of technology can be made humane. But it seems unlikely that social control can be exerted at the point of the generation of knowledge and technique.

Finally I return to the essential elements of planning itself, and the impact of these developments upon its conduct. The turbulence which is thought to be associated with a period of rapid technological change certainly raises the importance of planning — especially for the Third World countries which appear to be falling further behind relatively and sometimes absolutely. This consciousness and the constant improvement of technical means for planning give some hope for more effective processes.

We have not solved the problem of setting goals for society and achieving consensus on them. This essentially political problem can be informed but not solved by modelling and by planners. I would feel that effort in this field on the technical side might be more effective than addressing the political questions directly, as planners.

We must hold fast to the idea of exploring possible futures, either by the use of models or by the special means of scenario writing — which I feel turns out to be a certain form of modelling. If our exploration of these futures is systematic, then we tend to move in the direction of optimisation, which almost by definition presents insuperable problems of search in large-scale social systems. Constant consciousness of the value context of optimisation can keep this process on track, and broadening the social base of planning can provide a quasi-network of people with enormous computational power. The tools of modelling which we may provide at this point must be sharp and adapted to their purposes, and these we must help uncover.

PART EIGHT

THE FUTURE URBAN SYSTEM

23. PROBABLE URBAN FUTURES
P. Newton and M. Taylor

Opinion appears sharply divided on the value of studies which attempt to forecast the future. On the one hand we have those such as Ackoff (1981:ix) who argue that 'To the extent that we can control the future we do not have to forecast it... To the extent that we can respond rapidly and effectively to changes that we neither control nor expect... we need not forecast them'. Others (e.g. May 1982) argue for more future-oriented planning where the typical objective is to generate a number of probable scenarios in order to understand the implications of future movements for the present (i.e. to identify those policy and planning decisions required now in order to avoid or achieve possible future conditions). Yet in so far as the future is open to change by human planning, can it be open to forecasting (see Vickers 1981)?. If we follow the logic of Bell and Mau (1971) then the answer is probably yes, so long as the model of the future is probabilistic rather than purely deterministic because, until the future has become the present, some alternative possibilities remain open.

The position we hold on the matter (after Bell and Mau 1971) is that images of the future are real and deserve examination in that they tend to orient human behaviour and social action and thereby provide an insight into what alternative futures are being prepared in the present. This is particularly so under the liberating conditions that techno-logically advanced society makes possible, where the population is not wholly concerned with meeting subsistence needs and where the desire for self-determination is increasing (although uncertainty often exists as to what society's goals and objectives should be). With this come new burdens of responsibility to modern society in terms of knowing that both livelihood and environment may become, in important respects, what it makes of them. Advanced industrial and post-industrial societies then are confronted with alternative futures (appearing at accelerated rates) and with the power to choose among them. Increasingly the study of images of the future will be linked to social engineering whereby simulations of probable scenarios are undertaken in order to explore various hypotheses about the future and the role of intervention (typically by the state) in shaping it. The task of future-oriented studies is therefore twofold (after Sarre *et al.* 1973): first to decide which future is most probable and then evaluate its desirability (see e.g. the study by Textor 1978); and/or secondly, to identify a possible or desirable future and attempt to provide a programme to achieve it.

Methodological Approaches to the Study of Future Patterns of Urban Development

Characteristically then, the approaches available to the forecaster can be classified as either of two types: anticipatory or exploratory (Hall 1977; also termed 'top down' and 'bottom up' by Jones and Twiss 1978).

Anticipatory Scenarios

Here the objective is to establish whether a specific normative goal or objective might be achieved (i.e. a particular urban development form — such as the 'core city', the 'dispersed sheet', the 'star', the 'ring', the 'multi-centred net', the 'galaxy'; see Lynch 1962 and Chapter 25). The objective set for or by the planner may result from a national policy or vision (see Marien 1977). Initially it might be merely a desirable target without there being any clear idea of how it could be achieved in practice. Successive steps are then instituted to determine alternative ways by which the objective might be achieved and which of the alternative routes should be followed.

Exploratory Scenarios

The urban planner is concerned with the management of a complex urban system, the evolution of which is the outcome of the joint operation of numerous factors which are located in the present (and past) but which may evolve in a variety of ways in the future. A range of methods have been devised to assist in forecasting. These have recently been discussed and evaluated by Rescher (1981) and include: trend extrapolation, cyclical analysis, consensus methodologies such as Delphi, scenario construction, analogy, model-building and simulation.

The methodology employed in the present chapter is aligned to the exploratory approach and its suite of techniques; that is an exploration of probable urban futures. In the following chapter Klaassen pursues the alternative approach by considering which technological (and urban form) developments could be seen as desirable from a society's point of view.

Urban Futures Survey

This particular project was undertaken on the premise that the form of future urban activity and development may not be identified simply as an extension of existing trends and relationships. New technologies and a range of social and economic forces may emerge and be of a kind not evident from an extrapolation of past situations. The objective of the futures survey was to identify those factors and trends which may result in events and impacts not previously foreseen and which are capable of changing the direction of urban development via changing space needs and locational requirements. As such the study was concerned with first, an identification of emerging technological and socio-economic trends considered likely to have begun to exert an influence on urban areas by the year 2000; and secondly, a specification of the likely impact of particular trends on national settlement systems, individual cities, industrial sectors and population sub-groups.

The scope of the study thereby presented a range of research questions and problems concerning its formulation, conduct and associated analyses. These included constraints of space, time, value and knowledge.

Spatial Constraints. Researchers, and observers of society in general, occupy a particular position in space and time. Consequently their perceptions usually form only a small part of the universe of data, and insights are reliable only to the extent that a representative segment of society has been sampled. Miller (1957) points to the fact that most theories of social change are largely reflections based on Western society.

Temporal Constraints. Time is also an elusive dimension (What is a 'long time'? What is 'fast'?) in relation not only to interpretation of historical rates of change but to realistic forecast periods. In relation to the latter, Boniecki (1980) suggests that 10-15 years seems the most distant practical horizon that contemporary Westerners may see as related to their own life experience and to issues in planning. Also, the issues of the present (e.g. current economic climate) probably exert a significant (but so far unmeasured) influence on assessments of future paths of change.

Value Constraints. What any researcher sees of the world depends partly on his or her status position as well as on the experiences and ideas accumulated through life. In future-oriented studies, the issue of values assumes even greater significance. In addition to different value systems operating among a particular panel of 'experts', there is the likelihood that futurists' values and future values will not coincide. As Fowles (1977) puts it: 'Present views and plans for the future, however well-intended they might be, must to some extent be at odds with the values of those who will be subjected to them'.

Knowledge Constraints. The scope of this particular study (the future form and functioning of urban areas) suggests that a wide range of interacting factors — technological, political, economic, social and demographic — are relevant to an understanding of urban development and change. Identification of 'experts' with appropriate multi-disciplinary experience constitutes a major concern in futures studies.

The above issues had to be addressed, for the most part, in the sampling phase of the study and were associated with decisions to internationalise the study, consider replication in a future time period, assess the value positions of respondents and ensure a representative panel of 'experts'.

Methods for data collection and analysis also required careful consideration in view of the innovative nature of the study, the absence of a previously established methodology, possible difficulties in statistical inference and the extrapolation of survey results into more general conclusions. The approach adopted involved three principal stages: existential, correlational and explanatory — based on Singer's (1971) 'three levels of knowledge' in scientific investigation and Cavallo's (1982) general systems problem-solver framework.

Existential. The existential knowledge sought in the initial phase involved the identification and collation of ideas, factors and trends related to future changes in built forms, urban activity and settlement patterns. Following the guideline recommended by Martino (1972) for Delphi-type studies, the first phase was designed to be open-ended and far-ranging,providing an opportunity for respondents(a panel of experts chosen on the basis of demonstrated expertise in the field of urban analysis and socio-technical systems) to speculate about future urban development. At this level, however, any relationships between variables remained indeterminate. The replies to the first round questionnaire (for survey details and sample schedule see Taylor and Newton 1983) were used to frame the trend and impact statements used on the subsequent survey round.

Correlational. After a synthesis (via content analysis) of responses from the first exploratory survey, a second survey was instituted in order to establish broader-based estimates of the importance, and direction of operation of a set of trends and, via associative analyses (e.g. regression) establish preliminary relations between the trend and impact attributes. Interpretation of cross-impacts as correlations can be helpful to the forecasting of future conditions, but, as Helmer (1981) among others suggests, it is essential to have some insight into the cause-effect relationships between trends and resultant changes.

Explanatory. At the next epistemological level an attempt is made to specify (causal) linkages and structural relations between the trend-impact variable set. Here we, as researchers, may construct images of the future by any number of heuristic or systems dynamics devices. The likelihood (or, if goal-oriented, the desirability) of such future developments occurring would be evaluated against surveys of the values of relevant populations. Finally, to the extent to which the study of images of the future could be linked to social engineering, simulations are performed testing various hypotheses about the future and especially the role of deliberate action in shaping it.

Exploratory Survey: Methods and Results

The exploratory survey was distributed in September 1982 to 153 experts from 26 countries and 57 (37 per cent) usable replies were received. A synthesis of the responses led to the definition of a set of 90 trends considered likely to influence urban form and a set of 20 spatial impacts representing the manifestations of those trends in urban areas. To extract information from open-ended responses in such a way as to permit at least some basic form of quantitative analysis required application of content analysis methodology (see Holsti 1968, for a discussion of operational procedures). The most common version of content analysis and the one employed here is that which uses the frequency of occurrence of certain content characteristics (usually key words or phrases) as being relevant for purposes of inference. A microcomputer-based programme was devised for the content analysis of responses to the exploratory futures survey (for a description of the program, see Taylor and Newton 1983). In devising a coding system for the automated text scanning programme, three basic decisions had to be made.

The Major Categories of Analysis. These categories constitute the 'pigeonholes' into which the content of the expert comments are to be classified. Our conception of the major influences on urban development suggested use of the following exogenous dimensions:

Figure 23.1 Schema for Developing an Urban Systems Model

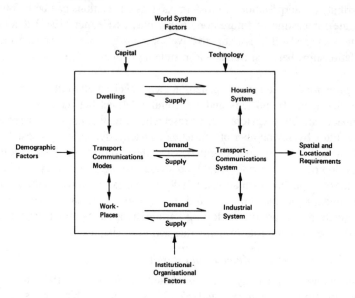

demographic change, world economic system influences, technology and energy; together with several endogenous structural dimensions comprising industry, housing, transport and governance factors (represented diagrammatically in Figure 23.1).

The Indicators. As categories are often quite generalised, they usually require the designation of specific indicators which represent the categories, yet refer directly to the particular content under analysis (energy indicators typically include variables such as 'real price of oil', 'substitution of alternative energy sources for oil' and so forth).

The Unit of Enumeration. Having decided upon a set of categories and indicators, the content of responses to the exploratory survey can be searched for the presence of any of the listed indicators. Every occurrence of a given indicator is tallied.

The results of the content analysis are displayed in Table 23.1. The table reveals the frequency with which particular factors were cited. No directionality is indicated as this was to be a principal objective of the second survey when a larger panel of experts were involved in

Table 23.1 Content Analysis of Responses to Exploratory Futures Survey: Top 25 Responses

Rank	Subject	Per cent of respondents identifying subject
1	Real price of oil.	46
2	Unemployment.	28
3	Emphasis on environment and conservation of resources	25
4=	State of national economy.	23
4=	Diversity in, and substitution of, transport modes (ranging from low technology modes such as walk/cycle, through individual and mass transit systems to high technology modes such as pipelines/guideways).	23
6	Application of telecommunications technology (e.g. satellite communication) in productive processes and the organization of industry.	21
7=	Substitution of telecommunications for some forms of travel (e.g. shopping-at-a distance via videotex).	19
7=	Level of social disorganization (e.g. crime, violence).	19
9=	Polarization of the population, emergence of 'two nation syndrome', with a wealthy elite minority and an economically disadvantaged majority.	18
9=	Application of computer technology (e.g. micro processors) in productive processes and the organization of industry).	18
9=	Ageing of the population.	18
12=	Size of households.	16
12=	Shift to labour-displacing (rather than labour-complementing) technology.	16
14	Leisure time available to workers.	14
15=	Income differentials between skilled, semi-skilled and unskilled occupations.	12
15=	Real value of wages and salaries.	12
15=	Private vehicle ownership, availability and use.	12
15=	Diversity of life styles.	12
19=	Rate of household formation (net effect of divorce/separation rate, marriage-remarriage rate, youth leaving parental home).	11
19=	Real cost of housing and land.	11
19=	Improved vehicle design (cost, safety, efficiency, emissions).	11
19=	Education level among the population.	11
19=	Changes in structure and operation of firms and their human organization.	11
24=	Level of government spending on urban infrastructure (e.g. roads, utilities).	9
24=	Rate of population growth.	9

evaluating a common set of factors. Twenty-two factors were cited by at least 10 per cent of respondents. Only one major category, namely world system influences, failed to attract a significant number of experts' 'votes'. Several of the principal long term primers of urban development, namely national economic performance, technological change (telecommunications in particular), the demographic cycle (age structure, household formation and household size), changing mode of transport and price of energy were identified. Important elements in the internal dynamics of metropolitan systems were identified for the following sub-systems: housing (costs); transport (diversity and substitutability — especially telecommuting); and industry (direct and indirect effects of technological change on structure and organisation of firms, including labour requirements, income differentials and so on).

Second Survey: Methods and Results

For the second stage of the study, a structured questionnaire was designed to appraise the 90 trends and factors and 20 spatial impacts which were nominated by the first phase respondents for further consideration. Respondents were asked to appraise the variables in relation to the largest urban system with which they felt familiar, and they were consequently asked to name this city. Appraisals of trends/factors were sought along two dimensions: first, the expected performance of the trend/factor from the present until the year 2000; and secondly, the anticipated degree to which the trend/factor will have initiated changes to urban form by the year 2000. For the spatial impacts, respondents were asked to indicate the likelihood that the impacts would have begun to emerge by the year 2000 (details of questionnaire design together with examples are given in Taylor and Newton 1983).

The required outputs from this phase were expectations of the direction, strength and importance of the trends and factors, and the expected directions and strengths of the spatial impacts. These data could be used to establish statistical relationships between variables, preparatory to a third phase on causal effects and linkages between variables.

The type of questionnaire and the forms of analysis prescribed for this phase of the study required an enlarged respondent panel from that used for the initial exploratory stage. The original panel was resurveyed (less any individuals who had asked to be excused), together with an additional panel selected along the lines indicated in Taylor and Newton (1983). This panel consisted of 670 experts from 48 countries. The questionnaire was distributed at the beginning of March 1983, and in all 323 responses have been received. The first 289 responses were analysed as a set, to define trend and impact directions.

Trend Performance by Region. In their study of images of the world in the year 2000, Ornauer *et al.* (1976) concluded that, while their respondents generally displayed a lack of consciousness about the future, the pattern of response that did emerge revealed the importance of national identity (responses varied more significantly between country than between sex, age or class divisions).

In the present study measures of central tendency and deviation on each trend factor suggest a considerable level of variability exists among the total set of respondents (for simplicity of presentation, distribution of total sample response only is displayed in Figure 23.2; detailed tabulations and analyses of data on a regional basis are presented in Newton and Taylor 1984). Not unexpectedly, perhaps, the respondents from less-developed countries diverged most strongly from their counterparts in advanced industrial societies (although caution should be taken in generalising from this sub-group given their small sample size). While risking criticism of participation in historicist futurology (Encel *et al.* 1975:56) whereby less developed countries are projected as being committed to follow a similar evolutionary pattern to that of Western industrial societies, the results from the futures survey (and the earlier work by Moore 1967:76) provide some basis for the concept of a development path along which all societies pass, at different times and rates. For example, in less-developed countries it was anticipated that cost of technology relative to cost of human labour would be increasing, as would number of years spent at work; government incentives for industrial and technological development and infrastructure provision would be increasing at a faster rate than in advanced Western societies; and the employment share in manufacturing employment was likely to be increasing (compared with reductions in advanced Western societies). Increased demand for oil and its products, more intense traffic problems, and higher levels of new residential construction were also anticipated.

Although overall differences in mean response tended to be minor across most trend factors, for North American and Western European respondents, there were several areas where *rates* of change diverged. For example, number of hours worked per week were expected to decline, but at a slower rate in North America (this is reinforced by the data on leisure time); income differentials were likely to increase in the

Figure 23.2 Trend Profiles

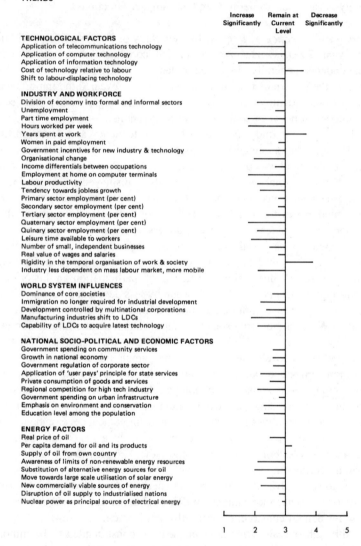

TRENDS

future, but at a slower rate in North America; employment at home on computer terminals was considered likely to increase significantly over the next 15 years, but more so in North America than in Western Europe; labour productivity and jobless growth were both expected to

Figure 23.2 Trend Profiles (continued)

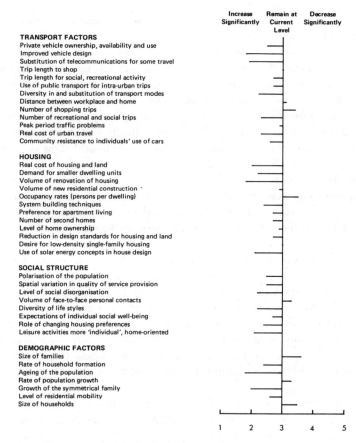

Note: The mean scores for each Trend are based on the pattern of response to a 5-point scale
(1 = increase significantly; 3 = remain at current level; 5 = decrease significantly)

increase, but at lesser pace in North America; and demand for smaller dwelling units was expected to grow, with higher rates of growth likely in North America. In reflecting upon these trends it is probable that a number of the differences in the future rates of change could well be attributable to variations in 'initial conditions' between the regions involved (e.g. in North America the stock of apartments is less than in Western Europe, hence the potential for growth in this section of the housing market is greater).

Trend Performance Under Variable Economic Conditions. Not only does interest in the future *per se* appear to be an inverse function of positive increases in affluence (interest declines during 'good times', according to Evered 1977), but national and international economic conditions could be expected to exert considerable influence on phenomena listed for evaluation in Delphi-type studies (e.g. Chen *et al.* 1981 developed three scenarios of US national development based on the economic alternatives of balanced growth, rapid growth and stagflation). In a cross-sectional study such as this and in a period where all countries surveyed were experiencing depressed economic conditions, evaluation of the 'economic influence' was limited to a cross-classification of the indicator 'Growth in National Economy' with the remaining 89 trend statements. Several trends appeared to be sensitive to their economic context. Under a declining national economy changes were anticipated with respect to: unemployment (increasing), real value of wages and salaries (decreasing), level of government spending on community services (decreasing), level of private consumption of goods and services (decreasing), level of government spending on urban infrastructure (decreasing), expectations of individual social well-being (decreasing) and level of residential mobility among urban populations (decreasing). In relation to the future role of government during recession, respondents were suggesting the likelihood of a shift to private sector-led recovery. Apart from this perhaps controversial speculation, the remaining future-states appear for the most part, as Clark (1978) has put it, as rational projections of *contemporary* possibilities in the major Western industrial nations.

Spatial Impacts by Region. Uniformity in pattern of response — as revealed by measures of central tendency — again tends to be characteristic of the spatial impacts elicited by 'experts' from different regions (see Figure 23.3 — again total sample trends are presented; regional profiles are presented in Newton and Taylor 1984). The principal contrasts appeared between the more youthful and decentralised Australian and North American regions and the longer-established European centres in regard to direction of change in density of residential development: the former group is likely to evidence reduction in housing space per person and associated increase in density of residential development. Spatial segregation is expected to increase at faster rates in less-developed countries. Examination of spatial changes under variable economic futures indicated that only one of the 20 spatial dimensions was affected, namely that of spatial segregation

Figure 23.3 Spatial Impacts

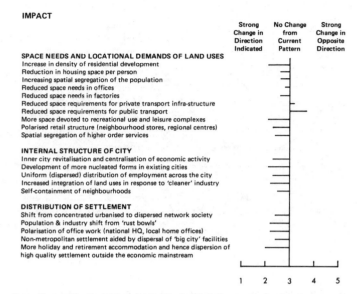

IMPACT

	Strong Change in Direction Indicated	No Change from Current Pattern	Strong Change in Opposite Direction

SPACE NEEDS AND LOCATIONAL DEMANDS OF LAND USES
Increase in density of residential development
Reduction in housing space per person
Increasing spatial segregation of the population
Reduced space needs in offices
Reduced space needs in factories
Reduced space requirements for private transport infra-structure
Reduced space requirements for public transport
More space devoted to recreational use and leisure complexes
Polarised retail structure (neighbourhood stores, regional centres)
Spatial segregation of higher order services

INTERNAL STRUCTURE OF CITY
Inner city revitalisation and centralisation of economic activity
Development of more nucleated forms in existing cities
Uniform (dispersed) distribution of employment across the city
Increased integration of land uses in response to 'cleaner' industry
Self-containment of neighbourhoods

DISTRIBUTION OF SETTLEMENT
Shift from concentrated urbanised to dispersed network society
Population & industry shift from 'rust bowls'
Polarisation of office work (national HQ, local home offices)
Non-metropolitan settlement aided by dispersal of 'big city' facilities
More holiday and retirement accommodation and hence dispersion of
high quality settlement outside the economic mainstream

1   2   3   4   5

Note: The mean scores for each Impact are based on the pattern of response to a 5-point scale
(1 = strong change in direction indicated; 3 = no change from current pattern; 5 = strong change
in opposite direction to that indicated in statement)

of the population (expected to increase under a declining national economy).

Scenarios of Metropolitan Development to Year 2000

Present estimates suggest that by the year 2000 approximately 80 per cent of the population in advanced industrial societies will live in urban centres. A majority of these people will live in large metropolitan areas. Guiding such development will constitute an enormous burden for decision-makers in both the private and public sectors, given the uncertainties surrounding the impacts that a range of exogenous factors such as energy price and new technologies may exert on future urban systems.

Given the complex nature of urban systems and the broad variety of factors considered to influence their course of development (viz. previous section on trends and impacts), the derivation of a model which hypothesises a structure inherent in the web of interrelationships

Figure 23.4 Urban Systems Model

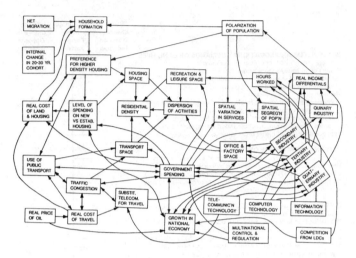

permits the generation (via simulation) of alternative urban scenarios. The model developed for this study belongs to the general class of systems dynamics models (see Forrester 1971). Figure 23.4 presents a model which connects a group of exogenous factors (technology, immigration, world economic system influences and energy price) with the principal urban sub-systems of housing, transport and industry (and their institutional or governmental linkages) and a set of spatial outcomes, namely space requirements (housing, transport, workplace and leisure outside the home) and locational conditions (dispersion of urban activity, residential density, population segregation and spatial variation in services).

Trends Integrator Procedure

The Trends Integrator Procedure (TIP) developed by Dickey and Doughty (1981) provides one means of tracing out both short- and long-term impacts of socio-technical factors on the built environment. Two major categories of variable are employed in TIP: *external factors* and *impact factors*.

External factors include those exogenous variables which are not influenced by a particular urban system and that affect, but are assumed not to be affected by, others in the system. The exogenous factors are assumed to be self-contained (e.g. telecommunications technology is assumed to 'grow on itself' at the rate of 6 per cent per year for the simulations depicted in Table 23.2, and is not affected by other variables in the model).

Impact factors have a built-in growth factor (as with the external factors) as well as influencing and being influenced by other impact factors. For example, the substitutability of telecommunications for travel is dependent upon growth in telecommunications technology (external factor) in addition to traffic congestion and the real cost of travel (internal factors). Impact factors are calibrated by designating the following for each (the factor 'housing space' from Figure 23.4 and Table 23.2 is used as illustration):

— recent annual (compound) rate of change — 2 per cent;
— the magnitude of relationships of factors influencing each factor (except externals) — preference for higher density housing 0.20 (20 per cent) level of spending on new housing 0.05 (5 per cent);
— direction of change (+ or —) of relationships of factors affecting each factor — —, + respectively;
— the influence of a 'unique' factor, comprising all other relevant variables not included (analogous to unexplained variance in regression — 0.75);
— future annual (compound) rate of change of each unique factor — 0.5 per cent.

The relationships suggested in the second and third items above are between the change in a particular factor and changes in those factors (including the unique) influencing it. Dickey and Doughty (1981) represented this symbolically by:

$$DF(i) = \sum_{j=1}^{n} C(i,j)DF(j) - a(i)U(i)$$

where: D = change in any factor,
$F(i)$ = level of factor i,
$C(i,j)$ = 'technical' coefficient relating the influence of the change in $F(i)$ to the change in $F(j)$,
$a(i)$ = 'technical' coefficient indicating the influence of the change in the Unique Factor, $U(i)$, for factor i on the change in $F(i)$

where: $\sum_{i=1}^{n} a(i) = 1$

Table 23.2 Output from Trends Integrator Procedure
Simulation over 10 Year Cycle: Melbourne and
Sydney

Factor	Initial conditions (Time 0) Most recent change*	Current level	Final conditions: SIM1 (after 10 years) Most recent change	Final level	SIM2 Final level	SIM3 Final level
Dispersion of activities	3.0	100	−1.0	95.4	100.1	100.2
Spatial segregation	5.0	100	2.2	112.5	103.6	102.7
Spatial variation in services	5.0	100	0.9	106.2	102.8	98.6
Residential density	1.0	100	1.2	104.5	99.3	100.0
Living space	2.0	100	−0.7	93.8	99.9	99.7
Working space	1.0	100	−5.6	71.4	101.2	79.6
Transport space	0.0	100	−0.3	98.0	100.2	102.3
Leisure space	1.0	100	0.6	104.8	99.6	100.0
Real cost of housing and land	3.0	100	1.4	111.8	104.3	98.6
Preference for high density living	1.0	100	1.8	112.0	100.2	100.6
Proportion of housing $ spent on new housing	−4.0	100	1.6	108.4	101.9	100.6
Household formation	2.0	100	−2.5	86.5	100.2	88.9
Use of public transport	2.0	100	3.8	125.9	99.5	89.5
Real cost of travel	15.0	100	9.1	150.2	105.7	116.9
Traffic congestion	2.0	100	−3.5	81.6	99.9	103.5
Telecommunications/travel substitution	0.0	100	42.6	332.1	107.0	126.6
Polarisation of population	4.0	100	4.7	119.7	99.3	101.8
Income differentials	0.0	100	7.6	135.4	97.0	109.7
Secondary workforce	−5.0	100	−12.1	33.1	85.4	4.3
Tertiary workforce	0.0	100	−9.0	54.1	102.8	416.4
Quaternary workforce	2.0	100	48.1	351.5	227.9	606.5
Quinary workforce	2.0	100	2.4	112.9	100.1	100.4
Average hours worked/ week/adult	−1.5	100	0.2	100.6	98.4	74.4
Government spending in real terms	0.4	100	9.0	148.8	120.2	212.8
Growth in national economy (GDP)	1.0	100	3.5	118.6	117.9	181.8

Notes: SIM1: Simulations performed using values determined by authors;
Melbourne focus
SIM2: Simulations performed using values determined by Melbourne
respondents to Futures survey (N = 46)
SIM3: Simulations performed using values determined by Sydney
respondents to Futures survey (N = 30)

* Exogenous variables: Multinational control and regulation, 2.0; competition
from LDC's, 2.0; real price of oil, 2.5;
telecommunications technology, 6.0; computer
technology, 1.0; information technology, 5.0; net
migration 0.0.

The C(i,j)'s and the a(i)'s can be negative, showing that an increase in DF(j) can lead to a decrease in DF(i). The sum of the absolute values of the technical coefficients must equal unity to ensure that all (100 per cent) of the influences on each factor are taken into account.

TIP is employed recursively over selected calculation periods (DT) between the base and horizon years to forecast the new (future) levels of each factor. In the first step, base-year factor levels are set at 100. Next, recent changes in impact factors are calculated, based on rates of change in the immediate past. In the third step future changes in the unique and external factors are determined. These then provide the basis for the next step, in which the above equation is employed to estimate future changes in impact factors. Finally, the changes are added to the preceding levels to get the new levels. The latter three steps in the process can be repeated for as many time periods (DTs) as desired to reach the horizon year.

Futuropolis 1: A Personal Model of Melbourne's Future

In reviewing Berlinski's 'On Systems Analysis', Eden (1978:160) makes the point that 'a system is never self-evident to all; it is defined by the scientist. Chaos to one person is a system to another, reality is a construction'. We are all familiar with the concept of an individual's mental model of the social system or cognitive image of the city. Replies to the CIBW72 survey represented individual experts' conceptions of the future structure of large urban systems based on their knowledge of underlying mechanisms of change. In the process of model development we drew upon these conceptions within the framework outlined in Figure 23.1.

Initial calibration of this model was undertaken by the authors drawing upon information currently available on Melbourne together with their expectations for future change in that urban system. Simulation over a 10-year period suggests (see Table 23.2, SIM 1) several possible changes of note following from the authors' conceptual model.

Industry. The most marked changes are in respect of employment, with shrinkage of the secondary workforce by 67 per cent, and tertiary workforce by 46 per cent, while quaternary employment increases by approximately 250 per cent (albeit from a relatively small base) and quinary employment by 13 per cent. Income differentials increase and are reflected in increased polarisation of the population.

Transport. In the transport system, significant increases are projected for the cost of travel, with increased patronage of public transport and an increasing substitution of telecommunications for travel. Limited improvements in traffic congestion occur.

Housing. Real cost of housing increases as does predilection for apartment living (the latter being largely a function of inability of increasing numbers of households to purchase detached housing). This stimulates new construction, however, as Melbourne's housing stock is predominantly detached housing.

Spatial effects. Most spatial-locational changes are of the order of 10 per cent or less over the 10-year period. The decline in housing space reflects increased housing costs and a shift to apartment living. Residential densities increase concomitantly. Increased spatial segregation of population and spatial variation in service provision result from increases in income differentials and polarisation of population. The most dramatic effect relates to working space where a shrinkage by almost 30 per cent is anticipated, reflecting a decline in secondary industry and the 'space saving' capabilities of new technology in the secondary, tertiary and quaternary sectors (see Dickey, Chapter 13).

Futuropolis 2: An Expert Panel's Model of Melbourne's Future

Data for this analysis derived from the responses to the CIBW72 Second Survey by 46 experts who used Melbourne as their focus.

Technical coefficients required for all interrelated factors in the TIP model were estimated from regression coefficients for the set of variables contained in the urban futures model (see Figure 23.4) and the proportion of unexplained variance from the regression (the latter was taken as the influence of the unique factor for each variable). Initial conditions were as previously defined.

Comparison of the results of this simulation with that previously undertaken clearly reveal the more conservative outlook derived by 'group' assessment (see Sackman 1975, for his comments on the de-individualisation effect of Delphi rounds and group decisions).

Major changes are anticipated in relation to employment with a decline in secondary employment forecast at 18 per cent. In contrast to the authors' model, however, Melbourne 'experts' foresaw only a marginal growth in tertiary employment and virtually none in quinary. Employment in the quaternary sector was seen as a major avenue for growth for the metropolitan workforce. Increases in housing and transport costs were anticipated, but at rates below contemporary levels of increase. National economic growth was forecast at levels slightly above those currently being experienced; it was expected that government spending would increase in real terms.

Notwithstanding these changes, virtually no change was forecast in space or locational requirements, again confirming the resilience or inertia of built forms over the short term.

An Expert Panel's Model of Sydney's Future

A similar analysis was conducted using data derived from the responses to the CIB W72 Second Survey by those 30 experts who used Sydney as their focus.

The profile for Sydney in the early 1990s (see Table 23.2) displays many of the archetypal attributes of the post-industrial city. It is likely to be a city without much secondary industry (see Chapter 4 for a UK-based comparison), hence a shedding of associated working space. Workforce growth will be dominated by tertiary and quaternary sectors and income differentials are expected to increase within the overall context of a buoyant national economy (and an increasing involvement by the state). Real cost of travel is forecast to increase with the consequence that patronage of public transport declines, while increased substitution is made of travel by telecommunications (also dampening the demand for working space and transport space). However, while predicted changes have been marked for some urban sectors (generally, and also in comparison with Melbourne) overall change in the urban fabric (population and land use distributions) is not expected to occur in the short term future.

Scenario Generation

In generating scenarios of future metropolitan development based on a model such as that outlined in this chapter, the forecaster is confronted with the issue of whether to accommodate all combinations of all the parameters that may play a role in the future of that city. For example, if there are 25 factors as is the case here, and if three values are allocated to each, then it is possible to generate approximately 850 billion future scenarios just by combining these factors and values.

Clearly it is infeasible to accommodate all combinations. The approach adopted here is to examine the impact of four exogenous variables namely: price of oil, application of telecommunications, computer and information technologies, each of which takes three different values (the technology variables assumed annual change rates of 0, 5 and 10 per cent; oil took values of minus 2, 0 and plus 5 per cent). Even here we are dealing with 81 scenarios; so a methodology is required where these scenarios can be presented in an interpretable form. Such a methodology is outlined in Newton and Taylor (1984). What follows is a summary of the results of the simulations, with a focus on the influence of technological change and price of oil on space needs for living, working, intra-urban travel, leisure (outside the home) and future locational patterns *within the Melbourne urban area*.

Living Space. The principal effect on living space is exerted through oil prices, where the greater the increase in price of oil, the greater the reduction in living space. Higher oil prices dampen demand for land on the periphery of the metropolitan area, the traditional focus for the majority of new (detached) residential construction activity. Technological change appears to be exerting a secondary effect, whereby increased availability of information technology tends to suppress living space requirements (TV-videotext oriented) while increased growth of telecommunications technology tended to increase living space requirements for particular groups (reflected in an increase in incidence of home-based employment; residence in urban fringe on cheaper land and larger house, telecommuting). 'Computer technology' per se appears to exert no influence and is, perhaps, too diffuse a concept, embodied as it is in the more concrete technologies of information and telecommunications technologies.

Working Space. Beaumont and Keys (1982:167) suggest that work- or business-related trips are more likely to be substituted by telecommunications than domestic (shopping, leisure) trips. In our simulations for Melbourne we find that greatest reductions in working space do in fact occur with higher rates of change in telecommunications technology.

Transport Space. Future increases in transport space are found to be associated with a reduction in the real price of oil and zero growth in telecommunications.

Leisure Space. Decline in leisure space use (external to place of residence) occurs in the context of significant rates of increase in both information and telecommunications technology (changes appear indifferent to the price of oil). This suggests increasing expenditure of leisure time inside the house and less in active sports requiring special community facilities or attendance at sporting fixtures. Reduction in demand for leisure space becomes a significant contributor to increasing density and less-dispersed metropolitan development.

Dispersion of Activities. Dispersion of activity is linked most strongly to lower oil prices. The combination of increased application of telecommunications and information technologies exerts a centralising effect at metropolitan level (even under conditions where there is a reduction in the real price of oil). Telecommunications and information technologies appear to exert land saving influences in the present metropolitan model (see Chapter 13). The dispersive influence of these technologies is likely to find greatest impact at inter-metropolitan level (Simon 1980).

Residential density. The simulation results suggest that under conditions of increased oil prices and increases in application of new technology, especially in the area of telecommunications, Melbourne's residential density will increase (i.e.improved telecommunications will occur within a proximal environment).

Spatial Segregation of the Population. When level of technology is held at current level and oil prices are varied between positions of growth and decline, no significant changes are evident in degree of spatial segregation of the population. With increased technological development, major increases in levels of segregation become apparent, suggesting that access to new technology-based employment (and its remuneration) becomes more difficult for a growing proportion of the population.

Spatial Variation in Services. The pattern of linkages identified in Figure 23.4 suggests similar outcomes could be expected as occurred with spatial segregation of the population. This was found to be the case.

An identical set of simulations performed on the Melbourne experts' model revealed a narrow band of variability around the spatial outcomes.

Conclusions

The time perspective and methodology of this chapter are characteristic of the transition to 'intellectual technology' considered typical of the post-industrial period (Bell 1980:167). In terms of time perspective (future orientation) and 'methodology', forecasting and planning succeeds the *ad hoc* adaptiveness and experimentation of the industrial period of societal development; and the empiricism of contemporary and earlier periods makes way for abstract theory, models, simulations, decision theory and systems analysis.

The problems confronted in adopting a futures perspective to a complex, multi-dimensional phenomena such as urban development are well-known (Sackman 1975) and this study attempted to address these as the project unfolded. As there are no future facts (despite what some Delphi proponents may claim) our decision has been to focus on anticipated changes (tendencies) across a wide range of factors associated with metropolitan development. In selecting respondents for the CIBW72 surveys, the panel consisted largely of academics with a demonstrated background in socio-technical and urban systems (via publication, academic position or presence on advisory committees). Self-assigned levels of expertise produced no statistically significant variations in future perceptions in subsequent analyses (a similar finding to that of Sackman 1975 and Bureau of Transport Economics 1982). Regional variation tended to be restricted to several issues and here resulted in contrasts between developed industrial and less developed societies (rather than between the several advanced industrial societies represented).

Simulations using the urban systems model developed for this study suggest the following speculative conclusions. First, it is apparent that while the impact of new technology on individuals may be revolutionary (rapid changes over short periods of time affecting significant segments of the population), its impact on large organisations and social systems (which include cities) is more likely to be evolutionary. Complex systems tend to be more resistant to change. Secondly, if urban change is most likely to be evolutionary, what direction or pattern is this evolution likely to take? Recognition has already been given to the fact that information and telecommunications technology force neither centralisation nor decentralisation *per se* and can be used to effect essentially any level of centralisation that an organisation or a society may wish (Simon 1980; Beaumont and Keys 1982). In the Melbourne metropolitan context, the emerging technologies embedded in the city's industrial and governmental institutions are expected to exert centralising tendencies, albeit at a slow pace (dispersal will become evident at regional and state level). Internal reorganisation of space is occurring at a more rapid pace, however, as social groups benefiting from change as well as those suffering as a result of technological change compete, on unequal terms, for a share of urban resources. The modelled scenario for Melbourne's urban future is probable: many of its elements are undesirable. The challenge is to devise a desirable future.

References

Ackoff, R.L. (1981) *Creating the Corporate Future*, Wiley, New York

Beaumont, J.R. and Keys, P.L. (1982) *Future Cities: Spatial Analysis of Energy Issues*, John Wiley, New York

Bell, D. (1980) 'The Social Framework of the Information Society' in M.L. Dertouzos and J. Moses (eds) *The Computer Age: a Twenty Year View*, The MIT Press, Cambridge, Massachusetts

Bell, W. and Mau, J. (1971) 'Images of the Future: Theory and Research Strategies' in W. Bell and J. Mau (eds) *The Sociology of the Future*, Russell Sage Foundation, New York

Boniecki, G. (1980) 'What are the Limits to Man's Time and Space Perspectives?' *Technological Forecasting and Social Change*, *17*, 161-75

Bureau of Transport Economics (1982) *The Future of Urban Passenger Transport: a Delphi Study*, AGPS, Canberra

Cavallo, R. (1982) 'Science, Systems Methodology and the "Interplay Between Nature and Ourselves"' in R. Cavallo (ed.) *Systems Methodology in Social Science Research*, Kluwer Nijhoff Publishing, Boston

Chen, K., Jarboe, K. and Wolfe, J. (1981) 'Long-Range Scenario Construction for Technology Assessment', *Technological Forecasting and Social Change*, *20*, 27-40

Clark, I.F. (1978) 'Prophets, Predictors and Public Policies, 1870-1970', *Futures*, *10*, 71-75

Dickey, J.W. and Doughty, J.C. (1981) *TIP. The Trends Integrator Procedure*, Division of Environmental and Urban Systems, Virginia Polytechnic Institute and State University (mimeographed)

Eden, C. (1978) 'Taking Systems Theory to Pieces', *Futures*, *19*, 159-61

Encel, S., Marstrand, P. and Page, W. (eds) (1975) *The Art of Anticipation, Values and Methods in Forecasting*, Martin Robertson, London

Evered, R. (1977) 'Interest in the Future', *Futures*, *9*, 285-95

Forrester, J.W. (1971) *World Dynamics*, Wright-Allen Press, Cambridge, Massachusetts

Fowles, J. (1977) 'The Problem of Values in Futures Research', *Futures*, *9*, 303-14

Hall, P. (1977) *Europe 2000*, Duckworth, London

Helmer, O. (1981) 'Reassessment of Cross-Impact Analysis', *Futures*, *13*, 389-400

Holsti, O.R. (1968) 'Content Analysis' in G. Lindzey and E. Aronson (eds) *The Handbook of Social Psychology*, Addison-Wesley, Massachusetts

Jones, H. and Twiss, G. (1978) *Forecasting Technology for Planning Decisions*, Macmillan, London

Lynch, K. (1962) 'The Pattern of the Metropolis' in L. Rodwin (ed.) *The Future Metropolis*, Constable, London

Marien, M. (1977) 'The Two Visions of Post-Industrial Society', *Futures*, *9*, 415-31

Martino, J. (1972) *Technological Forecasting for Decision-Making*, Elsevier, Amsterdam

May, G. (1982) 'The Argument for More Future-Oriented Planning', *Futures*, *14*, 313-18

Miller, D.C. (1957) 'Theories of Social Change' in F. Allen *et al.* (eds) *Technology and Social Change*, Appelton-Century-Crofts, New York

Moore, W.E. (1967) *Order and Change: Essays in Comparative Sociology*, John Wiley, New York

Newton, P.W. and Taylor, M.A.P. (1984) *The Impact of Technological Change on Urban Form: Report of the CIB Futures Study*, CSIRO Division of Building Research, Melbourne

Ornauer, H., Wiberg, H., Galtung, J. and Sicinski, A. (eds) (1976) *Images of the World in the Year 2000*, Humanities Press, New Jersey

Rescher, N. (1981) 'Methodological Issues in Science and Technology Forecasting: Uses and Limitations in Public Policy Deliberations', *Technological Forecasting and Social Change, 20*, 101-12.

Sackman, H. (1975) *Delphi Critique*, D.C. Heath & Co., Lexington

Sarre, P., Blowers, A. and Hamnett, C. (1973) *The Future City*, The Open University Press, Milton Keynes

Simon, H.A. (1980) 'The Consequences of Computers for Centralization and Decentralization' in M.L. Dertouzos and J. Moses (eds) *The Computer Age: a Twenty Year View*, The MIT Press, Cambridge, Massachusetts

Singer, J.D. (1971) *A General Systems Taxonomy for Political Science*, General Learning Press, New York

Taylor, M.A.P. and Newton, P.W. (1983) 'Exploring the Impacts of Technology Change on Urban Form', *Proceedings of the Second International Conference on New Survey Methods in Transport*, Pokolbin, NSW, September

Textor, R.B. (1978) 'Cultural Futures for Thailand', *Futures*, *10*, 347-60

Vickers, G. (1981) 'Editorial Balance Between Credos', *Futures*, *13*, 67-70

24. A DESIRABLE URBAN FORM
L. Klaassen

Among the elements that make a town function, the transport system is essential; it comprises the infrastructure for private conveyance as well as the infrastructure and services of public transport. If the transport system is inadequate the spatial organisation does not function as expected: traffic facilities may be under-utilised in one place and unable to satisfy requirements elsewhere. The only way to avoid such a state of affairs is to integrate (simultaneously and in mutual consideration) planning of the spatial organisation and the transport system.

Of great importance is the objective envisaged: the spatial organisation and the transport system together should offer a framework in which the actions of individual consumers and producers — individually optimum by definition — also bring about a global or societal optimum. The framework should do justice to individual preferences, prevent conflicts among individual or group interests, and in particular remain satisfactory over the long term. To that end, an understanding of both individual preferences and the conflicts among them and a vision of the (distant) future are required.

The organisation of space and the creation of a transport system largely determine the structure of an urban area and are irrevocable to a high degree. This implies anticipating in many respects the situations and values of a (distant) future, especially in so far as they diverge from what is valid today. A great deal of courage and imagination are thus required, particularly for towns that are still in an early stage of urbanisation.

To allow the many heavy contingencies to discourage us would be a grave mistake; they should, on the contrary, stimulate us to use our imagination in conjunction with a well-endowed state apparatus. The state apparatus is concerned with furnishing the country with houses, greenery, employment, leisure facilities, traffic and transport infrastructure, and with the way that infrastructure is used. By its nature the state apparatus is more or less compelling, by its effect either stimulating (subsidies, injunctions) or restraining (levies, prohibitions). Some functions or arms of the state may intervene directly in urban infrastructure investments and the use that is made of them, or work indirectly by creating the frameworks within which, and setting the criteria by which, investments are made and their utilisation is governed.

Central and local governments possess collectively the authority to steer the optimisation process and keep budgets balanced. They control the construction, maintenance and use of the technical and the socio-economic infrastructure, and can, by a differentiated system of levies, to some extent guide its use in the direction they desire. Nevertheless, in practice the results of government intervention fail to pass the criteria of an integrated policy. Several causes can be mentioned. Nobody has clear, overall responsibility. Responsibilities are dispensed by statutory authorities, both geographically and functionally. A coherent system of criteria by which to test policy and serving as an internally binding element is lacking (internal norms). Lacking also are any externally limiting criteria, such as could be derived from spatial planning, environmental hygiene, social interests, well-being (external norms).

In other words, two kinds of problem mark the present situation: the administrative structure is not tailored to the problems, and there are no coherent systems of norms to govern policy.

The Structure of the Problem

Traditionally, national as well as urban traffic studies have tried to assess the optimum network to satisfy traffic needs whose structure is determined by a spread of population and activities assumed *a priori*. Such an approach is evidently one-sided and indeed questionable as soon as high traffic densities are at stake. Very high densities are known to make the cost of traffic soar, especially on certain sections of the network, and the question arises whether in the long run this congestion will not influence the spatial distribution of people and activities. In that case, the principle of an *a priori* determined distribution that used to guide traffic investigations has to be abandoned. Or, to express it in traffic lore: the traffic matrix used to be a fixture, independent of the degree of congestion. For areas outside the agglomerations that assumption is still acceptable. There are many places where the road network can be extended in proportion to the needs without incurring extraordinary expenses, and in such places the conventional procedure will hardly entail grave mistakes. But in the large urban agglomerations the same procedure may bring about unacceptable situations. There, one cannot go on expanding the infrastructure as if it were at constant marginal costs, but will have to face the consequences of increasing congestion in *use* of the infrastructure.

There is general agreement that both public and private transport infrastructure in urban areas is used in an essentially highly inefficient way. Not only is traffic concentrated in a relatively small number of hours, but its alternating pattern also leads to the actual capacity being greatly under-utilised. The capacity of infrastructure required at a given volume and structure of traffic can be expressed in a simple formula:

$$C = \frac{Rd}{\sigma \bar{\iota}}$$

in which
- C = infrastructural capacity required;
- R = total number of trips;
- $\bar{d}$ = average trip length;
- σ = coefficient of spatial distribution, defined as the utilisation by direction, i.e. as the quotient of the maximum observed traffic flow measured in both directions and the maximum possible flow in both directions;
- $\bar{\iota}$ = coefficient of temporal distribution, defined as the utilisation by time unit, i.e. as the average flow in both directions.

The maximum value of σ and $\bar{\iota}$ is one. If $\sigma = 1$, the maximum observed flow in both directions is equal to the maximum possible flow in either direction; in other words, the infrastructure is equally utilised in each direction. If $\bar{\iota} = 1$, the road is occupied equally all through the day; $\sigma = 1$ and $\bar{\iota} = 1$ indicate a fully utilised infrastructure.

Now we can define our problem as the minimisation of C, in other words: given a certain volume of traffic, what is the least amount of infrastructure required to deal with that volume, or, in a formulation perhaps more corresponding to urban traffic problems: how can a given infrastructure be used optimally? According to the definition of required infrastructure capacity, planning measures will contribute to the minimisation if they result in fewer trips (R), a shorter average trip length ($\bar{d}$), an improved structure of traffic (σ), and an improved temporal structure ($\bar{\iota}$). In the next section these criteria are used to judge societal developments and measures taken by the public authorities or others (business enterprise, for instance) in relation to urban transport infrastructure.

General Trends

Our society is devolving in a way which partly supports and partly conflicts with the requirement of minimising the need for infrastructure. Progressive growth of areas outside the large urban agglomerations is conducive to minimisation. Increased motorisation and prosperity, promoting suburbanisation trends and thus leading to more and longer trips, works against minimisation.

In fact, the general tendencies involve all four elements that supposedly determine the capacity of infrastructure needed. The influences are in part positive and in part negative. Therefore, a traffic policy aimed at minimising the need for infrastructure must, on the one hand, support some general tendencies, and on the other take measures to counter any undesirable developments. So let us look closer into each influence.

Decentralisation, tending to evolve in several stages, sets in when people begin to leave the centre of the town, moving to the outskirts. So long as employment lags or fails to follow that movement, the traffic volumes will increase as a consequence of the larger home-to-work distance. Decentralisation also increases in association with a decrease in the average number of people per residential unit. As soon as people begin to consider moving beyond the outskirts of the town to places farther afield, the second decentralisation phase sets in. Progressive suburbanisation, caused by greater mobility as a result of car ownership and higher incomes, increases the average trip length and will also make it difficult for public transport to serve adequately the dispersed population. Moreover, at this stage, economic activities will also have begun to decentralise. Recognising the fact that the town centre is becoming less and less accessible to motorised traffic, many companies will resort to more accessible sites elsewhere. That marks a beginning of a degeneration of the centre. The word degeneration is chosen here to indicate an uncontrolled and unprepared process which, left to itself, could lead to the same deplorable situation that many American and some European towns are currently encountering.

The ultimate stage is marked by a declining population of the agglomeration and a progressively increasing one in municipalities at some distance from the historical centre. In this stage, demographic decentralisation, followed after some time by economic activity, thus has grown from an urban into a regional problem.

The expected increase in number of trips, in some ways an autonomous trend, will also depend on increasing car ownership. These trips lie in part outside the sphere of home-to-work travel; they are made to visit friends and relations, shops, restaurants, and so forth. Could some of them be replaced with telecommunication, in other words, could increasing congestion induce people to ring their contacts instead of visiting them? These questions have been discussed on several occasions, but the fact is that, with the exception of telegrams, a new means of communication has never yet diminished the use of older ones. Traffic (face-to-face contact) has grown irrepressibly, letters continue to be written since the introduction of the telephone, which in turn enjoys increasing popularity. Our society seems to have a growing need for communication, and to want to make use of all the means available. Indeed, individuals who have a telephone available communicate more by letter than those who have not. Apparently, the greater one's need for communication, the more one tends to use all available means.

Decentralisation Policy at Town Level

Imagine a town where a majority of employment is located in the centre and the majority of houses elsewhere. In such a town the structure of work-residence travel is such that in the morning the roads leading to the centre are fully occupied; likewise in the afternoon those leading away from the centre. The concentration of working hours causes a high peak (and therefore a low $\bar{t}$) and the separation of living and employment together with the concentration of employment causes a one-sided use of the infrastructure (low σ). In the long run, such an unfavourable structure causes congestion on the road network and a failure by public transport to meet the demand for an enormous capacity during a short part of the day. The lack of service and comfort in public transport is the result rather than the cause of the losses suffered by public transport companies. That is not to say that only business economics should be considered in deciding whether public transport ought to be maintained, contracted or expanded; environmental and especially social factors play a role too.

If, then, the present unfavourable traffic structure springs in essence from an unfavourable spatial structure, attempts to improve it by dispersing certain forms of employment, logically come first to mind. But how far can employment be spread without damage to the firms involved? Two points have to be considered more closely to find an adequate answer.

First, the links that bind companies together are most important for their functioning, and cannot be broken without affecting their profitability. Although we do not yet know with certainty how far such links make it necessary for establishments to locate near to one another, more and more research results point towards the existence of so-called blocks or bundles of companies, defined as groups within which inter-company communication is significantly more intensive than links with companies of other blocks. An investigation carried out in London has clearly proved the existence of a financial block, a shipping and transportation block, an insurance block, a newspaper and printing block, a wholesale block and so forth (Goddard 1968). Given that such blocks exist, we are then confronted with the question of their optimum location. Knowing that the different blocks need not necessarily locate in close proximity to each other, how can we best distribute them across the town?

Two criteria are important in that connection. First, are the blocks 'employment' or 'visitors' blocks? To determine their character we divide the number of visitors, for instance in a day, by the number of people employed in the block (V/W-ratio). Obviously, a block with high V/W creates traffic regularly spread through the day, and essentially needs space for short-time parking outside peak hours. A low V/W block generates traffic concentrated within a few hours and with space requirements for long-time parking. Clearly, blocks with a low V/W-ratio should not be located in a town centre, for they tend to cause high morning and afternoon peaks and monopolise parking space. Moreover their nature makes them unfit for town-centre location; essentially they are like industry parks, which are also concentrations of employment with a low V/W ratio.

The ranking of a block by its level of provision of goods and services is the second criterion. For a block with a low level of provision (say a shopping centre for daily necessities) a centre location is evidently undesirable. For high-ranking blocks, representing unique activities, a location within the town should be chosen with great care. Combination of the two criteria produces the following result:

	V/W Ratio	
Ranking	High	Low
High	centralise	concentrate at accessible points
Low	disperse	disperse

A low ranking makes dispersion across the town desirable irrespective of the V/W-ratio; at the local area (municipal) level a separation of high- and low-V/W blocks may be desirable. High ranking combined with a low V/W ratio makes concentration in secondary specific centres satisfying high-accessibility requirements desirable. Finally, a high V/W-ratio combined with a high ranking characterises a typical centre activity. Complicating factors arise in relation to the above approach in the sense that employment blocks, too, create visitors; for example, at noon, office workers considerably enhance and even stimulate the liveliness of a town centre. In other words, workers are visitors also, if only during a short time of the day. That is undeniable, but then workers in 'visitors blocks' can also be visitors; shop assistants, too, help to make the town centre function, not only during the noon interval, but also while they are working. Should a spatial urban structure make it possible to locate an employment block outside the town centre but at walking distance from it, then the two elements can be combined.

The question arises as to why the actual distribution of blocks (defined as we have done) is not in accordance with the pattern just sketched. Indeed, if that distribution is so preferable, why doesn't it come about of its own accord? The answer is that the traffic factor, or, more correctly, accessibility, while very important for blocks with a high V/W-ratio (whose profitability depends on it directly) is much less so for blocks with a low V/W-ratio. For the latter, traffic costs, consisting of the transportation costs of their staff, plus the cost of investing in road infrastructure, plus the deficits of public transport, are external costs not affecting the business results; therefore, they tend to choose their location without heed to these costs. Understandably, they will prefer a representative site in the town centre to one elsewhere in the country. An office that chooses the wrong site — from a traffic point of view — might have recruiting difficulties. Because society always suffers the traffic consequences of such 'wrong' choices, government clearly has to introduce the measures that may lead to a more acceptable distribution.

The next question, logically following from the foregoing, is whether urban governments are able to implement a locational programme as sketched above. To answer that question, a negative and a positive tendency have to be distinguished.

In many municipalities, the areas in or directly surrounding the town centre are being redeveloped, which mostly means that residential quarters are demolished to make room for offices. Offices, as we have seen, essentially have a low V/W-ratio which makes them unfit for central location. Moving people to the suburbs has a double-negative effect on traffic. To the extent that they previously worked in the centre they created little traffic in going from home to work. To the extent that inner-area residents used to work elsewhere, they used the under-utilised portion of traffic or road to go to work. In both cases their living in the town centre was favourable. In the new situation employment in the town centre has increased while residents have decreased and thus the flow in the unfavourable sense is reinforced and in the favourable sense diminished. Both the spatial and the temporal structure have changed for the worse. The conclusion must be that moving housing away from the centre is unfavourable in all respects and should be avoided as much as possible. The clear implication is that developments tending to weaken a town centre's residential function should be stopped. A measure to that effect can be taken quickly and its effects are instantaneous.

The question is, however, whether local policy should be content with stopping unfavourable developments — as it certainly can — or should act in a more active fashion, stimulating the town's residential function as well as the decentralisation of establishments already present in the inner town. The law should essentially make it possible for municipalities to prohibit the location of, say, certain kinds of offices in the town centre. At one time industries used to be admitted in towns and houses could be built in leisure areas, but measures have been taken to prevent such things (for example, zoning regulations can be made to enforce such measures). The important point is how the financial consequences of active decentralisation can be borne. Expanding a town centre's residential function means that houses have to be built or renovated, and that perhaps the cost of moving industries has to be paid out of collective means. Financial sacrifices are involved in both cases.

The Quality of Life in a Town

In the preceding sections we have presented a mixture of possible measures and societal factors which affect a town's development and in the long run might bring about a more acceptable structure than the present one. Its acceptability depends largely on the desirability of decentralisation, or rather, on the degree to which people accept decentralisation.

To approach urban problems otherwise than has been done so far, the significance of the town centre and in particular, its essential functions will have to be re-assessed. The town centre should be a meeting centre, a place to look at people, to shop without buying, to appreciate historic buildings, streets and squares, a place, in short, to do all those things that are not immediately connected with the town's economic functions. It should offer intimacy and quiet living, it should be accessible to traffic, but also be screened from its unpleasant impact. The space should be both accessible and sheltered. The town centre need not be large; it is the quality that counts.

To describe properly the essential functions of a town, we ought perhaps to take inventory of all there is and delete from it all that is not a genuine town-centre activity. The construction of pedestrian zones, the location of secondary centres, the reservation of space for underground garages, are all matters to consider carefully, as they will certainly become urgent in the coming 10-20 years.

In general we shall have to think about what activities we really want to keep or promote as town-centre functions, how much space is required for their functioning, and how the available space can best be organised to keep and stimulate these activities. Once the magnitude and the spatial structure of the inner-town functions (living included) are defined, we must work to realise them gradually. The process is an essential part of the wider decentralisation process. Both not only serve traffic, they also serve to prevent traffic from immobilising or destroying desirable structures. Indeed, such measures should not be taken for the sake of traffic, but for the sake of preserving the town centre, the place that makes a town what it really is.

References

Goddard, J. (1968) 'Multivariate Analysis of Office Location Patterns in the City Centre: a London Example', *Regional Studies*, 2, 69-85

PART NINE

OVERVIEW AND PLANNING IMPLICATIONS

25. FORCES FOR SPATIAL CHANGE
N. Pressman

Many experts and citizens living in metropolitan areas are beginning to believe that the future is beyond the reasonable control of man. Indeed, with major advances in the fields of systems engineering and analysis and the rapid technological change which has evolved during the last 5-10 years, one is hard pressed to keep up with the broad spectrum of post-industrial developments occurring in the more developed nations. Many people believe that the future is technologically determined and is, in fact, inevitable. They feel there is little that urban managers can do other than accept the 'facts' and help us to adjust to the new realities with a minimum of stress and inconvenience.

It will be the intent of this chapter to explore the various forces at work which are influential in transforming urban life styles and the fundamental spatial patterns emerging in response to urban growth trends. The ideas presented are for purposes of encouraging vigorous discussion, for the author is firmly convinced that people must remain in control and that technological progress must be channelled in the best interests of society. Planners must be concerned with what 'ought to be' rather than merely with accommodation of trends — even though this must also be incorporated into the planning process.

Some Sources of Urban Growth

People require several basic things from their physical environment (after Eberhard 1977). *Shelter* is required for living, working, playing, worship, etc. It may assume a variety of shapes and forms depending upon the economic and physical resources available in a given society. *Movement* is required between various shelter systems and by varying modes, including two and three dimensional organisation in space. *Information-communication systems* are necessary to interconnect people. These can be via face-to-face contacts or through mechanised systems such as telephones, radios, cable TV, video-conferencing, electronic mail. *Management systems* are required for controlling the 'metabolism' of human settlements. These regulate the flow of raw materials, food, and water into heat, light, energy and processed goods required by society.

The above 'hardware' requirements which are designed, built or physically manifested are complemented by the 'software' requirements of organisations, skilled people and institutions. Together, these two factors normally form the knowledge base which influences future urban patterns.

Since human intercourse has traditionally been the major *raison d'être* for the existence of cities, and as face-to-face interaction has been the key mode of communication until very recently, the dominant urban envelope which accommodated these actions and behaviour systems was that of the concentrated or compact variety (the historic model). The motivation for dwelling together was to minimise travel time and distance which gave rise to a compact urban form. However, in recent times important counter-processes have occurred which, while simultaneously enhancing opportunities for social intercourse, are also deconcentrating cities and perhaps diminishing their roles. Rapid technological developments in transportation and communication are making high-density settlement unnecessary for high-quality connectivity: 'Mechanised transport and the use of airplanes and telephones on a massive scale have so lowered costs of connectivity that people and businesses can now move almost anywhere and still enjoy intimate associations with those who stayed behind' (Webber 1982:148-9). An effective international communications network has permitted specialisation within the tertiary and quaternary employment sectors and has even tended to develop cities with specialised roles on a global basis:

> Most experts in retailing predict that much shopping, in the near future, will be via closed-circuit TV, which will obviously transform the configurations of today's and yesterday's shopping centers ... Spectator sports and other forms of entertainment seem increasingly to be brought to us via the tube, rather than face-to-face. There will be further predictable shifts in intra-urban, suburban and rural patterns. (Blake 1982:159)

In the US, one of the post-industrial, high-technology nations par excellence, the detailed results of the 1980 Census have demonstrated some dramatic changes between 1970 and 1980. For the first time, the population of rural areas grew as fast as that of urban areas, and the population of many rural areas grew sufficiently for them to be classified as urban (with the attractiveness of rural areas for industrial location being largely responsible for this trend). Furthermore, the geographic expansion and coalescence of urban areas have led to an increase in the number and appearance of 'supercities' (Long and De Are 1983). This deceleration of urban growth — widespread but not geographically uniform — has resulted in US urban areas becoming larger and less densely populated. These trends suggest that less concentrated forms of urban settlement may be on the horizon:

> City expansion in the late twentieth century is taking place in those locales where natural environments and climates are most amiable, where opportunities for leisure-time activities are plentiful and where the undesired side-effects of older high-density settlements have not yet accumulated. (Webber 1982:149)

Since the traditional constraints of industrial and service sector location are no longer applicable to any significant extent, and since new jobs are free to follow managerial talent and skilled personnel who tend to locate in high-amenity suburban locations, we have an emerging phenomenon which parallels the old adage 'population follows jobs', which can now be expressed as 'jobs follow population'. This is a cyclical process which appears to be less constrained than ever in the past. The recent American trends in urbanisation can be summarised as follows (Hall 1980): decline or stagnation (especially in number of inner-city jobs due to industry moving to the periphery) of larger urban areas; regional shifts from frostbelt to sunbelt; growth of non-metropolitan areas; deconcentration of people and of jobs with central cities losing populations and employment to suburban rings with a vastly increased proportion of growth occurring outside metropolitan areas.

The typical urban pattern that has emerged during the second half of the twentieth century has been eloquently expressed by Ithiel de Sola Pool (1980):

> a proliferation of hubs, some of them within the old city but away from the bull's eye, some of them planted beyond the city in green fields, some of them subsidiary downtowns, such as Neuilly or Shinjuku, and some of them specialised single-purpose developments like shoppers' malls or rural industrial parks. The Los Angeles metropolitan area is prototypic of what is likely to develop where there is cheap, good, and universal motor transport and telecommunications ... a highly differentiated, geographically dispersed structure of centres and subcentres with complex inter-relations among them.

'Technology Fix' Elements Likely to Direct Future Development

There are a number of current and soon-to-be diffused technologies which will have a probable impact on the future form of metropolitan areas. Without being absolutely certain of these impacts, the trends will be toward even greater diffusion or deconcentration than we have henceforth experienced — for better or worse. Communications facilities by the year 2001 are likely to be quite different from what we presently know them to be with the coming availability of abundant, low-cost bandwidth (made available through fiber optics developments) and the low cost of digital switching (made possible through progress in microchip electronics). The implied benefits of these technologies suggest that the future telecommunications system — by affecting the production, storage, handling, use and dissemination of information so essential to a knowledge-based economy — is likely to eliminate the disparities in the quality of communications service now found in different locations, (de Sola Pool 1980:9-10). An additional speculation made by de Sola Pool is that it will pay many large investment corporations, in many situations, to substitute investment in sophisticated communications for the expense of travel — given the increasing costs of transportation which might normally generate a counter-trend toward urban concentration in central cities and inner suburban locations.

New Technologies and Their Impacts on Lifestyles

There are a number of technological devices which, once widely diffused, will have short-range effects on the way the city functions and long-range effects on the structures, organisations and institutions of the urban region. The summary that follows is based on the work of Coates (1982):

Telematics Devices & Systems	Probable Impacts (1980-2001)
Microcomputers; Large-scale integrated circuits;	Movement away from centralised office space to suburban locations, homes and small work sites.
New memory systems; solid state laser, bubble, backend processes;	Home work-study centre and around-the-clock focus of the household used for entertainment and socialising with the outside world.

Morpheme generator.

Software &	Large cohorts of population in voice-to-voice,
Significant Systems	face-to-face, or data communication at any
Information utilities —	place at any time.
The Source,	Decentralisation of offices, work-at-home,
Lockheed,	electronic cottages.
Prestel	Estimate that, by 2000, the average household
Teletext	will have an investment in telematics roughly
Videotext	equivalent to its present investment in the
Pattern recognition —	automobile. Greater public participation and
voice, signature	influence in the actions taken by governments.
Encryption	Computer-console shopping for durable goods.
	Rush-hour (peak commuting) a thing of the past
	as many work routines are integrated with
	work-at-home and flextime schedules.

Undoubtedly, technology will interact with other social and economic forces and trends to affect future spatial organisation. Some of these newly emerging elements can be described as follows (after Coates 1982):

Trend	*Impacts*
Increase of aged population	Migration to warmer climates. Demand for smaller physical facilities. Potential increase in group living. Growth of geriatric communities.
Single-parent families; Deferred marriage	Smaller, modular facilities and larger, multi-occupancy, innovative dwelling arrangements.
Work-at-home and flexi-time scheduling	Gradual disappearance of circadian rhythms ... all-night TV programming, food stores and cinemas open 24 hours, night shifts in banking and computer centres.
Large-scale entry of women into the labour force	Demand for quinary services reducing unnecessary household tasks and routines (explosion of convenience-oriented technologies). Increasing amounts of recreation-time created through time-saving devices.
Higher levels of education	Increased expectations, upgrading of taste, desire for greater diversity in decor, design, furnishings, eating, etc.

Changing technologies of education	Continuing education, multiple-skilled personnel, frequent career changes, vocational changes accelerated.
Continuation of inflation, structural unemployment, and high personal taxes	Shift toward a more intensive barter-economy. Use of informal labour for many tasks as well as larger-scale 'do-it-yourself' movement.
Improved quality-of-life awareness	Potential resurgence in bicycle use, greater pedestrianisation of urban movement systems, priority given to pedestrians over vehicles.
Technologically mediated information & advice services	Psychiatric/marital/family counselling will become routine; diagnostic health and human, social and sexual services will be made more broadly accessible. Analytical services and information-collection services will grow.

The Question of Future Settlement Pattern

What impact will the technological changes have on the settlement pattern of the metropolis, as we know it today? What can be expected of these new forces as they exert pressures on the shape and content of our future urban regions?

In so far as basic or generic urban forms (or spatial patterns) are concerned, there seems to be general agreement that eight such fundamental shapes are in evidence (based on Gibson 1977; note that some cities may embody characteristics found in several of the basic types):

1. DISPERSED SHEET (Orthogonal Gridiron)

Spread of generally undifferentiated growth, without significant, major focal centres. e.g. Los Angeles, Tokyo.

2. SPIDER WEB (Radio-concentric) or (Ring Radial)

One of the most common urban forms. A high-density, exhibiting vital centrality, with surrounding development is the distinguishing characteristic. e.g. Paris, Vienna, Dallas.

3. STAR (Finger)

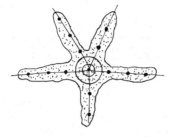

Basically a 'spider web' form with linear
radials usually defining some type of
open space. e.g. Copenhagen,
Washington, D.C.

4. SATELLITE (Cluster)

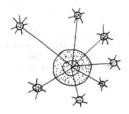

Variation of the 'galaxy' but with a
predominant central core or city
centre. e.g. Stockholm, London.

5. LINEAR

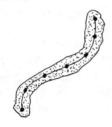

Development is organised along a
dominant 'corridor' (a single 'finger'
variation of the 'star' shape).
e.g. Cumbernauld, Ciudad Lineal
(Madrid), Megalopolis.

6. RING

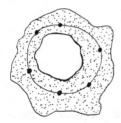

Linear form which closes upon
itself. It has a large open space
at the centre. e.g. San Francisco
Bay Area, Principal cities of the
Netherlands.

Note: Types 1 through 3 are normally produced by short-run, small-scale,
        individual entrepreneurial decision, whereas 4 through 6 forms
        require advance planning and careful control.

7. GALAXY

A series of linked 'cores' appropriated in the landscape at functional distances from each other. e.g. large urban regions, cities of Northern Germany.

8. POLYCENTRED NET

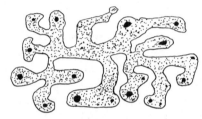

Diversely spread urban organisation with differentiated foci, dominant and minor arteries, built-up and open spaces — an articulated distribution. e.g. Detroit.

The numbers and distributions of the different nodal points (whether acting as central business districts, suburban centres or other functional purposes) are a measure of the degree of concentration or dispersal of the metropolitan system at large with economic, social, institutional and other forces tending to influence one or another of these options. Personal lifestyle preferences, opportunities and constraints (physical, economic or otherwise) are further factors to be considered in attempting to assess the prevailing trends which seem to embrace the 'dispersed' version of future city.

Impacts of Communications Technology

Two general trends of population distribution shifts have been identified (Colby 1959): a *centripetal* trend away from smaller towns toward the larger, more dominant urban centres; and a *centrifugal* trend away from the urban centres toward the suburban field or metropolitan periphery.

Without question, the new information technologies have been rendering a variety of jobs and their workers more footloose by facilitating the movement of information to people rather than through moving people to locations possessing the information. In other words, technology allows for an alternative *modus vivendi* to the actual spatial displacement of both goods and personnel. However, it is essential to stress that this possibility need not necessarily lead to deterministic conclusions about future urban patterns. We do not yet understand to what degree technological substitution can successfully replace human proximity and the real face-to-face interaction among people. Goddard (1980) suggests the 'possibility that by increasing the opportunities for interaction in society, the use of telecommunications can generate more travel than it substitutes for.'

Although we know that, especially in the US (and Australia, as well), population dispersal will most likely occur at a quicker pace in the 1980s than it has done in the past, we do not know precisely what influence information technologies have had directly on this phenomenon — although they enable more to happen in remote regions (Mandeville 1983). We are not yet capable of isolating precisely the many key variables which seem to be influencing a trend to the metropolitan fringe. Mandeville (1983:65) even goes so far as saying 'Unfortunately, so much of what is currently said about many aspects of the new information technologies is mere unsubstantiated assertion'.

The Future Form of the Metropolis

There are many forces which continuously work in simultaneous fashion (often at cross-purposes) to shape the future metropolitan pattern. Information technology is but one of these, albeit a significant one. In general, the two major trends influencing future urban-regional form appear to be working toward either a *dispersed urban pattern* or a more *concentrated city structure*. Some of the more important forces working toward one or another of these two directions are outlined below (based on a review of subject-matter presented in this book).

Forces Working Toward Dispersed Urban Pattern

— global manufacturing/international economic dependency;
— specialised job skills needed with multiple-skilled inhabitants emerging;
— influential human resources (personnel) moving to high amenity areas on the urban fringe, with jobs following these essential managerial groups;
— high technology-based corporations moving to suburban regions and medium sized towns (telecommunications now allow for the

provision of good education and medical facilities, high-level entertainment, and highly paid jobs away from the central city — attributes which were formerly available only in large urban centres);

— electronic communication reduces need for spatial displacement.
— the private motor car is here to stay and it can be readily assumed that continuing public investment in transportation infrastructure which is car-oriented will be made;
— manufacturing and other tertiary, quaternary and quinary forms of employment have been largely freed from the locational constraints of the past;
— 'preferred' lifestyle characteristics perceived to be localised in out-of-town, lower density, rural-character environments;
— large-scale, highly centralised white-collar central area work forces rapidly becoming obsolete as it becomes both more practical and desirable for 'information workforces' to disperse;
— increasingly heavy public-transport deficits (and concomitant lower quality service) are encouraging greater personal mobility thereby leading to increased deconcentration.

Forces Working Toward Concentrated Urban Structure

— continuing need for personal, face-to-face interaction despite the revolution in electronic communication;
— gradually and continuously increasing future energy costs with respect to business and personal travel demand;
— uncertain energy supply in the medium- and long-term future;
— huge public and private expenditures already directed and committed to commuting patterns from the peripheral areas towards the centre;
— anti-technology attitude emerging (technology too authoritative, acts as job-killer, etc.);
— anticipated decrease in real disposable income for large sectors of the society;
— re-emerging trend toward central city decay and the decreasing tax base which will call for greater attention;
— perceived advantages by some groups of reduced commuting time, and good access to the central city;
— electronic hardware will not be accessible to all economic classes;
— considerable vacant land now available in central city areas awaiting urban infill;

— recognition that the city centre serves as a symbolic 'heart' of the urban organism accommodating a variety of types and sizes of micro-public space and encouraging diversity, proximity, complexity, spontaneity and civility of collective human experience;
— reduction of urban sprawl and its resulting costs.

Centralisation Versus Decentralisation

Although it is impossible to predict patterns of future development with any degree of certainty, it is likely that we might anticipate a 'constellation of relatively *diversified and integrated* cities' involving perhaps more concentration than the present form, but also providing a high degree of subregional integration, allowing particularly for people to live near their places of employment (van Til 1980:68). This pattern would seem to provide 'clear energy savings, without extensive ruralisation, for its social organisation could be maintained even in the face of very tight energy supplies'.

In the verbiage of the communications industry, we can also anticipate a new system of cities with functions quite different from traditional, historic cities — 'virtual cities'. These are 'communities, campuses, laboratories, or corporate offices, scattered across the earth but connected electronically so that the chain reaction of human stimulation catches fire' (Martin 1981).

These 'cities', analogous to Webber's (1967) nonplace urban realm, will assume new functions related to the 'telematic society' and, as they do so, the functions of the traditional cities will also change. Some of these 'virtual cities' will be located on the distant metropolitan fringe as well as in smaller, remotely situated towns and regions as they are not directly tied, for their existence, to the dependency of a parent-city.

Nevertheless, change will occur slowly, with spatial structure, and social and organisational adjustments being far outpaced by the information technologies:

the inertia of the built environment as well as existing organisational structures are likely to present formidable barriers to radical spatial change ... information technology is a 'necessary', though not sufficient, condition for locational change. (Mandeville 1983:69)

It has been clearly pointed out that while

> information technologies may have considerable decentralising
> potential ... technology facilitates both centralisation and
> decentralisation of tasks, and what actually occurs is determined by
> other factors altogether. (Mandeville 1983:69-70)

The growth of non-metropolitan areas will likely continue, made possible by rapidly developing technological change. As Blumenfeld (1982) has so eloquently put it:

> this universal 'urbanisation' of the countryside also means an
> increased 'ruralisation' of the urban population, with increasing
> numbers living in small municipalities rather than in cities ... an
> extension of the long-standing centrifugal trend ... It is, however,
> important to realise that the 'urban magnet' retains its power, as is
> evidenced by the fact that the metropolitan fringe is growing much
> faster than the area further away from the center. The trend toward
> concentration is not so much 'reversed' as submerged and obliterated
> by the continuing trend toward 'decentralisation'.

Conclusions

This chapter has attempted to deal with the forces, in particular those connected with information technology, which are most likely to dictate or influence future settlement patterns. What emerges clearly is that technological change will have a powerful impact. However, it may not necessarily determine the possible outcomes as other critical factors are simultaneously acting on the decision-making field. These are of a social, economic and political nature and may override some or many of the technological elements. What is crucial is how we will choose to make use of the technology which is evolving in the context of the types of urban worlds we view as desirable. Our knowledge and application of the linkages between use of space (land), energy and technology and how they impact on society will be the deciding factors. Whether the future is gloomy or bright will depend on our taking the correct decisions. These decisions will, to a considerable extent, have to be based on the socio-economic structures and values we consider crucial to the well-being of society.

References

Blake, P. (1982) 'The End of Cities? Are There Credible Alternatives' in *Cities — The Forces That Shape Them*, Cooper-Hewitt Museum, Rizzoli, New York

Blumenfeld, H. (1982) *Have the Secular Trends of Population Distribution Been Reversed?*, Research Paper 137, Centre for Urban and Community Studies, University of Toronto

Coates, J.F. (1982) 'New Technologies and Their Urban Impact' in G. Gappert and R.V. Knight (eds) *Cities in the 21st Century*, vol. 23, Urban Affairs Annual Review, Sage

Colby, C.C. (1959) 'Centrifugal and Centripetal Forces In Urban Geography' in H.M. Mayer and C.F. Kohn (eds) *Readings in Urban Geography*, The University of Chicago Press, Chicago

Eberhard, J.P. (1977) 'Advanced Urban Systems: A World Wide Opportunity' *Habitat*, 2, 9-10

Gibson, J.E. (1977) *Designing the New City*, Wiley-Interscience, New York

Goddard, J.B. (1980) 'Technology Forecasting in a Spatial Context', *Futures*, 90-105

Hall, P. (1980) 'New Trends in European Urbanization', *The Annals of the American Academy of Political and Social Science*, 451, 45-51

Long, L. and De Are, D. (1983) 'The Slowing of Urbanization in the US' *Scientific American*, 249, 33-41

Mandeville, T. (1983) 'The Spatial Effects of Information Technology', *Futures*, 65-70

Martin, J. (1981) *Telematic Society*, Prentice-Hall Inc., Englewood Cliffs, New Jersey

de Sola Pool, I. (1980) 'Communications Technology and Land Use', *Annals of the American Academy of Political and Social Science*, 451, 1-12

Til, J. van (1980) 'A New Type of City for an Energy-Short World', *Futurist*, June, 64-70

Webber, M.M. (1967) 'The Urban Place and the Nonplace Urban Realm' in M.M. Webber (ed.) *Explorations into Urban Structure*, University of Pennsylvania Press, Philadelphia

Webber, M.M. (1982) 'Urban Growth: What are its Sources?' in *Cities — The Forces That Shape Them*, Cooper-Hewitt Museum, Rizzoli, New York

26. OPTIMISM AND PESSIMISM IN FUTURE PLANNING
P. Hall

Trying to describe the general flavour of the rich feast of theories and models presented in this book, I have three separate but related impressions. The first is how little we have addressed the specific remit, to discuss the impact of technological change upon urban form; of technological change itself we read much, of urban form relatively little. The second is that the chapters really address the situation only in the advanced industrial countries, and a relatively narrow group of advanced countries at that. The third is the overwhelming impression of pessimism, of passivity in the face of rapid technological, economic and social change. I should like briefly to ask why our contributions are like this, and what if anything we could do in further work to reduce or remove these limitations.

The first stricture is in part unfair; some chapters, those with a more technical modelling approach, do specifically address the question of urban form. But they do so, as traditionally work in this genre has done, at a macro-level, in terms of the broad distribution of activities in urban areas. The more general exploratory papers do not for the most part focus on urban form at all, even at this broad level. Entirely missing from both is any discussion of urban form as the person-in-the-street would understand it, in terms of the shapes and sizes and locations of buildings and the spaces between them. Urban impacts tend to enter indirectly, through the back door, via discussions of the impacts of technological change on urban society; the evolution of urban form is treated as the spatial expression of changes in that society. That is hardly surprising, given the bias of our education and our approach to the understanding of cities; but it is, in the strict sense of the word, remarkable.

The second impression, of geographical bias, simply reflects the economic determinants of urban research. The new version of Engels's Law states that only nations above a certain level of GDP per capita can afford to devote significant resources to support academics like ourselves to do theoretical urban research. Countries below this line have to concentrate on making things to sell to people like ourselves or, if they are able to spend on research, to concentrate it on better ways of making those things to sell. That is inevitable, but it does mean that we must beware that our findings may not readily be generalisable to most of the world.

There is however a greater geographical limitation than this, in that effectively we are an Anglo-American-Australian-Canadian-Northwest European group. The nations discussed here represent the core of the advanced industrial world but not the whole of it; they exclude France and Japan, for instance. They also exclude any representative from that important group of newly industrialising countries that includes such examples as Singapore, Hong Kong, Taiwan, the Republic of Korea and Mexico. This is significant because most of the nations represented are precisely those in which economic growth has most spectacularly faltered in the last decade. It is even more significant, because in general (with one or two exceptions) these nations are currently wedded to a political philosophy that denies any possibility of effective state action to counteract the failure.

That in turn helps powerfully to explain the third feature: the general tone of pessimism. The chapters tell us of powerful, even inexorable, changes transforming the world economy. Known technologies diffuse ever more easily and speedily from advanced industrial countries to less advanced ones, allowing the latter to compete with the former in the production of mass industrial goods. Older-established industrial sectors in the advanced countries are therefore under permanent threat of destruction from floods of cheap mass-produced goods from the newly industrialising world. The speed at which this is happening precludes any coherent strategy of adaptation. Within the advanced world individual industries, and individual industrialists, react as best they can: by process innovations which substitute capital for labour and newer more-modern plants for older less-efficient ones. This has drastic effects on employment in these sectors, particularly in the older plants that tend to be concentrated on older industrial cities and in the inner rings of metropolitan areas.

The new conventional wisdom argues that the only effective long-term adaptive strategy is to exploit the information revolution by developing high-technology manufacturing and producer services, in which the information-rich advanced countries have a natural competitive advantage. But this tends to aid only certain sections of the labour force, in certain socio-economic groups and in certain geographical locations; and these are generally opposite to those experiencing mass unemployment due to the decline of the older sectors. All this is inevitable, and with the best will in the world government can make only a limited difference, at least in the short run. This is the general trend of the argument in many of these chapters.

Faced with these limitations, our logical concluding question must be: in further co-operative work on this subject, how might we work to overcome them? Experience shows that speculative forecasting ventures of this kind suffer inherent methodological problems; but it may be possible to learn from the experience of related projects. In our international forecasting study *Europe 2000*, carried out between 1969 and 1976 (Hall 1977), we adopted a simple but reasonably effective approach to the problem. We first tried to project forward the broad technological, economic, social and cultural trends of the recent past, on the assumption that within some reasonably short time span (say, 10 years) these were unlikely to be rudely upset. We then asked what social and political responses to these trends might be expected over the medium-term forecasting future (say, 10-25 years) to produce a rather different world, and a different set of trends, in the longer term (roughly, more than 25 years). This method, applied qualitatively — that is, without any attempt at spurious numerical precision — proved relatively robust; the results, so far as we can judge them nearly a decade after the work, have been broadly borne out by actual experience.

Part of that work dealt specifically with urban futures. These were joined with predictions in other areas to give a synoptic view of likely trends in the economy, society, culture and politics. For the short run this produced a gloomy scenario dominated by an extension to other countries of the trends already then noticeable in Great Britain and the US: out-migration of jobs and of the more affluent sections of the population, with resulting concentrations of under-privileged people left in the cities; poor levels of physical and social environment; widespread manifestations of crime and social malaise; growing segregation and alienation as between the middle-class majority and the permanent under-class minority.

For the medium-term reaction the scenario produced a new assertion of the values of conviviality and community, coupled with the creative exploitation of new technologies by small-scale groups. But, it stressed, these technologies would make possible an ever-widening freedom to locate economic activities almost anywhere, in what were formerly remote rural locations. So the longer-run result might be that the new freedoms were exploited by the more affluent, while the under-class were left even more isolated and even more trapped than before.

That scenario does not seem any less plausible now than when it was developed, and it seems also to accord with the conclusions of a number of the chapters in this book. Any effort to predict how to reach the Good Society, to put it another way, must start by facing squarely the prospects for a Bad Society. It must show not merely where present trends will most likely take us, but must also show us a plausible set of social reactions that might cause those trends to change course.

Writing history in reverse suffers with exceptional force from a problem that is experienced less severely by all social scientists: the fact that the analyst is part of the object of analysis. Making and publicising a prediction may influence the likelihood of that prediction becoming true. This problem is basic and will not go away. Engels said something like this about Marx's prophecies, when he commented that they could not influence the likelihood of revolution but that they could shorten or lessen the birth pangs of the new order. Similarly, forecasters can argue that the general reaction of society to a series of events will take a particular form, but that — dependent on the advance publicity their analysis gives to these events — the entire process may be faster or slower.

It might be possible to go further, and to argue that such an analysis might affect not merely the pace, but also the direction, of events. If societies were able to recognise key issues clearly enough in advance, so this argument runs, they could guard against tendencies that might otherwise take them inexorably down paths that they would wish to avoid. This argument has merit in relation to some of the great turning points of history, where by altering consciousness the prophet might be able to avoid tragic outcomes. But whether to accept it will depend on a person's basic philosophic or ideological viewpoint.

In any event, whether determinist or believer in free will, the historian-in-reverse could accept that advance enlightenment would have some effect on the course of history. In that sense, speculation on the future impacts of technology could be more than an agreeable academic parlour game. And it might be worth more extended investigation than the present colloquy has been able to devote to it.

We might thus now attempt to distil and to utilise the product of the chapters, presented in this volume, in a second stage of our work. We might synthesise the results to form a picture of the state of the urban world towards the end of the 1990s. We could then ask what kinds of reaction society in general — and in particular that part of society that helped make policy — might have to this state of the world. In this way we might speculate on the ways in which urban society might then evolve into the next century. That would be a major speculative endeavour, but perhaps one worth making.

Reference

Hall, P. (ed.) (1977) *Europe 2000*, Duckworth, London

EDITORS AND CONTRIBUTORS

John F. Brotchie	Chief Research Scientist, Commonwealth Scientific and Industrial Research Organization, Melbourne
Peter W. Newton	Principal Research Scientist, Commonwealth Scientific and Industrial Research Organization, Melbourne
Peter Hall	Professor of Geography, University of Reading, and Professor of City and Regional Planning, University of California, Berkeley
Peter Nijkamp	Professor of Economics, Free University, Amsterdam
Michael Batty	Professor of Town Planning, University of Wales Institute of Science and Technology, Cardiff
Phil H. Bly	Senior Principal Scientific Officer, Transport and Road Research Laboratory, Crowthorne
John W. Dickey	Professor, Urban and Regional Planning Program and Center for Public Administration and Policy, Virginia Polytechnic Institute and State University
Marshall M.A. Feldman	Assistant Professor, Department of Urban Studies, Cleveland State University
Len Gertler	Professor and Director, School of Urban and Regional Planning, University of Waterloo
Britton Harris	UPS Professor Emeritus of Transportation Planning and Public Policy, University of Pennsylvania
Mieke Kesik	Assistant Professor of Economics, University of Waterloo
Leo H. Klaassen	President, Netherlands Economic Institute and Professor of Economics, Erasmus University, Rotterdam
John Levy	Associate Professor, Urban and Regional Planning Program, Virginia Polytechnic Institute and State University
Alan Lodwick	Research Officer, Institute for Transport Studies, University of Leeds

Lars Lundqvist   Head of the Research Group for Urban and Regional Planning, The Royal Institute of Technology, Stockholm

Roger L. Mackett   Senior Research Fellow, Institute for Transport Studies, University of Leeds

Edward J. Malecki   Associate Professor of Geography, University of Florida

Richard L. Meier   Professor of Environmental Design, Departments of City and Regional Planning, Architecture, and Landscape Architecture, University of California, Berkeley

Norman E.P. Pressman   Associate Professor of Urban and Regional Planning, University of Waterloo

John R. Roy   Principal Research Scientist, Commonwealth Scientific and Industrial Research Organization, Melbourne

Uwe Schubert   Associate Professor of Economics, Institute of Urban and Regional Studies, University of Vienna

Ron Sharpe   Principal Research Scientist, Commonwealth Scientific and Industrial Research Organization, Melbourne

Michael A.P. Taylor   Principal Research Scientist, Commonwealth Scientific and Industrial Research Organization, Melbourne

Wal van Lierop   Assistant Professor of Economics, Department of Economics, Free University, Amsterdam

Michael Wegener   Senior Research Fellow, Institute of Urban and Regional Planning, University of Dortmund

Mark Wigan   Chief Scientist (Transport), Australian Road Research Board, Melbourne

INDEX